THE COMPANION TO
THE MECHANICAL MUSE: THE PIANO, PIANISM AND PIANO MUSIC, c. 1760–1850

For Jan,
a more constant Companion

The Companion to
The Mechanical Muse: The Piano,
Pianism and Piano Music,
c. 1760–1850

DEREK CAREW

ASHGATE

Published by
Ashgate Publishing Limited
Gower House
Croft Road
Aldershot
Hants GU11 3HR
England

Ashgate Publishing Company
Suite 420
101 Cherry Street
Burlington, VT 05401-4405
USA

Ashgate website: http://www.ashgate.com

British Library Cataloguing in Publication Data

Carew, Derek
     The companion to The Mechanical Muse: The piano, pianism and piano music, c.1760–1850
     1. Piano music – 18th century – History and criticism 2. Piano music – 19th century – History and criticism 3. Musicians – Biography
     I. Title II. Carew, Derek. Mechanical use
     786.2'09033

Library of Congress Cataloging-in-Publication Data

Carew, Derek.
     The companion to The Mechanical Muse: The piano, pianism and piano music, c.1760-1850 / Derek Carew.
     p. cm.
     ISBN: 978-0-7546-6311-9 (alk. paper)
1. Piano music – 18th century – History and criticism. 2. Piano music – 19th century – History and criticism. 3. Musicians – Biography. I. Carew, Derek. Mechanical muse. II. Title.
ML700.C36 2007
786.209'033–dc22

                                                                                    2007014776

ISBN: 978-0-7546-6311-9

Printed on acid-free paper

Typeset in Times New Roman by Jonathan Hoare, Northwood, Middx
Printed and bound in Great Britain by MPG Books Ltd, Bodmin, Cornwall

Introduction

This Companion is intended to supplement the information given in *The Mechanical Muse* and to provide additional information which, for reasons of space, was not possible to include there. Although this book follows alphabetical order, it includes information of several kinds. There are biographies of all the relevant **persons** mentioned who were active during the period (*c.* 1760) or who affected it (for example J.S. Bach); this is confined to those of importance in the musical field. Separate entries are also given to important **works** and other **relevant matters** such as descriptions of musical forms, characteristics of dances and so on, as well as a small amount of **technical information** on music and some **technical terms** pertaining to keyboard instruments and ways of playing them.

It is not intended to replace the existing dedicated reference-books such as *Grove*, *Die Musik in Geschichte und Gegenwart*, etc. to which the specialist reader will always turn, but will be, I hope, useful for those who desire to know more about a particular topic and do not have access to more specialist reference works, or time to visit large or specialist libraries.

For that reason I have laid out the biographical entries under specific headings: name, profession and biographical details followed by a biography, a list of principal works and a section on further reading so that anyone who wishes to pursue an individual or a topic may do so. None of these, especially the last two, is intended to be exhaustive, but concentrates on the most accessible material in English, although some specialist studies and important books in other languages are included where necessary or desirable. Again, readers requiring further information are directed to more specialist works.

Dates

General

A single date in parenthesis denotes the date of completion of the work, e.g. (1828), sometimes qualified by '*c.*' (*circa*), giving the approximate date(s), e.g. (*c.*1828). Two dates hyphenated give the period during which the work was created, e.g. (1789–1800), either or both of which may be qualified by *c.*

Additional

Musical works

The date of first (or earliest known) performance may be given in addition to, or instead of, the date of completion, e.g. (perf. 1828), and/or date of first (or first-known) publication, e.g. (pub. 1828).

People

Birth and death are given as 'b.' and 'd.' or 'bap.' (baptized) if the birth-date is not known and 'bur.' (buried) if the date of death is not known: the date and the year are given in figures, the month is given in abbreviated form – the initial three letters – together with the place and, if obscure, the nearest well-known centre, qualified by 'nr' ('near'), as in '(b. 5 Mar 1838, Hoddesdon, nr Ware, Hertfordshire)' or sited with a larger better-known area given in parentheses, as in 'Cavaillon (Vaucluse)'. Occasionally, some of this information is missing, and in other cases, only general dates of part of a life is known, e.g. '*fl.*1828–32' denoting that the person was known to be active – '*floruit*' ('flourished') – at the date or during the dates given, with location(s) where known.

The names given in bold format are the commonest by which the person is now known; second and third, etc. names which are authentic but not normally used are given in bold type in parentheses, and alternative names or versions of names are given in square brackets, followed by titles, where appropriate: e.g. '**San Rafaele** [San Raffaele], **(Carlo Luigi Baldassare) Benvenuto Robbio,** Count of' refers to Count Benvenuto Robbio San Rafaele (also spelt San Raffaele) whose extra names are Carlo Luigi and Baldassare.

Abbreviations and Cross-References

Bibliographical

In the 'Further reading' sections, the reader is occasionally referred to one or more sources which are standard, or standard within the context and scope of *The Mechanical Muse*; these are given here in the same abbreviated form, *viz.*

AmZ:	*Allgemeine musikalische Zeitung.*
AMZ:	Allgemeine Musik Zeitung.
Bie/HISTORY:	Oskar Bie, *A History of the Pianoforte and Pianoforte Players* (New York, 1966).
Boalch/HARPSICHORD:	Donald Howard Boalch, *Makers of the Harpsichord and Clavichord, 1440–1840* (London, 1956, rev. 2/1974).
Burney/PRESENT:	C. Burney, *The Present State of Music in Germany, the Netherlands and the United Provinces* (London, 1773, 2/1775), ed. P. Scholes as *Dr. Burney's Musical Tours* (London, 1959).
Carew/MUSE:	Derek Carew, *The Mechanical Muse: The Piano, Pianism and Piano Music, c.1760–1850* (Aldershot, 2007).
Cole/PIANOFORTE:	M. Cole, *The Pianoforte in the Classical Era* (Oxford, 1998).
Ehrlich/PIANO:	C. Ehrlich, *The Piano: a History* (London, 1976).
EMDC:	*Encyclopédie de la Musique et Dictionnaire du Conservatoire.*
Fétis/*BIOGRAPHIE*:	F.-J. Fétis, *Biographie universelle des musiciens* (2/1860–65).
Harding/PIANO-FORTE:	Rosamond E.M. Harding, *The Piano-forte: its History Traced to the Great Exhibition of 1851* (Cambridge, 1933, rev. 2/1973).
Hipkins/PIANOFORTE:	A. J. Hipkins, *A Description and History of the Pianoforte* (London, 1896, rev. 3/1929/R1975).
Hubbard/HARPSICHORD:	F. Hubbard, *Three Centuries of Harpsichord Making* (Cambridge, MA, 1965).
JAMS:	*Journal of the American Musicological Society.*
Loesser/MEN:	A. Loesser, *Men, Women and Pianos* (New York, 1954).
Marmontel/*PIANISTES*:	A.F. Marmontel, *Les pianistes célèbres* (Paris, 1878).

Maunder/KEYBOARD:	R. Maunder, *Keyboard Instruments in Eighteenth-Century Vienna* (Oxford, 1998).
MGG:	*Die Musik in Geschichte und Gegenwart.*
ML:	*Music and Letters.*
MMR:	*The Monthly Musical Record.*
MQ:	*The Musical Quarterly.*
MR:	*The Music Review.*
MT:	*The Musical Times.*
Newman/SBE:	W.S. Newman, *The Sonata in the Baroque Era* (Chapel Hill, NC, 1959).
Newman/SCE:	W.S. Newman, *The Sonata in the Classical Era* (Chapel Hill, NC, 1963).
Newman/SSB:	W.S. Newman, *The Sonata Since Beethoven* (Chapel Hill, NC, 1969).
Pollens/EARLY:	Stewart Pollens, *The Early Pianoforte* (Cambridge, 1995).
PRMA:	*Proceedings of the Royal Musical Association.*
Russell/HARPSICHORD:	Raymond Russell, *The Harpsichord and Clavichord* (London, 1959, rev., 2/1973).
SIMG:	*Sammelbande der Internationalen Musikgesellschaft.*
SMZ:	*Schweizer Musikzeitung.*

General

adj.	adjective
ad lib	*ad libitum* ('at will')
anon.	anonymous(ly)
b.	born
bap.	baptized
bur.	buried
cm	centimetre(s)
¢	alla breve time-signature (2/2)
compl.	completed in, or by
d.	died
diss.	dissertation
ed.	editor / edited by
eds	editors
Eng.	English
equiv.	equivalent [to]
fl.	(Lat. *floruit*. 'flowered/flourished') (see 'People' above)
Fr.	French
Ger.	German
Gk.	Greek (classical)
hc	harpsichord

Ir.	Irish
It.	Italian
Lat.	Latin
m	metre(s)
mm	millimetre(s)
nr	near
perf.	performed
pf	pianoforte
plur.	plural(s)
Pol.	Polish
posth.	posthumous(ly)
pub.	published
R	reprinted (i.e. without revision or addition)
rev.	revised
Sp.	Spanish
tr.	translator / translated (by) / translation
U.	University
vol(s).	volume(s)

Cross-references

On their first mention in a section, key-words and surnames which have their own entries elsewhere in the Companion are asterisked, e.g. '*mode', '*Beethoven'. If there is more than one individual of musical relevance with the same surname, the *initials* are asterisked – whether or not there are entries for those others in this volume or not, e.g. '*J.S. Bach', '*C.P.E. Bach', *C.M. von Weber'; these are also asterisked in subsequent sections if an entry is in more than one section.

The Companion

A

Abel, Carl [Karl] Friedrich

German composer, viola da gamba player (b. 22 Dec 1723, Cöthen; d. 20 Jun 1787, London).

Son of a composer and viola da gamba player who gave him his first musical instruction, he may have studied in Leipzig with *J.S. Bach after his father's death in 1737. As a gamba player in the court orchestra in Dresden (under Hasse) he would have had contact with W.F. Bach (who was organist there) and J.S. Bach (who was court composer) and composed his first pieces. A few years of travel brought Abel to London where he became prominent in the city's musical life for his own concerts and his involvement (usually as director) in those of others. He was granted a royal privilege as a music-publisher in 1760. In 1763, he and *J.C. Bach became associates, having both been appointed chamber musicians by Queen *Charlotte and instigating the 'Bach-Abel' series of concerts – between 10 and 15 per annum. These were a fixture in London musical life for some 15 years and their success led to the building of the Hanover Square concert room, which opened in 1775. The series, which featured many continental musicians, thanks to Abel's travels, finished in 1782 in the face of rivalry from other series. Several of these continental musicians remained in England and included the violinist Wilhelm Cramer and the oboist J. C. Fischer and, after a visit to Germany, Abel gathered these and others of his nucleus of players for another series which lasted until his death in 1787, caused by excessive drinking and rich food.

Abel's instrument, the viola da gamba, was obsolescent during his lifetime and did not survive long after his death. His music is light and cheerful with a tendency to vary the rather four-square phrasing so characteristic of the pre-Classical era. His interests extended to art and artists and counted Gainsborough (who painted a fine portrait of him) and Cipriani, and the engraver Bartolozzi among his friends. He taught the pianist *J. B .Cramer.

Works

These are mostly instrumental and, apart from some works for viola da gamba, included the sonatas for flute (sometimes substituting violin) and harpsichord (sometimes substituting piano) opp. 2 (pub. 1760), 13 (pub. 1777) and 18 (pub. 1784), trios (which, cleaving to common practice in the period, he called 'sonatas'), and string quartets, such as his opp. 8 (pub. 1769), 12 (pub. 1775) and 15 (pub. 1780). He also wrote orchestral works – symphonies or 'overtures' in sets of six (opp. 7 (pub. 1767), 10 (pub. 1773) and 17 (pub. 1783)), and concertos (five for harpsichord op. 11 (pub. 1774) and seven for flute) – and a small number of vocal works.

Further reading

S.M. Helm, *Carl F. Abel, Symphonist: a Biographical, Stylistic and Bibliographical Study* (diss., U. of Michigan, 1953). W. Knape, *Karl Friedrich Abel: Leben und Werk eines frühklassischen Komponisten* (Bremen, 1973). M. Charters, 'Abel in london', *MT*, cxiv (1973); *The Bach-Abel Concerts* (diss., U. of London, 1978). S. McVeigh, *Concert Life in London from Mozart to Haydn* (Cambridge, 1993).

Action

The mechanism by which sound is produced on a keyboard instrument (involving strings or pipes) when the *key is depressed.

Additional Keys
Instigated by *William Southwell on one of his pianos (Dublin, 1794) these were extra keys added to either end of the piano's keyboard during the late eighteenth and early nineteenth centuries, thus widening the instrument's range. The number varied but rarely exceeded half an octave. The term, however, is used almost exclusively with reference to the higher end, where most of the musical activity took place. Published music was frequently provided with alternative notes or (usually very short) passages so that it was playable on instruments 'with or without additional keys'. An example can be seen in Plate 6 in *The Mechanical Muse*.

Aeolian mode (see *Mode)

Affections, Doctrine of the [Affects, Theory of] (Ger. *Affektenlehre*)
A *Baroque aesthetic following Greek and Latin authors, in which the various devices of oratory were employed to control and direct the emotions ('affections', *'affects') of the listeners. These emotions were rationalized – anger, love, sadness, jealousy, etc. – following the texts of vocal works, and musical means sought to express them. One result was that, up until about 1740, compositions, movements or discrete sections expressed only a single affection or emotion, thus imparting rationality and unity.

Affects
A term used during the eighteenth century to describe the emotions when aroused by artistic means. (See *Affections, Doctrine of.)

Agricola, Johann Friedrich
German composer, organist, singing master, conductor, musicographer (b. 4 Jan 1720, Dobitschen, Saxe-Altenburg; d. 2 Dec 1774, Berlin).
Son of a government agent and jurist, the boy began his musical studies early and was taught by *J.S. Bach and in Leipzig while he was at the University there. He moved to Berlin in 1741 and was taught by *Quantz, getting to know, among others, *C.P.E. Bach and Graun and became greatly interested in music theory and criticism, for which he is mostly remembered now. Agricola was involved in the publication of several important musical treatises but failed to appreciate the importance of *Gluck's operatic reforms. He corresponded with Padre Martini, Lessing and Adlung, and published pamphlets on musical taste in Italy and in France. Agricola took issue with Marpurg, who favoured French music, while he himself was a fully Italianized opera-composer and enjoying, at that time, the support of *Frederick the Great, who appointed him a court composer in 1751, following the success of his *intermezzo, Il filosofo convinto in amore* (The Philosopher found guilty of Love) the year before. However, he incurred Frederick's displeasure when, against the latter's rule that all the opera singers should remain single, he married one of the sopranos and was punished by having their joint salary greatly reduced. When the chief court opera-composer, Graun, died in 1759, Agricola was appointed musical director of the opera but was denied the title of *Kapellmeister*. The quality of his composition began to decline also, something of which Frederick, a composer and performer himself, was keenly aware.

On the other hand he was successful as a teacher and very highly regarded – the best organ-player in Berlin and the best singing-teacher in Germany, according to *Burney. His translation of an Italian treatise on the teaching of singing, with his own notes and commentary, was welcomed as a watershed in music education. He is counted as a member of the First *Berlin *Lied* School.

Works

Some dozen operas and *intermezzi*, including *Il filosofo convinto in amore* (1750) and *Cleofide* (1754). A dozen oratorios, cantatas and many songs and odes as well as keyboard sonatas and descriptive pieces and some chorale preludes for organ. His writings include *Anleitung zum Singekunst* (*Instructions in the Art of Singing*, a tr. of Tosi's *Opinioni de' cantori antiche e moderno* of 1723, with commentary and notes, pub. Berlin 1757), *Musica mechanica organoedi* (with Adlung, 1768), 'Nekrolog [J.S. Bachs]' (with C.P.E. Bach) in *Musikalische Bibliothek*, iv (Leipzig 1754) and articles for F. Nicolai's *Allgemeine deutsche Bibliothek* (Berlin 1765–96).

Further reading

H. Wucherpfennig, *J Fr Agricola* (diss., U. of Berlin, 1922). H. Löffer, 'Die Schüler J.S. Bachs', *Bach-Jahrbuch*, xl (1953). E.E. Helm, *Music at the Court of Frederick the Great* (Oklahoma, 1960). A. Dürr, 'Zur Chronologie der Handschriften Johann Christoph Altnikoils und Johann Friedrich Agricolas', *Bach-Jahrbuch*, lvi (1970). Burney/PRESENT.

Alberti, Domenico

Italian composer, harpsichordist, singer (b. *c.*1710, Venice; d. 14 Oct 1746, Rome).

A page to the Venetian ambassador to Spain, 1736, his singing was admired by the celebrated *castrato* Farinelli. He was reputed to have studied singing and counterpoint with Biffi and Lotti. He later joined the court of Marquis Molinari in Rome and is chiefly remembered for the *Alberti* Bass, the accompanimental device of closely-textured arpeggiated chords which feature prominently in his sonatas.

Works

Fourteen complete two-movement harpsichord sonatas survive from over twice that number. *Galant* in style, the first movements are in primitive sonata form and the others dances. There are also single movements for harpsichord and some vocal works.

Further reading

W. Wörmann, 'Die Klaviersonate Domenico Albertis', *Acta musicologica*, xxvii (1955). D.E. Freeman, 'J.C. Bach and the Early Classical Italian Masters', *Eighteenth-Century Keyboard Music*, ed. R.L. Marshall (New York, 1994). Newman/SCE.

Alberti Bass (see Alberti)

Alkan [Morhange], (Charles-) Valentin

French composer, pianist (b. 30 Nov 1813, Paris; d. 29 Mar 1888, Paris).

A child prodigy; won the Paris Conservatoire's *premier prix* for *solfège* at seven years of age, followed by those for piano (1824), harmony (1827) and organ (1834). He studied with Dourlen (harmony) and P.-J. Zimmermann (piano), was influenced by *Berlioz and taught *solfège* part-time at the Conservatoire (1829–36). Alkan became a close friend of *Chopin and was part of his and George Sand's circle. He visited London in 1833 and his life includes several periods of (undocumented) withdrawal from public life and similar gaps in compositional output. He was reclusive and introverted, and the popular story that he died under a falling bookcase seems to have no factual basis.

An admirer of earlier music – the Classical period, as well as *J.S. Bach and *Handel, transcriptions of both whose works he published – Alkan was recognized as being among the foremost virtuosi of his time and most of his output is piano-oriented. He was unusual (for his period) in giving greater prominence to others' works than his own in his performances. He championed the *pedalier* (*pedal-piano) and the music of *Beethoven's late period and that of *Schubert, neither of which was fashionable. He was a composer of striking originality, which occasionally overflowed into notation, for example, using triple-sharps, in tonality, and in rhythm, using time-signatures of five and seven beats.

Works
Funeral March on the Death of a Parrott, a comical work for choir & woodwind (1859); two Concerti da camera for pf solo (c.1832 and pre-1834); Piano trio (1841). For piano: *Nocturne* (1844); *Saltarelle* (1844); *Vingt-cinq préludes* (in all major and minor keys) (pf/organ, 1847); *Grand sonate: Les quatres âges*; many transcriptions and sets of variations.

Further reading
J. Bloch, *Charles-Valentin Alkan* (Indianapolis, 1941). R. Lewenthal, Introduction to *The Piano Music of Alkan* (New York, 1964). H. Macdonald, 'The Death of Alkan', *MT*, cxiv (1973); 'The Enigma of Alkan', *MT*, cxvii (1976). D. Hennig, *Charles-Valentin Alkan* (diss., U. of Oxford, 1975). R. Smith, *Alkan* (London, 1976–87). Fétis/*BIOGRAPHIE*. Marmontel/*PIANISTES*.

Alla turca (see *Turca, alla*)

Allegro (It.: 'lively', 'cheerful')
Used to denote a fast pace and, as a noun, to refer to the first fast movement in a composite work (suite, symphony etc.) in the *Classical Period, which was invariably so headed.

Allemande
*Baroque instrumental dance, one of the core movements of the *suite, together with the *courante*, *sarabande* and *gigue*. In common Baroque usage, a medium-paced dance in quadruple time with an anacrusis and a tendency towards a *style brisé* texture and motivic interplay.

Allgemeine musikalische Zeitung
German musical periodical published by Breitkopf & Härtel in Leipzig and issued weekly. The first series, edited by Friedrich Rochlitz, was in 50 vols (1798/99–1848), and the second, and third, edited by S. Bagge, were in 3 vols (1863–65) and 17 vols (1866–82) respectively, the last under a different publisher. The periodical was accompanied by occasional supplements.

Andante (It.: 'walking')
A musical term used, from the middle of the eighteenth century, to indicate a relaxed, easy *tempo. Qualified by *Molto* (It. 'very' or 'much') or *Più* (It. 'more') it usually means slower than *andante*. There is also a diminutive form, *Andantino*, which is normally taken to mean a slightly faster tempo that *Andante*, although some have taken it to imply the opposite.

Andantinetto (similar to *Andantino*) is also found. *Andante* is also used as the title of a (usually short) piece.

Andante favori (It.: 'favourite *Andante*') A name applied to a number of pieces by a number of composers headed *Andante* as a result of their popularity. The name is particularly applied to *Beethoven's piece of that name in F major, WoO 57 (1803) which was originally the slow movement of the *'*Waldstein*' Piano Sonata (no. 21 in C major, op. 53, 1803–4).

An die ferne Geliebte, op. 98
Song-cycle (six songs) by *Beethoven composed 1815–16 to poems by Alois Jeitteles: 1. 'Auf dem Hügel' ('On the Hill'); 2. 'Wo die Berge so blau' ('Where the Mountains so Blue'); 3. 'Leichte Segler in den Höhen' ('Light Swift on High'); 4. 'Diese Wolken in den Höhen' ('These Clouds on High'); 5. 'Es kehret der Maien, es blühet die Au' ('May Appears, the Meadow is in Bloom'); 6. 'Nimm sie hin denn, diese Lieder' ('Then take away these Songs').

There are also two other Beethoven songs with similar titles, which are unconnected with the cycle: 'An die fernen Geliebten' from Six Songs op. 75 (1809; words by Reissig) and 'An die Geliebte' WoO 140 (in two versions, 1811 and ?1814; words by J.L. Stoll).

Anticipations of ... (see *Recollections of ...)

Apollosaal (Apollo-Säle, Apollosäle)
(Ger.: 'Apollo-Room(s)')
A lavishly-appointed suite of ballrooms opened in Vienna in 1808, catering for 4,000, some say 6,000. The accommodation included five great pillared dance-halls with mirrored walls and crystal chandeliers, together with a couple of dozen rococo-styled drawing rooms, three glass-domed gardens with waterfalls and swans, and thirteen kitchens, including private drawing-rooms, gardens and kitchens.

'Appassionata'
Title given by his publisher to *Beethoven's piano sonata in F minor no. 23, op. 57 (1804–1805, dedicated to Count von Brunsvik) because of its passionate first movement and especially its opening.

Appoggiatura (It. pl. and Fr. *appoggiature*; Ger. *Vorschlag*)
A musical decoration by which a note is preceded by another, accented, note moving by *step, thus displacing the main note, as in F—E or te—doh. The appoggiatura itself must be approached by a note of the same pitch as itself or by one more than a step away. (If it is approached by a note a step away it is an accented *passing note.) The appoggiatura can be chromatic or *diatonic, and upper or lower, but not unaccented.

Archduke Rudolph of Austria (see *Rudolph)

Aria (It.: 'air', 'tune')
A song for solo voice, but the term tends to be reserved for such a piece within the context of a larger vocal piece (opera, *oratorio, *cantata, etc.). It is also applied to a lyrical instrumental solo or chamber piece or a slow movement of a larger work (often a *concerto).

Armonica [Glass (h)armonica, Musical Glasses]
An instrument in which glasses of different sizes are graded and struck,

bowed, or stroked to produce a musical sound; it is thought to have been of Oriental origin. There are late medieval references to such an instrument, and an illustration of a 'Pythagorean experiment' in which glasses are filled with varying amounts of liquid and stroked with sticks to produce different notes. The instrument came into its own in serious music during the eighteenth century, with glasses being struck with a (sometimes muffled) stick and in 1744 an Irish player, Richard Pockrich, used glasses of different sizes with water to fine-tune them, the wetted rims of which he stroked. *Gluck is reported to have played a concerto on the instrument two years later at a concert in London and again in 1749 in Copenhagen, while its popularity had made the London newspapers by the middle of the century. Ann Ford, the wife of Gainsborough's biographer Thicknesse, was a fine performer and published a *method for it (the first one known) in 1761, going into fine detail. Benjamin *Franklin heard the armonica being played on a visit to England in 1761 and was so captivated that he determined to work to improve it. He took great care with the grading of the glasses and, by placing them closer together, could produce runs and chords much more easily than before. It was he who suggested the name 'armonica' in deference to the legendary Italian love of music. Within a short time, a trough of water was placed below the rotating – by means if a treadle – glasses so that they were constantly moist. The armonica was much more popular in Europe than in the New World and a British *virtuosa*, Marianne Davies (who was welcomed in the highest social circles), was heard by the *Mozart family on their visit to London in 1773 and *Leopold Mozart expressed his interest. Another devotee was Anton

Mesmer, the inventor of mesmerism or 'Animal Magnetism', who used it to lull his subjects into relaxation and who was also friendly with the Mozarts. Wolfgang wrote the beautiful Quintet in a K617 for the instrument in tandem with flute, oboe, viola and cello in 1781 for a renowned blind *virtuosa*, Marianne Kirchgessner. It seems that both versions of the instrument, the glasses and Franklin's more mechanized version, continued to be used side by side. The sweet tone was praised by many, including Goethe, but there were cases of listeners' nerves being adversely affected by the sound and it was banned in several German towns. Various improvements were tried on the armonica, but none lasted.

The vogue of the instrument began to wane in the 1830s, although the technique was revived in the twentieth century, facilitating the recording of Mozart's quintet.

Further reading
C. Sachs, *History of Musical Instruments* (New York, 1940). A.H. King, 'Some Notes on the Armonica', *MMR*, lxxxvi (1945–46). B. Hoffmann, 'Glasharmonika und Glasharfe', *Musica*, iv (1950). B. Matthews, 'The Davies Sisters, J.C. Bach and the Glass Harmonica', *ML*, lvi (1975).

Arnaut Manuscript
A manuscript in the Bibliothèque Nationale, Paris (lat. 7295) dating from 1440, written by the Netherlander Henri Arnaut de Zwolle. It contains a description of a hammered *dulcimer although Arnaut admits to basing his description on a manuscript from the end of the previous century. The particular instrument described is a mechanized form of dulcimer, the *dulce melos*, in

which a keyboard causes hammers to strike the strings. No such instrument has survived.

Arne, Thomas Augustine

English composer, violinist, keyboard player (b. 12 Mar 1710, London; d. 5 Mar 1778, London).

Son of a line of upholsterers his father intended him for law after his education at Eton College, but was won over by the boy's musical talent and dedication. He was taught the violin by Michael Festing – there is a possibility that he also had lessons with Geminiani – and heard *Handel improvise on the organ in Oxford (1733). He taught his sister – later to become the wife of Theophilus Cibber, whose father, Colley taught her acting – and his brother to sing and the family gave a performance of Handel's *Acis and Galatea* and became involved in a bid to set up an English opera. When the group split up soon after, Arne set up on his own at the Haymarket Theatre, producing his own works (*Dido and Aeneas*) with some success, which led to his engagement at Drury Lane. Arne also wrote incidental music, commissioned by his brother-in-law, and in 1735 married a singer for, apparently, professional reasons. His masques *Comus* (based on a Miltonic text) and *Alfred* (which contained the subsequently famous tune *Rule Britannia*) were huge successes. When his sister's marriage failed and she left London for Dublin, Arne and his wife visited her soon after, making plans for subsequent seasons in the city.

In 1755 Arne and his wife separated, she remaining in Dublin and Arne paying her an allowance. Back in London he spent much time preparing his music for publication, while still composing and producing stage works, including his greatest success, *Artaxerxes* (perf. 1762), which remained in the British repertory for many years.

When his popularity in dramatic works declined, he turned to writing catches and glees, giving annual 'concerts'. He had financial troubles, however, but continued to have some stage successes. He was reconciled with his wife in 1777 and died, after an illness, the following year.

Arne's contribution to eighteenth-century British music was his gift for simple melody, an 'agreeable mixture of Italian, English and Scots', as *Burney put it, very much in tune with the burgeoning interest in vernacular music and *opera buffa* and its national variations.

Works

Many are lost or destroyed in one of several fires. Dramatic (masques): *Dido and Aeneas* (perf. 1734); *The Fall of Phaeton* (perf. 1736); *Comus* (perf. 1738); *Alfred* (including '*Rule, Britannia') (perf. 1740); *The Arcadian Nuptials* (perf. 1764); *The Fairy Prince* (perf. 1771). Dramatic (operatic): *The Country Lasses* (perf. 1751); *Eliza, The Sheepshearing* (both perf. 1754); *Thomas and Sally* (perf. 1760); *Artaxerxes, Love in a Village* (both perf. 1762); *May-Day* (perf. 1775). Instrumental: *VIII Sonatas or Lessons* (harpsichord, pub. 1756); *Six Favourite Concertos* (organ/harpsichord/pf, c.1787))

Further reading

R. Fiske, *English Theatre Music in the Eighteenth Century* (London, 1973). S. Sadie, 'The Chamber Music of Boyce and Arne', *MQ*, xlvi (1960). T.J. Walsh, *Opera in Dublin (1705–1797)* (Dublin, 1973). R. Langley, 'Arne's Keyboard Concertos', *MT*, cxix (1978). M. Burden,

The British Masque 1690–1800 (diss., U. of Edinburgh, 1991).

Arpeggione

A string instrument invented by J.G. Staufer in Vienna in 1824, and, simultaneously, by P. Teufelsdorfer in Pest, it was also called 'guitar violoncello', as it was fretted and tuned (like the modern guitar) to E-A-d-g-b-e, but was bowed. The principal performer on the instrument, Vincenz Schuster, is remembered as having played a work which *Schubert wrote for it, the *Arpeggione Sonata in A minor, D.821, which is now normally played on the cello, and which gave the instrument its name after it was published in 1871.

Arpeggione Sonata

The sonata in A minor (D.821) written for *arpeggione and piano by *Schubert (1824, pub. 1871) but now usually played on the cello (with piano). Its movements are (i) Allegro, A minor, 4/4; (ii) Adagio, E major, 3/4 leading to (iii) Finale: Allegretto, A major 2/4.

Arpicembalo

A keyboard instrument invented by *Cristofori the name of which appears in a manuscript inventory of instruments at the court of Prince Ferdinand of Tuscany in Florence, dated 1700. Its full description is 'Arpicembalo di Bartolomeo Cristofori di nuova inventione, ... con ... martelli, che fanno il piano, et il forte' ['A large keyboard instrument by Bartolomeo Cristofori, of new invention, ... with ... hammers, that produce soft and loud'] and this is taken to refer to the pianoforte.

Artaria

Austrian music publishing house (also iconography, maps, engravings and lithographs) (1765, Mainz – 1858, Vienna).

The firm issued works by all Classical and early *Romantic composers, with large collections by *J. Haydn, *W.A. Mozart and *Beethoven (but only three by *Schubert, who published with the related but separate firm of Matthias Artaria), as well as *Clementi, *Boccherini, *Gluck, Salieri, *Pleyel, *J.B. Cramer, *Hummel, *Moscheles and *Rossini.

art de préluder, L' (*The Art of Preluding*) op. 300

Treatise by *Czerny; Part Two of his *School of Extemporaneous Performance*.

art de toucher le clavecin, L' (*The Art of Playing the Harpsichord*)

Treatise by *F. Couperin published in 1716 and in a revised second edition in 1717. The result of Couperin's first-hand experience as a dedicated teacher of harpsichord, the work is unlike its only predecessor in French (the *Principes de clavecin* by *Saint-Lambert) and many following in that it does not proceed from first musical principles, but deals with such matters as fingering (in which the writer takes some more modern developments of his time into account), *ornamentation and performance practice. Much of it is specifically directed at the author's own works and includes eight specially-composed pieces to illustrate points made. The treatise was, and remains, very influential, and *J.S. Bach is known to have used it.

art du chant appliqué au piano, L' (*The Art of Singing Applied to the Piano*)

Title of a pedagogical work by Sigismond *Thalberg – his op. 70 – which uses his own piano-arrangements of operatic arias to teach piano technique. *Czerny and

Bizet produced a later simpler edition with an extra twelve numbers.

Art of Playing the Harpsichord, The
(see *L'Art de toucher le clavecin)

Athenaeum, The: Journal of Literature, Science, the Fine Arts, Music and the Drama
British periodical in English published in London, 1827–1921.

Athenäum, Das
German periodical; (May 1798 – Aug 1800, 6 numbers).

Consisting largely of essays and *Fragmente* ('fragments', or short pithy aphorisms), produced in Berlin by Friedrich and August Wilhelm Schlegel to publicize their ideas, and those of their group, the *Frühromantiker*, including Tieck and Schleiermacher.

Attwood, Thomas
English composer, organist (bap. 23 Nov 1765, London; d. 24 Mar 1838).

Son of a coal merchant who played viola and trumpet in the King's Band, the boy became a chorister at the Chapel Royal and so impressed the Prince of Wales that he funded his studies, in Naples (1783–85), with Felipe Cinque and Gaetano Latilla, and in Vienna (1785–87), with *W.A. Mozart. On his return, he was appointed as music teacher to the Duchess of York (1791) and the Princess of Wales (1795) and became organist at St Paul's Cathedral, London and composer to the Chapel Royal in 1796. He wrote much for the stage and was a founder-member of the *Philharmonic Society (1813), organist to King George IV (1821), a professor of the *RAM (1823) and organist to the Chapel Royal in 1836. He was a close friend of *Felix Mendelssohn who stayed with him on several of his London visits and who dedicated several pieces to him, including his Three Preludes and Fugues op. 37.

Works
Many theatrical pieces, religious vocal works and glees. Three Piano trios op. 1 (?1787); three Piano Sonatas (with *ad lib* violin and vc) op. 2 (1791) and chamber music giving equal importance to all instruments. He also wrote pieces for winds and arrangements of others' works for piano. His didactic works include *Easy Progressive Lessons for Young Beginners* (pf/hc, c.1795) and *A Short Introduction to the pianoforte* (?1805).

Further reading
M. Kelly, *Reminiscences*, ed. R. Fiske (London, 1975). E. Hertzmann, 'Mozart and Attwood', *JAMS*, xii (1959). C.B. Oldman, 'Thomas Attwood, 1765–1838', *MT*, cvi (1965); 'Attwood's Dramatic Works', *MT*, cvii (1966). N. Temperley, ed., *Music in Britain: the Romantic Age 1800–1914* (London, 1981).

Augmentation
A device by which the notes of a melody are proportionally lengthened, such as being doubled, a minim and a crotchet becoming a semibreve and a minim, for example. The device is often used in *contrapuntal forms, such as *fugue or *canon.

Augurio Felice, L' ['The Happy Portent']
Title given by Domenico *Corri to his piano sonata in B♭ major published in 1808.

Auxiliary (note)
A note which moves by *step (i.e. a semitone or a tone) from a given note

and immediately back to that note, as in G—A—G, D—C#—D, ray—me—ray, etc. The auxiliary may be chromatic or *diatonic and accented (on the strong beat) or unaccented.

Ayrton, William
English composer, writer, music critic, impresario (b. 24 Feb 1777, London; d. 8 May 1858, London).

Son of an organist and composer, he married in 1803 and was a successful impresario in the field of Italian opera in London, also writing critical and general articles on music for various periodicals, including the *Harmonicon*, which he edited 1823–33.

Ayrton was a founder-member of the [Royal] *Philharmonic Society; Fellow of the Royal Society and of the Royal Society of Antiquaries. He was responsible for first British staging of *W.A. Mozart's *Don Giovanni* in 1817 and *Rossini's *La gazza ladra* in 1821, and he boosted the careers of several singers, such as Mme Pasta and Mme Camporese.

Works
Edited and contributed to the monthly musical periodical the *Harmonicon* (London, 1823–33), *The Musical Library* (London, 1834–37) and *The Madrigalian Feast* (London, 1838).

Further reading
W.T. Parke, *Musical Memoirs* (London, 1830). A.H. King, *Some British Collectors of Music* (Cambridge, 1963).

B

Bach, Carl Philipp Emanuel

German composer, keyboard-player (b. 8 Mar 1714, Weimar; d. 14 Dec 1788, Hamburg).

Emanuel was taught music by his father, *J.S. Bach, attended the Lutheran seminary in Cöthen and studied again under his father (and J.M. Gesner and J.A. Ernesti) at the Thomasschule, Leipzig, since the family followed their father's appointments to Cöthen and Leipzig (1723–34), where he studied law at the university; he spent a further four years in legal studies at the University of Frankfurt an der Oder. A position accompanying a young aristocrat on his European travels was abandoned in favour of an appointment harpsichordist to the soon-to-be *Frederick the Great of Prussia at his musically well-staffed court in Berlin, where he remained from 1738 to 1768. His musical colleagues included, as well as two of his pupils (J.F. *Agricola and C. Nichelmann), C.F.C. Fasch, Franz and Johann *Benda, C.H. and J.G. Graun and, following Frederick's prime musical interest, the flute, J.J. *Quantz.

He married the daughter of a wine merchant in 1744 and had three children, none of whom were musicians and none of which had any children. His house was ever open to visitors, who included *Galuppi, although his friends did not include many musicians, being literary figures – such as the poets Gleim, Ramler and Lessing – and the banking family, the Itzigs, including Sara Levy, *Felix Mendelssohn's great-aunt. His pupils *Schulz and Fasch lived in and his father visited him twice, the second being the occasion which led to the latter's composing the *Musikalisches Opfer ('*Musical Offering') for Frederick. When his father died in 1750, he inherited a third of the musical estate, some of which he sold. His widowed mother lived in some need, which seems to have been ignored by her children, Emanuel included. His post at Frederick's court remained that of an accompanist during his 30 years of service to the King, although in practice it embraced many other duties, but he had ample time to pursue his other interests, teaching and composition as well as writing. When he threatened to resign in 1755, because his pupils' salaries were greater than his own, he received a 66 per cent increase, bringing his salary to 500 thalers; unfortunately, because of devaluation during the Seven Years War (1756–63), the increase was negligible in practice. When the war finished in 1763, he began to look around for a more lucrative appointment and, after several failures, the death in 1767 of his godfather, *Telemann, created a vacancy which interested him. In spite of Frederick's reluctance to let him go, in 1768 he was appointed to succeed Telemann in the post of Kantor of the Johanneum (Lateinschule) and music director of five churches in Hamburg where he remained until his death in 1788. In spite of his salary remaining modest (600 thalers), there were fees attached to many aspects of the post which made him quite comfortably off for the first time in his life and he received many visitors to his home, including Lessing, Klopstock, Gerstenberg, Sturm, *Reichardt, Lotti and Baron van Swieten, whose championing of Emanuel's music and that of his father, Sebastian, influenced *W.A. Mozart in Vienna. He died of a long-standing chest ailment in 1788.

Bach was a prominent member of the First *Berlin Lied School. Although a champion of the clavichord, Emanuel recognized and respected the qualities of the early piano in the later part of his life. He was the chief exponent of the *empfindsamer stil* ('highly sensitive' style) or **Empfindsamkeit*. An important didactic strain in his output includes the *Versüch* (see *Works*), and he tended to tailor his compositional style according to the audience at which it was aimed, whether for a patron or the public, or for his own private use. His music (especially chamber) shows clearly the transition from late-*Baroque to *Classical.

Highly influential as a teacher, he taught his half-brother, *Johann Christian Bach as well as J.A.P. *Schulz and F.W. Rust, *Hérold, Schörring, *Hüllmandel and probably *J.L. Dussek. His treatise on keyboard-playing, the *Versüch* (see *Works*), was possibly the most influential treatise of the eighteenth century and a vital source for performance practice. Bach's keyboard works (in particular) influenced *W.A. Mozart, *Beethoven and, especially, *J. Haydn.

Works

A huge amount of keyboard (clavichord and harpsichord) music: sonatas (including *Sechs Sonaten mit veränderten Reprisen* ('Six Sonatas with Altered Repeats') W50 (H126, 136-40; 1760); fantasias, rondos, variations, dances and character-pieces and the series of mixed collections (such as those '*für Kenner und Liebhaber*' ('for Connoisseurs and Amateurs')); many of the keyboard pieces are revisions or re-workings. His chamber works include many trio-sonatas and works with equally-participating keyboard parts as well as many in the *continuo vein; here he was greatly constricted for much of his life by the taste of his arch-conservative employer *Frederick the Great. Orchestral

music includes sets of symphonies (including the six of W182 written for van Swieten), a body of harpsichord concertos (ten of which were arranged for non-keyboard instruments but transcend mere 'arrangements'), several for two harpsichords and a number of Sonatinas for two and one harpsichord and orchestra as well as a delightful *Concerto doppio* (Double Concerto) in E♭ for harpsichord and fortepiano W47 (1788). The bulk of his sacred music (largely cantatas and passions) dates from the last part of his life in Leipzig, and his theoretical work is crowned by the treatise, **Versuch über die wahre Art das Clavier zu spielen, mit Exempeln und achtzehn Probe-Stücken in sechs Sonaten erläutert* (pub. Berlin 1753); Eng. tr. and ed. by W.J. Mitchell as *Essay on the True Art of Playing Keyboard Instruments* (New York, 1949).

Further reading

O. Vrieslander, *Carl Philipp Emanuel Bach* (Munich, 1923). H. Miesner, *Philipp Emanuel Bach in Hamburg* (Heide, 1929, rev. 1969). A.E. Cherbuliez, *Carl Philipp Emanuel Bach 1714–1778* (Zurich and Leipzig, 1940). Burney/PRESENT.

Bach, Johann [John] Christian [the 'London Bach']

German composer, performer, impresario (b. 5 Sep 1735, Leipzig; d. 1 Jan 1782, London).

The youngest son and tenth child of *J.S. Bach by his second wife Anna Magdalena, he was taught by his father and possibly by Johann Elias Bach (his cousin) in Leipzig. On the death of his father J.S. Bach, he moved from Leipzig to Berlin to live with his brother *C.P.E. Bach (with whom he studied composition and keyboard), and then to Italy (1755–62) where he studied with

Padre Martini in Bologna (1757) and gained the post of second organist in Milan Cathedral in 1760; he converted to Catholicism about this time. The success of the operas he composed at this time led to a commission for two operas for the King's Theatre in London, where he moved in 1762. Notwithstanding the works' great success, a change of management of the theatre in 1763 was not in Bach's favour and, in spite of offers in Europe, he chose to remain in London. He dedicated his op. 1, a set of six harpsichord concertos, to Queen *Charlotte (who was also German) and became her music master from 1763. Christian became friendly with the young *W.A. Mozart (whose style he influenced) during the latter's fourteen-month stay in the city, 1764–65. He played a solo on one of *Zumpe's pianos in a concert on 2 June 1768 – apparently the first solo public use of the piano in London. A friendship with another compatriot already settled in London – Carl Friedrich *Abel, with whom he shared lodgings – led to the instigation of a series of concerts, later called the Bach-Abel concerts which continued until 1774. A brief incursion into the oratorio market was not a success financially and in 1772 he accepted a commission for an opera to celebrate the name-day of the Elector Carl Theodor in Mannheim. The resulting work, *Temistocle*, was a huge success and he produced his *Lucio Silla* for the following year which was less of a success, though Mozart thought highly of it. In 1773 he married the soprano Cecilia Grassi and in 1778 had the first of two of his portraits painted by his friend Gainsborough. Bach's music was well known in Paris and the Académie Royale de Musique commissioned him to write an opera, *Amadis de Gaule*, which

was performed before Marie Antoinette in 1779, but was not greatly successful. Back in London, in spite of – or perhaps partly because of – the venture to build a new concert-hall (the Hanover Square Rooms) the Bach-Abel Concerts were declining in prestige and at the box-office and the absconding of his housekeeper with £1,000 (equivalent to some £25,000 today) plunged Bach seriously in to debt. His health began to decline in 1781 and on New Year's Day of the following year he died almost without public comment.

One of the most important exponents of the *style galant*, in which most of his music is cast, and much of which is in that style's characteristic two-movement form, the second frequently a minuet. Although conservative in his operas, most of which cleave to the Metastasian *opera seria* type, his symphonies show the development from the Italian opera-overture, though he never adopted the four-movement shape, and the first movements also show the transition from a *binary to *sonata forms. He was important in crystallizing the layout of the classical solo concerto, and followed contemporary trends in including sets of variations on popular tunes (including *God Save The Queen). His keyboard and chamber music was mainly didactic and for amateurs and he was an important early influence on *W.A. Mozart. His op. 5 set of sonatas was the first London publication to give the option of piano in their title.

Works

[T numbers refer to those used by C.S. Terry (see *Further reading*)] His operas include *Artaserse* T217:xl (perf. 1760), *Temistocle* T283/3:xlviii (perf. 1772), *Lucio Silla* T232:xlv (perf. 1774), *La*

Clemenza di Scipione T229:xliv (1778), and *Amadis de Gaule* T215:xxxiii (perf. 1779), many of whose extracted songs and arias enjoyed popularity in subsequent individual publications. There are many sacred works and songs, symphonies, overtures and *sinfonie concertante*; three sets of six keyboard concertos (op. 1 for harpsichord (pub. 1763) and op. 7 (pub. 1770) and op. 13 (pub. 1777) both for harpsichord/piano. There is much chamber music with keyboard as well as solos and duets for harpsichord.

Further reading
C. Terry, *John Christian Bach* (London, 1929). E. Warburton, *A Study of Johann Christian Bach Operas* (diss., U. of Oxford, 1969). B.A. Mekota, *The Solo and Ensemble Keyboard Works of Johann Christian Bach* (diss., U. of Michigan, 1969). M.A.H. Vos, *The Liturgical Choral Works of Johann Christian Bach* (diss., Washington U., 1969). M.R. Charters, *The Bach-Abel Concerts* (diss., U. of London, 1978). F.C. Petty, *Italian Opera in London 1760–1800* (Ann Arbor, MI, 1980). S.W. Roe, *The Keyboard Music of J.C. Bach* (New York, 1989). Fétis/ *BIOGRAPHIE. MGG.*

Bach, Johann Christoph Friedrich
[the 'Bückerburg Bach']
German composer (b. 21 Jun 1732, Leipzig; d. 26 Jan 1795, Bückerburg).

The eldest surviving son of *J.S. Bach and his second wife Anna Magdalena, he studied music in Leipzig with his father, and possibly had a brief spell studying law in Leipzig university. After his father's death in 1750, he left Leipzig and was appointed harpsichord-player in the small court orchestra at Bückerburg in 1750, where he married in 1755 and became *Concert-Meister*

officially in 1759, having been fulfilling the post's duties for three years previously. Although on good terms with the count (who consented to become godfather to Bach's first son) and despite his attempts to change his compositional style to fit in with the Count's Italianate taste, the latter seems not to have been impressed with Friedrich's compositions. The appointment of *Herder for a brief spell as court pastor was compensation for the provincialities of the court and they became friends and collaborated on a series of dramatic and vocal works during the period 1771–76, when Herder accepted Goethe's invitation to Weimar. Friedrich, together with his eldest son, visited his brother *J.C. Bach in London in 1778, where they enjoyed the thriving concert life and when Bach returned home, leaving his son in Christian's care, he brought with him a piano and a good deal of new music. He remained in post in Bückerburg until his death, in 1795, from a chest complaint possibly brought on by depression over the death of his half-brother *Carl Philipp Emanuel the same year.

Like his two great brothers, Johann Christoph well illustrates the transition from serious *Baroque *contrapuntality to a lyrical *homophonic Classical style, partly through their influence but also from his operatic productions of *W.A. Mozart and *Gluck. His chamber music shows great appreciation of parts' individual integrity.

Works
Much sacred music for soloists, chorus and orchestra, though much of his music is lost or destroyed as a result of the Second World War. Similarly, only eight of his 20 symphonies as well as four of his five keyboard concertos survive. There is

also chamber and keyboard – piano or harpsichord – music.

Further reading
H. Wohlfarth, *Johann Christoph Friedrich Bach* (Berne, 1971). G. Hey, 'Zur Biographie Johann Friedrich Bachs und seiner Familie', *Bach-Jahrbuch*, xxx (1933). *MGG*. Newman/SCE.

Bach, Johann Sebastian
German composer, keyboard-player (b. 21 Mar 1685, Eisenach; d. 28 Jul 1750, Leipzig).

His general education was at the Lateinschule in Eisenach, and it is most likely that his father taught him string playing but not keyboard, which he learned from his relative Johann Christoph Bach in Ohrdruf and possibly organ-building also. His general education continued at one of the schools attached to the Michaeliskirche, Lüneburg, where he was influenced by the organist-composers Georg Böhm, Reincken, Bruhns, Buxtehude and later by Kerll, Pachelbel, Froberger, Fux, Caldara, Frescobaldi, Fischer, Strungk, the Grauns, Zelenka, Keiser, Hasse, Telemann, Handel and Vivaldi. He had no formal teacher(s) of composition.

After his childhood in Eisenach, Bach went to school in Lüneburg (*c*.1700–?1702) and appears to have been a freelance musician in Weimar (?1702–1703) before being appointed as organist of the Neukirche in Arnstadt (1703–1707). His duties allowed him plenty of time for composition and practice, and he undertook his epic journey – on foot – to Lübeck to hear Buxtehude play, extending his allowed leave of one month to four. This and other matters caused friction with his superiors and he was glad to be appointed organist of the Blasiuskirch at Mühlhausen on the same salary as Arnstadt. Although he got on well with the council, it seems that the congregation found the music he was producing – and not just his own compositions – a little too 'modern' for their taste. In any case, he cited this in his letter of resignation, prompted by the offer, by the Duke of Weimar, of a post at his court, the better terms of which no doubt swayed Bach, whose wife – he had married his cousin, the singer Maria Barbara in 1707 – was pregnant. The council reluctantly accepted, asking only that he supervise the overhaul of the St Blasius organ, to which he agreed. He became court organist at Weimar in 1708 and became friendly with J.G. Walther. His promotion to *Konzertmeister* in 1714 (with appropriately enhanced salary) was the result of an offer of the post of organist at Halle, where the organ was over twice the size of that at Weimar; this is even after the enlargement and improvements which Bach had already made to the Weimar instrument. Most of his organ music was written during this period and it is also worth mentioning that Bach had already built up a reputation as an advisor for building, improving and refurbishing organs and has been described as 'the famous Weimar organist' in a book by *Mattheson, who mentioned his compositions as well. It was also at this time (1717) that Bach, visiting Dresden, was persuaded into challenging the French keyboard virtuoso Louis Marchand, to a harpsichord – it was later said to be an organ – 'duel', but Marchand absconded before the event.

Matters at Weimar – rivalry and bad feeling generally between the Duke and his nephew – soured the environment and this, perhaps coupled with Bach's growing awareness of his regard in the wider world, caused him to look around for another post. When he was offered the higher-paid post of *Kapellmeister* at the court of Prince Leopold at Cöthen (1717–23), he accepted; his new master, Prince Leopold of Cöthen, was the brother-in-law of Duke Ernst of Weimar and clearly was to some extent party to negotiations. Perhaps this fact prompted Duke Wilhelm of Weimar to withhold his release. After his visit to Dresden, however, and his pyrrhic victory over Marchand, his letter of request caused such annoyance to Wilhelm that he had Bach imprisoned for almost a month. He finally took up post in December 1717.

At the Cöthen court, Bach found himself in a much more relaxed environment, with a young lover of music – who also understood it – as Duke. The latter had studied music with J.D. Heinichen in Rome while on the Grand Tour and played harpsichord, violin, and viola da gamba as well as sang. The court had, at the time of Bach's arrival, 18 musicians and the bulk of his chamber and orchestral music dates from his sojourn there. The fact that he was also on good personal terms with Prince Leopold was apparent in a number of ways, apart from the fact that his salary was twice that of his predecessor's: the Prince, for example, stood godfather to one of Bach's sons (named after the Prince), and when a room was needed for the orchestra to rehearse, Bach was paid rent when his own home was used. When the Prince took the waters at Carlsbad, he took some musicians (including Bach) and instruments with him. It was on returning from one of these visits that the composer found his wife, at 36, dead and buried. This unsettled him in more than the obvious way and he became interested in the post of organist at Hamburg, which had a four-manual Schnitger organ sporting some 60 *stops. Although offered the post, Bach refused. Now aged 36, he married a 20-year-old singer, Anna Magdalena Wilcke, daughter of a court trumpeter. Less auspicious for Bach was the Prince's very festive marriage in December 1721 to a lady who was uninterested in any of the arts and affected the composer's relationship with her husband. Most of Bach's work at Cöthen consisted of secular cantatas, at least half of which are lost; of the 47 extant, 10 have no surviving music. Also from this period date a number of didactic works, the *Clavierbüchlein* ('Little Keyboard Book') for his new wife Anna Magdalena, of which a third (25 leaves) survives and a similar work for his son *W.F. Bach, the *Clavier-Büchlein*, although they contain earlier music also. It seems as if he also began his great collection of preludes and fugues, *Das *wohltemperirte Clavier* ('The Well-tempered Clavier') in Cöthen.

The circumstances of Bach's next appointment, as *Kantor* at the Thomaskirche in Leipzig, have gone down in history as one of the most stinging indictments of philistine small-town government, in spite of the post being one of the most prestigious in Germany and in a thriving and prosperous city. Telemann was the most favoured – and by far the most famous – of the six-strong shortlist, but withdrew as he was offered an increase in salary in his extant post, a state of affairs which also applied to the next best, Graupner. After several other candidates dropped out for various reasons, and only Bach and two others remained, Bach was reluctantly offered the post, on the basis that, according to Councillor Platz, one of the appointing committee, the best musicians being unavailable, a mediocre one would have to do(!). In spite of being attached to the Thomaskirche, the

Kantor's duties actually included the four main churches in Leipzig, the musical education of the selective Thomasschule and a number of musico-civic duties also. His compositional burden centred on church music (mostly a cantata of about half an hour's duration) for Sundays, principal feasts and some other occasions, and a yearly cycle comprised of some 60 cantatas; Bach completed – almost certainly, since a good deal is lost – five complete cycles. The only other music he composed during his first six years at Leipzig were his six Harpsichord *Partitas* and some pieces for his occasional virtuoso organ-recitals.

In 1729, in addition to his other duties, Bach took over the *collegium musicum*, a voluntary instrumental body involving university students as well as professional musicians giving weekly concerts on a regular basis and, occasionally, extra ones. Many works of Bach's own, frequently earlier, works in revised form, and those of other composers, were performed, with occasional visits (by special invitation) from musicians from outside. His output in sacred music was only slightly diminished, including the Passions and some of the Masses (the great B Minor Mass among them) as well as motets, etc. His music for the Dresden court earned him the title of *Hofkomponist*.

Bach's difficulties with authority, including arguments over various kinds of precedence and clashes with others over scholastic and musical matters, surfaced in Leipzig, becoming, at times, quite acute. He gave up the *collegium musicum* in 1737 and took on a number of private pupils. The same year, his compositional style (not his performance) was publicly criticized in the journal *Der critische Musikus* by J.A. Scheibe and, in spite of vociferous factions gathering behind

the two, matters were somewhat left in the air. Bach took over the *collegium musicum* again in 1739, but five years later its 40-year life ended because of lack of accommodation.

Bach continued to produce instrumental music during this period – the '*Goldberg' Variations and sets of *chorale preludes for organ. He also developed an interest in the piano, no doubt following from his admiration of the work of Gottfried *Silbermann, with whose excellent organs he was well acquainted and who also made pianos; the composer's suggestions were incorporated into Silbermann's mechanisms. He also acted as an agent in selling one of the pianos, which he praised publicly.

It was this connection which gave rise to one of his last great works. When, in 1747, he accepted an invitation to *Frederick the Great's court at Potsdam to see his son Carl Philipp Emanuel, the harpsichordist at the court, he played on a series of Silbermann's pianos, improvising in various genres, including on a theme given him by the King, the result of which was acclaimed by all present. On his return to Leipzig, he composed the *Musikalisches Opfer ('*Musical Offering*'), based entirely on the King's theme. He had this printed the same year and dedicated to Frederick. In spite of an eye cataract, Bach was engaged in another correspondence controversy, this time about the place of music in schools. He became completely blind, and an operation (1750) by the British eye-specialist John Taylor was only partly successful; a repetition of the surgery failed. Taylor's performance of the same operation on Handel, however, was a success. Bach, much weakened, died after a stroke shortly afterwards. The other great work from his last years, begun in the mid-1740s, was *Die Kunst der Fuge* ('*The Art of Fugue*') which remained unfinished (by less than half a movement, it seems) at his death.

Bach transformed just about all of the extant compositional genres during his lifetime except opera and he created the keyboard concerto. His influence on subsequent music is incalculable. In terms of personal influence, he taught, as well as members of his own family, J.M. Schubart, J.C. Vogler, Krebs, *Agricola, Kirnberger, *Abel, Altnikol, *Gerber, Schübler, Kittel, Nichelmann, Müthel, Doles and G.G. Wagner. The 'Bach revival' of the first half of the nineteenth century (for which *Felix Mendelssohn was largely responsible) brought his music to many composers – Mendelssohn himself, *Schumann, *Chopin, *Brahms, etc. – none of whom escaped his influence.

Works
Religious: 200 surviving cantatas, representing about three-fifths of his total; four Passions (Sts Matthew, John, Mark and Luke; the Easter and Christmas Oratorios; motets; hundreds of chorales. Instrumental music includes many organ works (six trio sonatas, preludes and fugues, the *Orgelbüchlein* ('Little Organ Book') (BWV599-644), the 'Schübler' Chorales (BWV645-60)); chamber works: the Suites and *Partitas* (three of each) for solo violin, the six Solo Cello Suites and works for violin and for flute with harpsichord. For harpsichord: *Das *wohltemperirte Clavier* (48 Preludes and Fugues, BWV846-69), *Italian Concerto*, *Goldberg Variations*, 2- and 3-part Inventions; various concertos for violin, and for harpsichord and four Orchestral Suites. The **Musikalisches Opfer* ('Musical Offering') and *Die Kunst*

der Fuge ('The Art of Fugue') date from his last years, and the latter remained unfinished at his death.

Further reading
Too numerous to mention; a good general introduction is C.M. Boyd, *Bach* ('The Master Musicians' Series, London, 1983).

Bach, Wilhelm Friedemann [the 'Halle Bach']
German composer, keyboard player (b. 22 Nov 1710, Weimar; d. 1 Jul 1784, Berlin).

Eldest son (and favourite child) of *J.S. Bach, he was taught by his father and at the Lateinschule (Cöthen) and, at the age of 13, he entered the Thomasschule when the family moved to Leipzig in 1723. He also studied the violin for a year with J.G. Graun in Merseburg and philosophy, mathematics and law at the University of Leipzig (1729–33). Friedemann visited *Handel in Halle in 1729 to invite him to visit J.S. Bach and the family in Leipzig, but Handel was unable to accept; in fact these two greatest German composers of the period never managed to meet. In 1733, the year in which Friedemann's studies (mathematics, law and philosophy) at Leipzig University ended, he was appointed organist (part-time) at the Sophienkirche, Dresden where the *Kapellmeister*, Pantaleon *Hebenstreit, had the greatest respect for him. He also became friendly with other musicians – Hasse (and his wife), Buffardin and the lutenist Silvius Weiss. By this time Friedemann was recognized as the best organist in Germany and this, together with his father's influence, helped him to gain the prestigious post of organist at the Liebfraukirche, Halle, in 1746, which carried with it the responsibility for music (with orchestra) at Halle's three main churches. Friedemann accompanied his father on the latter's visit to one of his other sons, *C.P.E. Bach at the court of *Frederick the Great in Potsdam, on which occasion Bach senior's *Musikalisches Opfer ('Musical Offering') was conceived. Such visits, no doubt, contrasted sharply with the strict pietism of Halle, which was beginning to become burdensome to the fun-loving, free-thinking and newly-married composer. On top of this, there was a degree of friction with his employers and the advent of the Seven Years War (1756–63) subjected Halle residents to huge taxes. Although offered the post of *Kapellmeister at the Darmstadt court, he failed to take it up for reasons which are unclear; this, by common consent, appears to be the beginning of the erratic behaviour for which he became known afterwards (although exaggerated in some quarters). He finally resigned his Halle post in 1764 and taught privately until 1770, when the family moved to Brunswick for four years, becoming friendly with his father's biographer, Forkel. It was here that financial pressures caused him to begin the dispersal of his father's manuscripts with little regard for their destinations; many have never been recovered. The last ten years of his life (1774–84) were spent in Berlin in illness and poverty and he died of lung disease, leaving his wife and daughter in dire financial straits.

Friedemann was greatly gifted musically, but wayward. Unlike his brothers, he never managed work through the *Baroque or to combine it with later styles, resulting in strangely hybrid works in which old and new styles sit side by side, sometimes happily, sometimes not. He also did not help his reputation, or publishability, by neglecting popular forms such as the rondo, the variation-set, and the lied. Yet, there is plenty of beauty of melody and harmonic daring, and the 12 fine keyboard *Polonaises are expressive enough to place them among the progenitors of *Romanticism. Among his pupils were Nichelmann, Rust and Sara Levy (the *Mendelssohns' great-aunt). His father wrote the first book of the '48' (Das *wohltemperirte Clavier) for him and it was unfortunate that this was one of the manuscripts which he sold and which has never come to light.

Works

Sonatas, fugues and short pieces for harpsichord including 12 *Polonaises F12 (c.1765); some harpsichord concertos and chamber, orchestral and sacred works.

Further reading

W. Nagel, 'W. Fr. Bachs Berufung nach Darmstadt', SIMG, i (1900). M. Falck, Wilhelm Friedemann Bach: sein Leben und seine Werke, mit thematischen Verseichnis und zwei Bildern (Leipzig, 1913, rev. 1919). P. Wollny, Studies in the Music of Wilhelm Friedemann Bach: Sources and Style (diss., Harvard U., 1993).

Backers, Americus

Dutch or German piano- and harpsichord-maker (fl. London 1763–78; d. Jan 1778, London).

Almost nothing is known about Backers except that between the years given he worked at 22 Great Jermyn Street in London. The invention of the *'English' grand action in 1772 is attributed to him by James Shudi Broadwood, possibly with the collaboration of John *Broadwood and Robert *Stodart. One harpsichord (1766) survives, owned by Lord Hylton, and a piano of his is in the Benton Fletcher

Collection at Fenton House, London, and another – the earliest example of the *'English' grand action with the date 1772 on the nameboard – was owned by the Duke of Wellington (now on loan to Edinburgh University).

Further reading
W.H. Cole, 'Americus Backers: Original Forte Piano Maker', *English Harpsichord Magazine*, iv/4 (1987). Cole/PIANOFORTE.

Bagatelle (Fr.; Ger. 'trifle')
A short, light piece, usually for keyboard and associated with no particular musical form. The name first appears as a title for a piece ('Les bagatelles') in *F. Couperin's tenth *ordre* for harpsichord (pub. 1717). It became well known after its use by *Beethoven, as the title for his sets of pieces for piano, opp. 33 (1801–1802), 119 (1820–22) and 126 (1823–24), the later pieces of which transcend the expected triviality to become comparable with his more serious piano works. His famous miniature *Für Elise* is also a bagatelle. Later composers have also written sets of bagatelles (some individual pieces of which have been given titles) such as Saint-Saëns (the six of op. 3, pub. 1856), Sibelius and Bartók. Some have also departed from the solo-piano format, as in the case of Dvořák, whose four of op. 47 are scored for two violins, cello and harmonium and Webern's six for string quartet of 1913.

Bagpipe
A wind instrument whose sound, in the simplest terms, is produced by air passing through a pipe with a reed or reeds. The air is fed from a bag (usually goatskin or sheepskin) produced by blowing or by a small bellows strapped to the player.

Whereas the instrument can have as many as seven pipes (not including that used to blow it), it is very rare to find less than two, the chanter (producing the melody) and the drone, or drones, each producing a continuous single note, usually the key-note and/or its fifth (dominant). (The most advanced bagpipes, the Irish *Uileann* Pipes, also have two or three 'regulators', producing several notes by keys, which can be tuned to give chords). The instrument, an important component in *folk music, is of great antiquity and exists in many local variations of the basic type. The most common are (apart from the Irish instrument mentioned), the well-known Great Highland Pipe (Gaelic *píob mhór*), the Northumbrian small-pipes, the Breton *biniou*, the French *cornemeuse* and *musette*, the Italian *zampogna* and *cornamusa*, the Germanic *Dudelsack*, and a number of Middle and Eastern European types (*gajda, kozioł, dudy, diple, piva*, etc.). Their main shared characteristics, the drone(s) and the 'warblers' (grace-notes), were imitated in art-music including piano-music, in pieces with folk connections, ranging from the French *clavecinistes* through *Chopin (especially in the *Mazurkas) and on to later figures such as Bartók.

Balbastre [Balbâtre], **Claude-Béninge**
French composer, organist (b. 22 Jan 1727, Dijon; d. 9 May 1799, Paris).
He received organ lessons from his father and perhaps C. Rameau in Dijon. When the family settled in Paris in 1750, he received lessons from J.-P. Rameau (composition) and P. Février (organ) and frequently played organ at the *Concerts Spirituels (his own concertos and transcriptions of others' works). He was appointed organist at St Roch (1756) and part-time at Notre Dame (1760).

In 1776 Balbastre became organist to Monsieur (later Louis XVIII) and also taught the children of the nobility and of other important figures (including Marie-Antoinette and Thomas Jefferson). He remained until the Revolution and was reduced to poverty for the remainder of his life after the fall of the monarchy.

Balbastre wrote sets of keyboard pieces with character-names after the manner of *F. Couperin. He is credited with the invention of the *peau de bouffle* (a set of harpsichord quills of leather, giving a less metallic tone), and of the 'fortepiano organisé' (a combined piano and organ); although he is quoted as having an antipathy to the piano, he appears to have had a conversion.

Works
Include *Pièces de clavecin, 1er livre* (pub. 1759); *Recueil de noëls formant 4 suites* (harpsichord/pf, pub. 1770); *Sonates en quatuor* (harpsichord/pf, two violins, cello, and two horns *ad lib*, pub. 1779) and organ concertos (now lost).

Further reading
J. Gran, *L'orgue et les organistes en Bourbogne et en Franche-Comté au dix-huitième siècle* (Paris, 1943). M. Frécot, *La vie et l'œuvre de Claude-Benigne Balbastre (1727–1799)* (diss., U. of Paris, c.1950). H. Cripe, *Thomas Jefferson and Music* (Charlottesville, VA, 1974). C. Pierre, *Histoire du Concert spirituel 1725–1790* (Paris, 1975). Fétis/*BIOGRAPHIE*. Burney/*PRESENT*. *MGG*.

Ballad (from Lat. *ballare*, 'to dance')
(1) *The *folk ballad* A species of folk-song characterized by a dramatic narrative style. It was known from the Middle Ages and was originally used for dancing-songs (the *carole*, for example),

but later came to describe a narrative solo song. The genre exists throughout Europe and possesses a power and craftsmanship which places occasional examples on a par with art-poetry and song. Ballads frequently deal with the supernatural and are an important repository of folk belief from various historical stages in the last 800 years. They came into prominence in the mid-eighteenth century and during the *Romantic period with the growing interest in the vernacular.

Three collections were influential in Britain: the 'Broadside Ballads', whose words, of folk origin, and often dealing with contemporary sensations, were printed on large sheets of paper called broadsides, were sold on the streets and at fairs and were hardly ever accompanied with musical notation, and the 'Child' Ballads were collected by the American scholar F.J. Child and published in 5 volumes (1882–98) as *English and Scottish Popular Ballads*, which included several variants of many of the poems. The third collection is the subject of the following section.

(2) *The German art-ballad* In 1765, Bishop Percy published a collection of manuscript ballads which he found in his house. It had great influence in Germany subsequently, with imitations by the leading poets of the time and translations into German by figures such as *Herder (in the 1770s). The form occupied an important place in the work of Goethe and Schiller and was also prominent in the work of the first *Berlin *Lied* School, of *Reichardt, *Zelter and (especially) *Zumsteg, who influenced *Schubert and *Loewe as well as later composers. The ballad thus became an important component in the German *lied tradition in the nineteenth century. Goethe's poem

Erlkönig is well-known, especially in its settings by *Schubert and others.

(3) *The English sentimental ballad* Another type of ballad can be seen in the output of British composers from the late eighteenth century – Dibdin and Horn, for example – usually appearing in operas, of which they were often the most popular numbers. They were sentimental and homely and became the mainstay of the drawing-room musicians, hence the sub-genre 'drawing-room ballad'. They became the basis of a huge industry in Britain and America, associated not so much with their composers, as with their singers who, together with the publishers made large sums of money from them. One of the best-known of all was *Bishop's *'Home, sweet home' (1823).

(4) See *Ballade.

(5) See *Ballad-opera.

Ballade
(1) Together with the *virelai* and the *rondeau*, one of the standard verse-forms of late medieval French poetry and song, with each verse ending with the same refrain-line.

(2) A type of early-nineteenth-century instrumental piece (usually for piano). The earliest use of the name in this sense was probably the first of *Chopin's four ballades – op. 23 in G minor, 1831–35 pub. 1836. The others are no. 2 in F major op. 38 (1836–39), no. 3 in A♭ major op. 47 (1840–41) and no. 4 in F minor (1842). They share the characteristics of having compound time-signatures, being similar in cut and content to the heroic *folk-*ballads and having a discursive narrative style based less on the standard musical forms of the period than on a kind of thematic metamorphosis suggestive of an extramusical (literary) programme. The suggestion that they were influenced by the ballads of his friend, the Polish poet Adam Mickiewicz, was not alluded to by Chopin, and the feeling is of a more general balladry than specific models or stories. Later composers also used the form, such as *Brahms, in his *Four Ballades* op. 10 (1854), the first of which is headed 'After the Scottish ballad "Edward"' in *Herder's 'Stimmen der Völker', and Grieg. Vieuxtemps wrote a Ballade and *Polonaise for violin and piano, and Fauré one for piano and orchestra.

Further reading
J. Samson, *Chopin's Ballades* (Cambridge, 1995).

*Ballad-opera
A theatrical and musical entertainment in English which grew up in Britain during the first third of the eighteenth century, with connections to the earlier French *vaudeville*. The dialogue was spoken, like the *Singspiel*, which influenced subsequently, and the music consisted of separate songs sung by the actors and accompanied by harpsichord. These were adapted from *folk-songs, ballads, popular songs and, occasionally, opera-arias with new words in keeping with the subject-matter. This was comic, usually satirical, vernacular and topical, one of the reasons for the growth of the ballad-opera being the hegemony of Italian opera in Britain which, because of the language, style and costliness, was a minority and upper-class pursuit. The most famous of them was the first, John Gay's *The Beggar's Opera*, with music selected and arranged by J.C. Pepusch, produced in 1728. The

subject is London's low-life criminal class, with much of the action being set in Newgate Prison. It is also a satire on London's high-life and, particularly, the Prime Minister, Sir Robert Walpole and, similarly, several characters are based on other real individuals such as the recently-executed highwayman Jack Sheppard, who was the prototype for the hero, Captain MacHeath. The opera was a huge success and spawned some ninety imitations within a decade, although the fashion was soon superseded with the reinstatement of Italian opera, *Handel being one of its main champions. The form did survive, however, without its satirical bite, as the country opera, with a rural or village backdrop to a story-line of love and deception. Important representatives of this type are C. Johnson's *The Village Opera* (perf. 1729), I. Bickerstaffe's *Love in a Village* (perf. 1763) and J. O'Keefe's *The Highland Reel*, with music by William Shield.

Baroque

From as early as the thirteenth century, the term 'baroque' was used in art and literary criticisms a derogatory term with connotations of grotesquery and absurdity, supposed to have been derived from the Portuguese word *barroco* (an irregular pearl). It became a term of respectable criticism in the mid-nineteenth century when applied to the art and civilization of the seventeenth century, although it is still used (with a small-case 'b') to imply an over-decorated fussiness.

In music, the term designates the period between the Renaissance and the *Classical, roughly (and in several phases) 1540–1750, although it must be remembered that this does not take into account geographical location or stylistic overlap. The traits associated with the term are an expression of individuality (shown in the development of the concerto, for example), the preponderance of *polyphony as opposed to *homophony (though in a freer sense than dictated by the Renaissance), a more-or-less equal balance between harmony and *counterpoint, a strong tendency towards unification on various levels (such as, in emotional terms, that dictated by the contemporary *Doctrine of Affections) and the use of florid *decoration.

Barrington, Daines

British lawyer, naturalist, writer, antiquary (b. 1727, London; d. 14 Mar 1800, London).

Son of a viscount, he attended Oxford university, but left without a degree. He was called to the Bar and held several public offices. His many interests included music and the phenomenon of the child prodigy, examining and testing, among others, the young *W.A. Mozart, reporting his findings to the Royal Society in 1769 (see *Works*).

Works (concerning music only)
'Account of a Very Remarkable Musician. In a Letter from the Honourable Daines Barrington, F.R.S. to Matthew Maty, MD. Sec. R.S.', *Philosophical Transactions of the Royal Society*, lx (1770) the results of his tests on the 13-year-old *W.A. Mozart in 1769; 'Experiments and Observations on the Singing of Birds', *Philosophical Transactions of the Royal Society*, lxiii (1773); *Miscellanies* (London 1781) with accounts of contemporary musicians.

Further reading
Obituary in *Gentleman's Magazine*, lxx (1800). J.C. Kassler, *The Science of Music in Britain 1714–1830* (New York, 1979), vol. 1.

Bartolozzi, Therese (see *Jansen, Therese)

Basso continuo (see *Continuo)

Battle of Prague, The
A hugely successful piece by *Koczwara first published in Dublin, c.1788, for piano trio. It was reprinted may times throughout Europe and America in many arrangements, including its best-known form as a solo piano piece.

Battle-piece (Fr. *bataille*; It. *battaglia*)
A piece of *programme-music popular from the sixteenth to the nineteenth centuries depicting a particular (named) battle. Famous examples are orchestral, *Beethoven's *'Battle Symphony' (op. 91, 1813) and Tchaikovsky's *1812* overture (op. 49, 1880) – both inspired by the Napoleonic wars – and *Liszt's *Hunnenschlacht* (*Battle of the Huns*). The name is also applied to a genre of piano-piece, exemplified by *Koczwara's *The Battle of Prague*, which follows the progress of a battle from the forebodings through rallying-calls, national anthems, sounds of guns and ammunition and 'cries of the wounded' to the final triumphal march. Such pieces were particularly suited to the early piano because of its wide range in pitch and in sonic possibilities, but also because of the use of the various *stops and *pedals which, when present (as they often were) could further alter the sound. Many examples of the type can be found, including those by *Lemière de Corvey, J. Blewitt and J. Gildon.

'Battle Symphony'
An orchestral *battle-piece by *Beethoven, op. 91 (1813) the full title of which is *Wellingtons Sieg oder Die Schlacht bei Vittoria* (*Wellington's Victory, or the Battle of Vittoria*). The last word is Beethoven's mis-spelling of 'Vitoria', the town in northern Spain where the battle took place during the Peninsular War on 13 June 1813, resulting in Wellington's decisive victory over Napoleon's troops.

Bebung
A performance device peculiar to the clavichord, in which the constant contact which the tangent – and indirectly the finger – had with the string allowed the pitch to fluctuate when the key was shaken from side to side, or quickly pressed up and down, without re-sounding.

Beethoven, Ludwig van
German composer (bap. 17 Dec 1770, Bonn; d. 26 Mar 1827, Vienna).
  The son of a local court musician who taught him piano and violin, he also learned piano from T. Pfeifer and organ from Willibald Koch, Zenser and G. van den Eeden (who may have given him composition lessons also) and he attended the Bonn *Tirocinium* (public school). Beethoven's father's harshness and savage discipline resulted in an unhappy childhood; his most significant teacher in Bonn was the court organist, Christian Gottlob *Neefe, who taught him composition, c.1779–92 and whom, by 11 years of age, he was assisting as deputy organist and by playing orchestral harpsichord. His mother died of tuberculosis when he was 17 and his father's drink problem put the family in financial jeopardy, upon which he petitioned their employer, the Elector, for half of his father's salary, which was granted. His work – he was by now also playing viola in the court and other orchestras – brought him into close contact with the orchestral musicians

such as Franz Ries (with whom he studied violin and whose son, *Ferdinand Ries, he later taught), Andreas and Bernhard Romberg, Nikolaus Simrock (with whom he studied the horn) and *Antoine Reicha. He also made some important non-musical connections, with Count Waldstein (dedicatee of his eponymous Piano Sonata in C major op. 53) who became a loyal patron and friend and the young widow, Frau von Breuning, who was a second mother to him.

Beethoven went to Vienna in 1792 on an allowance from the elector and remained for the rest of his life, much of it supported by his aristocratic friends. His lessons with *J. Haydn did not satisfy his rigour and he took others in secret, with J. Schenck and probably *W.A. Mozart, also with Albrechtsberger (counterpoint) and Salieri (vocal composition).

J. Haydn, however, was always on hand to encourage him and speak on his behalf. Because of his aristocratic connections and the fact that the Austro-Hungarian and German nobility were particularly literate and cultured musically, his career advanced quickly and, in spite of his antisocial and rude manner, he was much in demand as pianist and composer. He published a set of three piano trios as his op. 1 – in spite of Haydn's advice to omit the last because of its novelty – and dedicated them to Prince *Lichnowsky in whose house he was staying and who remained a staunch patron; the publication made the young composer a tidy profit. In February 1796 he and the prince embarked on a concert-tour of Prague, Dresden (playing for the Elector of Saxony) and Berlin (appearing several times before Friedrich Wilhelm II, King of Prussia and meeting Himmel, *Zelter and Fasch). The arrival of the French emissary Général Bernadotte with the

celebrated violinist Rodolphe Kreutzer followed and they are credited with the suggestion that the composer should write a heroic symphony celebrating the young French general Bonaparte, who was Beethoven's age at the time; this would become his third, the 'Eroica', in E♭ major, op. 55 (1803). His outward life seemed very happy: he was surrounded by a circle of (mostly rich and titled) friends who were generous in their care and financial assistance and whom he occasionally treated abominably, his works were eagerly awaited by publishers and listeners alike, he felt his performance on the piano had improved; by now he was regarded as the best in Europe.

But he was nurturing a dark secret. For a few years, Beethoven had begun to be aware of approaching deafness, which he kept to himself until the middle of 1801, when he wrote to two of his friends. After his death, a document (afterwards called the 'Heiligenstadt Testament', after the village in which he spent the summer of 1802) was found among his papers which shows his feelings of suicidal despair at this time (1802). His third symphony ('Sinfonia eroica') was originally entitled 'Bonaparte' but, when the general proclaimed himself emperor (May 1804), Beethoven famously tore the work's title-page in half. His compositions continued unabated – the fourth, fifth and sixth symphonies, the three 'Rasoumofsky' quartets op. 59, the two piano trios op. 70, the Mass in C major op. 86 and the fourth piano concerto. There were also a few love affairs at this time, mostly involving ladies above his social station and it may have been the failure of these that began to interest him in a more permanent, and salaried, position. Count Lichnowsky was already paying him an allowance and, when he received an offer of a *Kapellmeister*ship from Napoleon's youngest brother, Jérôme (whom he had installed as King of Westphalia), his noble friends rallied around to keep him in Vienna. Three of them – the Archduke Rudolph (who remained a close friend until his death), Prince *Lobkowitz and Prince Kinsky – guaranteed him an annuity-cum-pension and he did, indeed, remain in Vienna for the rest of his life. He travelled a little at this time, however, in search of cures for his ill-health, meeting Goethe in Teplitz, falling in love with his physician's 18-year-old daughter (he himself was now 40) and writing the famous letter to the 'Immortal Beloved', whose identity has been the subject of much intrigue, but is most plausibly Antonie ('Toni') Brentano, ten years younger that Beethoven, and unhappily married. Again, nothing came of the relationship, although there is evidence that at least on this occasion, the love was requited. Beethoven entered a period of some three years of depression which curtailed his creative output. On top of this, his annuity was reduced drastically (to less than half) by the devaluation of the currency due to the Napoleonic wars, Kinsky was killed in a riding accident and Lichnowsky's estate much reduced because of mismanagement; so Beethoven was financially less than comfortable. His brother, Caspar Carl, was seriously ill at this time and requested that the composer take responsibility for Caspar's son, Karl, then aged 6, to which Beethoven consented. To celebrate Wellington's victory at Vittoria, he composed a *'Battle' symphony. This was one of several pieces performed at concerts during the *Congress of Vienna (November 1814 – June 1815). Beethoven made a good deal of money, in various ways, and even though his annuity was restored to its former value, his letters of the time show him to be full of financial insecurity. In late 1815, a series of events began which would dominate practically the rest of his life. His brother Caspar Carl died and the custody of his nephew, Karl (nine years of age) was not, as the previous document had stated, given to Beethoven, but, in a codicil, divided between him and the boy's mother. Beethoven was determined to have the boy removed to his sole custody and, by a process of vilification, succeeded and in January 1816 he had the child removed to a boarding school. In 1818 he took Karl into his own home and hired a tutor for him, but a few months later he placed him in a village school, from which the boy was soon expelled for speaking against his mother (encouraged by none other than Beethoven). After four years of legal wrangling he finally (1820) regained custody of his nephew, very much a mixed blessing.

By this time Beethoven was completely deaf and his conversations with others were carried out *via* notebooks, containing the other side of the conversations. Unfortunately, Anton *Schindler, who was for some years a kind of factotum of the composer's, took it on himself to destroy two-thirds of them and falsify to some extent what remained, such was his 'devotion' to the great man. His nephew Karl, now at university, had moved in with him and the relationship was not an easy one; Beethoven was possessive and jealously suspicious of the young man's friends and the eventual result was Karl's attempted suicide in 1826. Beethoven was extremely affected and afterwards became prey to several physical conditions including abdominal and joint pains and eye troubles.

However, he gradually began to emerge into if not quite society at least the streets of Vienna and although he was by no means in sympathy with Vienna's musical fashions, he was persuaded, by a deputation of friends and admirers, to conduct a public concert. This comprised of an overture, part of the C Major Mass and the Ninth Symphony; the event was very well attended and the music well received. Beethoven, according to several later reminiscences, remained at the conductor's desk engrossed in his score until told about the tremendous applause going on behind him, upon which he turned and bowed. The last three years of his life were confined to the string quartet and his ailments became progressively worse. The *Philharmonic Society of London sent him a gift of £100 and he was continually visited by friend and well-wishers. He died about 17.45 on 26 March 1827 and his funeral was a huge public event with some 10,000 mourners. He left his estate to his nephew Karl.

Works
Nine symphonies (including the 'Eroica', no. 3 in E♭ major op. 55 (1803), the 'Pastoral', no. 6 in F major op. 68 (1808) and the *'Choral', no. 9 in D minor op. 125), a *'Battle Symphony', overtures (including *Coriolan* op. 62 (1807), *Leonora* no. 1 op. 138 (1806–1807)), dances and incidental music; five mature piano concertos (no. 1 in C major op. 15 (1795, rev. 1800), no. 2 in B♭ major op. 19 (1793–98), no. 3 in C minor op. 37 (?1800), no. 4 in G major op. 58 (1805–1806) and no. 5 in E♭ major (*'Emperor' op. 73 (1809)); 18 string quartets (including the six of op. 18 (1798–1800), the three *'Rasoumofsky' Quartets op. 59 (1805–1806), and the *Grosse Fuge* in B♭ major op. 133 (1825–26)); piano trios, violin sonatas (including the 'Spring' in F major op.

24 (1800–1801) and the *'Kreutzer' in A minor op. 47 (1802–1803)), five cello sonatas; 32 piano sonatas (including no.8 in C minor op. 13 (the *'*Pathétique*', ?1797–98), no. 14 in C♯ minor, op. 27/2 (the *'Moonlight', 1801), no. 15 in D minor op. 28 ('Pastoral', 1801), no. 17 op. 31/2 in D minor (*'Tempest', 1802), no. 21 in C major op. 53 (*'Waldstein', 1803–1804), no. 23 in F minor op. 54 (*'Appassionata', 1804–1805) and no. 29 in B♭ major op. 106 (*'*Hammerklavier*', 1817–18)); sets of variations and shorter pieces for piano (including 15 Variations and a Fugue on an Original Theme op. 35 ('Eroica Variations', 1802) and 33 *Variations on a Waltz by *Diabelli op. 120 (1819; 1822–23)), smaller piano pieces (including sets of *Bagatelles); many songs (including the cycle *An die ferne Geliebte*) and folksong arrangements; masses (inc. *Missa solemnis* in D major op. 123 (1819–23)) and cantatas.

Further reading
There is a huge body of literature, but a good start could include M. Solomon, *Beethoven* (New York, 1977); H.C.R. Landon, *Beethoven: a Documentary Study* (London and New York, 1970); ed., *The Beethoven Companion* (London 1987). D.W. Jones, *Beethoven* (London, 2003).

Behrent, Johann (see *Brent, John)

Bel canto (It. 'beautiful song)
A term applied to singing (usually female voices) and to *arias which were of the Italian fluid, lyrical (rather than dramatic) sort of the eighteenth and early nineteenth centuries. By implication, the term has been applied to a style of piano playing, texture or melody which exhibited similar properties, such as in the *nocturnes of

*Field and *Chopin. The main models were *Rossini, Donizetti and, especially, *Bellini.

Bellini, Vincenzo
Italian composer (b. 3 Nov 1801, Catania; d. 23 Sep 1835, Puteaux, nr Paris).

The oldest of seven children of a *maestro di cappella*, organist and composer, he learnt the piano from his father and composition from his grandfather, and his general education was entrusted to a local priest. He was much influenced by *W.A. Mozart, *Rossini and by his native *folk-music. Bellini left Catania at 17 (1819) as the municipal government paid for his further studies at the Naples conservatory, where he worked with G. Furno, C. Conti, G. Tritto (counterpoint), Zingarelli, the director (composition and *solfège*) and G. Crescentini (theory of singing). He was commissioned to write an opera (*Il pirata*) for La Scala, Milan, where he moved in 1827. The opera was a great success and he became friendly with its librettist, Felice Romani, with whom he produced some of his greatest operas, and also friendly with the tenor G.B. Rubini who became his collaborator for some nine years. Bellini was accepted in the higher social circles and was able to support himself by writing operas alone, unlike many of his opera-composing counterparts, such as Rossini and Donizetti. It was around this time (*c*.1830) that the first signs of the gastro-enteritis which would kill him began to show itself. His operas were occasionally unsuccessful, mainly because of their novelty, but their worth was soon recognized.

His work was now being performed around Europe and the years 1833–35 were divided between London and Paris, where he made the acquaintance and friendship of *Rossini, *Chopin, Heine and others. It was also where he died, while in quarantine for suspected cholera although it was in fact the gastro-enteritis which had already been a problem.

His beautiful, simple and approachable melodies were based on his native Sicilian folk music and he had an instinctive response to prosody, together with the ability to construct long curving lines from short, often two-bar, units. This *bel canto* melodic style was adopted by many *Romantic composers, especially the piano virtuoso-composers, *Hummel, *Field and *Chopin.

Works
A good deal of vocal, as well as a small amount of instrumental and orchestral music are of little significance compared to his operas which include: *Il pirata* (perf. Milan, 1827), *La straniera* (perf. Milan, 1829), *I Capuleti e i Montecchi* (perf. Venice, 1830), *La sonnambula*, *Norma* (both perf. Milan, 1831), *I puritani* (perf. Paris, 1835).

Further reading
F. Schlitzer, 'Vincenzo Bellini', *Mondo teatrale dell'Ottocento* (Naples, 1954). L. Orrey, *Bellini* (London and New York, 1969). H. Weinstock, *Vincenzo Bellini: his Life and his Operas* (New York, 1971). M. Adamo and F. Lippmann, Vincenzo Bellini (Paris, 1981). J. Rossellini, *The Life of Bellini* (Cambridge, 1996).

Benda, Franz [František]
Bohemian composer, violinist (bap. 22 Nov 1709, Staré Benátky; d. 7 Mar 1786, Nowawes, nr Potsdam).

After two years at St Nicholas's in Prague where he was a chorister, Benda ran away at the age of 11 (1720), and sang at the Hofkapelle in Dresden, where he also studied the violin. Returning to Prague in 1723, he joined the Jesuit seminary where he sang also and, after his voice broke, concentrated on the violin and composition. The years 1726–29 were spent in Vienna but, following some trouble, he and some friends hastily departed for Warsaw, joining a chamber ensemble until 1732 when he became a violinist in the royal orchestra. He studied composition with J.G. Graun in Ruppin (1733–36) and afterwards with his brother C.H. Graun. The Prussian crown prince *Frederick – later The Great – appointed him as his violinist and he moved with him to Potsdam on his accession as emperor in 1740, where he got on well with his colleagues, who included *C.P.E. Bach and J.J. *Quantz. Benda was appointed Frederick's *Konzertmeister* in 1771.

Benda founded a new school of violin playing, specializing in affecting *cantabile* playing and in *decorating the given melody-lines. He taught, among others J.W. Hertel, F.W. Rust and J.P. *Salomon, friend of *J. Haydn, and responsible for bringing him to London.

Works

His chamber music centres on the violin and includes duos and trios; in some cases the flute can substitute for the violin. There are 17 symphonies and 17 violin concertos. Some of his works are collaborative and some misattributed. Quite a number are lost.

Further reading

F. Berten, *Franz Benda: sein Leben und seine Kompositionen* (Essen, 1928). E.E. Helm, *Music at the Court of Frederick the Great* (Norman, 1960). T.C. Murphy, *The Violin Concertos of Franz Benda and their Use in Violin Pedagogy* (diss., U. of Southern California, 1968). D. Heartz,

'Coming of Age in Bohemia: the Musical Apprenticeships of Benda and Gluck', *The Journal of Musicology*, vi (1988). Burney/PRESENT.

Benda, Georg (Anton) [Jiří Antonín] Bohemian composer, brother of *Franz Benda (bap. 30 Jun 1772, Staré Benátky; d. 6 Nov 1795, Köstritz).

He attended high school and (1739–42) the Jesuit college at Jičín and emigrated with his family to Prussia in 1742 where, like his brothers, he became a violinist in the court orchestra of Prince *Frederick – to be The Great – of Prussia. In 1750 he was appointed as *Kapellmeister* to Duke Friedrich III of Saxe-Gotha, receiving six months' leave to study in Italy (1765–66), meeting Hasse in Venice and visiting Bologna, Florence and Rome. He returned home to a new title, *Kapelldirector* in 1770. The death of his master and the accession of a new one in 1772 began a period of opera-composition, including *Singspiels* and the *melodramas *Ariadne auf Naxos* and *Medea*. After a visit to Vienna, where his work was a success, he retired to Gotha on a pension, during which time he directed a performance of *Ariadne* in Paris and visited Mannheim several times. He died in 1795.

Benda created the first successful *melodramas which particularly impressed *W.A. Mozart, who rated his music highly. He was also remembered for his *Singspiels*, several of which were of a serious nature, and was admired by Hiller, *Gerber and *Burney.

Works

A body of stage works including the *Singspiels, Der Jahrmarkt* (perf. 1775), *Walder* and *Romeo und Julie* (both perf. 1776) and the *melodramas *Ariadne auf Naxos*, *Medea* (both perf. 1775)

and *Pygmalion* (perf. 1779). There are many vocal works and instrumental works including *c.*30 symphonies, six harpsichord sonatas and sonatinas, and some chamber music.

Further reading
A.S. Winsor, *The Melodramas and Singspiels of Georg Benda* (diss., U. of Michigan, 1967). E.V. Garrett, 'Georg Benda, the Pioneer of the Melodrama' in *Studies in Eighteenth-century Music: a Tribute to Karl Geiringer* (London, 1970). J.D. Drake, 'The Songs of Georg Benda', *MT*, cxiii (1972). T. Bauman, *North German Opera in the Age of Goethe* (Cambridge, 1985).

Benedict, Sir **Julius**
German (naturalized English) composer, conductor, teacher (b. 27 Nov or 24 Dec 1804, Stuttgart; d. 5 Jun 1885, London).

Having been taught by J.C.L. Abeille, he left for Weimar at 15 (1819) to study with *Hummel and was introduced to *Beethoven and, from 1821–25, studied with *C.M. von Weber in Dresden on Hummel's recommendation. He gained the post of conductor at the Kärntnertortheater in Vienna (1824) with the help of Domenico Barbaia, who took him to Naples the following year as a theatre conductor, staying there for nine years. Benedict went to London *via* Paris in 1835 and remained there until his death in 1885. He was appointed conductor at the Lyceum Theatre (1836), musical director at Drury Lane (1838–48), accompanied Jenny Lind on her American tour (1850) and was appointed conductor at Her Majesty's Theatre in 1858, producing his own and others' operas. He also was very active on the provincial festival circuit and conducted the Liverpool Philharmonic Society

(1876–80) and at the Crystal Palace for ten years. He was knighted in 1871.

In spite of Italian influences, Benedict cultivated an 'English' *folk-like style in the manner of Balfe and Wallace. His piano compositions are of the 'Viennese' virtuoso style and he wrote an important biography of C.M. von Weber.

Works
Operas include *The Gypsy's Warning* (1838), *The Brides of Venice* (1844), *The Lily of Killarney* (1862); cantatas, songs and partsongs; a symphony, overtures, two one-movement Piano Concertinos (op. 18 in A♭ major (pub. 1831), op. 39 in E♭ major (pub. 1833); later, each was expanded into a piano concerto); two violin sonatas; two piano sonatas, op. 2 (*c.*1823), op. 4 (*c.*1825), Rondo in A major op. 3 (*c.*1825), Rondo brillant in A♭ major op. 5 (*c.*1827); fantasias on popular and operatic tunes. Other publications include *Beethoven's Works for the Piano* (London, 1858), *Carl Maria von Weber* (London, 1881, 5/1899) and *A Sketch of the Life and Works of the late Felix Mendelssohn Bartholdy* (London, 1850, 2/1853).

Further reading
J. Warrack, *Carl Maria von Weber* (London, 1968, 2/1976). N. Temperley, ed., *Music in Britain: the Romantic Age 1800–1914* (London, 1981).

Bennett, Sir **William Sterndale**
English composer (b. 13 Apr 1816, Sheffield; d. 1 Feb 1875, London).

His mother died when he was two, and his stepmother a year later. He was sent to Cambridge with his sisters to live with grandparents 1820–24 and was taught music by his grandfather. Two years later he was admitted to the *Royal Academy of Music in London as a prodigy, studying with Oury and Spagnoletti (violin and piano), and composition *Crotch and *Potter (both composition). He began to switch his main instrument from violin to piano and his first piano concerto (1832–33) impressed many, including Queen Victoria and Prince Albert, and *Felix Mendelssohn, who invited him to visit him in Germany, which he did for almost nine months, becoming part of Mendelssohn's circle, earning also the friendship and admiration of *R. Schumann. In 1837, back in London, he began teaching privately and at the *Royal Academy of Music, but this began to interfere with his composition. His marriage brought with it the need for a more permanent post, but despite Mendelssohn's recommendation he was not appointed Professor of Music at Edinburgh. He was offered the conductorship of the Leipzig Gewandhaus concerts in 1853 but declined; however, he did accept that of the *Philharmonic Society in London after Wagner's resignation. Bennett was elected professor of music at Cambridge in 1856, and introduced examinations for degrees as opposed to 'exercises'. In 1866 he gave up conducting and was made principal of the *RAM. He was knighted (on the recommendation of Gladstone) in 1871. He died in early 1875 and is buried in Westminster Abbey.

Bennett sought to perpetuate the *Classical School – especially *W.A. Mozart and Mendelssohn and their 'English' followers including *Clementi and *J.B. Cramer – in his teaching, and in his own compositions and strongly resisted the new school of *Thalberg and *Liszt, and *Berlioz, as well as the more innovative contributions of *Chopin and *R. Schumann, in spite of the latter's championing of him in his youth. He

had a deep and idiomatic understanding of the piano and its possibilities. He conducted the first English performance of *J.S. Bach's *St. Matthew Passion* in 1854. He was also active as an editor of earlier music, and of the *Chorale Book for England* (1863).

Works

His orchestral works include: six symphonies, six piano concertos (including no. 1 in D minor op. 1 (1832), nos 2 in E♭ major op. 4 and 3 in C minor op. 9 (1834), no. 4 in F minor op. 19 (1838) and one in F minor (1836)); concert overtures. His chamber music includes a sextet in F♯ minor op. 8 (1835), a piano trio in A major op. 26 (1839), a cello sonata in A major op. 32 (1852). Works for piano include character pieces, *6 Studies in the Form of Capriccios* op. 11 (1834–35), *3 Impromptus* (1836), *Fantaisie* op. 16 (1837), *Suite de pièces* (1842), Sonata in F minor op. 13 (1837). There are various choral works, songs, partsongs and glees.

Further reading

N. Temperley, *Instrumental Music in England, 1800–1850* (diss., U. of Cambridge, 1959); 'Mendelssohn's Influence on English Music', *ML*, xliii (1962); 'Sterndale Bennett and the Lied', *MT*, cxvi (1975). G. Bush, 'Sterndale Bennett: the Solo Piano Works', *PRMA*, xci (1964–65); 'Sterndale Bennett: a Note on his Chamber and Piano Music', *MT*, ciii (1972).

Berger, Ludwig
German composer, pianist (b. 18 Apr 1777, Berlin; d. 16 Feb 1839, Berlin).

Son of an architect, he studied flute and piano in his youth, first living in Templin and Frankfurt and later in Berlin

(1799–1804), where he had composition with Gürrlich. He met and became friendly with *Clementi, travelling to St Petersburg with him in 1804, and remaining there for eight years, where he married, and was influenced by *Field's music. He fled to London in 1812 because of Napoleon's advance and his playing was well received there. Berger returned to, and died in, Berlin. His pupils included *Felix Mendelssohn – whose *Lieder ohne Worte* were inspired by his *Etudes* – Taubert and *Henselt.

Works
A piano concerto in C major, seven piano sonatas including op. 18 in C minor and the *Sonata-Pathétique* op. 7 in C minor (following *Beethoven's op. 13); 29 studies including the *Etudes*, opp. 12 and 22 and piano variations.

Further reading
D. Siebenkäs, *Ludwig Berger: sein Leben und seine Werke unter besonderer Berücksichtigung seines Liedschaffens* (Berlin, 1963). *MGG*.

Bériot, Charles-Auguste de
Belgian violinist, composer (b. 20 Feb 1802, Leuven; d. 8 Apr 1870, Brussels).

His first teacher, J.-F. Tiby, became his guardian after he was orphaned young, and he appeared in public as soloist in a concerto by Viotti at the age of nine. In 1821 he met the composer – then director of the Paris Opéra – in Paris who encouraged, but did not teach him. Bériot attended the Conservatoire classes in violin (with Baillot), but found it difficult. Nevertheless, he had great success shortly after with his débuts in Paris and London (1 May 1826) and was made solo violinist to King William I of the Netherlands.

In 1829 he met the singer Maria *Malibran and they travelled on many concert-tours over six years, culminating in their marriage in 1836; the singer died six months later in Manchester, causing Bériot to abandon his playing career. He resumed in 1838 with another concert-tour and remarried. He refused the offer of a professorship at the Conservatoire, accepting the headship of the violin faculty in the Brussels Conservatoire, which he held from 1843–52, when he retired due to failing eyesight.

Bériot combined the elegance of the Parisian style of violin-playing with a Paganinian technique, producing a new more *Romantic style, the Franco-Belgian School, which left its mark on *Felix Mendelssohn's Violin Concerto in E minor. His compositions are rarely heard today.

Works
Ten violin concertos and a dozen *Airs variés* as well as shorter pieces, including the *Scène de ballet* op. 100 and Duos brillants for violin and piano. He also wrote some teaching works, the *Méthode de violon* (1858) and the *Ecole transcendente de violon* (1867), and taught Vieuxtemps.

Further reading
P. Soccanne, 'Charles de Bériot', *Le guide du concert* (Paris, 1937) E. Heron-Allen, *A Contribution towards an accurate Biography of de Bériot and Malibran* (London, 1894). M. Goldstein, 'Charles-Auguste de Bériot', *Cahiers Ivan Tourgéniev, Pauline Viardot et Maria Malibran*, x (1986).

Berlin *Lied* Schools
The name given to the song-outputs of two successive groups of German

composers centred on Berlin in the second half of the eighteenth century. The songs were characterized by strophic settings, a *folk-like style and simple piano accompaniments. Some were collected and published in *Oden mit Melodien* (1753–55) by Ramler and *Krause, representing the First Berlin *Lied* School. Without compromising the spirit of the school, the songs of a later generation (The Second Berlin *Lied* School) were more elaborate, such as those by *Reichardt, *J.A.P. Schulz (*Lieder im Volkston*, 1782) and *Zelter (*Lieder, balladen und Romanzen*, 1810).

Berlioz, (Louis-) Hector

French composer (b. 11 Dec 1803, La Côte-St-André, Isère; d. 8 Mar 1869, Paris).

His general education – particularly literature (French and Latin) and geography – was mostly given by his father, a well-respected doctor, but he also taught him flageolet and he learnt flute and guitar with local teachers. On his own, he studied harmony treatises by Rameau and Catel and *romances* by French composers, using them as models for his own works. After his first degree in Grenoble (1821) he was sent, at his father's behest, to the Ecole de Médecine in Paris. He heard many operas in Paris (*Gluck, *Méhul, *Boieldieu, Salieri) and studied with Le Sueur (1822–26) at the Conservatoire. He pursued medicine for two years, gaining a basic qualification, but decided to take up music as a career, in spite of his parents' opposition; this led to reduction and, at times, cancellation of his allowance, causing him hardship and debt. At the Conservatoire he continued with Le Sueur (composition) and with *Reicha (fugue and counterpoint), winning the *Prix de Rome* at his

fourth attempt. Berlioz was fired by performances of Shakespeare's plays by a visiting troupe from London and fell in love with the Irish actress Harriet Smithson, whom he eventually met; they married in 1833 and were estranged nine years later. Winning the *Prix* provided Berlioz with the opportunity to visit Italy – 15 creatively important months – with an income for a few years, and he became reconciled with his parents, whom he visited in 1831.

Back in Paris, he learned from the works of *C.M. von Weber and *Rossini, heard *Beethoven symphonies conducted by *Habeneck; was inspired by Goethe (*Faust*), and by the poetry of *Moore, Scott, Byron, Chateaubriand, *Hoffmann, Fennimore Cooper, Vigny, Musset, Hugo, Gautier, Flaubert and Balzac. Lack of recognition, of a musical post and of commissions caused him to earn his living as a musical critic. After a local conductor botched a performance of *Harold en Italie*, Berlioz decided to conduct his own works himself thenceforth, and became one of the earliest 'career' conductors. He wrote several operas with little success – his music was 'too difficult' – and songs, mostly written with, or arranged for, orchestral accompaniment. The rest of his life was spent mainly in writing music and criticism, and touring Europe as conductor of his own and others' works. The contrast between his reception abroad and in Paris became acute, and he abandoned the city for sojourns in Russia and – avoiding the perils of the 1848 revolution – England, where he was warmly received. His last 15 years were spent in death-obsessed morbidity, lonely disillusionment and almost constant physical pain, due to intestinal neuralgia. He is buried in Montmartre Cemetery in Paris.

As well as his musical works Berlioz is remembered for his critical writings in, especially, the periodical the *Revue et gazette musicale* and the newspaper, the *Journal des débats*, and for his raising of the status of conducting to an international profession – enshrined in his *Le chef d'orchestra: théorie de son art* (Paris, 1852) – as well as for his *Mémoires* and his *Grand traité d'instrumentation et d'orchestration modernes*, op. 10 (Paris, 1843) only the second, but most influential, of its kind.

As a composer, he enjoyed almost no influence in France during his lifetime or later, and outside, affected mostly minor figures. His orchestration technique did, however, find disciples in *Liszt, R. *Strauss, Mahler, Balakirev, Rimsky-Korsakov, Tchaikovsky and, in spite of themselves, Debussy and Ravel.

Works
Operas: *Benvenuto Cellini* (1834–37, perf. Paris, 1838), *Les Troyens* (1856–58, perf. Paris, 1863), *Béatrice et Bénédict* (1860–62, perf. Baden-Baden, 1862). Orchestral: overtures, inc. *Waverley, Le roi Lear, Le carnaval romain, Le corsaire*; symphonies, inc. *Symphonie fantastique* op. 14 (1830, pub. 1845), *Harold en Italie*, for va and orchestra, op. 16 (1834, pub. 1848), *Roméo et Juliette*, for voices and orchestra, op. 17 (1839, pub. 1847), *Grande symphonie funèbre et triomphale*, for military band, orchestra and voices *ad lib*, op. 15 (1840, pub. 1843). Many choral works and songs with orchestral accompaniment. No works for solo piano and few chamber works – all lost or incorporated into other larger works.

Further reading
E.T. Cone, *Berlioz: Fantastic Symphony* (New York, 1971). J.-M. Bailbé, *Berlioz:* *artiste et écrivain dans les Mémoires* (Paris, 1972). H. Macdonald, *Berlioz* (London, 1982, 2/1991). D.K. Holoman, *Berlioz* (Cambridge, MA, 1989). *Berlioz Society Bulletin*.

Bertini, Henri(-Jérome)
French pianist and composer (b. 28 Oct 1798, London; d. 30 Sep 1876, Meylan).

Brought up in Paris until the age of 13, he was taught by his father and brother (Auguste), who had been a pupil of *Clementi. He then toured, as pianist with his father, to Belgium, Holland, Germany, England and Scotland. He resettled in Paris in 1821 and spent his life teaching and composing.

Bertini's performance style was of the early 'classic' *Romantic school (Clementi, *Hummel, *Moscheles, *et al.*).

Works
There are many solo piano works: rondos, fantasias, variations and studies, including *25 Etudes Faciles et Progressives* op. 100; a number of smaller and larger chamber works include a nonet, op. 107 and three unpublished symphonies for piano and orchestra.

Further reading
P. Beyls, *Henri Bertini 1798–1876: pianiste virtuose et compositeur de musique* (Grenoble, 1999). Marmontel/PIANISTES. Fétis/*BIOGRAPHIE. MGG*.

Beyer, Adam
Piano-maker (b. 1774).

He had a workshop in Compton Street, Soho, London. His instruments were based on *Zumpe's.

Biblical Sonatas
A set of sonatas in several movements forming the last of four published volumes

of keyboard music by the German composer and keyboardist Johann Kuhnau (1660–1722). The volume is entitled *Biblische Historien* (*Biblical Stories*) and contains six programmatic sonatas illustrating biblical themes: 1. *The Fight between David and Goliath*; 2. *Saul cured by David through Music*; 3. *Jacob's Wedding*; 4. *Hezekiah, Sick unto Death and Restored to Health*; 5. *Gideon, Saviour of Israel*; and 6. *Jacob's Death and Burial*. Kuhnau's point was to show that emotional states could be depicted on the keyboard without recourse to a poetic text. The various movements have Italian subtitles, such as 'The tranquil and contented soul of Saul' heading the last (3rd) movement in the second sonata, *Saul cured by David through Music*.

Bichord [bichord-strung, bichord stringing]

Of the piano or harpsichord, having two strings with the same tuning for each note of the same pitch sounded simultaneously with a single *jack or hammer.

Biedermeyer

A term used originally to describe the interior design and furniture of a particular kind of bourgeoisie in the German-speaking countries during the first half of the nineteenth century. The term comes from the name of a fictitious teacher created by Ludwig Eichrodt during the 1850s. It became a derogative term to denote the comfortable, dull, reactionary, unimaginative and politically conservative in that class, and was lampooned by *R. Schumann at the end of *Carnaval* with the use of the *Grossvatertanz*.

Binary form

A musical form which was, as the name implies, in two sections, labelled as A and B, each of which was usually repeated. The same, or recognizably similar melodic material was used for each section, the first of which modulated to, and cadenced in, the dominant (in a major-key work) or the relative major (in a minor-key one). The second section often began in this same key and modulated back to the tonic, using the A material or a close relative.

Melodic material (and sections)	‖:A	:‖: B	:‖
Key (major)	I___	V V	_I__
Key (minor)	i___	III III	_i__

Between the V (or III in the minor-key version) and the I of the second section there were often brief excursions to related keys and, if these were notable, the term 'rounded binary' was often used. Most of the instrumental dances in the *Baroque *suite were cast in binary form.

Bishop, Sir Henry R(owley)

English composer (b. 18 Nov 1786, London; d. 30 Apr 1855, London).

He had little education as a child but, by 13 years of age, he was partner in his cousin's music-selling business in London's Soho and had published some songs and piano pieces. He went to Newmarket to train as a jockey, but was unsuitable and his patron agreed to pay for music lessons back in London, where the teenager studied harmony with Francesco Bianchi. Bishop wrote ballets and an opera and was appointed musical director of Covent Garden theatre in 1810. He was a founder-member of the *Philharmonic Society and one of the original professors of the *RAM, a post which he exercised very little. He left Covent Garden in 1824 for a similar position at the Drury Lane theatre and a few years later became director and composer to Vauxhall Gardens, which was beginning to fail. He took a BMus degree at Oxford in 1839 and was appointed Reid Professor at Edinburgh in 1841; he resigned two years later, having given only two lectures. He was knighted in 1842 on the recommendation of Prince Albert, succeeding *Crotch in the chair of music at Oxford in 1848, and died of cancer in 1855.

Bishop was an indefatigable composer of English dramatic music in a time of decline, and of songs of the '*folk/popular' type in the period. His market required plagiarism of the Greats and his mutilations of *W.A. Mozart etc. are scorned, yet he was considered a very gifted composer in his time. Most of his music is in the form of incidental music to plays (particularly Shakespeare) and semi-musical works, both his own and others'. Many of his songs have survived, encapsulating a kind of English/Celtic 'folk'-style.

Works
Instrumental works; ballets (*Love in a Tub* (perf. 1808), *Mora's Love* (perf. 1809); farces; operas (*The Maniac* (perf. 1810), *The Lord of the Manor* (perf. 1812), *The Farmer's Wife* (perf. 1814), *Lionel and Clarissa, The Maid of the Mill* (both perf. 1814), *Maid Marian* (perf. 1822), *Aladdin* (perf. 1826); hundreds of glees and songs, of which *Home, Sweet Home* (with words by the American poet John Howard Payne) is best remembered.

Further reading
F. Corder, 'The Works of Sir Henry Bishop', *MQ*, iv (1918). R. Northcott, *The Life of Sir Henry R. Bishop* (London, 1920). P.M. Young, *A History of British Music* (London, 1967). N. Temperley,

ed., *Music in Britain: the Romantic Age 1800–1914* (Oxford, 1981).

Black Joke, The
Title of an Irish *folk song used by *Clementi as the theme for two sets of *variations, a freestanding one (1771) with twenty-one variations, and the other forming the finale of his op. 1 no. 3 piano sonata (?1781) with eight. All of these are taken from the free-standing set, but are rendered more difficult to play. The sets throw interesting light on early-nineteenth-century variation technique.

Blanchet
Family of French harpsichord- and piano-makers of which the most important figures were François-Etienne II (b. *c*.1730, Paris; d. 1766, Paris) and Armand François Nicolas. The former's harpsichords were much in demand, although he altered other makers' instruments (such as those of Ruckers) and incorporated parts from other makers' instruments into his own. Under him, the firm was appointed *facteur des clavessins du Roi* in the 1750s and Blanchets were owned by, among others, *François Couperin, *Taskin and *Balbastre, who played one to *Burney. Armand François Nicolas Blanchet (b. 1763, Paris; d. 1818, Paris) made pianos and wrote a *Méthode abrégée pour accorder le clavecin et le forte-piano* (Paris pub. 1797–1800, R/1976). He went into partnership with a German maker in Paris, Jean (Johannes) Roller who, after his retirement in 1851, was replaced by Nicolas's son P.A.C. Blanchet; the latter became head of the firm on his father's death four years later. Blanchet et Roller took the piano-buying public by storm in the Paris Exhibition of 1827 (in the Louvre) when they exhibited a small 'piano droit' (see *piano) of

a metre high and 1.30m wide which was obliquely strung. The action was improved three years later and copied by many others. Another type of upright action of theirs (1829) was improved in 1860 and was also taken up widely.

Further reading
Boalch/HARPSICHORD.
Harding/PIANO-FORTE.
Hubbard/HARPSICHORD.
Russell/HARPSICHORD.

Boccherini, (Ridolfo) Luigi

Italian composer and cellist (b. 19 Feb 1743, Lucca; d. 28 May 1805, Madrid).

Born of an artistic family, he studied with his father and a local musician, first appearing in public as a cellist at 13 years of age. He went to Rome to study with G.B. Constanzi in 1757 and the same year he and his father were appointed to the court theatre in Vienna. Boccherini returned to Lucca for three years in 1764 and, since his name and his works (in manuscript copies) were becoming known outside of his home country, he embarked on a concert-tour with a violinist friend. In Paris, in 1767, he gained an aristocratic patron and published already-written chamber, as well as orchestral works. He settled in Madrid in 1769 and was appointed composer and performer to the Infante, Don Luis in 1770. Reports of his being in Germany at the court of Friedrich Wilhelm II are likely to be incorrect, though he was appointed chamber composer there, carrying out his duties *in absentia*; he remained in Spain until his death. He had several patrons after the death of the Don Luis, but after Friedrich Wilhelm's death, his successor did not continue his appointment and refused him a pension. Boccherini died of tuberculosis in poverty and distress, although his condition was no doubt exacerbated by the death of all his four daughters and both his wives within a short time.

Boccherini is credited with instigating the first public performances of string quartets (1765) and is seen as the chief representative of Latin chamber music during the *Classical period. He was a strong devotee of the rare string quintet, in which he doubled the cello rather than the viola (as in the case of *W.A. Mozart) and possibly influenced him in his own string quintets.

Works
A small amount of vocal music, 26 symphonies (including C minor op. 41 (G519, 1788) and D minor, op. 37/3 (G517, c.1787)); 11 cello concertos and one for harpsichord in Eb major, G487; some 300 chamber pieces, including string trios, quartets and quintets.

Further reading
G. de Rothschild, *Luigi Boccherini: sa vie, son œuvre* (Paris, 1962; Eng. tr., rev. 1965). E.I. Amsterdam, *The String Quintets of Luigi Boccherini* (diss., U. of California, Berkeley, 1968). V. Terenzio, 'Immagine dei Boccherini', *Quadrivium*, xiv (1973). Y. Gérard, *Thematic, Bibliographical, and Critical Catalogue of the Works of Luigi Boccherini* (London, 1969). R. Coli, *Luigi Boccherini* (Lucca, 1988, 2/1992). L Della Croce, *Il divino Boccherini: vita, opere, epistolario* (Padua, 1988). Fétis/*BIOGRAPHIE*.

Böhner, (Johann) Ludwig (Louis)

German pianist, composer, conductor (b. 8 Jan 1787, Töttelstedt, Gotha; d. 28 Mar 1860, Gotha).

Best known for being the personality which inspired *E.T.A. Hoffmann's

'Capellmeister Kreisler', in turn inspiring *R. Schumann's *Kreisleriana*, op. 15 (1838), the highly talented child learnt violin, keyboard and composition from his father, a local Kantor, and later from *Spohr. He moved to Jena and became friendly with Goethe and Hoffmann and became director of the Nuremberg theatre until 1815. After several concert-tours he suffered a nervous breakdown from which he never recovered, although he continued to compose. He was a pioneer in being an early writer of concert overtures and integrating the Germanic hunting style into opera, influencing *C.M. von Weber's *Der Freischütz*.

Works
Several concert overtures, some pieces for solo clarinet and orchestra and six piano concertos as well as operas, including *Dreiherrenstein* op. 107 (unpub.), songs and chamber music and solo piano pieces (variations, etc.).

Further reading
F.K. Bolt, *Johann Ludwig Böhner, 1787–1860: Leben und Werke* (Hildburghausen, 1940). A. Beer, 'Johann Ludwig Böhner: E.T.A. Hoffmanns Kapellmeister Kreisler?', *Festschrift Christoph-Hellmut Mahling*, ed., A. Beer, K. Pfarr and W. Ruf (Tutzing, 1997).

Boieldieu, (François-) Adrien
French composer (b. 16 Dec 1775, Rouen; d. 8 Oct 1834, Jarcy, Seine et Oise).

Son of a clerk, he was taught by the local abbot, an ardent Classicist, and the choirmaster at Rouen cathedral, but his most important musical training – piano, organ, harmony and composition – was from the cathedral organist, Charles Broche, who had studied with Séjan and Padre Martini. Boieldieu was appointed organist at a local church in 1791 and gave his first public recital. The favourable reception of two of his *opéras comiques* in Rouen (where there was a strong tradition of such works) and of his sets of romances for violin and piano after their publication in Paris in 1794, encouraged him to move to that city in 1796. He soon became one of the country's chief dramatic composers and he was appointed to the Conservatoire to teach piano (1798–1803), where *Fétis was one of his pupils. The breakup of his marriage to a free-living dancer caused him to accept a post in the Russian imperial court in St Petersburg in 1803 and the Tsar made him director of the French Opera. After nine years he resigned and returned to Paris where he re-established himself musically and received several important tokens of public esteem, being appointed court composer and accompanist in 1815, made a member of the advisory board of the Académie Royal de Musique in 1816 and becoming a member of the Académie des Beaux-Arts the following year. After the success of his opera *Le petit chaperon rouge* in 1818, he went to his country house because of bad health and wrote little for seven years. Then the arrival of *Rossini in Paris in the early 1820s threw the city into musical turmoil, with pro-Italian and pro-French operatic factions being set up, of which Boieldieu was the prime representative of the French, in spite of his admiration for Rossini. His *opéra comique*, *La dame blanche* (1825) from a tale by Scott to a libretto by Scribe was a huge success all over Europe. A further opera was less successful, causing him financial problems and he was also developing acute laryngitis, losing his voice completely. He died in 1834 and was given a state funeral before being buried in Rouen.

Works

His operas include *La fille coupable* (1793); *La famille suisse* (perf. 1796); *Le petit chaperon rouge* (1818); *Les voitures versée*s (perf. 1808, rev. 1820); *La dame blanche* (perf. 1825); *Les deux nuits* (perf. 1829). There are nine piano sonatas, concertos for piano (in F major, pub. 1792) and harp (in C major, pub. 1801), chamber works, and some hundred and forty *romances* for voice and piano, piano with violin (sometimes *ad lib*) or two violins.

Further reading

H. Gougelot, *La romance française sous la Révolution et l'Empire* (Melun, 1938). G. Favre, *Boieldieu: sa vie, son œvre* (2 vols, Paris, 1944–45). K. Pendle, *Eugène Scribe and French Opera of the Nineteenth Century* (Ann Arbor, MI, 1979). Fétis/*BIOGRAPHIE*.

Bolero

A Spanish *song-dance in triple metre of moderate tempo derived from the *seguidilla*, but appropriating steps from several Spanish dances, it was popular during the last quarter of the eighteenth and the nineteenth centuries. Characterized by a triplet in the latter half of the first beat, or forming the second, it was danced by a couple, who came together in the first and last of its three sections, and had interspersed solos in the second, faster one. Each of the three sections began with an introductory promenade (the *paseo*) and the *bien parado* (the momentary holding of a set pose) coincided with the ends of sections, or occasionally, phrases, of the dance. Musically it was of A—A—B shape and a number of composers used it in operas (*C.M. von Weber's *Der Freischütz* (1817–21), and his incidental music to *Preciosa* (1820), *Méhul's *Les

deux aveugles de Tolède (perf. 1806), and *Berlioz's *Benvenuto Cellini* (1834–37)), and as piano-pieces, such as *Chopin's *Bolero* in C major op. 19 (1833), as well as Ravel's famous *Boléro* of 1928 (though originally called *Fandango*).

Bösendorfer

Austrian firm of piano-makers.

Ignaz Bösendorfer (b. 28 Jul 1796, Vienna; d. 14 Apr 1859, Vienna) was apprenticed to the Viennese maker Joseph *Brodmann and received his permit as a manufacturer in 1828 and received the title of *K. u. K. Hof- und Kammerklavierverfertiger* from the emperor in 1830. The resilience of Bösendorfer's instruments under the hands of *Liszt ensured their international fame. Ignaz's son, Ludwig (b. 15 Apr 1835, Vienna; d. 9 May 1919, Vienna) moved to a new factory in 1860 and patented a new action. Staunchly conservative and resistant to modernism in types and techniques, the firm made pianos with Viennese actions as well as those with British until *c.*1900 and continues to make some of the finest of pianos today.

Further reading

C. Ehrlich, *The Piano: a History* (London, 1976). A. Liversidge, 'Of Wood and Iron Wrought: the Making of Bösendorfer', in J.R. Gaines, ed., *The Lives of the Piano* (New York, 1981).

Bourrée (Fr.; It. *borea*; Eng. boree, borry)

A French *folk-dance, court dance and instrumental dance. Still known in many parts of France – the Auvergne (where it is thought to have originated from the *branle*) Berry, Bourbonnais, Cantal, Languedoc and Limousin. Although the folk-dance exists in both duple/quadruple and triple *metres, its stylized form is duple/quadruple with a crotchet upbeat, a medium to fast tempo and four-bar phrasing, with frequent syncopations of the second beat. In this it is similar to the *rigaudon which was, however, more lively. The *bourrée* occurs in orchestral music by *J.S. Bach, Lully, Fischer and Georg Muffat, and in keyboard music by J.S. Bach, d'Anglebert, Purcell and *D. Scarlatti.

Brace (see *Bracing)

Bracing
A method of strengthening the frame of a *piano with braces, to counteract any possible deformation due to string tension and atmospheric factors such as dampness. Wood was used at first, but metals of various kinds were also applied, as in the *Compensation Frame, until iron framed instruments became standard.

Brahms, Johannes
German composer (b. 7 May 1833, Hamburg; d. 3 Apr 1897, Vienna).

He received his early musical education from his father and studied piano with O.F.W. Cossel, and theory with Eduard Marxsen, in Hamburg, studying *J.S. Bach, *Beethoven and some more recent piano-virtuosos; he appeared in public as a pianist at 15 years of age. Brahms, already a great lover of *folk-tales, came into contact with the Hungarian *quasi*-folk styles in music in 1848 and had first-hand experience during a concert-tour with the Hungarian violinist Reményi (Eduard Hoffmann, 1828–98), meeting the violinist Joseph *Joachim in Göttingen and *Liszt at Weimar. Although a packet of compositions which he sent to *R. Schumann for comments was returned unopened, he deeply impressed the Schumanns at Düsseldorf in 1853, with both his playing and his compositions, giving rise to Schumann's famous article 'Neue Bahnen' in the *Neue Zeitschrift für Musik*. On returning to help the Schumanns during Robert's nervous breakdown, he fell in love with *Clara, who was 14 years older, but nothing came of this – or of any other of his romances – although they remained lifelong friends. In 1859 Brahms settled in Hamburg and he and Joachim publicly expressed opposition to the 'New German School' of Liszt and his circle, an action which created professional difficulties for him. He moved to Vienna in 1862, where he remained for the rest of his life, making many influential and close friends. His hopes of becoming conductor of the Philharmonic Concerts in his home city of Hamburg came to nothing and he accepted the position of director of the Berlin *Singakademie* in 1863. He was appointed by a majority of one vote, but soon resigned due to administrative difficulties; at the same time, his parents' marriage was breaking up and he was unable to save it.

He settled permanently in Vienna in 1868 and the following year was strongly attacked by Wagner in a periodical article, no doubt because the latter feared rivalry. Brahms did not reply, but any hope of amicability was shattered. He went on several concert-tours and in 1872 – after three years of waiting – was persuaded, to accept the conductorship (choral as well as orchestral) of the Vienna *Gesellschaftskonzerte*, where he presented the Viennese public with concerts of early music – *J.S. Bach and *Handel and before. In spite of their success, Brahms wanted more time to compose and he resigned in 1875. He was given the use of the famous Meiningen court orchestra by its conductor, Hans von Bülow, to try out his compositions, and he spent much time there as the guest of the Duke and Duchess, who became lifelong friends. He finished his *Deutsches Requiem* ('German Requiem') after news of his mother's death and its first performance, given during the Franco-Prussian War, was invested with political significance, marking the composer as a patriot. He also began to be honoured abroad: Cambridge University offered him a doctorate in music in 1876, which he refused, although he accompanied Joachim (who accepted his doctorate) to the University and brought with him the newly-composed first symphony in C minor op. 68 (1855–76) which was performed there. Brahms refused the offer of a doctorate from Cambridge again in 1892.

He spent his summers at various resorts composing, and the winters giving concerts. In 1881 a rift developed between him and Joachim over the latter's (unfounded) accusations against his wife, whose side Brahms took; although this was healed six years later, they were never as close again. His frequent visits to Meiningen, whose duke and duchess were close friends as well as being patrons, enabled him to work in peace and comfort and resulted in the last two symphonies, while his visits to the summer chamber-music festival at Hofstetten inspired the late chamber music. In 1891 his meeting with the clarinettist Mühlfeld gave rise to his last instrumental works, the Trio, Quintet and two sonatas for clarinet. He died, as did his father, of liver cancer.

Brahms had a keen interest in music of the past, playing, editing and presenting them in public whenever the opportunity arose. Although a *Romanticist, he preserved a sense of *Classical poise, restraint and formal concern in his work.

He was generous and helpful to younger musicians (e.g. Dvořák).

Works

Orchestral Four symphonies (no. 1 in C minor op. 68 (1855–76), no. 2 in D major op. 73 (1877). no. 3 in F major op. 90 (1883) and no. 4 in E minor op. 98 (1884–85)), two piano concertos (in D minor op.15 (1854–58) and B♭ major op. 83 (1878–81)), a violin concerto in D major op. 77 (1878), a concerto for violin and cello in A minor op. 102 (1887), two serenades, variations on a theme by *J. Haydn op. 56a (1873).

Chamber three piano trios, three piano quartets, three string quartets, two string quintets, two string sextets, the piano quintet in F minor op. 34 (1861–64), the clarinet quintet in B minor op. 115 (1891), trios for horn, and for clarinet, sonatas for violin, for cello, and for clarinet.

Piano Three sonatas (no. 1 in C major op. 1 (1852–53), no. 2 in F♯ minor op. 2 (1852) and no. 3 in F minor op. 5 (1853), variations (including his op. 9 on a theme by *Robert Schumann in F♯ minor (1854), the *Variations and Fugue on a Theme by G. F. *Handel* in B♭ major op. 24 (1861), and the *Variations on a Theme by *Paganini* in A minor op. 35 (1862–63)); ballades, sets of pieces (eight of op. 76 (1878), seven fantasias, op. 116, three *Intermezzos*, op. 117, six of op. 118, four of op. 119 (all 1892–93))

Vocal and choral works Many, religious and secular, inc. *Ein deutsches Requiem* op. 45 (1857–68), the *Alto Rhapsody* op. 53 (1869), [15] *Romances* from Tieck's 'Magelone' op. 33 (1861), *Vier ernste Gesänge* [Four Serious Songs], op. 121 (1896).

Further reading
From an enormous literature: J. Burnett, *Brahms: a Critical Study* (London, 1972). M. MacDonald, *Brahms* (London, 1990). J. Swafford, *Johannes Brahms* (New York, 1997). M. Musgrave, *A Brahms Reader* (New Haven, CT, 2000).

Brent, John
No biographical information is available; he built the first indigenous piano in America, a square, in 1775.

Bridge
(1) In a *piano (or other stringed instrument) a piece, or several pieces, of carved wood fixed – usually glued – to the *soundboard and supporting the strings, so that the sound of the latter's vibrations is conducted to the soundboard to amplify the sound.

(2) A musical passage joining two more obviously thematic areas, as in *Sonata Form. Its function often includes that of modulation to another key. It is also called a 'transition' (passage).

British Grenadiers[' March]
The official regimental march of the British Grenadiers. It dates from the late seventeenth century, although the tune is (probably much) older. Sometimes a later version mentioning the Battle of Waterloo is used instead.

British Piano
A preferred term, used throughout *The Mechanical Muse*, for what is called the 'English Piano' in recognition of the vital contribution made by Scottish (*Broadwood, etc.) and Irish (*Southwell) makers; as well as being geographically correct it is also politically so, since both countries were part of the United Kingdom. Its characteristics, compared with the '*Viennese' piano of its period – with which for a while it vied for popularity, until makers began to amalgamate the best qualities from each during the nineteenth century – were a sonorous tone, a deeper *key-dip, a heavier *action and larger hammers, slightly inefficient damping which, however, allowed for a very expressive legato *touch. It was largely *trichord (as opposed to the *bichord of the 'Viennese' model) with thicker strings and had a heavier and convex (downwards in the grands) soundboard. In addition, the case was integral to the instrument (unlike the 'Viennese') which conveyed the sound to the (mostly wooden) floor thus strengthening it. The instrument became associated with the music of the *'London piano School', which is misleading, as most of them were Austro-German and therefore used to playing the 'Viennese'; in point of fact, virtuosi became used to playing both kinds, like *Hummel (who owned the first British grand in Vienna) and prized each for their own distinctive qualities.

Broadwood, John
Scottish piano-maker (b. 6 Oct 1732, Cockburnspath, Scotland; d. 1812, London).

Trained as a joiner and cabinet-maker in Scotland, moving to London in 1761 to work in the firm of Burkat *Shudi. Broadwood married Shudi's daughter in 1769, becoming his partner in 1770. Not long after he arrived at Shudi's workshop, Broadwood collaborated with Americus *Backers and Robert *Stodart on the 'English grand action', then turning his attention to the *square piano, the early models of which he based on *Zumpe's, but he soon experimented with various features patenting changes in 1783. Although Shudi's son continued the partnership after his father's death three years later, Broadwood was the senior of the two and managed the firm singlehandedly from 1782. He then turned his attention to grands, based on the examples of *Backers, and, on *Clementi's advice, consulted the scientists Thomas Gray and Tiberius *Cavallo, resulting in greatly improved instruments by the late 1780s and impressing *J. Haydn, who visited the workshops in 1794. The firm's output increased greatly in the 1790s – some 400 squares and 100 grands a year and 1,000 and 400 respectively by the 1820s.

Broadwood's pianos were used by all the leading musicians in the early nineteenth century and his business, using some of the factory-based production-practices of the period sparingly, grew and prospered. Iron *bracing was applied in the 1820s in various ways to counteract the increased tension and power of the strings.

Further reading
Hipkins/PIANOFORTE.   Harding/
PIANO-FORTE. Loesser/MEN. Ehrlich/
PIANO. D. Wainwright, *Broadwood by Appointment* (London, 1982).

Brodmann, Joseph
Viennese piano-maker about whom there is little information except that Ignaz *Bösendorfer, founder of the firm of that name, trained in his workshop.

Browne-Camus, Count Johann Georg von
Patron of *Beethoven (b. 1767, Livonia; d. 1827).

Scion of an old Irish family, he was in the Russian Imperial Service in

Vienna and, like so many others among Beethoven's patrons, squandered his huge fortune. He showed the young composer great generosity – Beethoven called him 'the foremost Maecenas of my muse' – and received the dedication of the op. 9 String Trios (which the composer described as the best of his works to date), the piano sonata in B♭ major op. 22 and the *Gellert-Lieder* op. 48. His wife was also dedicatee of several works. He seemed to combine spirituality, generosity and talent with lack of will and depravity. After a mental breakdown, he was confined to a mental institution for some years.

'Bückerburg Bach', The (see *Johann Christoph Friedrich Bach)

Buff stop (see *Stop (3) and (4))

Bunting, Edward
Irish pianist, teacher and folksong collector (b. Feb 1773, Armagh; d. 21 Dec 1843, Dublin).

The son of an English engineer who married and settled in Ireland, Edward moved to Belfast and became a piano-teacher – later much celebrated – and the organist of St Anne's church at the age of 11; two years later was appointed organist in two other churches. He acted as scribe during a meeting of harpers in the city in 1792, thus helping to preserve the remnants of a dying traditional musical art. He helped in the organization of the visit of Catalani (1809) and the Belfast Music Festival (1813). Bunting founded Belfast Harp Society (1808–13) and the Irish Harp Society (1819–39). His notation of the performances of some of the last representatives of the Irish harp tradition during their meeting in Belfast in July 1792 was of enormous significance in preserving the remnants of a great musical tradition and the results were published in *A General Collection of Ancient Irish Music*, the first of its three volumes of which appeared in London 1796, the second in 1809 (with a dissertation on harps) and the third in Dublin 1840 (with a dissertation on Irish music history). He also collected *folk-music in the field. Bunting moved to Dublin on his marriage in 1819 and was appointed organist of St Stephen's Church. He died there in 1843. The *Collection* was liberally used by Thomas *Moore in his *Irish Melodies*.

Further reading
C.M. Fox, *Annals of the Irish Harpers* (London, 1911). M. McNeill, *The Life and Times of Mary Ann McCracken, 1770–1865: a Belfast Panorama* (Dublin, 1960). G. Yeats, *The Harp of Ireland* (Belfast, 1992).

Burney, Charles
English music historian and composer (b. 7 Apr 1726, Shrewsbury; d. 12 Apr 1814, London).

He moved to Chester as a child, but returned to Shrewsbury at 16 and was stimulated by visiting organists to undertake musical study, especially violin (and French) with Nicola Matteis the younger. He met *Arne at 18 in Chester and began a harsh two-year apprenticeship with him in London, where he met *Handel and the harpsichord-maker *Kirckman, who recommended him in 1746 to the wealthy aristocrat Fulke Greville as his musical tutor/companion. Burney gained much from this two-year exposure to high society. He married in 1749 and became organist of St Dionis', Backchurch, played harpsichord and composed for theatrical productions, becoming a close lifelong friend of Garrick. Following illness, he

and his family moved to King's Lynn as organist but returned to London in 1760 and Burney became established as a popular private teacher. He was awarded a DMus (Oxon) in 1769, without, however, attendance at any lectures.

His wife having died, he visited Paris to arrange his two daughters' schooling – one, Esther was a very talented keyboard player, the other was the writer, Fanny – and took the opportunity to visit continental libraries, which stimulated him to write a history of music, and in 1770 he undertook a tour of the main cities of France and Italy, writing up and publishing his diaries (see below) and making firm friends with Padre Martini. Two years later he paid the Germanic countries a similar compliment (see below), meeting Metastasio, *Gluck, Hasse and *C.P.E. Bach, and heard *Frederick the Great as a flautist. He had various posts as organist, and his home attracted musicians, writers and artists from all over Europe, his Sunday-evening concerts becoming famous. His *History* was published in four volumes between 1776 and 1789. He was much involved in the Handel Commemoration of 1784, and saw a great deal of *J. Haydn during the latter's London visits between 1793 and 1795. He wrote the music articles for Rees' *Cyclopaedia*.

Works
His musical compositions, including a number for keyboard, are competent enough, but it is his literary output which has kept his name in currency. These include, *The Present State of Music in France and Italy: or the Journal of a Tour through those Countries, undertaken to collect Materials for a General History of Music* (London, 1771); *The Present State of Music in Germany, the Netherlands, and*

the United Provinces, or, the Journal of a Tour through these Countries, undertaken to collect Materials for a General History of Music (London, 1773); *A General History of Music from the Earliest Ages to the Present Period, to which is prefixed, a Dissertation on the Music of the Ancients* (London, 1776–89).

Further reading
P.A. Scholes, *The Great Dr Burney* (Oxford, 1948); *Life of Sir John Hawkins* (London, 1953). J. Hemlow, *History of Fanny Burney* (Oxford, 1958). R. Lonsdale, *Dr Charles Burney: a Literary Biography* (Oxford, 1965). K.S. Grant, *Dr. Burney as Critic and Historian of Music* (Ann Arbor, MI, 1983).

Burns, Robert
Scottish poet and songwriter (b. 25 Jan 1759, Alloway, Ayrshire; d. 21 Jul 1796, Dumfries).

Son of a cotter, he laboured and ploughed on the several farms tenanted by his father. Nevertheless, his attendance at various schools gave him a grounding in the classic authors, French and mathematics and he read copiously whenever possible. Influenced greatly by the poetry of Robert Fergusson he began to compose poetry in great quantity after his father's death in 1784, much of it in Scots dialect as well as English. Financial and domestic problems prompted a plan to emigrate to Jamaica, but the publication (in Kilmarnock) and immediate success of his *Poems, Chiefly in the Scottish Dialect* in 1786, resulting in his becoming the darling of Edinburgh literary and aristocratic society, changed his mind. He gave up farming with some relief and became an excise officer and, as well as his continuing original writing, he used his professional travels as an opportunity to collect *folk-tunes and words in the Scottish Highlands and the Borders (in English and Scottish Dialect). In 1788 he married his youthful – though by no means only – sweetheart Jane Armour and died of rheumatic heart disease in 1796.

He remains an iconic working-class poet and had a widespread influence, especially after his early death, his works being set by most of the leading composers of the period, including *R. Schumann and *Felix Mendelssohn.

Works
Poems, Chiefly in the Scottish Dialect (Kilmarnock, pub. 1786), including 'The Cotter's Saturday Night', 'To a Mouse', 'Holy Willie's Prayer'; 350 songs with original words and/or tunes (though based on folk originals) many of which appeared in James Johnson's *The Scots Musical Museum* and *Thomson's *Select Collection of Original Scottish Airs* (5 vols, 1793–1818), the best-known of which include 'Auld lang Syne', 'O my luve's like a red, red rose', 'Ye Banks and Braes', 'Scots wha hae'.

Further reading
T. Crawford, *Burns: A Study of the Poems and Songs* (Stanford, CA, 1960). R.D.S. Jack and A. Noble (eds), *The Art of Robert Burns* (London, 1982). R. Bentman, *Robert Burns* (Boston, MA, 1987). J.A. Mackay, *Burns: A Biography of Robert Burns* (Edinburgh, 1992). K. Simpson, ed., *Burns Now* (Edinburgh, 1994).

Burton, John
English keyboard-player and composer (b. 1730, Yorkshire; d. ?3 Sep 1782, Portici, nr Naples).

A pupil of John Keeble, little information available on his life. He toured Germany as a performer in 1754, probably coming into contact with the piano. He played organ concertos between the acts of plays at Drury Lane Theatre in London. His set of *Ten Sonatas* (see below) has one of the earliest known references to the piano on an English-language title-page.

Works
Include *Ten Sonatas for the Harpsichord, Organ or Piano-forte* (London, pub. 1766), keyboard concerto in A major (1767) and *12 Italian Canzonetts* for voice and harpsichord op. 3 (*c.*1770).

Further reading
C.L. Cudworth, 'The English Organ Concerto', *The Score*, 8 (1953). C. Burney, 'Harpsichord', *Rees's Encyclopaedia* (London 1819). J. Ingamells, ed., *A Dictionary of British and Irish Travellers in Italy, 1701–1800* (New Haven, CT, 1997).

BWV [-number]
A method of numbering the works of *J.S. Bach, as BWV769; it is an abbreviation for *Bach-Werke Verzeichnis* (Index of Bach's Works) compiled by the German scholar W. Schmieder and published in Leipzig in 1950.

C

Cadenza (It.: 'cadence')

A virtuoso passage interpolated into a concerto, near the end of a movement, usually preceded (in the *Baroque and *Classical periods) by a second-inversion (or 6-4) chord. It stems from the practice of *Baroque singers of embellishing – more or less elaborately – the final cadence in a piece. This passed into instrumental concerto usage and was very often improvised by the soloist or soloists, but from the second third of the nineteenth century onwards, tended to be written-in by the composer. Occasionally a particular virtuoso's *cadenza* (or *cadenze* (plural)) became attached to a particular work in subsequent performances, such as *Joachim's for the *Brahms Violin Concerto. The term is also applied to shorter, more *decorative, passages, whose insertion in *Baroque and *Classical usage is often indicated by a pause-mark, or to an embellished cadence.

Cancrizans (Lat.: 'crablike'; Ger. *Krebsgang* 'crab motion')

A musical device which involves a melody, or melodic material, being played or sung backwards; it is more commonly known as 'retrograde' and its use (rare nowadays) is mostly confined to *contrapuntal music of the pre-Classical period.

Canon (from Gk. *kanon*, 'rule')

A musical *contrapuntal device (or form) whereby a single musical line is more-or-less strictly imitated by one or more additional lines, usually beginning after the previous one. These are traditionally called 'voices' even though they may be instrumental and this is an indication of canon's antiquity, which extends back to at least the fifteenth century and it has always been prized as an academic exercise, occasionally surfacing into the musical mainstream (as, for example in the works of *J.S. Bach). A very good example of a canon is the familiar catch or round, *Three Blind Mice*. Since the opening voice is imitated by the other two voices exactly – i.e. each interval is exactly the same as that in the corresponding place in the tune – it is a 'strict canon', and since each entry begins on the same note (or its octave), it is a 'canon at the unison' (or 'at the octave'). Because there are three voices in the canon, each based on a single melody (the familiar tune), it is also an example of a 'canon three in one'. Canons can be further categorized by the number of bars which elapse between the entries; in this case, each voice enters two bars after the previous one – making it a 'canon of two bars' – and since it can theoretically go on for ever, it can be called a 'perpetual canon'.

The form is subjected to many other devices in the hands of skilled composers. The musical intervals of entry are most commonly the unison, octave, fourth or fifth, the last two reckoned upwards from the first voice, even though they may enter an octave lower; thus, if a canon begins in its first voice on a C and the second voice takes up the tune beginning on a G, the canon is always 'at the fifth' even though the G may be that *below* the first voice (i.e. a fourth below). Other intervals between the entries also occur, a famous example being the very beautiful fourteenth variation in *Brahms's set (op. 9, 1854) on a theme of *R. Schumann, where the second of the two voices enters at the interval of a semitone. Within *tonal music, it would be impossible to have a strict canon under these conditions (implying simultaneous keys a semitone apart) and so it is an example of a 'free canon' where intervals between the voices' versions of the tune are frequently a semitone out, a tone in one, for example, being answered by a semitone in the other(s) or a major 3rd answered by a minor 3rd etc. (It will be appreciated that 'free' is very comparative in this sense.) A canon, like *Brahms's mentioned, may be accompanied by one or more free parts or voices, i.e. they do not partake of the canon itself, although they may occasionally quote some of its material. Free parts are useful in covering up any thinnesses in the harmonic texture which may well arise due to the rigorousness of the form.

As well as the aforementioned types, there are other procedures also available to the composer of canons. The subsequent voices may manipulate the original material in a number of strict ways, for example by *augmentation or *diminution and/or by *inversion or *cancrizans (i.e. retrograde). *J.S. Bach's *Musikalisches Opfer ('Musical Offering') is compendium of such esoteric canons, very often presented as 'puzzle canons', the 'tune' being given on one single line only with the procedures to be followed stated verbally – 'canon by augmentation in contrary motion – but the performer or reader is left to fathom out exactly what goes where. It was common for composers of all periods to write short canons for amusing their (usually composer-) friends, often set to meaningless, frivolous or even (as in the gentlemen's-only musical clubs of the eighteenth century and earlier) risqué or scurrilous words.

Canon, The
A constructed succession of composers (or, indeed, any body of individuals bound together by a common worthy, but usually artistic, pursuit) judged, by 'general consent', to be of superior quality ('The Great Composers', 'Artists', etc.) in chronological order, implying an exclusive band of guardians of quality influencing each other and perpetuating a Great Tradition.

Cantabile (It.: 'in a singing style')
The term is used as a musical direction to imply a 'vocal' style, although this is restricted to the more leisurely aspects such as smoothness of melody and delivery, graded dynamics, leisurely *tempi* and beauty of tone. Piano-composers of the late eighteenth and early nineteenth centuries (*Field, *Hummel and *Chopin particularly) developed a piano technique – the 'cantabile-decorative' style – based on contemporary operatic performance involving florid decoration of a more-or-less simple vocal line over a slow harmonic rhythm and unobtrusive accompaniment. It came into its own in slow movements, especially in *concertos.

Cantata (It.: 'sung'; Fr. *cantate*; Ger. *Kantate*)
Originally used to distinguish a sung piece from an instrumental one ('*sonata' or *toccata), it was a work for a solo voice with or without chorus and with accompaniment, often orchestral. It could be secular or, as in the bulk of such works during the later *Baroque period (exemplified by *J.S. Bach's cycles of cantatas) religious. They could be described as operas without action or costume, although there was usually some unifying idea or mood-type. The genre all but died out after the Baroque period.

Canzonet (see *canzonetta)

Canzonetta [canzonet] (It. diminutive form of *canzona*; song, and used also in Eng. and in the form canzonet)

A term applied to short vocal pieces in dance-like form from the sixteenth to the eighteenth centuries, when it was used to describe a light solo song. In the nineteenth century it was used to describe a lyrical instrumental piece, such as the slow movement of Tchaikovsky's Violin Concerto.

Cappi

Nineteenth-century Austrian music-publishing firm.

Founded by **Giovanni Cappi** (1765–1815), an employee in the firm of *Artaria who became a partner and resigned to set up on his own *c*.1800. Published younger contemporary composers, particularly *Beethoven (opp. 25–7 and '29' [=31]) and, after reorganization by the cousins Carlo and Pietro as Cappi & Comp., it became *Schubert's principal publisher.

Capriccio (It., 'fancy', 'whim'; Fr. *caprice*)

A piece which implies a degree of freedom and *improvisation, often involving *fugato or *fugue. The name was occasionally applied to the *cadenza in eighteenth-century concertos. A famous example is *J.S. Bach's *Capriccio On the Departure of a Beloved Brother* BWV992.

Caprice (see *Capriccio*)

Carillon (Fr.; Eng. (imported from the French); Ger. *Glockenspiel*; It. *campanelli*, *campanette*)

A set of at least 23 tuned – chromatically, except for the three lowest – bells either in a Church or civic spire or on a wooden frame, which were played by hand with beaters or by large *keyboard with rounded separate wooden *keys ('baton' keys) and sometimes having similarly-shaped keys. In the nineteenth century there were attempts made to provide it with a piano-type keyboard but the amount of finger-pressure required was a problem. Partly for this reason and partly because the closely-guarded secret of making accurately-tuned bells died out in the nineteenth century with the last of the bell-makers' families, the instrument was already part of the nostalgic past, with connotations of the passing of time and the peal of the Angelus. The piano was well-suited to producing a kind of muted carillon sound in passages in the upper register when the dampers were raised. It was a fairly popular effect and occurs in the last movement of *J.B. Cramer's E♭ major Piano Sonata, op. 25/3, which is a 'Rondo en Carillon' showing several different 'carillon' textures and in no. 2 of Moscheles' *4 grandes Etudes de concert* ('Le Carillon', Allegro giocoso). The use of the German *Glockenspiel* for carillon must not be confused with its use to refer to a different, later (percussion) instrument, with rows of metal (usually steel) bars laid out like the black and white notes of the piano, a kind of metal xylophone.

Carnaval

A set of piano pieces by *R. Schumann (op. 9, 1833–35, pub. 1837) with the subtitle *scènes mignonnes sur quatre notes*. Its 21 numbers depict various characters in the context of the Venetian carnival and include real living people as well as fictional ones. The pieces are 1. Préambule. 2. Pierrrot. 3. Arlequin. 4. Valse noble. 5. Eusebius. 6. Florestan. [5 and 6 referred to aspects of Schumann's own personality, with which he sometimes signed his musical reviews] 7. Coquette. 8. Replique. [no number] Sphinxes [three musical motifs which he directs are not to be played]. 9. Papillons. 10. ASCH-SCHA (Lettres dansantes). 11. Chiarina [referring to *Clara Wieck, his wife-to-be]. 12. *Chopin. 13. Estrella [referring to a lady-love of his, Ernestine von Fricken]. 14. Reconnaissance. 15. Pantalon et Columbine. 16. Valse allemande. 17. Intermezzo: *Paganini. 18. Aveu. 19. Promenade. 20. Pause. 21. Marche des Davidsbündler contre les Philistins.

Case

The outer 'shell' of a keyboard instrument, usually made of (hard) wood. It can be part of the instrument – i.e. mortised into it or otherwise fixed – or separate, in the sense that removing it would not significantly damage the instrument or alter its tone.

Casework

The decoration (wooden, ivory, plastic, plaster or metal) on the case of a keyboard instrument.

Castil-Blaze [Blaze, François-Henri-Joseph]

French writer on music, composer, librettist, arranger (b. 1 Dec 1784, Cavaillon (Vaucluse); d. 11 Dec 1857, Paris).

Son of a novelist and amateur composer, he went to Paris to study law in 1799, but also attended the Conservatoire (newly-founded), for *solfège, harmony and instrumental studies. He decided to become an administrator, the *Inspecteur de la Librairie* in the Vaucluse, and had some songs published. In 1820 he resigned and returned to Paris to become involved with music as a critic and wrote for several journals, which attracted much attention,

as did his monograph *De l'opéra en France* (1820). This was followed a year later by one of the first music dictionaries in French, his *Dictionnaire de musique moderne*. He was director of the Théâtre de l'Odéon from 1824 to 1829 and his translations of *W.A. Mozart's operas and *C.M. von Weber's *Der Freischütz* (as *Robin des Bois*) into French were very successful. Later Weber translations, however, were failures, as were his own operatic compositions, and he set up a publishing firm and became editor of the journal *Le ménestrel*, aided, and finally succeeded, by his son.

Castil-Blaze treated criticism as a professional pursuit, rather than an amateur interest, furnishing it with its own more meaningful vocabulary. He took an anti-*Berlioz stance because of the latter being outside of and opposed to the lyric French tradition, preferring to support *Meyerbeer. In his translations of W.A. Mozart's, C.M. von Weber's and *Rossini's operas into French he occasionally incorporated foreign material (sometimes of his own composition) and changed characters' names and settings; his bowdlerizations were derogatively referred to as 'castilblazades'.

Works
De l'opera en France (pub. Paris, 1820, 2/1826); *Dictionnaire de Musique Moderne* (pub. Paris, 1821, 2/1825), one of the first musical dictionaries in French; *Le piano: Histoire de son invention* (pub. Paris, 1840); articles in the *Journal des débats*, *Le constitutionnel*, *Le ménestrel* (which he later edited), *La revue de Paris*, *La revue et gazette musicale de Paris*.

Further reading
F. Fétis, 'De l'opéra en France', *Revue musicale*, i (1827). D.G. Gislason,

Castil-Blaze, 'De l'opéra en France', and the Feuilletons of the 'Journal des débats' (1820–1832) (diss., U. of British Columbia, 1992). K. Ellis, *Music Criticism in Nineteenth-Century Paris: la Revue et Gazette Musicale de Paris, 1834–80* (Cambridge, 1995). Fétis/*BIOGRAPHIE.*

Cast-iron frame

An iron *piano frame cast in one piece, whose strength and rigidity allowed for higher string tension, resulting in a louder sound and a greater compass than previously. Intended for a *square piano, it was invented in Boston by Alpheus Babcock and patented in 1825. Several European countries produced similar patents, but the first for a grand piano was by Chickering in 1843, also in Boston. These were viewed with some suspicion, especially in Britain, Germany and Austria and it was not until the firm of *Steinway in New York exhibited a cast-iron frame with *overstringing and acceptable volume and tone that the doubters were won over.

Cavallo, Tiberius

Italian (English naturalized) natural philosopher and inventor (b. 1749, Naples; d. 1809 England).

He settled in England before 1775 and was made Fellow of the Royal Society in 1799. Cavallo investigated, and experimented with, electricity, magnetism and chemistry, and was consulted by John *Broadwood about methods of stringing and *striking-places in his pianos. He invented several electrical (non-musical) instruments and wrote on electricity and magnetism.

Cembalo (It., Ger.)

A name for the *Harpsichord.

Characteristic [Piano] Piece (see *Character Piece)

Character Piece (Fr. *pièce caractéristique*; Ger. *Charakterstück*)

A usually short piece of music, often for solo piano, which encapsulates a particular mood, character or idea. It is associated with nineteenth-century *Romanticism, although there is a long tradition of French keyboard pieces (for harpsichord) which have a similar programmatic function and fanciful titles. These include works in *suites (*ordres) by *François Couperin (e.g. 'La Ténébreuse' ['The Moody One'] and 'Les Abeilles' ['The Bees']) and Rameau. The *Romantic equivalents include such works as *Beethoven's *Für Elise*, *Hummel's *La bella Capricciosa*, *Schumann's set *Carnaval* and many pieces by *Heller, while the genre is continued in the *œvre* of composers like Smetana (*Rêves* (1875)), Sibelius (*Characteristic Impressions* op. 103 (1924)) and, of course many of Debussy's pieces.

Further reading

E. Bodky, *Die Charakterstück* (Berlin 1933).

Charlotte [Sophia], Queen

Queen of Mecklenburg-Strelitz (b. 1744, Germany; d. 1818, London).

She married George III in London on 8 Sep 1761, was crowned as his queen on 22 Sep 1761 and managed the royal household on a number of occasions when the King was temporarily incapacitated (due to what was then thought to be madness). She patronized her fellow-German musicians, especially *J.C. Bach, who dedicated his op. 1 harpsichord concertos (pub. 1763) to her and was her music-master from 1764. Her patronage boosted the popularity of the piano in England.

Cherubini, Luigi (Carlo Zanobi Salvadore Maria)

Italian composer teacher theorist (b. 14 Sep 1760, Florence; d. 15 mar 1842, Paris).

Taught by his father, a keyboard-player in a Florence theatre, and by other local musicians, the boy had composed some 18 works by his late teens, including a cantata performed at Florence Cathedral for the future Emperor Leopold II. The latter awarded him a grant to study for three years with Sarti, in Bologna and Naples, during which time he had his first opera premiered in 1779. When he returned to his home city two years later he worked to a number of operatic commissions with great success.

Cherubini decided to visit London in 1784 and was composer for the King's Theatre from 1784 to 1786 where his works were well-received and he came to the notice of the Prince of Wales.

On a visit to Paris in 1785, he met *Marmontel and Viotti who presented him to Queen Marie Antoinette; he settled in Paris in 1786, sharing an apartment for half a dozen years with Viotti. Although his first opera for the city was not a great success, he was engaged by Viotti as music-director of an operatic company with royal and aristocratic patronage, the Théâtre de Monsieur in the Tuileries. His first opera for the company, the heroic comedy Lodoïska (perf. 1791), was an enormous success and *Grétry, then of advanced age, publicly thanked the composer. The opera, an early instance of the rescue-opera (of which probably the best-known example is *Beethoven's Fidelio), chimed in well with the ideals of the Revolution and ran for some 200 performances, making Cherubini's reputation. Political developments, however, made it unsafe for the composer and he fled to rural Normandy; when he returned to Paris in 1793, he married, in spite of social and financial insecurity, and became a triangle-player in a military band. The leader, Bernard Sarrette, was charged with setting up the Institut National de Musique and made Cherubini head of instruction and when the government decreed that it should become the Conservatoire in 1795, he was appointed one of the five inspectors (under Sarrette), the others being Gossec, Grétry, Le Sueur and *Méhul. Although he wrote the statutory revolutionary hymns, his advancement was hampered at this time because he and Napoleon did not get on, due to the latter's dislike of 'noisy music'. In public, however, the composer continued to be successful, with the operas Medée (perf. 1797) and especially Les deux journées (perf. 1800).

His fame had already spread well beyond France and after a season of his works in Vienna, he was invited to visit in 1805, where he was given a great reception by the court and the principal musicians, including *J. Haydn and *Beethoven; he attended the first performance of the latter's rescue-opera Fidelio and began working on an operatic commission, Faniska (perf. 1806). To add to his triumph, when the victorious Napoleon entered the city in 1805, he sought Cherubini out, appointing him to direct a series of concerts and wishing him to come back to Paris in the near future.

On his return, however, Cherubini plunged into a depression – not the first – which so undermined his musical confidence that he began to take up other pursuits, such as botany and painting, enjoying more than a little success in both. While convalescing, his friend, the composer Auber, suggested he compose a mass and Cherubini's earlier interest in sacred music resurfaced. His church music was the source of his compositional success henceforth, while his sporadic opera-compositions were not very well received, due to a shift in public taste. Appointed *surintendant de la musique du roi* (Superintendent of the King's Music) under the Bourbons, his career blossomed and he was made a *Chevalier* of the Légion d'honneur by Louis XVIII in 1814. The following year brought a commission for several pieces from the new Philharmonic Society and he was made superintendent (with Le Sueur) of the royal chapel, and in 1822 he became director of the restructured Conservatoire. Finally, five years after the composition of his great D minor Requiem (1836, perf. 1838), he was appointed Commander of the Légion d'honneur (1841) and, at the age of almost 81, the first musician to be so honoured. He died the following year.

Cherubini's operas were a happy combination of *opera buffa, opera seria* and the forms of *opéra-comique* but held together by a well-developed sense of structure. The symphonic cut and independence of the orchestral writing, and the use of reminiscence themes, were important forerunners of later procedures, including the Wagnerian *leitmotiv* and the nineteenth-century music-drama in general, and his operatic finales were comparable to *W.A. Mozart's – unknown in France until later – in their dramatic sweep and development. *Lodoïska* broke new ground in that it moved beyond the restricted mythical world of Classical Antiquity and ascribed the same heroism, emotions and 'nobility' to ordinary humans in recognizable settings, and his musical technique on all levels was more than capable of doing them justice. His pupils included *Boieldieu, Auber and Halévy and his general influence extended widely, on *C.M. von Weber, *Felix Mendelssohn, *R. Schumann, *Hummel – whose cause he championed in France – *Brahms and Wagner, while Beethoven, also strongly influenced, described him in 1805 as the foremost composer of dramatic music in Europe and his greatest contemporary.

Works

His fame rests on his operas which include *Olimpiade* (c.1783, to a text by Metastasio), *Démophon* (perf. 1788), *Lodoïska* (perf. 1791), *Médée* (1797), *Les deux journées, ou Le porteur d'eau* (perf. 1800), *Faniska* (perf. 1806) and *Pimmalione* (perf. 1809). His masses include those in F major (1808–1809), in D minor (1811) and the Solemn Masses in C major (1816), E major (1818) and G major (1819, intended for the coronation of Louis XVIII) as well as the two Requiems (that in C minor, 1816 for the anniversary of Louis XVI, and that in D minor, 1836, for male voices only, which was performed at his own funeral). There is a large body of other sacred and ceremonial works – odes, *chants*, motets and Revolutionary *hymnes*. His instrumental music includes marches and *contredanses* as well as six string quartets and a string quintet with some piano music, including six harpsichord sonatas (1780), two *romances* (1808), *La rose, romance* (1809), and a Fantasia in C major (1810). There is also the influential pedagogical *Cours de contrepoint et de fugue* (*Course in Counterpoint and Fugue*, pub. 1835, with an English tr. 1837).

Further reading
C.F. Reynolds, *Cherubini* (Ilfracombe, 1963). B. Deane, *Cherubini* (London, 1965). W. Dean 'Opera under the French Revolution', *PRMA*, civ (1967–68). M.S. Selden, 'Cherubini and England', *MQ*, lx (1974). S. Willis, *Luigi Cherubini: A Study of His Life and Dramatic Music 1795–1815* (diss., Columbia U., 1975). E.J. Dean, ed., *The Rise of Romantic Opera* (Cambridge, 1976). O. Heidemann, *Luigi Cherubini: Les Abencérages, ou l'étendard de Grenade* (Munster, 1994). D. Charlton, *French Opera 1730–1830: Meaning and Media* (Aldershot, 2000). Fétis/*BIOGRAPHIE*.

Chollet, Jean Baptiste (Marie)

French tenor and amateur composer (b. 20 May 1798, Paris; d. 10 Jan 1892, Nemours).

He was largely self-taught in his early years but later studied at the Conservatoire in Paris, where he spent the greater part of his life, singing in the chorus of several opera-companies and then high baritone parts in French-speaking opera centres. He joined the Opéra-comique as a tenor in 1826 and was much acclaimed in the première of *Hérold's Marie, subsequently creating the title-roles in the latter's *Zampa* (perf. 1831) and Auber's *Fra Diavolo* (perf. 1830), with its wide range from G below Middle C to A♭, two octaves above. After a deterioration in his voice due to an illness in 1844, he directed at various theatres, although he still sang on occasion, including a visit to London (St James's Theatre) in 1850.

Works
Some piano variations.

Further reading
A. Laget, *Chollet* (Toulouse, 1880).

Chopin, Fryderyk Franciszek [Frédéric François]

Polish composer and pianist (b. 1 Mar 1810, Żelazowa Wola, nr Warsaw; d. 17 Oct 1849, Paris).

His mother was Polish, and his father, though a Frenchman, lived in Poland and became a naturalized Pole. The family moved to Warsaw in the year of Chopin's birth and his general education was first given at home by his father, by a tutor, and then at the local school in Żelazowa Wola. He was taught piano (with emphasis on *J.S. Bach and the Viennese Classics) with local Warsaw teacher and composer Wojciech *Żywny (Adalbert Ziwny) 1816–22. Being a precocious pianist, he began to perform in the city's aristocratic *salons*. He first appeared in public, at eight, playing a *Gyrowetz concerto. While at high school, he studied with with Józef *Elsner, the director of the Conservatory, where he became a full-time student for three years after leaving school in 1826, learning harmony, *counterpoint and composition. At this time he also heard and absorbed the *folk-music of local peasants and the music and performance-style of *Hummel, *Felix Mendelssohn and *Kalkbrenner and some of *Handel and *Rossini's operas. He made a brilliant performing debut in Vienna in 1829 and shortly afterwards went on tour in Germany and Italy, during which his performances of Polish-folk-oriented compositions gave him the aura of a Polish national composer. He intended to travel to London *via* Vienna and Paris, but remained in Paris for good after his arrival in September 1831. His first concert five months later was a great critical and public success and he became a central figure in Paris musical life, making friends with Hiller, *Meyerbeer, *Bellini, *Liszt and *Berlioz (though he disliked his music!), being patronized by the Rothschilds and becoming the most fashionable piano teacher. This last helped to maintain his lifestyle and freeing him to compose without having to give public performances, to which career he was temperamentally and physically unsuited; he did appear in later performances, but never as principal. Becoming friendly with the Polish refugees from the failed 1830 revolt, he joined the Polish Literary Society and was already acquainted with figures such as Balzac, Musset, Delacroix, Heine and Mickiewicz. Various visits abroad brought him into contact with *Felix Mendelssohn and the *Schumanns. He visited London with the Parisian piano-maker Camille *Pleyel in 1837, playing only once, and in private, and keeping almost completely to himself. Back in Paris, after initial reluctance, he allowed himself to be drawn into an affair with the novelist Aurore Dudevant – who published as George Sand – and this stimulated his creativity for nearly a decade. Their three-month stay (with her two children) on Majorca produced the final version of the *Préludes, and considerable headway was made with the C♯ minor Scherzo and the *Polonaise in C minor op. 40/2. On their return he enjoyed his first stay at Sand's country house at Nohant, beginning a summer habit that would last until 1846. In Paris he began to feel the effects of the tuberculosis which had long been with him, and from which he would die. The acrimonious separation from Sand aggravated the situation and the revolution of February 1848 caused him to accept a long-standing invitation from his wealthy Scottish pupil Jane Stirling to visit England, where he was immediately taken up by aristocracy and royalty and even gave a few semi-public concerts. This social and professional round weakened him further, as did the financial necessity to play in Manchester on his way to Scotland, and Glasgow and Edinburgh when he arrived. Returning to his beloved Paris, and unable to support himself by composing or teaching, the Stirlings' generous gift of money saw him through. His funeral was attended by some 3,000 and he was buried in the cemetery of Père-Lachaise, Clésinger's monument to him being unveiled a year later.

Chopin was a gifted melodist with great improvisatory talent, an adventurous harmonism, and possessed of an intuitive sense of musical structure. He had a fundamental understanding of the piano, its *tonal and technical possibilities, which he broadened greatly, and the instrument is present in all his compositions. He transformed the spirit, while remaining true to the letter, of *salon* music in, particularly, his waltzes.

His influence was widespread and long-lasting, on *Liszt and Wagner as well as many later French composers (Saint-Saëns, Franck, Fauré, Debussy) and the nationalists of various countries including many of the Russian composers, especially those with a strong piano orientation (e.g. Rakhmaninov and Moszkowski).

Works

Solo piano Four *Ballades*, in G minor op. 23 (1831–35), in F major op. 38 (1836–39), in A♭ major op. 47 (1840–41), in F minor op. 52 (1842); *Barcarolle* in F♯ major op. 60 (1845–46); *Berceuse* in D♭ major op. 57 (1843–44); *Fantaisie* in F minor op. 49 (1841); three *Impromptus*, in A♭ major op. 29 (1837), in F♯ major op. 36 (1839), in G♭ op. 51 (1842) and the *Fantaisie-impromptu* in C♯ minor op. 66 (1835); four Scherzos, in B minor op. 20 (1831–32), in B♭ minor op. 31 (1837), in C♯ minor op. 39 (1839), in E major op. 54 (1842); *Etudes*, 12 in op. 10 (1829–33), 12 in op. 25 (1832–37) and the *Trois nouvelles études* (1839) for *Moscheles' Méthode*; three Piano Sonatas, in C minor op. 24 (1828), in B♭ minor op. 35 (1839), in B minor op. 58 (1844); Bolero in C major op. 19 (1833); *Tarantelle* in A♭ major op. 43 (1841); 24 *Préludes* op. 28 (1836–39); *Nocturnes, *Polonaises (inc. the *Polonaise-fantaisie* in A♭ major op. 61 (1845–46), *Mazurkas, *Waltzes, *Variations.

Chamber Introduction, theme and Variations in D major (two pianos, 1836); *Rondo in C major op. 73 (2 pianos, 1828); Piano Trio in G minor op. 8 (1828–29); Cello Sonata in G minor op. 65 (1845–46).

Piano and orchestra Concertos, no. 1 in E minor op. 11 (1830), no. 2 in F minor op. 21 (1829–30); Variations in B♭ major on *Mozart's 'Là ci darem' op. 2 (1827); Fantasia on Polish Airs in A major, op. 13 (1828); *Krakoviak* (rondo) in F major op. 14 (1828); Grand *polonaise in E♭ major op. 22 (1830–31).

Vocal 17 songs op. 17 (written throughout his life and pub. 1857).

Further reading
G. Sand, *Un hiver à Majorque* (pub. Paris, 1842, 5/1929; Eng. tr. 1956 ed. J. Mallion and P. Salomon, Meylan, 1985, 2/1993); *Histoire de ma vie* (pub. Paris, 1854–55). F. Liszt, *F. Chopin* (Paris, 1852; Eng. tr. 1877). G. Abraham, *Chopin's Musical Style* (London, 1968). A. Walker (ed.) *The Chopin Companion* (New York, 1973). J. Samson, *The Music of Chopin* (London, 1985). J.-J. Eigeldinger (tr. N. Shohet, ed. R. Howat), *Chopin: Pianist and Teacher*

(London, 1986). A. Orga, *Chopin: his Life and Times* (Tunbridge Wells, 1976, 2/1978). Z. Chechlińska, 'Ze studiów nad źródłami do Scherz F. Chopina' ['A source study of Chopin's Scherzos'], *Annales Chopin* , v (1960). A. Zamoyski, *Chopin* (London, 1979).

Chorale

The hymn sung by the congregation in Protestant church services. It has a long and varied history, the term being originally applied to Latin *plainsong melodies but then transferred to the Lutheran vernacular hymn. Indeed, Martin Luther (1483–1546), whose teachings were, of course, very congregationally based, himself adapted melodies from a number of sources (*folksongs, popular songs, plainsong, extant hymns) adding appropriate vernacular words, and so laying down a corpus of chorales for the Protestant liturgy which was used by later composers and to which they added. The melodies appeared on their own or in choral settings, ranging from complicated *monophonic ones to the more-or-less simple block-chordal settings with which we tend to associate the chorale from the middle of the seventeenth century. These melodies tend to keep vestiges of their plainsong (and/or, in some traditions, folk) origin in being largely syllabic (one note to a syllable allowing the words to be clearly articulated), moving by *step and in uncomplicated rhythms, so that they can be easily learned and sung by a musically-unlettered congregation. It was also common for the choir to harmonize with other parts and/or to alternate *monophonic verses with choral ones. Many composers, as well as adding their own original melodies, undertook settings of chorales in plain block-harmonization, of which the many by *J.S. Bach are the most famous. Chorales were included in many larger compositions, such as masses, *oratorios and *cantatas and were used as the basis of musical elaboration, such as in the case of the chorale prelude (Ger., *Choralvorspiel*), developed by the north German composers (Böhm and Buxtehude, for example) of the seventeenth century. In this form, the basic chorale melody (plain or *decorated) became the principal strand in a *contrapuntal elaboration; again, Bach's as the best-known, the greatest example being the collection in his *Orgel-Büchlein* (*Little Organ Book*).

Chorale prelude (see *chorale)

Cimbalom [kimbalom]
A Hungarian *dulcimer played with wooden or covered beaters, the sound of which is characterized by grace-note skip and a 'roll' or '*tremolo*' used to sustain the notes. Both of these have found their way into music – especially piano-music – suggestive of Hungarian or Magyar *folk-influence, for example, *Schubert's Hungarian Melody, D817 (1824) and *Liszt's Hungarian Rhapsodies (issued as *Magyar rhapsodiák* or *Rhapsodies hongroises*, and composed between 1839 and 1847). See Carew/MUSE, Chapter 21.

Cinti-Damoreau [neé Montalant], Laure (Cinthie) ['Mlle Cinti' using the Italianized version of 'Cinthie']
French soprano (b. 6 Feb 1801, Paris; d. 25 Feb 1863, Paris).
   She lived in Paris all her life, studying piano and singing at the Conservatoire and making her debut at 14. After a London season (1822), her subsequent ten-year engagement at the Paris Opéra (1825–35) resulted in her creation of

the principal soprano roles in *Rossini's *Le siège de Corinthe*, *Moïse*, *Le Comte Ory*, and *Guillaume Tell* as well as in Auber's *La muette de Portici* and Isabelle in *Meyerbeer's *Robert le diable*. Her marriage to the tenor V.C. Damoreau took place in 1827. During her next engagement, at the Opéra-Comique (1836–41), she appeared in several of Auber's new operas and toured America in 1844. She taught singing at the Conservatoire, 1833–56, and published several singing manuals including *Méthode de chant* (1849); she also composed and published some songs. She was especially famed for her purity of voice, justness of intonation and her capacity for embellishment.

Further reading
A. Caswell, 'Mme Cinti-Damoreau and the Embellishment of Italian Opera in Paris: 1820–1845', *JAMS*, xxviii (1975).

Classical (Lat.: the highest class of citizen or writer; Fr. *classique*; Ger. *Klassik*, *klassisch*)
(1) A term generally used to describe something as the best example of its kind, a model of excellence, suitable for emulation.

(2) It can also be used in the sense of being characterized by, or emulating, the values of the civilizations of Classical Antiquity (Greece and Rome principally). These values embodied serenity, nobility, simplicity and a sense of community and shared aesthetic experiences.

(3) In general musical usage, a term used to distinguish art-music (often inappropriately called 'serious music') from popular forms of music (including jazz and ethnic musics), implying standardization and a degree of

permanence as opposed to the supposed transience of the popular market.

(4) Music of the Classical period, which was reckoned to show traits akin to those of Classical Antiquity, expressed in restraint and formal balance. It is often used as an antithesis to *Romantic.

Classical Antiquity (see *classical (2))

Clavecin (Fr.) Harpsichord

Clavecin à maillets (Fr.: 'harpsichord with hammers')
A series of keyboard instruments invented by Jean *Marius in Paris, four slightly different examples of which he submitted to the Académie Royale des Sciences in 1716. The strings were struck by small hammers, as the name suggests, but in the more direct manner of the *clavichord tangent – which is where Marius's idea came from – than the piano as we later find it. The hammers appear not to have been covered and there is no *damping or *escapement.

Clavecinistes
School of French composers who played the harpsichord (often to virtuoso standard) and wrote music for it in the hundred years after *c.* 1650. They include Jacques Chambonnières, Jean-Henri D'Anglebert, Jean-Philippe Rameau and several Couperins, including probably the greatest in this sphere, *François Couperin ('le grand').

Clavicembalo (It.) Harpsichord

Clavichord (Fr. *clavicorde, manicorde*; Ger. *Clavichord, Klavichord*; It. *clavicordo, manicordo*; Lat. *clavicordium*)
The simplest keyboard instrument though capable of great subtlety of tone-colour. It was in continuous use from probably the fourteenth, certainly the fifteenth centuries up to the early nineteenth. Its shape is that of an oblong box with the keyboard inset in the longer side or projecting from it. The strings are parallel to the keyboard, are struck by small metal blades ('*tangents') attached to the keys, causing them to vibrate. The player's finger is in close and constant contact with the string as long as the note is sounding. This results in several characteristic features of the instrument: (a) there is a great feeling of intimacy between player and instrument; (b) the volume and tone can be regulated by *touch; and (c) a '*Bebung' (vibrato) effect can be obtained. As against these, however, is the lack of sustaining power, since the tangent is in continuous contact with the string while it is sounding, and the low level of volume. Although larger clavichords were built, it is at its best in an intimate domestic setting.

Until the eighteenth century, clavichords were 'fretted'. This was a process familiar to lute and guitar players, whereby a string is stopped by the finger (pressed against the fret on the neck) at prefixed lengths giving the notes. Similarly on early clavichords, a string, touched by tangents at different lengths along its length, could serve for several notes; a disadvantage is, of course, that those notes could not sound simultaneously. Thus, an early clavichord of, say, four octaves (representing some 45 notes, as these instruments often miss out the lowest chromatic notes) could be accommodated on 17 strings. During the eighteenth century, the instrument became 'unfretted', i.e. each note had its own string (or strings, since some were *bichord instruments). The clavichord was *J.S. Bach's favourite keyboard instrument apart from the organ and

*C.P.E. Bach was praised for the feeling and beauty of his playing on it. It was associated with his *empfindsamer Stil ('feeling style') and was a favourite in northern Germany where it lasted longer than elsewhere. In later times, interest was rekindled in the clavichord by those built by Arnold Dolmetsch at the very end of the nineteenth century.

Further reading
H. Neupert, *Das Klavichord* (Kassel, 1948, 2/1955; Eng. tr., 1965). E.M. Ripin, 'The Early Clavichord', *MQ*, liii (1957). K Cooper, *The Clavichord in the 18th Century* (diss., Columbia U., 1971). R. Troeger, *Technique and Interpretation on the Harpsichord and Clavichord* (Bloomington, IN, 1987). B. Brauchli, *The Clavichord* (Cambridge, 1998).   Boalch/HARPSICHORD. Russell/HARPSICHORD.

Clavier

(1) (Fr.) The keyboard of a keyboard instrument.

(2) (Ger.) Keyboard instrument in general. It is in this sense that the *Colt Clavier Collection is named.

(3) The silent 'practice pianos' or 'dumb claviers' used by pianists.

'*Clavier-Instrument*'
A hammered keyboard-instrument built by Christoph Gottlieb *Schröter in Dresden, *c*.1721, which may be a proto-piano.

'*Claviola*'
Keyboard instrument invented by *John Isaac Hawkins in which the strings were bowed. It was played in public in Philadelphia (1802) and in London (1833), where it became popular for a time.

Claviorgan (Fr. *clavecin organisé*; Ger. *Orgelklavier*; It., Sp. *claviorgano*; quasi-Lat. *claviorganum*)
A keyboard instrument combining strings (harpsichord, clavichord, piano) and pipes (organ). The principle was used for a long time and instruments of the kind are described as early as the 1540s, but the English term appears to date from the end of the nineteenth century. As suggested, the term covers many combinations, including German court organs which contained sets of harpsichord strings, but the late eighteenth and early nineteenth centuries produced a large number – among a rash of more fanciful instruments – and included examples from the most respected of makers, *Broadwood, *Merlin and *Taskin among them. Such an instrument, combining a piano and an organ played by the same keyboard, by Merlin (1784) is in the *Colt Clavier Collection (See Carew/MUSE Pl. 20).

Claviorganum (see *Claviorgan)

Clementi, Muzio [Clementi, Mutius Philippus Vincentius Franciscus Xaverius]
Italian composer, keyboard player, teacher, music publisher and piano-maker (b. 23 Jan 1752, Rome; d. 10 Mar 1832, Evesham, Worcestershire).
    Son of a silversmith, he studied as a child under various teachers in Rome, including Antonio Burone, Giuseppe Santarelli and possibly Gaetano Carpani. He became organist at the local church at the age of 13, being noticed that year (1766) by a wealthy English traveller, Peter Beckford (cousin of the novelist William Beckford), who brought him from his father for seven years and took him to his country estate in Dorsetshire,

England. Nothing is known of this period, except that he appears to have been studying alone, but in about 1774 he moved to London, appearing in public as a harpsichordist early the following year, and he was also 'conducting' from the harpsichord at the King's Theatre in the Haymarket. The immediately popular six op. 2 sonatas were published in early 1779 and the year after, Clementi began a Continental tour, being well received in Paris and participating in the famous performance 'duel' with *W.A. Mozart in the presence of Joseph II in December 1781. Clementi's report of Mozart's playing ('spirit and grace' according to *Berger) was not reciprocated by his rival ('not a *kreuzer*'s worth of taste or feeling ... a mere *mechanicus*'). Returning to London in autumn of 1783, he took on *J.B. Cramer as a pupil and at the height of a concert series in which he was the main keyboard soloist, rushed to Lyons and an attempted elopement with one of his French ex-pupils failed. He was back in London in mid-1785, where he settled until 1802, having a thriving career as performer, conductor, composer, publisher and piano-maker. Like most of the London composers, the success of *J. Haydn's two visits to the capital (1791–92 and 1794–95) adversely affected Clementi's career, but not as a piano-teacher and he continued to teach not only the wealthy and titled but also career-musicians (see below). In 1802 he began another European tour, this time as publisher, to secure the rights of publication from Continental composers and publishers, to publish some of his own music, and to drum up business for his pianos. He was accompanied for part of the journey by the young John *Field, the gifted Irish composer/performer, whom he employed in his London warehouse

to demonstrate his pianos. Over the next nine or ten years, Clementi visited Europe many times – in spite of the perils of the Napoleonic wars – reaching Russia on more than one occasion, where he and Field eventually parted company. He married and was widowed within a year, and negotiated the publication rights with *Beethoven for some of the latter's greatest works – the '*Rasoumovsky*' *Quartets* op. 59, the *Coriolanus* overture, the 4th Symphony, 4th Piano Concerto and the Violin Concerto. His affairs in London prospered greatly and he married again, at almost 60, and fathered four children. Subsequent visits to Europe to arrange and present performances of his symphonies (including those at the *Concert Spirituel in Paris, 1816–17 and the Gewandhaus in Leipzig, 1822) were not greatly successful. He retired in 1830 and, after a stay in Staffordshire, the family moved to Evesham, where he died at the age of 80. He was buried, after a huge funeral, in the cloisters of Westminster Abbey.

His music combines an Italianate lyricism with a Germanic craftsmanship and a keyboard style which can be associated with the *British piano and the *London Piano School. Even his early works have *Romantic foreshadowings and pre-echoes of pieces by several composers (Mozart and Beethoven in particular). Issued first editions of Beethoven's works and was an important piano-teacher, piano-maker and author of didactic works in London.

Clementi influenced Beethoven, in terms of compositional and early keyboard styles. As a piano-teacher, his pupils included Field, J.B. Cramer, *Theresa Jansen, Benoit-Auguste *Bertini, Carl Zeuner, Alexander Klengel, *Berger and *Kalkbrenner, and he had contacts with younger musicians, such as *Herz and *J.L. Dussek.

Works

Many piano sonatas and other pieces for piano, including *The Black Joke with 21 Variations*, wo2 (1777), the G minor sonatas op. 7/3 (pub. 1782), op. 34/2 (pub. 1795) and op. 50/3 (*Didone Abbandonata*) (pub. 1821), the op. 13/6 in F minor (1785) and the F# minor op. 25/5 (1790). His didactic works, *Introduction to the Art of Playing on the Piano Forte* (pub. 1801), the Six Progressive Sonatinas op. 36 (pub. 1797), and the collection of 100 pieces in three vols entitled *Gradus ad Parnassum* (pub. 1817–26) had enormous influence on contemporary and later pedagogy and are still of great value today.

Further reading

J.C. Graue, *Muzio Clementi and the Development of Pianoforte Music in Industrial England* (diss., U. of Illinois, 1971). H. Truscott, 'The Piano Music I', in ed. D. Arnold and N. Fortune, *The Beethoven Companion* (London, 1971). L. Plantinga, *Clementi: His Life and Music* (London, 1977). Newman/SCE. Loesser/MEN.

Cocks, Robert

English music publisher (b. 1798; d. 7 Apr 1887, London)

He began his career as a concert manager at the Hanover Square Rooms. He founded his publishing firm in London in 1823, where he employed a staff of musicians, including his two sons, to edit and compile music. The firm's publications included *J.S. Bach's keyboard works in *Czerny's edition, *Beethoven's string quartets and music by Czerny, Rode, *Hummel, *Spohr and others. He also had a circulating music library. The firm of Augener bought the company in 1898 and its name changed in 1904.

Further reading

C. Humphries and W.C. Smith, *Music Publishing in the British Isles* (London, 1954, 2/1970). O. Neighbour and A. Tyson, *English Music Publishers' Plate Numbers in the First Half of the Nineteenth Century* (London, 1965). J.A. Parkinson, *Victorian Music Publishers: an Annotated List* (Warren, MI, 1990).

Colt Clavier Collection

A collection of historic keyboard instruments collected over some fifty years by C.F. Colt. It is housed in Bethesda in Kent, Great Britain.

Combination instruments

These are keyboard instruments in which the actions of several different types are combined, such as piano-harpsichord in which one or more sets of strings can be plucked or struck with hammers, and the piano-organ, a very popular combination in which a piano included an organ mechanism; this was also called *'organised piano' and '[forte]piano organisé' and enjoyed widespread use in France. (See the *claviorgan ('Claviorganum') by *Merlin in *The Mechanical Muse*, Plate 20.)

Compass (Fr. *étendue*; Ger. *Umfang*)

The pitch-range available between the extremes (lowest to highest notes) of an instrument (usually fixed) or voice (variable). Although the *piano's compass is more-or-less standardized today, it varied greatly during earlier periods, but showed a general trend of widening in both directions as time went on. The most common method of showing the pitch range is that of the acoustician Helmholtz, in which *middle C is given as c′ (small-case and with a single dash), the octaves above being c″, c‴, etc., and those below being given as C′ (upper-case C with a single dash), C″, C‴, etc. A common variant of this is to use numbers instead of dashes for the upper octaves (c1, c3, etc.) and repeated capitals for the lower (c, then C, CC etc.). The letter-names of the other notes follow suit in both systems. (See also *Tessitura.)

Compensation frame

A method of *bracing the frame of a *piano using tubes of the same metal as the strings (brass or iron) so that changes in temperature and humidity causing expansion or contraction of the strings would be compensated for and the tension of the strings would remain substantially the same, preventing breakage and preserving tuning. It was invented and patented by the *Stodart firm in London in 1820. Its function was obviated by the adoption of the *cast-iron frame after 1850.

Concert, Benefit

A concert common in Britain in the late eighteenth and early nineteenth centuries for the 'benefit' of an individual (or, more rarely, group or organization) in which the musicians involved pledged to forgo their usual fees, thus allowing the benefactor to keep all or most of the profits. This could be particularly lucrative if one or more of those involved were of international standing, especially visiting virtuosi.

Concertino

(1) A diminutive form of *concerto, implying a lighter and technically easier work.

(2) The smaller of the two groups in the *concerto grosso.

Concerto (It. and Eng.; Fr. *concert*; Ger. *Konzert*)

An instrumental musical genre in which an instrument or small group of instruments is combined and contrasted with an orchestra or larger instrumental group. The derivations of the word reflect this two-pronged meaning: *concertare* (Lat.), 'to contend, debate, dispute' and *concertare* (It.) 'to agree, arrange collect together'. During the *Baroque period, it had two forms, the *concerto grosso, in which a smaller and a larger body of instruments were involved, and the solo concerto. The latter normally meant a solo instrument and orchestra, but because of formal differences between the solo and grosso types, 'solo' could also mean the double (with two solo instruments) or the triple (with three). It was rare to find larger solo groups; such a work was usually found in the *Classical period and designated a *'sinfonia concertante'.

The solo concerto of the Baroque and Classical eras was a work of virtuosity for the soloist(s) in three movements, basically fast-slow-fast. Very generally speaking, during the Baroque, the first movement was dramatic and in *ritornello form, and in the Classical and *Romantic in modified *sonata form; it has been argued that *W.A. Mozart's concertos show characteristics of each. The orchestra usually began with a *tutti stating the main thematic material and the entry of the solo instrument(s) was something of an event, thereafter, alternation and interplay between soloist(s) and orchestra became the focus, with some solo passages, notably the *cadenza towards the end of the movement. The 'slow' movement, for the most part, showed the lyrical aspect of the instrument(s) in a rondo or slow-movement *sonata-form. It was *aria-like, although there were occasional dramatic interpolations and solo passages; occasionally variation-form was used. In the Romantic period, there was a tendency to link the second and third movements, which sometimes resulted in truncation of the former. The finale was almost always lively and virtuoso in rondo, sonata-rondo or, occasionally, variation-forms.

There are, inevitably, exceptions to almost all of the foregoing, among them the fact that many early concertos lack a slow movement (*J.C. Bach, *Field) and some have a fourth (*Brahms's Second Piano Concerto and Litolff's), while *Liszt's and R. *Schumann's are in a continuous movement with sections corresponding, more-or-less, to the separate-movement forms.

Further reading
D. Tovey, *Essays in Musical Analysis*, III: *Concertos* (London, 1936). A. Veinus, *The Concerto* (New York, 1944, 2/1964). M.F. Bukofzer, *Music in the Baroque Era* (New York, 1947). R. Hill, ed., *The Concerto* (London, 1952). A Hutchings, *The Baroque Concerto* (London, 1961, R3/1973). C.V. Palisca, *Baroque Music* (New Jersey, 1968). D. Forman, *Mozart's concerto Forms* (London, 1971). P.H. Lang, ed., *The Concerto 1800–1900* (New York, 1969). J.A. Meyer, 'The Idea of Conflict in the Concerto', *Studies in Music*, viii (1974). *MGG*.

Concerto Grosso (It.: 'large concerto')
A form of *concerto peculiar to the *Baroque period in which a small orchestra or group of instruments alternated and played with an orchestra or larger group of instruments. The smaller body was called the 'concertino' and the larger the 'ripieno' or 'concerto grosso'. A favourite form of the concertino in Italy consisted of two violins and a cello, sometimes with its own continuo. This combination began in the op. 6 concerti grossi of Corelli and was subsequently used by *Handel in his opp. 3 and 6. Several of *J.S. Bach's 'Brandenburg' Concertos are of this type, but do not use this concertino makeup. The concerto grosso tends to have more than the three movements which became standardized for the solo concerto and often include dance-movements and *fugues. The *sinfonia concertante of the *Classical period, with its group of four or more soloists, could be seen to be a revival of the spirit of the concerto grosso and later works have also used the principle, such as Stravinsky's 'Dumbarton Oaks', Vaughan Williams's *Fantasia on a Theme by Thomas Tallis*, and the various 'Concertos for Orchestra' – which highlight not one fixed, but several different groups to alternate with the orchestra – by such as Bartók, Kodály, Hindemith and Tippett.

Concerts of Ancient [Antient] **Music**
A concert-giving society in London during the eighteenth century. Founded in 1776 by aristocratic amateurs who rotated as its directors, its intention was to promote older 'learned' music, particularly that from before the seventeenth century and to this end it formally banned music less than 20 years old. Later in the century it began to feature more and more the music of *Handel, culminating in the close collaboration with the organization of the great Handel Commemoration of 1784. This took place at Westminster Abbey and the Pantheon with over 500 musicians in the orchestra and

choir and was attended by George III, lending considerable kudos to the proceedings and the organization itself. The festival remained an annual fixture for seven years, *J. Haydn attending the last on his first visit to London in 1791. The organization was disbanded in 1792.

Concert spirituel (Fr.: 'sacred concert') A series of concerts founded in 1725 in Paris by Anne Philidor to promote instrumental music and sacred vocal works in Latin, although later, secular works and works in French were introduced. The concerts played a large and important part in Paris's musical life, along with the Opéra and the organization was discontinued after 1790. The title enjoyed a revival in 1805 and was used for similar concerts by concert organizations throughout Europe.

Conductor
A director of a musical performance who uses gestures to ensure unanimity of execution and interpretation. This is usually considered as the sole contribution to the performance, but before the *Baroque period, the principal musician – leading or highest-voiced singer, principal string player, etc. – was responsible for time and *tempo and to an extent, interpretation and ensemble. The rise of the *continuo in the *Baroque period passed the function to its player – who was often the composer – in smaller ensembles and was shared between the continuo and the principal musician – usually the first string player – in larger ones. As late as the 1790s in London, Joseph *Haydn 'presided' at the piano during performances of his 'London' Symphonies in this sense – indeed, almost thirty-five years later, *Felix

Mendelssohn was induced to do the same. In the nineteenth century the function of the conductor was gradually detached from other functions and became the profession we recognize today. It is the virtuoso violinist Louis *Spohr who is credited with the first use of the baton – as opposed to a scroll of paper or manuscript, which had long been used in France – in a concert in London in 1820, although, it was more likely to have been his violin bow. The principle, however, had been established and was particularly apposite for larger and more diverse orchestras and the increasing complication of orchestral scoring after the *Classical masters, all of which would continue during the later nineteenth and the twentieth centuries.

Conductor's piano (see *Piano)

Congress of Vienna (see *Vienna, Congress of)

Continuo [*basso continuo*] (It.: 'continuous bass'; Eng. thoroughbass (obsolete); Ger. *Generalbass*)
A type of instrumental accompaniment, primarily associated with the *Baroque period, the point of which was to free the non-bass melodic parts or voices from having to represent all the notes of a given harmony. It consisted of a melodic line played by a bass instrument, such as a cello, providing the foundation of the piece's harmonies and a series of figures. These gave further information, such as the type of chord (major, minor, with added notes such as sevenths, etc.) and its position, and were produced by another, harmony-instrument – i.e. one capable of producing chords – such as keyboard (harpsichord, organ) or lute-type instrument, such as (in earlier times) the lute itself or the *chitarrone*.

The interpretation ('realization') of this code, was seen as something of an art, ranged from strumming the basic chords to producing a fully-fledged additional part, as some of *J.S. Bach's extant realizations show.

Contrapuntal (see *Counterpoint)

Contredanse (Fr.; Ger. *Contratanz, Kontretanz*; It., Sp., *contradanza*) Eighteenth-century French dance enjoying widespread popularity based on the English Country Dance of the preceding century, from which the name derives. The English original was a line-dance, based on the interaction of the dancers rather than any regular system of *steps, but the French version (which may have been influenced by another dance *Le cotillon*) was a square set which took its choreography from the noble dance-styles. The *cotillon* was subsequently used in English-speaking countries to denote the square French style of the Country dance. The popularity of the *contredanse* grew in France, while the *minuet became increasingly more formal, stylized and aristocratic. Later in the century, the steps became simplified and smaller groups of dancers were used, sometimes the minimum of four, hence the alternative names of *cadrille* or quadrille. Several composers wrote sets of *contredanses* for dancing, notably *W.A. Mozart and *Beethoven.

Coolin, The (Ir., *An Cúilfhionn* ('the fair-haired' [boy]))
Irish *folk song popular with composers in the first half of the nineteenth century, especially as a subject for *rondos or sets of *variations. It also appears in *Moore's *Irish Melodies* as 'Though the last glimpse of Erin'.

Corri, Domenico
Italian composer, teacher and music publisher (b. 4 Oct 1746, Rome; d. 22 May 1825, London).

Corri moved from Rome, where he learnt singing, violin and harpsichord, to Naples for four years (1763–67) studying with Nicola Porpora but returned to Rome where he married one of his pupils and met *Burney. It was the latter's good opinion which resulted in an invitation from the Musical Society of Edinburgh to conduct for them in 1771, where the family remained until 1790, managing the Vauxhall pleasure gardens and the Edinburgh Theatre Royal. Around 1790, in financial difficulties, he moved to Soho in London and founded a music publishing business which – after his daughter, Sophie, married *J.L. Dussek – became Corri, Dussek & Co. The firm ran into financial difficulties around the turn of the century and Dussek fled his creditors; Corri, however, continued on and was joined by his son, who took over the business in 1804. Corri wrote several successful operas and continued as a teacher also. His health began to fail and he was having fits of madness at the end of his life. At a time when *figured bass was falling out of use, he devised a system of skeleton accompaniments which point towards the later use of arpeggiated basses in song accompaniments.

Works
He composed operas (including *Alessandro nell'Indie* (perf. 1774), *The Cabinet* (perf. 1802) and *The Travellers* (1806), all in London) as well as vocal pieces (3 volumes of *A Select Collection of the most Admired Songs, Duetts* (c.1779)) and keyboard pieces, including 21 sonatas, some of which are accompanied and some with titles such as

Nelson's Victory, a Characteristic Sonata with Tambourine Accompaniment (pub. *c.*1800) and a piano concerto in A major (pub. 1880).

Further reading
C. Humphries and W.C. Smith, *Music Publishing in the British Isles* (London, 1954, R/1970). W.C. Smith, *The Italian Opera and Contemporary Ballet in London 1789–1820* (London, 1955). H.C.R. Landon, *Haydn: Chronicle and Works, Haydn in England 1791–1795* (London, 1977).

Cottage piano
A small type of upright piano designed for houses with limited space and lower incomes. (See the cottage piano by *Broadwood in Plate 23 in *The Mechanical Muse*.)

Counterpoint (adj. **contrapuntal**)
The art of simultaneous combination of melodies.

(1) *Free counterpoint* So-called to distinguish it from strict counterpoint (see (2) below), it is the combination of simultaneous melodies with no other rules than that the part-writing is 'correct' according to the theoretical precepts of the period. The emphasis is on the horizontal, or linear aspect of the music although the resultant harmonic basis must also be 'correct'. This kind thrived in the *Baroque period and one of the consequences of any possible thin-ness in the harmonic sense was the use of the *continuo which provided a constant harmonic underlay, thus providing any harmony-notes lacking and ensuring that the progression of the harmony was clear at all times. Various academic devices were used, one of which was counterpoint

at certain intervals, thus a skilful contrapuntist could ensure that a melody which 'went' with another (different) melody a third away from it would also 'work' if it were put a sixth away from it; this is 'counterpoint at the third and sixth' or whatever intervals are in question. Another device is that of *invertible counterpoint*, where the added voice will work above or below the original one – by no means a foregone conclusion. An extreme form of counterpoint is *canon, where the same melody is used in several parts (like a round).

(2) *Strict counterpoint* This is the name given to the type of counterpoint used in the Renaissance period when what appears to us nowadays as a very strict code of rules was in operation. It is also called polyphony (adj. polyphonic).

Country dance (see *Contredanse*)

Couperin, François [*le grand*]
French composer, harpsichord-player, organ-player (b. 10 Nov 1668, Paris; d. 11 Sep 1733, Paris).
    The greatest member of a great musical dynasty, he was trained by his father who died when the boy was ten and his father's post as organist at St Gervais passed to him when he was 18. In 1693 he was appointed teacher to Louis XIV and one of his four court organists (who each served annually for a quarter of a year); he was also granted a royal privilege as a music printer and vendor. He wrote a set of trio sonatas which became the nucleus for his later set *Les nations*, published in Paris in 1726, showing his love for, and knowledge of, the Italian *Baroque composers, notably Corelli, to whose memory he later wrote the *Apothéose de Corelli*. He taught many

aristocrats at court and was ennobled (by buying his own coat of arms, as recently allowed by the king) after three years and made *Chevalier de l'Ordre de Latran* in 1702. Soon his compositions were being performed at court and elsewhere, and several published, such as his *Concerts royaux* (1722) and *Les goûts réünis* (The Tastes Reunited, 1724). He soon became recognized as the leading French composer of his time.

In spite of his onerous duties at court and at St Gervais – where he was still organist for nine months of the year – in 1713 he acquired a twenty-year licence to publish music and set about publishing his harpsichord pieces in *ordres (suites) grouped together in a series of books (*livres*) and, in between, the first (1716) and second (revised, 1717) editions of his treatise *L'art de toucher le clavecin*. That same year, he took over D'Anglebert's duties as the king's harpsichordist also. His health began to fail – a fact which he mentions several times in prefaces to his published works – and he arranged for his daughter, Marguerite-Antoinette, a very talented musician, to succeed him as harpsichordist – the first woman in such a royal post – G. Marchand to take over his duties in the royal chapel, and his cousin Nicolas was also provided work. He also took out another privilege for printing and publishing his remaining works, but this was not carried out after his death with the result that much of his chamber and sacred music has been lost.

In spite of his fame, there is little documentation on Couperin's life and less on his personality. His style managed to fuse Italian and French traits into a successful hybrid and what he may have lacked as a *contrapuntal writer – which was not in great favour in France – he made up for with clear linear writing of charm and beauty; he was the musical equal of his two great compatriots, Racine (literature) and Watteau (painting).

Works
Four *livres* (books) of harpsichord music, containing between them 27 *ordres (suites), in turn containing *character-pieces of real people, fictitious people and depicting abstract human qualities. There are chamber works also, including *Concerts royaux* (*Royal Concerts*, pub. 1722) and *Nouveaux concerts* (*New Concerts*, pub. 1724), *Apothéose de Corelli* (pub. the same year) and *Apothéose de Lully* (pub. the following year). A large body of sacred music survives as well as his *method, *L'art de toucher le clavecin* (*The Art of Playing the Harpsichord*, pub. 1716, rev 2/1717) and *Regle pour l'accompagnement* (*Rule[s] for accompanying*) which remains in manuscript.

Further reading
W. Mellers, *François Couperin and the French Classical Tradition* (London, 1950 2/1987). P. Citron, *Couperin* (Paris, 1956, 2/1996). T. Dart, 'On Couperin's Harpsichord Music', *MT*, cx (1969). P. Beaussant, *François Couperin* (Paris, 1980; Eng. tr., 1990). D. Tunley, *Couperin* (London, 1982). O. Baumont, *Couperin, le musicien des rois* (Paris, 1998).

Coupled, coupling, coupler

The temporary combining of two or more sets of strings on a *harpsichord (or ranks of pipes on an *organ) so that they can be played simultaneously by the same set of *keys (or by a different set of keys than those usual for those particular strings or pipes). This is usually achieved by *stops or *pedals (or occasionally some other form of lever) called 'couplers'.

Some pianos were also provided with this kind of mechanism and in *combination instruments the different mechanisms were also coupled in this way.

Courante (Fr.: 'running', 'flowing'; It. *corrente*; Eng. corant, coranto)
A dance of obscure origin in triple time which existed in two forms by the beginning of the eighteenth century: the French *courante*, *contrapuntal, majestic and stately with metrical ambiguities (especially hemiola) and prescribed choreography, and the Italian *corrente*, a faster simpler *homophonic courtship dance with provision for improvised steps. As a piece of music, the *courante* became one of the staples of the *Baroque *suite and, because of its adoption by, notably, *Handel and *J.S. Bach, the faster Italian version is seen as more characteristic, in spite of the French titling.

Cramer, Henri
French pianist.
   Little is known of him except that he was active in Paris after 1840 and was very prolific as a composer.

Works
Mostly for piano, they include *rondos, *fantasies, *caprices, marches, *waltzes and a huge number of pieces based on operatic themes.

Cramer, Johann [John] Baptist
German (British naturalized) composer, pianist and publisher (b. 24 Feb 1771, Mannheim; d. 16 Apr 1858, London).
   Son of a violinist who taught him the instrument, he was taken to live in London at the age of three and, four years later, studied the piano with J.D. Benser and then J.S. *Schroeter (1780–83) and with *Clementi for a year before learning theory from C.F. *Abel. The boy was well-versed in their works as well as those of *J.C. Bach, *C.P.E. Bach, *Scarlatti, *Paradies, Müthel, *J. Haydn and *W.A. Mozart. Cramer made his public debut at ten in his father's benefit concert. He toured France and Germany, 1788–91, and was given some manuscripts of *J.S. Bach and published his earliest works. On his return to London, he began to establish himself as one of the city's leading pianists, composers and teachers, becoming acquainted with *J. Haydn during the latter's visits in the 1790s. Another tour (1799–1800) took him through the Netherlands, Germany and Austria, renewing his friendship with Haydn and meeting *Beethoven (whose sonatas he helped to introduce to the British public), *Hummel, *Cherubini, *Dussek, *Wölfl, *Weber and *Kalkbrenner. Apart from a Continental visit 1816–18, he remained in London 1800–1835, marrying twice, and becoming involved in various publishing partnerships – with Chappell, as Cramer & Keys, and as Cramer, Addison and Beale – before founding his own firm of J.B. Cramer & Co. Ltd., which is still trading. During these years he made the acquaintance of *Ries, *Felix Mendelssohn, *Czerny, *Berlioz and *Liszt. He was buried in Brompton Cemetery.
   One of the most admired pianists of the first half of the nineteenth century, especially for his legato playing, associated with the *London Piano School and winning the particular admiration of Beethoven. As a composer, he saw himself in the line of Mozart, although he combined this conservatism with more advanced keyboard figuration and technique. His pedagogical works were of widespread importance in the nineteenth century. He was one of the

founders of the *Philharmonic Society in 1813 and appointed to the board of the *RAM in 1822. His studies were admired by *Beethoven (who annotated and recommended them for his nephew's use and said they were the best preparatory training for his own works) and by *R. Schumann, who found them good 'for head and hand'.

Works
Nearly 70 piano sonatas, including op. 53 in A minor, 'L'ultima' (1812), and op. 62 in E major 'Le retour à Londres (bef. 1819); nine piano concertos and a Concerto da camera in B♭ major (piano solo, flute and string quartet, 1813) are extant as well as chamber music with piano. Pedagogical works include the *Studio per il pianoforte* (pub. 1804–10), *Instructions for the Pianoforte* (pub. 1812), *Dulce et utile* op. 55 (1818 or before), 16 études op.81 (pub. *c.*1835) and shorter works.

Further reading
J.B. Brocklehurst, 'The Studies of J.B. Cramer and his Predecessors', *ML*, xxxix (1958). P.F. Ganz, *The Development of the Etude for Pianoforte* (diss., Northwestern U., 1960). A. Tyson, 'A Feud between Clementi and Cramer', *ML*, liv (1973). J.C. Graue, 'The Clementi-Cramer Dispute Revisited', *ML*, lvi (1975). Fétis/ *BIOGRAPHIE*. Newman/SSB.

Cristofori, [Christofani, Cristofani, Cristofali] Bartolom[m]eo
Italian designer and maker of keyboard instruments, inventor of the *piano (b. 4 May 1655, Padua; d. 27 Jan 1731, Florence).

Little is known of his early life until his appointment as instrument-maker at the court of Prince Ferdinand de' Medici

in Florence from 1688 and an inventory of 1700 shows that he had already made at least one *piano. He never joined the guild to which the other local instrument makers belonged and received permission to work at home because he found the court workshops too noisy and distracting. He remained in Florence, until his death, 44 years later.

Works
Three *pianos are extant: 1720, in the Metropolitan Museum of Art, New York; 1722, formerly in Padua, now in Rome; 1726, in the Karl-Marx Universität, Leipzig. There are also a spinet (1693) (see *harpsichord), a *harpsichord of 1722 and some related instruments of doubtful authenticity.

Further reading
K. Restle, *Bartolomeo Cristofori und die Anfange des Hammerklaviers* (Munich, 1991). M. O'Brien, *Bartolomeo Cristofori at Court in Late Medici Florence* (diss., Catholic U. of America, 1994). Fétis/*BIOGRAPHIE*. Russell/ HARPSICHORD. Harding/PIANO-FORTE. Pollens/EARLY.

Cross-stringing (see *Overstringing)

Crotch, William
English composer, organist, painter and musical theorist (b. 5 Jul 1775, Norwich; d. 29 Dec 1847, Taunton).

A musical prodigy, as attested by Daines *Barrington and *Burney, Crotch, son of a master carpenter, was self-taught as a child. He played the organ in public and at Buckingham Palace at the age of three and was investigated by the Royal Society. Also proficient on the piano and violin and showing talent in painting and drawing, he attended Cambridge university 1786–88 and was appointed organist at Christ Church, Oxford, at the age of 15, gaining his BMus in 1794, a professorship in 1797 and the DMus in 1799. He gave the first course of formal music lectures in Oxford during the first four years of the new century and moved to London in 1807, becoming a well-known and respected teacher, composer and musical theorist. He was a member of the *Philharmonic Society and first principal of the *RAM 1822–32.

Crotch was capable of composition in a variety of styles, though little in sympathy with the music and performance styles of his own time. An important lecturer and pedagogical writer, he was instrumental in the revival of older, especially English, music and taught Sterndale *Bennett. He was also a fine painter and a friend of Constable; he also wrote on an immensely wide variety of non-musical subjects.

Works

There are many vocal and choral works, including the oratorios, *The Captivity of Judah* (1786–89) and *Palestine* (1805–11) as well as odes and Anglican chants. The instrumental music includes a piano/harpsichord concerto (1794), three organ concertos (*c*.1805); three keyboard sonatas, preludes and other pieces for piano; two violin sonatas, a string quartet (1788, rev. 1790). His pedagogical works include *Elements of Musical Composition* (pub. 1812, rev. 1833, 1856), *Rudiments of Playing the Piano* (pub. 1822), *Practical Thorough Bass* (pub. *c*.1825), *Lectures on the History of Music* (delivered at Oxford, 1798–1832).

Further reading

A.H. King, *Some British Collectors of Music c.1600–1960* (Cambridge, 1963); P.F. Williams, 'J.S. Bach and English

Organ Music', *ML*, xliv (1963); I. Fleming-Williams, 'Dr William Crotch, Member of the Oxford School and Friend of Constable', *The Connoisseur*, clix (May, 1965); B. Rainbow, *The Choral Revival in the Anglican Church (1839–1872)* (London, 1970); J. Rennert, *William Crotch* (Lavenham, 1975). S. Wollenberg, 'Music in 18th-Century Oxford', *PRMA*, cviii (1981–82). C. Ehrlich, *The Music Profession in England since the Eighteenth Century* (Oxford, 1985).

Czerny, Carl

Austrian composer, pianist, teacher and writer on music (b. 21 Feb 1791, Vienna; d. 15 Jul 1857, Vienna).

Born into a musical family, his father was a music-teacher and piano-repairer, and played several instruments; he taught his son *via* the music of *J.S. Bach, *W.A. Mozart and *Clementi and the boy also learnt languages (Italian, French, German) from some of his father's students. Carl made rapid progress under *Beethoven's tutelage, using *C.P.E. Bach's *Versuch* as a textbook; he became an excellent sight-reader and improviser. At the age of nine he made his public début in Mozart's C minor piano concerto (K491) and he could play all Beethoven's piano music from memory. He gave regular concerts devoted to Beethoven's works in his home, with the master in attendance on occasion, and played frequently for Prince *Lichnowsky, one of Beethoven's most faithful patrons.

Although much admired as a public performer, he retired from the platform (probably for health reasons, as he was of fairly weak constitution) and spent the rest of his life quietly in Vienna. Beethoven entrusted the musical education of his nephew, Carl, to Czerny. He became close friends with many of the leading musical figures of the day – including Beethoven's circle – *Hummel, *W.A. Mozart *fils*, *Streicher, *Clementi and *Chopin, and, being in great demand as a teacher, taught many of the following generation. Subject to illness in his last years, he died in 1857 and left everything to the *Gesellschaft der Musikfreunde*, which houses his manuscripts and library.

Czerny was celebrated for his interpretations of Beethoven and his writings are important and first-hand observations on the master's methods in performance, teaching and, to an extent, composition. He also produced editions of the keyboard works of Bach and *D. Scarlatti, and many arrangements. His influence as a teacher was enormous and his pupils included *Döhler, *Kullak, *Thalberg, *Heller, Leopoldine Blahetka and *Liszt.

Works
11 sonatas, 28 sonatinas and many sets of variations and potpourris for piano as well as works for piano duet. His chamber music includes sonatas and sonatinas for violin, eight piano trios, seven piano quartets and five string quartets. He also wrote six symphonies, six piano concertos and two piano concertinos, various vocal pieces and a huge quantity of didactic music for learners of all ages at all stages of pianism. His pedagogical works include the *School of Extemporaneous Performance* (2 vols, opp. 200 (1829) and 300 (1833)), *Complete Theoretical and Practical Pianoforte School*, op. 500 (1839; Eng. tr., 1939), the *School of Practical Composition* op. 600 (?1849–50), *Letters to a Young lady on the Art of Playing the Pianoforte*, and *Letters on Thorough-Bass* op. 815 (1842, pub. 1851).

Further reading
C. Czerny, *Erinnerungen aus meinem Leben* (1842, trans., *MQ*, xlii (1956)). D.W. MacArdle, 'Beethoven and the Czernys', *MMR*, lxxxviii (1958). P. Badura-Skoda, ed., *Carl Czerny: über den richtigen Vortrag der sämtlichen Beethoven'schen Klavierwerke* (Vienna, 1963). J. Mahr, 'Carl Czerny: das Genie des Fleisses', *Neue Zeitschrift für Musik*, 130 (1969). U. Mählert, 'Die Vortragslehre von Carl Czerny', *Musica*, 44 (1990). Newman/SCE and /SSB.

D

Dalberg, Johann Friedrich Hugo, Freiherr von

German author, amateur composer, pianist and aesthetician (b. 17 May 1760, Mainz; d. 26 Jul 1812, Aschaffenburg).

Of a noble family, studied theology at Göttingen and entered the Church, becoming a canon at Triers, Worms and Speyer, although most of his time was spent in study and music. His physical deformity did not deter him from becoming a virtuoso pianist and he travelled a great deal, in Italy and England in particular.

Dalberg studied composition with Holzbauer and his works were well regarded, as were his writings on Indian and ancient Greek music. His evocative novels are similar in style to the writings of *E.T.A. Hoffmann and he is seen as one of the first musicians of *Romanticism.

Works

Various sonatas and smaller pieces for harpsichord and/or piano; sonatas for violin, piano trios, a piano and wind quartet; songs and *Lieder* and sacred choral works.

Further reading

A. Weinmann, 'Zwei unechte Mozart-Lieder', *Musikforschung*, xx (1967). G. Wagner, 'Friedrich Hugo von Dalberg als Liederkomponist', *Mitteilungen der Arbeitsgemeinschaft für mittelrhenische Musikgeschichte*, ix (1993). M. Embach and J. Godwin, *Johann Friedrich Hugo von Dalberg (1760–1812): Schriftsteller-Musiker-Domherr* (Mainz, 1998).

Damper, Damping (see *Pedal)

Dance, William

English violinist, pianist (b. 1755, London; d. 5 June 1840, London).

Coming from an artistic family – a well-known architect for a grandfather and several other relatives who were painters and literary figures – Dance was a violinist at Drury Lane and the Kings Theatres, leading the orchestra during the *Handel Festival of 1790 and also playing concertos on the piano. He was one of the three instigators (with *Corri and *J.B. Cramer) and a founder-member of the Philharmonic Society, whose treasurer he remained for the rest of his life. *Felix Mendelssohn was a close friend of the family.

Further reading

W.T. Parke, *Musical Memoirs* (London, 1830).

Dance-suite (see *Suite)

Day, John

British soldier, ?piano-maker (*fl.* 1816). Nothing is known of him except that he was described (or described himself) as 'Lieutenant on Half Pay, of His Majesty's Eleventh Regiment of Foot' (Harding/ PIANO-FORTE, p. 444) and that he added a frame of musical glasses (see *armonica) to a cabinet piano for domestic use, patented in 1816. The glasses, hit by the hammers, could be played with or without the piano.

Decoration

A process by which notes or passages are added to the given music as embellishments, the implication that these added notes are superfluous (though desirable), rather than structural. Decorations can be written out by the composer, editor or performer, or left to the performer's discretion, either worked out beforehand or *improvised. They can also be conveyed through a system of signs added above or below (more rarely before or after) the note(s) (such as the *trill (*tr* ∿), or mordent (∿)). The realization of these signs tends to change – more or less – according to the period in which the music was written, and any added material must be appropriate to the period style. When the decoration is a series, or a passage, of notes, these are usually printed or written in smaller case than the main note(s).

Del Mela, P. Domenico
Italian piano-maker of whom almost nothing is known. He was a pupil of *Cristofori and one instrument by him survives, an upright piano – possibly the first of its kind – dated 1739.

Deutscher (Teutscher) (Ger.; It. *tedesca*) 'German' or 'in the German style'. A term applied to dances and to a form of madrigal in the fifteenth and sixteenth centuries, interchangeable with '**allemande*' in the *Baroque period. The *Deutscher* or *deutscher Tanz* was one of a series of triple-time vernacular dances (such as the **ländler*) which gave rise to the *waltz. Many composers wrote sets of these for public and private use, among them *W.A. Mozart, *Beethoven, *Schubert and *Hummel.

Diabelli, Anton
Austrian publisher and composer (b. 5 Sep 1781, Mattsee (Salzburg); d. 7 Apr 1858, Vienna).

He studied in Michaelbueren and Salzburg and entered the monastery at Raitenhaslach in 1800 but, after three years, moved to Vienna, making his name as a teacher of piano and guitar, and as

an arranger and composer. Becoming interested in music publishing, he set up shop with art-publisher Pietro Cappi as Cappi & Diabelli in late 1818 and had great success in popular music and arrangements for piano and guitar. He also published his own compositions with some success. He became associated with *Schubert and published his first works, **Erlkönig* ('op. 1') and **Gretchen am Spinnrade* ('op. 2') both in April 1821. He also published smaller works and the reissue of the late sonatas by *Beethoven, together with the **Diabelli Variations* op. 120, for which he was directly responsible and for which he wrote the theme. The firm continued publishing after his death before being bought up.

Diabelli used his knowledge of the market in publishing lucrative popular pieces to finance weightier works; he also gave *Schubert his first publishing 'break'.

Works
Masses and some piano and chamber works.

Further reading
L. Kantner, 'Anton Diabelli: ein Salzburger Konponist der Biedermeierzeit', *Mitteilungen der Gesellschaft für Salzburger Landeskunde*, xcviii (1958). E. Anderson, ed. and tr., *The Letters of Beethoven* (London, 1961). A. Weinmann, *Verlagsverzeichnis Anton Diabelli & Co., 1824 bis 1840* (Vienna, 1985).

'Diabelli' Variations
(1) A set of variations (50 with a coda) on a theme which, in 1819, the Viennese composer and publisher Anton *Diabelli sent to every Austrian composer he knew and valued. The aim was to create a patriotic compendium of short pieces which would

be bound to sell well. Although not all of those he contacted took part, those who did included Voříšek, *Czerny, *Kalkbrenner, *J.P. Pixis, *Moscheles, *Gelinek, *Hummel, *Sechter – a suitably *contrapuntal offering – *Mozart's son (also called *Wolfgang Amadeus), *Schubert, the Archduke *Rudolph and the 11-year-old *Liszt.

(2) To most people, however, the name refers to *Beethoven's *33 Variations on Waltz by Diabelli* op. 120 in C major (1819; 1822–23, dedicated to Antonie Brentano). His first reaction to the proposal was to contemptuously discard Diabelli's waltz as a 'cobbler's patch', but it began to stimulate his imagination and the set is widely regarded as one of the greatest sets of variations.

Diatonic

Broadly, referring to the notes within a given scale as implied by the key-signature, excluding any chromatic accidentals.

Dichterliebe (Poet's Love)
Song-cycle of 16 numbers by Robert *Schumann (his op. 48, 1840) to poems from *Das Buch der Lieder* (The Book of Songs, pub. 1827) by Heinrich Heine. The songs are 1. 'Im wunderschönen Monat Mai' ('In Beautifullest Month of May'); 2. 'Aus meinen Thränen' ('My Tears All Turn'); 3. 'Die Rose, Die Lilie' ('The Rose and the Lily'); 4. 'Wenn ich in deine Augen seh' ('When into Thy Dear Eyes'); 5. 'Ich will meine Seele tauchen' ('I Will Dip My Soul'); 6. 'Im Rhein, im heiligen Strome' ('In Rhine'); 7. 'Ich grolle nicht' ('I'll Not Complain'); 8. 'Und wüssten's die Blumen' ('And O If the Flowers'); 9. 'Das ist ein Flöten' ('There's Flute and Fiddle'); 10. 'Hör ich das Liedchen' ('When I Hear Others'); 11. 'Ein Jüngling liebt' ('A Lover Loves a Maiden'); 12. 'Am leuchtenden Sommermorgen' ('A Sunshiny Summer Morning'); 13. 'Ich hab'im Traum geweinet' ('In Dream I Lay'); 14. 'Allnächtlich im Traume' ('Each Night-Time'); 15. 'Aus alten Märchen' ('From Realms of Ancient Story'); 16. 'Die alten, bösen Lieder' ('The Bad Old Songs').

'Didone Abbandonnata' [*'Dido abandoned'*]
The title given to his *characteristic piano sonata in G minor op. 50/3 by *Clementi. It is a musical depiction of the story of Dido, Queen of Carthage, and Æneas, to whom she had given refuge and with whom she had fallen in love. The pair neglect their political duties as a result of their passion. When, after two reminders, Æneas is commanded by the Gods to leave Carthage; he does so without telling her. As she sees the Trojans setting sail she kills herself by falling on her sword. The sonata is unified by being based on the opening motif.

Die wahre Art das Klavier zu spielen
(see *Versuch über die wahre Art das Klavier zu spielen*)

Diminution

A device by which the notes of a melody are proportionally shortened, such as being halved, a minim and a crotchet becoming a crotchet and a quaver, for example. The device is often used in *contrapuntal forms, such as *fugue or *canon.

Dittersdorf, Carl Ditters von [Ditters, Carl]

Austrian composer and violinist (b. 2 Nov 1739, Vienna; d. 24 Oct 1799,

Neuhof (now Novy Dvur) nr Sobeslav, Bohemia).

Ditters was the son of a well-to-do costumier in the court theatre in Vienna. He attended the Jesuit school and received private instruction in music, French and religion, and learnt the violin with local teachers. After lessons with J.P. Ziegler, he played in the court orchestra and studied composition with Giuseppe Bonno using Fux's *Gradus ad Parnassum*. A trip to Italy with *Gluck in 1763, allowed him to meet Padre Martini and the *castrato* Farinelli amongst others. He became *Kapellmeister* to the Prince-Bishop of Grosswardein – the post having been vacated by *Michael Haydn – in 1765 and on the disbanding of the *Kapelle* four years later, was offered a similar position by the Prince-Bishop of Breslau in 1770, becoming a Knight of the Golden Spur at the Prince's instigation. He married the following year and was ennobled by the Empress Maria Theresa as a consequence of his appointment of *Amtshauptmann* of Freiwaldau in 1773, gaining the additional surname 'von Dittersdorf'. He remained in the Prince-Bishop's service until the latter's death in 1795, upon which his small pension induced him to accept a nobleman's offer of lodgings for himself and his family, where remained until his death.

Dittersdorf left an important body of symphonies, similar to *J. Haydn in their wit and their use of *folk elements and several of them are programmatic (see below). His Italian operas were performed at Esteráza under Haydn and his *Singspiels* are of great importance in crystallizing the genre for later composers.

Works
Included the programmatic 12 symphonies on the *Metamorphoses* of Ovid (of which 7–12 survive only in his own piano duet arrangements); four oboe concertos, 18 violin concertos, five viola concertos, one each for cello and double bass and five harpsichord concertos; much chamber music and some keyboard works and a sizeable body of dramatic works including the *Singspiels Doctor und Apotheker*, *Betrug durch Aberglauben* (both perf. 1786) and *Die Liebe im Narrenhause* (perf. 1787).

Further reading
J. LaRue, 'Dittersdorf Negotiates a Price', *Hans Albrecht in memoriam* (Kassel, 1962). F.O. Souper, 'The Music of Dittersdorf', *ML*, xi (1930). T. Bauman, *North German Opera in the Age of Goethe* (Cambridge, 1985). J. Lane, *The Concertos of Carl Ditters von Dittersdorf* (diss., Yale U., 1997). H. Unverricht, ed., *Carl Ditters von Dittersdorf, Eichstätt 1989* (Tutzing, 1997).

Divertimento (It.: 'diversion', recreation'; Eng.; Ger.; Fr. *divertissement*)
A piece of music primarily for entertainment or as background; often associated with outdoor music as exemplified in the Serenade, Cassation, *Notturno*, *Nachtmusik*, *Partita* and *Tafelmusik*. It is mostly found in chamber or orchestral, rather than solo form, although some for solo keyboard survive (by *J. Haydn, for example).

Doctrine of the Affections
(*Affektenlehre*) [see Affections, Doctrine of the]

Döhler, Theodor (von)
Austrian pianist and composer (b. 20 Apr 1814, Naples; d. 21 Feb 1856, Florence).

An infant prodigy, he was taught the piano by *Benedict and around 1829 went to Vienna for further study with *Czerny (piano) and *Sechter (composition). He toured as a virtuoso in 1836, staying in St Petersburg 1843–45. He was ennobled through the offices of his patron the Duke of Lucca and married a Russian Princess in 1846, retiring from the concert platform and moving to Florence in 1848.

Works
Mostly for piano including a concerto, op. 7 and an opera *Tancreda*.

Further reading
B.M. Antolini, 'Pianisti italiani a metà ottocento', *Nuova Rivista Musicale Italiana*, xxv (1991).

Dorian mode (see *modes)

Double, doubled
(1) Verb. Used on its own without qualification, it means to play or sing in unison or at one or more octaves with another voice or instrument.

(2) Verb. It may be qualified by an interval, such as 'doubled at the third' in which a part is played or is sung in parallel with another or several, at the interval of a third or a compound third (i.e. a third removed by one or more octaves). The interval at which the part is doubled – most commonly a third or a sixth – alternates between major and minor as desired by the composer.

Double (Fr. 'double')
In French music, especially in keyboard suites of the eighteenth century, a name used to denote a variation on an existing movement, which *ornaments the given melody in smaller notes over the same harmonic basis. It is usually given as a separate movement following its 'parent'.

Double concerto
A *concerto for two instruments.

Double-escapement
A form of *escapement, invented by Pierre *Erard and patented in England in 1821, by which the hammer could be re-used to strike the strings before it had returned to its place of rest. This allowed for much greater rapidity in repeating a note or notes.

Double-exposition (see *Sonata Form)

Double harpsichord
A *harpsichord with two *manuals (or *keyboards) which have independent sets of strings or can be *coupled together.

Double trill
A trill on two notes simultaneously.

Down-striking
Referring to a piano mechanism in which the hammers fall to strike the strings from above, as opposed to the more common up-striking action.

Dragonetti, Domenico (Carlo Maria) ['Il Drago']
Italian composer and virtuoso double bass player (b. 7 Apr 1763, Venice; d. 16 Apr 1846, London).
  According to some sources his father played double bass and guitar, which the boy practised secretly, also gaining knowledge of the violin from a local amateur, which he applied to the bass; he possibly studied also with a theatre-orchestra bass player, M. Berini. After making his name as a street-player,

he was appointed principal bass at the Opera Buffa in Venice at 13 and the same position at the Grand Opera Seria a year later. He moved to London in late 1794 and became *continuo player at the King's Theatre, Haymarket, although he soon began to acquire a reputation as a soloist in the London area. He visited *J. Haydn in Vienna in 1798 and when he returned ten years later, met *Beethoven and *Sechter. His performance of Beethoven's cello sonata op. 5/2 on the bass caused the composer to embrace both player and instrument. He was now building up a European reputation as a virtuoso, and his fees for performances were notoriously high. Dragonetti was a collector of musical instruments and antiques and a connoisseur of art, acquainted with many of the leading musicians of the day (*Liszt, *Rossini, *Hummel, *Paganini and *Spohr) and was a close friend of Vincent Novello.

Using a three-stringed instrument, Dragonetti focused attention on the double bass as a solo instrument and raised its status as a orchestral instrument.

Works
(Mostly unpublished, in manuscript in the British Library) for solo and accompanied – by piano or orchestra – double bass as well as eight or more concertos, over 30 string quintets with double bass, and other works.

Further reading
R. Slatford, 'Domenico Dragonetti', *PRMA*, xcvii (1970–71). A. Planyavsky, *Geschichte des Kontrabasses* (Tutzing, 2/1984). A.W. Thayer (ed. E Forbes), *Life of Beethoven* (Princeton, NJ, 1964, 2/1967). F.M. Palmer, 'Domenico Dragonetti and the Double Bass in London at the Turn of the Eighteenth Century', in M. Burden and I. Cholij (eds), *A Handbook for Studies in English Eighteenth Century Music*, iv (Edinburgh, 1993); *Domenico Dragonetti in England (1794–1846): the Career of a Double Bass Virtuoso* (Oxford, 1997).

Drechsler, Joseph
Bohemian composer, organist, conductor (b. 26 May 1782, Vlachovo Brě zí, nr Strakovice; d. 27 Feb 1852, Vienna).

Son of a *Kantor* and schoolmaster who first taught him music, he was a chorister in Passau and the Benedictine monastery at Florenbach, and in Prague. On his move to Vienna in 1807 he taught, composed and studied. He was appointed *répétiteur* at the Court Opera in 1810 and assistant *Kapellmeister* in 1812 or 1814. In 1815 he became organist at the Servitenkirche and opened a music school, and after spells as choirmaster in St Anna's and the Pfarrkirche am Hof, he was appointed *Kapellmeister* of St Stephen's Cathedral. *Beethoven recommended him to his pupil and patron the *Archduke Rudolph and his theoretical works were influential during his lifetime.

Works
Singspiels (*Die Feldmühle*, perf. 1812) and incidental music (e.g. to Raimund's *Der Diamant des Geisterkönigs* (1824) and *Das Mädchen aus der Feenwelt* (1826)); 16 masses, a Requiem, cantatas, *lieder*, piano sonatas and string quartets.

Further reading
C. Preiss, *Joseph Drechsler* (Graz, 1910). A. Orel, ed., *F. Raimund: Sämtliche Werke*, vi (Vienna, 1924). E. Kitzler, *Joseph Drechsler und seine Kirchenmusik* (diss., U. of Vienna, 1983).

Dreher (see *Waltz)

Dulce melos
(1) Latin for *Dulcimer.

(2) (Fr. *doucemelle*) A stringed keyboard instrument depicted in a treatise (*c.*1440) by Arnaut de Zwolle (*c.*1436–54). Basically a dulcimer with keys, its action appears similar to that of early pianos.

Dulcimer (Ger. *Hackbrett*)
The name given to multi-stringed zither-like instruments without keyboard. Many types have trapezoid shape and are unfretted. If it is finger-plucked, the instrument is called a *psaltery and if played with hammers, a dulcimer. It is widespread in usage, crossing cultures (Asia, the Orient), times (from the middle ages) and types of music (art, *folk). Pantaleon *Hebenstreit, a virtuoso, played a large dulcimer for Louis XIV, who decreed that it be called '*pantaleon' (or 'pantalon') in his honour. As an instrument with struck strings, its popularity may well have focused the attention of keyboard-makers onto the piano, then in its infancy.

Dulcken, (Marie) Louise [Louisa, Luise] (née **David**)
German pianist (b. 20 Mar 1811, Hamburg; d. 12 Apr 1850, London).
    Little is known of her life except that she was the younger sister of the German violinist Ferdinand David and made her public debut at the age of ten and played *Hummel's A minor Concerto at the age of twelve. After concert-tours with her brother, she settled in London after her marriage in 1828, becoming a very successful performer and teacher and keeping a popular *salon* which attracted a wide variety from the London intelligentsia. She taught Queen Victoria, was a close friend of *Moscheles and

played duets with Hummel during his visit in 1830.

Further reading
W. Kuhe, *My Musical Recollections* (London, 1896).

Dumont, (Jeanne-) Louise (see *Farrenc, Louise)

Duoclave
A type of *piano designed for duets with two *keyboards, or with provision for later addition of a second keyboard.

Duport, Jean-Pierre [*l'aîné*]
French cellist and composer (b. 27 Nov 1741, Paris; d. 31 Dec 1818, Berlin).
    Duport made his début at the *Concerts Spirituels in 1761 and was a frequent performer at later Concerts. He stayed in England and Spain and, in 1773, was appointed by *Frederick the Great as first cellist in the royal chapel, where he supervised concerts and taught Prince Friedrich Wilhelm II, 1787–1806. He was part of the court after the chapel was dissolved and received a pension. While on a visit to Potsdam in 1789, *W.A. Mozart wrote the set of 9 Variations in D K573 on a Minuet (from the cello sonata op. 4/6) by Duport. Later, *Beethoven and Duport performed at court and it is likely that the former's cello sonatas op. 5 (1796) dedicated to Friedrich Wilhelm II, were written for Duport.

Works
Three violin concertos (1792), a cello concerto and about 30 sonatas for cello and bass.

Further reading
S. Milliot, *Le violoncelle en France au XVIIIe siècle* (Paris, 1985). V. Walden,

One Hundred Years of Violoncello: a History of Technique and Performance Practice 1740–1840 (Cambridge, 1998). Fétis/*BIOGRAPHIE. MGG.*

Durchkomponirt (Ger.:
'through-composed)
A method of song-composition by which the music is independent of the poem's linear structure or verse form. Thus, instead of, for example, repeating the music more-or-less exactly for each stanza, as in a *strophic setting, it follows its own path, so that it can perhaps more faithfully reflect the nuances (on several levels) of the text. It is particularly well-suited to narrative and dramatic poetry and was generally preferred to strophic setting from the early nineteenth century onwards.

Dussek [Dusík, Dussik], **Jan Ladislaw** [Johann Ladislaus (Ludwig)]
Bohemian composer, pianist (b. 12 Feb 1760, Čáslav; d. 20 Mar 1812, St Germain-en-Laie or Paris).
Son of an organist and well-known composer, Dussek spent his early years in Iglau (now Jihlava) where he learnt piano and organ and trained as a chorister in the Minorite church, also attending the Jesuit Gymnasium there and then at Kutná Hora. He also attended school in Prague and spent a term at the University. After going to Malines (now Mechelen) to teach piano, he visited Holland and spent a year in The Hague, teaching the stadtholder's (William V) children. Dussek played in Hamburg and met *C.P.E. Bach – from whom he may have received lessons as well as advice – and performed at the court of Catherine II in St Petersburg in 1783. He became *Kapellmeister* to Prince Radziwill *c.*1782–84 and then embarked on a tour of Germany – including Berlin,

Dresden, Frankfurt am Main, Kassel – playing the glass harmonica (see *armonica) as well as piano. In 1786 he went to Paris attached to a diplomatic company and his performances during his three-year stay attracted the attention of Marie Antionette; he also met Napoleon. Dussek's aristocratic connections made his position in Paris difficult during the Revolution and he fled to England, spending the next 11 years there teaching and performing; he was particularly commended by *Haydn and married Sophia Corri, a talented singer, harpist and pianist. Dussek formed a partnership with her father and the publishing house of *Corri, Dussek & Co. was founded, publishing many of his works. He encouraged *Broadwood to extend the range of his pianos (from five to six octaves between 1791 and 1794) and himself wrote for this 'piano with *additional keys'. The business became debt-ridden and Dussek fled to Hamburg in late 1799, after which his father-in-law was jailed for bankruptcy; it is unlikely that he saw his wife or daughter ever again. He met *Spohr and played with the horn-player Giovanni Punto and gave three very successful concerts in Prague in which, according to *Tomášek, he was the first to place the piano sideways relative to the audience so that they could see his profile. (He was often referred to as 'le beau Dussek' on account of his good looks.) From 1804 to 1806 Dussek was *Kapellmeister* to Prince *Louis Ferdinand of Prussia – a good composer – and the pair were notorious in their wildness on their trips between various battlefields. The Prince was killed at the battle of Saalfeld (10 Sep 1806) and Dussek wrote his famous *Elégie harmonique* op. 61 (C211). In September Dussek was back in Paris in the service of Talleyrand, as well as teaching and giving many concerts. He died of gout (due to a drink problem) and his grave is unknown.

An unjustly neglected composer, Dussek exhibited many *Romantic traits in his music, especially in harmony and dynamics, and an unusual degree of chromaticism for his period. He also anticipated the piano style of the nineteenth-century virtuosos – indeed his music shows remarkable pre-echoes of specific composers such as *Beethoven, *Schubert, *R. Schumann, *Chopin, *Felix Mendelssohn, *C.M. von Weber, *Rossini, *Liszt and *Brahms.

Works
About 14 piano concertos (some harpsichord/piano) including the 'Military' op. 40 (C153) in Bb major (1798), and a few for harp as well as a double piano concerto. Many chamber works, violin sonatas, piano trios – with a number arranged as piano sonatas – and many including harp; numerous piano sonatas including the 'Farewell' in Eb major op. 44 (C178) (1800), the *Elégie harmonique* in F♯ minor op. 61 (C211) (1806–1807) and the Ab major op. 64 (also found as opp. 70, 71 and 77) (C221) called 'Le retour à Paris' and 'Plus ultra' (1807). He also wrote *Instructions on the Art of Playing the Piano Forte or Harpsichord* (London, 1796) published in French, in German and in many later editions.

Further reading
H. Truscott, 'Dussek and the Concerto', *MR*, xvi (1955). E. Blom, 'The Prophecies of Dussek', *Classics Major and Minor* (London, 1958). S.V. Klíma, 'Dussek in England', *ML*, xli (1960); 'Dussek in London', *MMR*, xc (1960). H.A. Craw, *A Biography and Thematic Catalog of the Works of J.L. Dussek* (1760–1812). A.L. Ringer, 'Beethoven and the London Pianoforte School', *MQ*, lvi (1970). O.L. Grossman, *The Solo Piano Sonatas of Jan Ladislav Dussek* (diss., Yale U., 1975). Newman/SSB.

E

Ecossaise (Fr.: 'Scottish'; Eng. ecossaise)

One of the *contredanses* of the eighteenth and early nineteenth centuries. The eighteenth-century moderately-paced version prevalent among the French aristocracy was replaced by the fast lively ninetteenth-century couple-dance, usually in 2/4. It was particularly popular in Vienna and *Beethoven, *Schubert, *C.M. von Weber and *Chopin wrote *écossaises*.

Éibhlín a Rúin (Ir.; Eng. 'Eileen Aroon' tr. 'Eileen, my secret', 'secret' being a term of endearment in Gaelic)

Irish *folk-song popular throughout Europe and America which appears in Moore's *Irish Melodies* as 'Erin! the tear and the smile in thine eyes'; it is also known as 'Robin Adair'.

Eine kleine Gigue

A *gigue* by *W.A. Mozart, in G major, K574. He improvised it in the notebook of the Leipzig court organist on 16 May 1789, which has survived. It was modelled on the *gigue* from *Handel's 8th Keyboard Suite in F minor, Mozart being particularly taken up with the older composer's music at the time.

Elégie harmonique *sur la mort du Prince Louis Ferdinand de Prusse* (*Harmonic Elegy on the Death of Prince Louis Ferdinand of Prussia*)

A piano sonata in F♯ minor op. 61 (C211) by J.L. *Dussek. It was written to commemorate the killing of his patron and friend Prince *Louis Ferdinand of Prussia at the battle of Saalfeld, 10 Nov 1806. There is an edition in *Musica*

Antiqua Bohemica, xx (1954), lxiii (1963) and an autograph of the first movement is in the Thüringische Landesbibliothek in Weimar.

Eliason, Edward

?British composer active in London in the early nineteenth century, who evidently knew *Paganini as his *6 Characteristic Caprices* are dedicated to 'mon ami Paganini' and have appended to them a *'Farewell caprice ded to Eliason by Paganini'*.

Elsner, Józef Antoni Franciszek
[Joseph Anton Franciskus; Józef Ksawery; Joseph Xaver]

German (naturalized Polish) composer, teacher (b. 1 Jun 1769, Grodków, Silesia; d. 18 Apr 1854, Warsaw).

Elsner sang in the church choir as a child and was a pupil at the Dominican school and the Jesuit *Gymnasium* at Breslau (now Wrocław); he also played the violin. He read theology and medicine at the University of Breslau and medicine in Vienna, but gave this up in favour of a career in music. Appointed to conduct the opera orchestra in Brno (1791–92) – which he did from the first-violin stand – he then went to Lemberg (now L'vov) 1792–99 concentrating on composition, before settling in Warsaw in 1799, where he spent a quarter of a century in charge of the Opera and teaching. In 1818 he became rector of the School of Elementary Music and Art, in 1821 rector of the Conservatory – where his distinguished pupils included *Chopin – and in 1826 of the Main School of Music. He also had a music engraving shop from 1802, and was elected to the Warsaw Society of Friends of Science in 1805, the year in which he organized a music club with *E.T.A. Hoffmann. Elsner founded the Society for Religious and National Music in 1814 and was a member of many Polish music societies and contributed many critical press articles and reviews. He was the correspondent of the *Allgemeine musik Zeitung* 1802–25 and gained various honours in his homeland.

Works
Many stage works, masses, eight symphonies, chamber music and music for piano.

Further reading
A. Nowak-Romanowicz, *Józef Elsner* (Kraków, 1957). M. Zduniak, 'W sprawie utworów Józefa Elsnera' [The Music of Jósef Elsner], *Muzyka*, xxii/2 (1977). A Swartz, 'Elsner, Chopin, and Musical Narrative as Symbols of Nation', *Polish Review*, xxxix (1994).

'Emperor'
(1) 'Emperor' Quartet (*Kaiserquartett*): nickname of *J. Haydn's string quartet op. 76 no. 3 in C major (1797) because of his use of his own *Emperor's Hymn* (**Gott erhalte Franz den Kaiser*, which was made the Austrian National Anthem) as the theme of the set of variations which comprises the slow movement.

(2) 'Emperor' Concerto: English name given (by whom is not known) to *Beethoven's Piano Concerto no. 5 op. 73 in E♭ major (1809; ?1811, dedicated to the Archduke *Rudolph). There is no record of any imperial connection in the composition or contemporary performances of the work, and the title may be a reference to the rather majestic opening and thematic material.

Empfindsamer Stil [see *Empfindsamkeit*]

Empfindsamkeit (Ger.: 'sensibility', 'sentimentality')
Also called ***Empfindsamer Stil***. It was a north German mid-eighteenth-century aesthetic movement associated with subjectivity, intimacy and sensitivity, and, in music, with simplicity, lack of obtrusive *decoration and including instrumental recitative. The movement was championed by *C.P.E. Bach, who included more-or-less rapid movement through various *affects, and ideally found in his *clavichord music.

Encyclopédie, L' (Fr.: The Encyclopedia)
A dictionary of universal knowledge published in 35 volumes between 1751 and 1776 edited by Diderot and D'Alembert. The articles were written by leading French intellectuals and *philosophes*, such as Voltaire, Montesquieu, Buffon and Turgot, with many of the music articles by *Rousseau. It remains a monument to the rationalism of the *Enlightenment and attracted the hostility of both church and state in its attacks on credulity and superstition. Its full title was *Encyclopédie, ou Dictionnaire raisonné des sciences, des arts et des métiers, par une société de gens de lettres* (Encyclopaedia, or analytical dictionary of the sciences, the arts and the professions, by a society of writers).

'English Piano' (see *British Piano)

'English Piano School' (see *London Piano School)

Enlightenment (Ger. *Aufklärung*, of which it is translation)
A movement of the eighteenth century characterized by the desire to combat prejudice and superstition in thought and politics, to replace dogma with

rationalism, and received wisdom with experimentation. This was to be done through dissemination of knowledge and a general rise in educational and literacy levels, and open debate. Originating in English empiricism (Locke and Newton), French rationalism (Descartes) and scepticism (Bayle). Its promulgators were the *philosophes*, Montesquieu (*L'esprit des lois* (*The Spirit of the Laws*, 1748)), Voltaire (*Lettres philosophiques* (*Philosophical Letters*, 1734)), Lessing, in his moralizing bourgeois dramas, Kant (Kritik der reinen Vernunft (Critique of Pure Reason, 1781)) and Diderot and d'Alembert's *Encyclopédie*.

Erard

French firm of piano- and harp-makers and music publishers. Its founder was **Sébastien Erard** (b. 5 Apr 1752, Strasbourg; d. 5 Aug 1831, Passy).

He was apprenticed to several Parisian harpsichord-makers, gaining aristocratic patronage. Taking *Zumpe as his model, he produced his first piano in 1777 and three years later went into partnership with his brother (J.-B. Erard), seeking and gaining the protection of Louis XVI in the case of obstruction by the hostile guild of luthiers; the firm subsequently grew and a workshop was established in London after the beginning of the Revolution, their first English grand being built in the middle of the 1790s. The firm went from strength to strength, enjoying French and English royal and aristocratic patronage and greatly improving the piano, culminating in the invention of the *double-escapement action by Sébastien's nephew, **Pierre Erard** (1796–1855) who had taken over the running of the firm, which was awarded a gold medal at the Paris exhibition of 1855. Ensuing conservatism allowed the

technological lead to pass out of the Erard firm and the London factory was closed in 1890 (although harps continued to be made at another site). The firm finally amalgamated with another in 1960.

Erard pianos were admired by many composers, particularly those settled in Paris, especially *Chopin and, in the twentieth century, Paderewski.

Further reading
A.J. Hipkins, *A Description and History of the Pianoforte* (London, 1989, rev. 1929, 1975). A. Dolge, *Pianos and their Makers* (California, 1911, rev. 1972). C. Hopkinson, *A Dictionary of Parisian Music Publishers* (Edinburgh, 1954). D. Wainwright, *The Piano Makers* (London, 1975). Ehrlich/PIANO. Cole/PIANOFORTE. Harding/PIANO-FORTE. Loesser/MEN. Fétis/*BIOGRAPHIE*.

Erlkönig (The Erl-King)
Song by Franz *Schubert (in G minor, D.328) to words by Goethe composed in several versions in 1815 and published as 'op. 1' in 1821. The poem is based on a ghost-story from Bürger's collection *Leonore* (1773) in which Death (personified as the 'Erl-King') chases a child and his father fleeing on horseback. The song is presented as a dialogue between the two, accompanied by fierce impassioned *tremolando* chords on the piano. Death, whom the father cannot see, but the child can, claims the latter at the end of the song.

Escapement [mechanism] (Fr. *échappement*; Ger. *Auslösung*; It. *scappamento*)
A component in the *action of a piano which allows the hammer to 'escape', or dislodge itself, from the mechanism

which propels it towards the strings just before it hits the latter. (See also *double-escapement.)

Esterháza (see *Eszterháza)

Esterházy
Hungarian noble family famous for their patronage of the arts, especially music. *J. Haydn served under four members of the family, the princes Paul Anton (22 Apr 1711 – 18 Mar 1762, reigning from 1734), his brother Nikolaus (Joseph) the 'Magnificent' (18 Dec 1714 – 28 Sep 1790), the latter's son (Paul) Anton (11 Apr 1738 – 22 Jan 1794) and his son Nikolaus (12 Dec 1765 – 25 Nov 1833). The ancestral castle was in Eisenstadt (Kismarton in Hungarian) and their summer residence was at *Eszterháza.

Eszterháza [Esterháza]
Summer residence of *J. Haydn's patrons, the Esterházy family, from 1766 until 1790. Intended to rival the palaces of Schönbrunn and Versailles, it enjoyed a rich cultural life with performances by famous troupes such as those of Carl Wahr (specializing in Shakespeare and Schiller) and the marionette group of Pauerbach, not to mention the other operatic casts for whom Haydn wrote.

Etude (see *Study)

Ewer
A British firm of music-sellers, publishers and importers based in London. Founded by John Jeremiah Ewer in 1823, it became Ewer and Johanning shortly after. Johanning left the firm around 1830 and it continued as J.J. Ewer & Co. until 1867, when it joined with Novello & Co., becoming Novello, Ewer & Co. In 1898 the name of Ewer was dropped. Ewer &

Co. were the main publishers of *Felix Mendelssohn's music in Britain and also had a large circulating library.

Exercise (Fr. *Exercice*; Ger. *Übung*; It. *essercizio*)
A practice-piece for voice or instrument, usually fairly short and concerned with one aspect of technique. The emphasis is very much more on the technical than the musical and such pieces are usually repetitive. The type became very popular in the early nineteenth century, especially applied to the piano and its widespread popularity as a domestic and amateur instrument.

Before the nineteenth century, the term (in various languages) was not used in anything more than a very general didactic sense and not specifically to do with technical matters of performance, such as *D. Scarlatti's '*essercizi*' (harpsichord sonatas) and *J.S. Bach's *Clavier-Übung*. Compare *study.

Expression marks
Words and signs within a musical score to aid expression; they may refer to particular notes or passages and are treated under this heading as distinct from *tempo markings. They are traditionally in Italian. The following is not intended to be exhaustive.

(1) *Words*
(a) *Fixed dynamics* these give information as to the volume of the note or [passage in question and range from *ppp* ['triple *piano*'] through *pp* (*pianissimo* [very soft]), *p* (*piano* [soft]), *mp* (*mezzo piano* [medium soft]), *mf* (*mezzo forte* [medium loud]), *f* (*forte* [loud]), *ff* (*fortissimo* [very loud]), *fff* ['triple *forte*']; occasionally *pppp* and *ffff* are found.

(b) *Graded dynamics* these include *crescendo* (abbr. *cresc.* [getting gradually louder], *diminuendo* (*dim., dimin.*) or *decrescendo* (*decresc.* [getting gradually softer]) often qualified by *più* [more], *meno* [less], *poco a poco* [little by little], *molto* [very (much)] etc.

(c) *Manner of performance (tempo)* (Some of these may be included in the *tempo direction over the beginning of the piece or section). There are many kinds, including *espressivo* [expressively] *accelerando* [getting gradually faster], *rallentando* (abbr. *rall.*) or *ritenuto* (abbr., *rit., riten.* [getting gradually slower, or held back]).

(d) *Manner of performance (other)* These include *legato* [joined together, i.e. smoothly], *staccato* [detached] etc. and the ending -*o* can be altered to -*issimo* [very]. Occasionally individual notes are marked with such indications as *fz* (*forzand, forzato*) or sf or sfz (*sforzando, sforzato* [forced, i.e. forcefully]).

(2) Signs
These range from the 'hairpins' ⊏ and ⊐ for *crescendo* and *diminuendo* or *decrescendo* respectively) and dots over or below the notes for staccato as well as a sideways 'v' (<, occasionally >) over or under a note for *forzato* etc.

Extempore, Ex tempore [performance]
(see *Improvisation)

F

F or Fa mode
Alternative names for the *Lydian mode.

Falsetto (It.; Fr. *Fausset*; Ger. *Falsett*,
Fistelstimme)
A treble range or *register – occasionally
thought of as 'unnatural' in the sense of
'artificial' – in the adult male voice. It is
a vocal *harmonic, where the vocal cords
vibrate at a shorter length than is normal. It
is used in *yodelling and in some Country
and Western music as well as being a
legitimate technique in certain twentieth
and twenty-first-century vocal techniques
(such as in Schoenberg's *Pierrot lunaire*
op. 21 (1912)). It is also common in
music of non-Western cultures, such as
that of the pygmies of Africa.

Fandango
A Spanish courtship dance from
Andalusia and Catalonia, in triple time
of medium pace, accompanied by guitar
and castanets (occasionally additional
instruments) or clapping; its typical
rhythm suggests syncopation. Its origins
are unclear, some scholars suggesting
Moorish, West Indian or Latin American
provenance. It is certainly derived from
popular dance and is first mentioned in
literature in the early eighteenth century.
By the end of that century it had become
a favourite in Britain, especially among
the aristocracy, and opened the way for
the introduction of the guitar into polite
drawing-rooms. Local Spanish variants
include the *malagueña*, *granadina*,
rondeña and *murciana*, and there is also a
slower, sadder sung version. *Fandangos*,
stylized or not, were written by Rameau,
*D. Scarlatti, possibly Soler, *Boccherini,
*W.A. Mozart (finale to the third act

of *Figaro*), *Gottschalk and Rimsky-
Korsakov, as well as the later Spanish
nationalists. There is a *fandango* in one of
*Beethoven's sketchbooks (1810) and it
was Ravel's original name for his famous
Bolero (1928).

Fantaisie (see *Fantasia*)

Fantasia (It., Sp., Ger., Eng.; Eng., Fr.,
Ger. *Fantasie*; Fr., Ger. *Phantasie*; Fr.
Fantaisie)
An instrumental piece (usually solo and
often for the keyboard) which is either
improvised, or the written result of an
*improvisation. During the *Romantic
period, it was also used to describe a large
multi-movement or multi-section work
analogous to the *sonata but freer, such
as *Schubert's *'Wanderer' Fantasy. The
same period also saw the proliferation of
the operatic fantasia, a fantasy based on
an air or, more usually, a sequence of airs,
from an opera in vogue or a perennial
favourite, such as those of *Thalberg and
*Liszt.

Fantasie (see *Fantasia*)

Fantasy (see *Fantasia*)

Farrenc, (Jacques Hippolyte) Aristide
French music publisher, flautist, scholar
(b. 9 Apr 1794, Marseilles; d. 31 Jan
1865, Paris).
    Farrenc departed from the family
tradition of business to pursue a musical
career, arriving in Paris in 1815 and
being appointed second flautist in the
orchestra of the Théâtre Italien. He
attended the reopened Conservatoire in
1816, also learning the oboe and was set
up as a teacher, composer and publisher
– principally the works of German
composers, especially *Beethoven and

*Hummel – by the early 1820s. He was very much involved in the second edition of *Fétis' *Biographie universelle*, using the results of his own research. His great interest in early music caused him to cease trading and devote the remainder of his life to research and he produced some original compositions also. With the assistance of his wife, *Louise Farrenc, he issued, a 23-volume collection of keyboard music, *Le trésor des pianistes*, covering 300 years of music, including contemporary composers. Louise completed the programme after his death.

Further reading
H. Barré, 'Farrenc (Jacques-Hippolyte-Aristide …)', *Les Bouches-du-Rhône: encyclopédie départmentale*, ed. P. Masson, II/xi (Marseilles, 1913). Fétis/ *BIOGRAPHIE*. Marmontel/*PIANISTES*. *MGG*.

Farrenc, (Jeanne-) Louise (*née* Dumont) French composer, pianist, teacher, scholar; wife of Aristide *Farrenc (b. 31 May 1804, Paris; d. 15 Sep 1875, Paris).

Born into a family with a long history of artistic achievement – her brother, Auguste Dumont was royal sculptor – she showed remarkable artistic and musical talent, reaching professional standard as a pianist by her mid-teens. She studied composition, theory and orchestration under Anton *Reicha at the Paris Conservatoire and married *Aristide Farrenc at 17 (in 1821), who published several of her compositions. She was appointed professor of piano at the Conservatoire in 1842, and, sharing her husband's passion for early music, inaugurated and, together with her students, participated in a series of *séances historiques*, historical concerts featuring early keyboard music. These stimulated interest in what might now be called 'authentic' performance of early music involving keyboard instruments, and her publications underlined this. She taught many gifted pianists at the Conservatoire, including her own daughter, Victorine, and remained there until her retirement in early 1873. She was the only woman to hold a full chair at the institution during the nineteenth century and her *Etudes* op. 26 were adopted as set works for the piano-students. Louise assisted her husband in the publication of *Le trésor des pianistes*, which she completed after his death in 1865, issuing the remaining 15 of the 23-volume set.

Works
These include many salon pieces for piano, sets of variations and rondos on popular operatic airs, 30 *Etudes* op. 36 (*c.*1839), 12 *Etudes brillantes* op. 41 (1858). Much chamber music, among it two piano quintets (in A minor, op. 30 (1842) and E major op. 31 (?1844–51)), two piano trios (in E♭ major op. 33 and D minor op. 34 (both ?1850–55)) and various chamber sonatas. There are also unpublished orchestral works, overtures, three symphonies and a piano concerto.

Further reading
B. Friedland, 'Louise Farrenc (1804–75): Composer, Performer, Scholar', *MQ*, lx (1974); *Louise Farrenc, 1804–1875* (Ann Arbor, MI, 1980). Marmontel/ *PIANISTES*. Fétis/*BIOGRAPHIE*. *MGG*.

Fay, Amy [Amelia] (Muller) American pianist, writer on music (b. 21 May 1844, Bayou Goula, LA; d. 28 Feb 1928, Watertown, MA).

Following studies with Tausig and *Kullak, she was a pupil of *Liszt, in Weimar. Afterwards, she lived in Boston where she had a high profile as a concert pianist, gaining even more recognition on her residence in Chicago (1878) as a lecturer, teacher and critic. She was also prominent in musical life generally, especially in women's organizations and was president of the New York Women's Philharmonic Society, dedicated to highlighting the musical achievements of women. Among her friends were Paderewski, Longfellow and J. Knowles Paine. Her diary, dealing with her European studies, was published as *Music Study in Germany* (Chicago, IL, 1880, R/1969) and provides important insights on Liszt during the period of her study with him.

Further reading
M.W. McCarthy, 'Amy Fay: the American Years', *American Music*, iii/1 (1985); *Amy Fay: America's Notable Woman of Music* (Warren, MI, 1995).

Ferrini, Giovanni
Italian harpsichord-maker (b. ?1699; d. 1758, Florence).

Italian keyboard-maker, pupil and co-worker of *Cristofori. Two authentic instruments of his remain, a spinet (1731) (see *harpsichord) and a combination of piano and harpsichord of 1745, the last remaining instrument from the school of Florence.

Further reading
S. Pollens, 'Three Keyboard Instruments Signed by Cristofori's Assistant, Giovanni Ferrini', *The Galpin Society Journal*, xliv (1991).

Fétis, François-Joseph
Belgian musicologist, critic, composer, teacher (b. 25 Mar 1784, Mons, nr Liège; d. 26 Mar 1871, Brussels).

Born into a family of musicians and instrument-makers, his father played organ in the local church, violin in the theatre and conducted locally. The boy, taught (including piano, violin and organ) by his father, was well-versed in the music of *C.P.E. Bach, *J. Haydn and *W.A. Mozart and by the age of nine had had a violin concerto of his own performed at one of his father's concerts. He left for Paris in 1800 to enter the Conservatoire, where he studied with *Boieldieu and Pradher (piano) and harmony with J.-B. Rey, using Rameau as his guide. He was also influenced by Catel and *Cherubini and became interested in early music, particularly that of Palestrina, and in music history generally, a subject which was not featured in the Conservatoire curriculum.

Fétis won a composition prize and married the 14-year-old daughter of the wealthy editor of the *Mercure national* in 1806, but, on the loss of his wife's fortune in 1811, the couple left Paris and settled in Douai (1813), where he taught harmony and singing and played the organ. He returned to Paris five years later and embarked on his career as composer, teacher and critic, writing comic operas and popular piano pieces; was appointed to teach counterpoint and fugue at the Conservatoire and published his *Traité* on these subjects in 1824; he was also librarian at the institution, 1826–31. He wrote critical articles for various newspapers and founded the weekly *Revue musicale*, which he edited and contributed to for six years. Appointed first director of the Brussels Conservatory in 1833, and was the dominant figure in Belgian musical life, directing the royal concerts for Leopold I as his *maître de chapelle*, and keeping in correspondence with musicians all over Europe. His most important publications came shortly after and he contributed to the *Revue et gazette musicale*, newly formed (1835) by the amalgamation of his own *Revue* and the *Gazette musicale de Paris*. He was an avid collector of treatises, books and musical instruments with a consuming interest in the musical past which, in spite of his (deserved) reputation for being dry and academic, he was insistent on being perceived as part of the then present's musical heritage and shown in living performances, organizing series of *Concerts historiques* in Brussels and Paris.

Fétis saw musical history, in which he penetrated, both in width and depth, farther than any of his predecessors or contemporaries, as the evolution of musical language; this led, for himself and for many, to a kind of 'alternative' to contemporary music, of which he was mistrustful. He also viewed harmony and counterpoint in an evolutionary guise, not so much in that there was 'progression' in the Victorian sense of 'improvement' but in changing rules appropriate to their period. His personal library and instrument collection are an important part of Belgian national musical heritage and his influence on subsequent perception of musical history and theory was great.

Works
Numerous articles and theoretical publications, including *Traité du contrepoint et de la fugue* (*Treatise on Counterpoint and Fugue*, Paris, 1824, enlarged 2/1846), *Biographie universelle des musiciens* etc. (*Universal Biographical Dictionary of Musicians*, Brussels, 1835–44, 2/1860–65, 1963) containing a vast amount of information from earliest to then-present times, but marred by errors; *Esquisse de l'histoire*

de l'harmonie considérée comme art et comme science systematique (*A Sketch of the History of Harmony, considered as an Art and as a systematic Science*, Paris, 1840); with I. *Moscheles, *Méthode des méthodes de piano* ([*The*] *Method of Methods for Piano*, Paris, ?1840, Eng. tr., 1841), *Méthode des méthodes de chant* ([*The*] *Method of Methods for Singing*, Paris, 1869).

Further reading
R. Wangermée, 'Les premiers concerts historiques à Paris', *Mélanges Ernest Closson* (Brussels, 1948); *Françcois-Joseph Fétis, musicologue et compositeur* (Brussels, 1951). L. Ayesterán, 'Fétis, un precursor del criterio etnomusicológico en 1869', *1st Inter-American Conference on Ethnomusicology: Cartagena, Columbia 1963*. C. Dahlhaus, *Untersuchungen über die Entstehung der harmonischen Tonalität* (Kassel 1967). H. Huys et al., *François-Joseph Fétis et la vie musicale de son temps: 1784–1871* (Brussels, 1972). B. Simms, 'Choron, Fétis and the Theory of Tonality', *JMT*, xix (1975). K. Ellis, *Music Criticism in Nineteenth-Century France: 'La revue et gazette musicale de Paris', 1834–1880* (Cambridge, 1995).

Field, John
Irish (Russian nationalized) composer and pianist (b. ?26 Jul 1782, Dublin; d. 23 Jan 1837, Moscow).

Born into a family which had been musical for several generations, his father was a violinist in Dublin theatre orchestras and taught him the violin; he also received lessons from his grandfather, an organist, and from the Italian composer Tommaso Giordani, who had settled in the Irish capital. A child prodigy, John gave his first public performance at the age of nine (1792) and the family moved to London the following year. Field was apprenticed to Muzio *Clementi for eight years and his father joined the Haymarket Theatre orchestra; the boy had his London début in 1793, and played a *Dussek piano concerto a year later. He learnt the violin, possibly from J.P. *Salomon and is mentioned in *J. Haydn's notebook. Clementi used him to demonstrate his firm's pianos and published some of his pieces anonymously. His performance of his own First Piano Concerto in 1799 (at the King's Theatre) propelled him into the musical world and when his apprenticeship expired later that year he was much in demand as a performer; his op. 1, three piano sonatas dedicated to Clementi, were published in early 1801. Field accompanied Clementi on an eight-year tour of Europe beginning in 1802, with the intention of publicizing his firm's pianos and securing publishing rights from European composers, *Beethoven included. The young virtuoso had great success in Paris, playing, among other things, *J.S. Bach's preludes and fugues, and studied briefly with Albrechtsberger (*counterpoint) in Vienna before reaching St Petersburg later in 1802. Clementi's meanness and harsh treatment towards Field is documented and may have been the reason the latter chose to remain when the former moved on in 1893; he did, however, make sure that his erstwhile *protégé* was introduced to the 'right people'. Field took the city by storm in his début concert of 1804 and enjoyed a prosperous time teaching, performing and publishing his *nocturnes and *concertos, moving between Moscow and St Petersburg and marrying a French *pianiste*-pupil, Adelaide Percheron in 1810. He finally settled in Moscow in 1821, introducing his illegitimate son, Leon, to the public

as a child prodigy, meeting and playing with the visiting *Hummel (1822) and becoming a close friend of Pushkin. The decade of the twenties, however, produced little in the way of composition and his addiction to alcohol, which was responsible for his terminal cancer, began to grow alarmingly. Impending medical bills caused him to undertake a concert tour with Leon, reaching London in 1831 where he was operated upon, with some success, and was warmly received by the British public, meeting *Felix Mendelssohn, Sterndale *Bennett and *Moscheles and being a pallbearer at the funeral of Clementi. He played with great success in many European cities, but on reaching Naples, was too ill to continue. After months of confinement, he was brought back to Moscow by a Russian aristocrat, recovering a little on the way and giving three concerts in Vienna, where he stayed with *Czerny. He composed his last series of nocturnes not long before his death in early 1837.

Field, as well as being a recognized virtuoso, differed from many of that ilk in his expressive, *cantabile* playing; he was called, among many similar titles, 'the singer among pianists', and this was partly due to his having been raised on the *British Piano, with its great possibilities for legato-playing. He also invented the nocturne, which was the perfect, though not the only, vehicle for his pianism. Field's innate understanding of the possibilities of the piano's sustaining pedal at an early stage in its usage was pioneering and contributed greatly to the effect of his playing.

He influenced a whole school of players, including Mendelssohn, Friedrich Wieck – who taught his daughter, *Clara Schumann and possibly *Robert Schumann himself to an extent, on Fieldian principles – and *Chopin, who was further influenced by his nocturnes, using them as models for his own. His successors in Russia were greatly in his debt, especially the Nationalist school, who were by no means unaware of his treatment of *folk and folk-popular music.

Works
Seventeen *nocturnes, four piano sonatas, fantasies, waltzes, variations (including the set on the song *Kamarinskaya*) and rondos as well as works for piano duet and a small number of chamber pieces, all including piano. There are also seven piano concertos

Further reading
F. Liszt, *Über John Fields Nocturne* (Leipzig, 1859). A. Kaminskaya, *John Field's works as a Performer and Teacher and his Piano Compositions* (diss., U. of Moscow, 1951). A. Nikolayev, *Dzhon Fil'd* (Moscow, 1960; Eng. tr., 1973). C. Hopkinson, *A Biographical Thematic Catalogue of the Works of John Field* (London, 1961). D. Branson, *John Field and Chopin* (London, 1972). P. Piggott, *The Life and Music of John Field* (London, 1973). R. Langley, 'John Field and the Genesis of a Style', *MT*, cxxvii (1982).

Figuralvariationen (Ger.: 'Figural variations') (see *Variation)

Figured bass (see **Basso continuo*)

Fingering
(1) The use of the fingers on musical instruments.

(2) An indication of which fingers to use in certain cases. These indications usually involve figures (principally keyboard),

letters (e.g. guitar) or other symbols, usually as part of some kind of tablature.

Folk Music
Definition – even 'working definition' – of this term is at best fraught with difficulties and at worst – especially in the days of mass media, the blurring of musical boundaries once considered decisive (art, folk, popular, pop, jazz and so on) and ethnic migration – impossible. It is perhaps easiest to discern in past times. Among its characteristics are its production by more-or-less untutored musicians, its transmission being largely oral, its preoccupation with everyday matters, its spontaneity, its rooting in the working classes with (in earlier times) strong rural and peasant connections, its lack of obvious sophistication, its occasional use of archaic forms, verbalizations and musical methods (modes and so on) and the fact that it is not professional. Clearly, any of these traits can be challenged, if not dismissed, and it is debatable whether the term has any real meaning or usefulness, but some of us think we know what we mean.

Forelle, Die [The Trout]
Song by Franz *Schubert, D550, which exists in five versions (*c*.1817 – *c*.1820). It was used as the theme of the set of variations making up the fourth movement of the Piano Quintet in A D.667 (1819) nicknamed '*Die Forelle*' (**'Trout' Quintet).

Fortepiano
Name commonly applied to the earlier forms of the *piano[forte]. It is best applied to those of the *Viennese school.

'Forty-Eight' (see *Wohltemperirte Clavier)

Franklin, Benjamin
American printer, scientist, statesman and musician (b. 17 Jan 1706, Boston; d. 17 Apr 1790, Philadelphia).

Apprenticed to his printer half-brother in early teens, but soon travelled to New York and Philadelphia and spent two years as a printer in London after which he opened his own printing press in Philadelphia in 1730. He printed several hymn-books and an almanac, becoming prosperous and, through his occasional writings, well-known. He founded the American Philosophical Society and the body that would become the University of Pennsylvania; his experiments with lightning and electricity are part of science history. He became a diplomat and visited England in 1757 as agent to the colonies, becoming friendly with many members of British intellectual society and was ambassador to France, living there for ten years. Franklin played the guitar, harp and glass dulcimer and perfected the *armonica, a form of musical glasses. He helped to draft the American Declaration of Independence and was an active scientist and *philosophe*.

Further reading
V. Meyer, 'The Glass Harmonica, Originally Designed by Benjamin Franklin, Currently being Built by Gerhard Finkenbeiner', *Experimental Musical Instruments*, ii/4 (1986). E. Stander, 'Notes for the Musical Glasses', *Experimental Musical Instruments*, vi/2 (1990).

Frauenliebe und -leben [A Woman's Life and Love]
*Song-cycle by *Robert Schumann (1840), a setting of eight poems by Adalbert von Chamisso from a set of the same name. It charts the progress of a young woman's love from first sight

through marriage, motherhood and widowhood. The songs are: 1. 'Seitich ihn gesehen' ('Ever since I saw him'), 2. 'Er, der Herrlichste von allen' ('He, the noblest of all'), 3. 'Ich kann's nicht fassen, nicht glauben' ('I cannot believe it'), 4. 'Du Ring an meinem Finger' ('Oh Ring upon my finger'), 5. 'Helft mir, ihr Schwestern' ('Help me, sisters'), 6. 'Süsser Freund, du blickest' ('Sweet friend, you look'), 7. 'An meinem Herzen, an meiner Brust' ('At my heart, at my breast'), 8. 'Nun has du mir den ersten Schmertz getan' ('Now, have you first hurt me').

Frederick the Great (See Frederick II, King of Prussia)

Frederick II, King of Prussia
[Frederick the Great]
'Enlightened' German king, military commander, artistic and intellectual patron, flautist and composer (b. 24 Jan 1712, Berlin; d. 17 Aug 1786, Potsdam).

Because the opposition of his father, William I (known as 'the barracks king'), to any of Frederick's leanings other than those directly geared to statesmanship and the military life, the young boy's education in other matters, such as the arts and music, were carried out in secret. He was, however, allowed to study thoroughbass and rudimentary vocal composition at the age of seven with the cathedral organist at Berlin. J.J. *Quantz, whom he heard play in Dresden, occasionally visited and gave him flute lessons. His father, as a result, became less tolerant and finally prohibited all such 'amusements'. In 1730 Frederick, now eighteen, tried to escape to England, but was caught and one of his entourage beheaded in front of him. He henceforth immersed himself in the pursuits of his father, finally gaining his approval and reluctantly submitting to a politically-arranged marriage in 1733. He had an entourage of resident musicians, however, and when he finally acceded to the throne in 1740, he was responsible for a number of political reforms and the foundation of several cultural institutions, including the Berlin Opera. His musical court featured Graun as *Kapellmeister and principal opera composer, J.F. *Agricola as court composer, *Quantz (from whom he had composition lessons) as flautist and *C.P.E. Bach as court cembalist (keyboard accompanist) as well as 40 instrumentalists and eight principal singers – including three *castrati* – not to mention set-designers, dancers, *costumiers*, librettists and administrative personnel.

The Seven Years War (1756–63) took its toll on all things and Frederick began to harden into the mould of his father, so that music began to languish somewhat, prompting the resignation of Nichelmann and C.P.E. Bach and the position of *Kapellmeister* became frozen for some time.

Frederick was an enlightened political reformer and patron of the arts as well as being a gifted military commander. He corresponded at length with Voltaire, and others and maintained a large and distinguished musical court with frequent concerts and opera performances, although he failed to appreciate the genius of C.P.E. Bach, preferring the works of his lesser employees. He is credited with having composed the theme upon which *J.S. Bach improvised on his visit to Potsdam in 1747, which became the basis for the later *Musikalisches Opfer* ('*Musical Offering*'), dedicated to Frederick.

Works

Four concertos and 121 sonatas for flute, arias and cantatas and some orchestral works, mostly in autograph, although a few have had subsequent publication.

Further reading

G. Müller, *Friedrich der Grosse als Musikfreund und Musiker* (Leipzig, 1898). E.E. Helm, *Music at the Court of Frederick the Great* (Norman, OK, 1960). N. Mitford, *Frederick the Great* (New York, 1970). C. Hogwood, *Music at Court* (London, 1977). D. McCulloch, *Aristocratic Composers in the 18th Century* (diss., U. of Surrey, 1990). Burney/PRESENT.

Friderici [Friederici, Friedrichs], Christian Ernst

German keyboard-instrument-maker (b. 7 Mar 1709, Meerane; d. 4 May 1780, Gera).

A very inventive craftsman, little is known of his life; he possibly learnt harpsichord- and organ-making from Gottfried *Silbermann. He established a workshop in Gera in 1737 and invented the first *Pyramid piano (1745) and one of the first *square pianos (1758). Both *C.P.E. Bach and *W.A. Mozart owned instruments by Friderici and thought highly of them.

Further reading

Boalch/HARPSICHORD. U. Dähnert, *Der Orgel und Instrumentenbauer Zacharias Hildebrandt* (Leipzig, 1962). F. Friedrich, 'Die Orgel- und Instrumentbauer Friderici', *Ars Organi*, xliii (1995).

Fuchs, Aloys [Alois]

Austrian musicologist (b. 22 Jun 1799, Raase [now Rázová, Moravia]; d. 20 Mar 1853, Vienna).

He learnt organ and cello before studying philosophy and law at Vienna

University and held various administrative posts. A bass singer and member of the court choir, he began collecting, transcribing and copying musical books and manuscripts – a great number of them autographs, including those of *J.S. Bach, *Handel, *Gluck, *W.A. Mozart and *Beethoven – from 1820 and his collection formed the basis of those in the *Gesellschaft der Musikfreunde* in Vienna – to the board of which he was appointed in 1829 – and the Staatsbibliothek in Berlin, as well as others. His many catalogues of composers' works remain of great value.

Further reading
R. Schaal, *Quellen und Forschungen zur Wiener Musiksammlung Aloys Fuchs* (Graz, 1966).

Fugato (see *Fugue)

Fugue (Eng., Fr.; Ger. *Fuge*; It. *fuga*)
At its most general, this is a musical *contrapuntal composition in which a theme (or *subject) undergoes a number of more-or-less traditional manipulations. The most characteristic of these occurs in the first of its three sections, the exposition, where the subject appears in all of the vocal or instrumental 'voices' (or parts – usually three to five) in turn, the even-numbered entries ('answers') in the dominant and, under certain circumstances, slightly altered from the subject. The entries, after the first, are accompanied by one or more countersubjects, which may be 'regular' (in that they henceforth tend to appear whenever the subject does) or 'free' (i.e. non-recurrent). The middle section usually consists of further appearances ('entries') of the subject in different keys separated by 'episodes' (which are usually derived from material from the exposition) and the closing section almost always presents the subject in terms of some sort of apotheosis. This section often includes a *pedal-point and stretto, overlapping entries in the manner of a *canon, although neither of these devices is necessarily confined to the closing section. Other devices, such as *augmentation, *diminution and *inversion of the subject may also occur.

The idea of fugue as a musical form (as outlined above) is rejected by some commentators, who claim that it is a device, or a procedure, or texture and there is some justice in this, given the many exceptions, even – one might say especially – in the greatest fugue-composers.

The use of a fugue-like exposition in works other than fugues is called *fugato*.

Fux, Johann Joseph (see *Gradus ad Parnassum*)

G

Galant [style] (Fr.; Eng.; It. *galante*)
A term used to describe a style of music
between the *Baroque and *Classical
periods as a reaction to the strictness
and *contrapuntality of the church style.
It was characterized by simple, well-
balanced, regularly-phrased melodies,
with unobtrusive, mostly *diatonic
harmonies. Its chief exponent was *J.C.
Bach. (See also *Style galant.)

Further reading
C. Cudworth, 'Cadence galante: the
Story of a Cliché', *MMR*, lxxix (1949);
'Baroque, Rococo, Galant, Classic',
MMR, lxxxiii (1953). D.A. Sheldon, 'The
Galant Style Revisited and Re-evaluated',
Acta Musicologica, xlvii (1975). *MGG*.

Gallenberg, (Wenzel) Robert, Graf von
Austrian composer and administrator (b.
28 Dec 1783, Vienna; d. 13 Mar 1839,
Rome).
    Member of a noble family, he studied
composition with Albrechtsberger
and gained recognition as a serious
composer. He married *Beethoven's pupil
Countess Giulietta Guicciardi (to whom
the latter dedicated his *'Moonlight'
Sonata) and moved to Italy a year later,
becoming known as a ballet-composer
and contributing largely to the music in
the celebration for Joseph Bonaparte in
Naples in 1805. On his return to Vienna
in 1822 he became entrepreneurially
involved in operatic ventures, the losses
from which resulted in his leaving the city
permanently for France and Italy in 1830.

Works
Many ballet scores, including *Wilhelm
Tell* (1810), *Die Silberschlange* (1821)

and *Arsena* (1822); pieces for piano,
overtures, marches, dances and songs.

Further reading
A. Bauer, *150 Jahre Theater an der Wien*
(Zurich, 1952).

Galop
A fast, lively and very simple dance in
2/4 time of German origin, suggested by
a horse's gallop. It was a couple-dance
in which the dancers (in close contact
as in the *waltz) sprang quickly through
the room. Many of the tunes were based
on operatic or popular sources and the
dance was very widespread in the 1820s
in Vienna and, a little later, in Britain and
France. It was popular as a finale-dance in
balls and ballets and occurs in many operas
including Balfe's *The Bohemian Girl*.

Galuppi, Baldassare
Italian composer, instrumentalist and
conductor (b. 18 Oct 1706, Burano, nr
Venice; d. 3 Jan 1785, Venice).
    Son of a barber who played the violin in
theatre orchestras from whom he received
his early training. After the failure of the
teenager's first opera, he was advised by
Benedetto Marcello and spent three years
studying keyboard and composition with
Antonio Lotti. After a year in Florence as
a theatre harpsichordist, he returned to
Venice to compose operas, his first success
being *Dorinda* with libretto by Pescetti.
His appointment as *Maestro di musica*
to the Ospedale dei Mendicanti resulted
in a great improvement in standards and
he also composed much sacred music.
He spent two years in London (1741–43)
as composer for the King's Theatre, his
works there being admired and performed
long after he had left. Back in Italy, he
held various appointments – including
Venice's highest, that of *maestro di*

cappella at St Mark's in 1762 – before his collaboration with the playwright Goldoni produced a stream of very successful *opere buffe* which greatly influenced the development of the genre throughout Europe. He generally raised the status of the orchestra in his dramatic works.

His fame having spread to Russia, he was granted three years' leave to become musical director at Catherine the Great's chapel, staging Italian operas and composing Orthodox Church music of a type which cast the prevailing Russian idioms in Italianate counterpoint which remained influential for subsequent composers of Russian Orthodox Church music. He returned in triumph to his post at St Mark's in 1768, between then and his death increasing his output of instrumental and religious, rather than his theatrical, works.

Works
Many operas, including *L'Arcadia in Brenta* (1749), *Il filosofo di campagna* (1754), *Idomeneo* (1756) and *Ifigenia in Tauride* (1768); many other oratorios and masses; six sonatas and other smaller works for keyboard, six chamber sonatas, sinfonias, overtures.

Further reading
D. Heartz, 'Hasse, Galuppi and Metastasio', *Venezia e il melodrama nel settecento* (Venice 1975); 'The Creation of the Buffo Finale in Italian Opera', *PRMA*, civ (1977–78). Burney/PRESENT. Newman/SCE.

Ganer, Christopher
German piano-maker (*fl.* 1774–1809).

Almost nothing is known of Ganer's life except that he arrived from Leipzig to work in Broad Street, London (1774–1809) and built mostly square pianos,

which survive in several collections – Fenton House and the Victoria and Albert Museum (London), the Russell Cotes Museum (Bournemouth), the *Colt Clavier Collection (Kent).

Gavotte (Fr.; O Eng. gavot; It. *gavotta*)
French *folk-dance, court dance and instrumental form widely used in ballets and very popular in *Baroque stage works. It was very common as a component of the instrumental *suite, especially that for keyboard, as can be seen in the works of *J.S. Bach and *Handel, where it is in 4/4 time and has a characteristic 2-crotchet upbeat, retaining something of its pastoral associations by being accompanied on occasion by a drone-bass. The *gavotte* is still danced on a wide scale in Brittany, and although its origins are from the south of the province (*Basse-Bretagne*, or *Breiz-izel*) it was also to be found in Provence and the Basque country.

Gebrauchsmusik (Ger.: 'functional music')
A term first used in the early twentieth century to describe music written for, or having a strong leaning toward, functional reasons other than purely artistic ones. Under this heading was grouped film music, music for radio or mechanical instruments, political music and music for amateurs and community music (which was also called *Gemeinschaftsmusik*). In our own day we could also add such music as that used while waiting for telephone extensions to answer and some of that used in shopping malls and superstores as well as some popular and light music.

Geib
German firm of piano- and organ-makers and music-publishers, working first in England and the in the United States.

Geib, John [Johann]

German piano-maker and founder of the Geib firm (b. 27 Feb 1744, Standernheim; d. 30 Oct 1818, Newark, NJ).

Geib migrated to London and is reputed to have been the first to make *'organised pianos' in Britain. He also patented a double action for the square which was later adopted for all such instruments in Britain. In mid-1797 he emigrated with his family to New York and took his twin sons into the business, John Geib & Co. and later & Son. He retired *c.*1816. The firm also published (mainly patriotic) music.

Further reading

O. Ochse, *The History of the Organ in the United States* (Bloomington, IN, and London, 1975). J. Ogasapian, *Organ Building in New York City 1700–1900* (Braintree, MA, 1977); 'New Data on John Geib', *The Tracker*, xxiii/4 (1979).

Geigenwerk

A keyboard instrument resembling a harpsichord in which the tuned strings (one per note) were brought into contact with a series of revolving wheels covered with parchment, operated by a treadle. The name was given to it by its inventor, Hans Haiden, working in the last quarter of the sixteenth century. There were still several examples in collections during the early eighteenth century.

'Geistertrio' ('Ghost' Trio)

Nickname for the first of Beethoven's two piano trios op. 70 in D major, composed in 1808. The three movements are i. Allegro vivace con brio (3/4 D major), ii. Largo assai ed espressivo (2/4 in D minor, whose piano *tremolandi* and sudden dynamic changes are the basis of the nickname) and iii. Presto (C in D major). It is dedicated to Countess Marie Dudy.

Gelinek [Gelineck, Jelínek], Joscf (Abbé)

Czech composer, pianist, piano-teacher (b. 3 Dec 1758, Sedlec, nr Sedlčany; d. 13 Apr 1825, Vienna).

He learnt music in his home town, at a Jesuit college and at Prague university. He entered the seminary in Prague in 1783, where he studied music as well as theological subjects and was ordained priest three years later. According to one of his biographers, he met *W.A. Mozart on the latter's visit to the city in 1787 and, after Gelinek improvised on one of Mozart's themes at the home of Count Kinsky (one of *Beethoven's main patrons), the older composer recommended him to the count. Gelinek was taken on as domestic chaplain and piano-teacher to the Kinskys, moving to Vienna with them around 1790, where he studied counterpoint with Albrechtsberger. He was very much in demand as a composer of fashionable piano-pieces and teacher for noble families, becoming friendly with *J. Haydn and the young Beethoven and it was Gelinek who introduced him to another teacher when his lessons with Haydn were unsatisfactory. He became domestic chaplain to Prince Nikolaus II *Esterházy *c.*1807, a post he held until the end of his life.

Works

Mostly variations on popular and operatic melodies for piano aimed at accomplished performers; many similar works are spuriously attributed to him. He also wrote two harpsichord concertos and about 30 chamber works, as well as being an excellent arranger of other composers' works for piano.

Further reading
P. Nettl, *Forgotten Musicians* (New York, 1951). G. Proier, *Abbé J. Gelinek als Variationenkomponist* (diss., U. of Vienna, 1962).

General Collection of Ancient Irish Music, A (see *Bunting)

Genouillères (knee-levers; see *Knee-pedals)

Gerber, Ernst Ludwig
German scholar, organist, composer (b. 29 Sep 1796, Sonderhausen; d. 30 Jun 1819, Sonderhausen).

He was taught music theory and organ by his father, the composer Heinrich Nikolaus Gerber, who had been a pupil of *J.S. Bach. After studying law in Leipzig University, he practised law in his home town and was tutor to the children of the local prince. Succeeding his father in 1775 as court organist, he also managed the prince's accounts and was his court secretary.

Although known as a composer and cellist he is remembered above all as a lexicographer and collector of music, resulting in his having one of the greatest private collections of its time, including his father's and some others' libraries. It was augmented by the gift of copies of most of its publications by the Breitkopf firm and included manuscripts as well as printed music. Building partly on the work of some other scholars, J.G. Walther and J.F. *Reichardt among them, his lexicons formed the unacknowledged basis for, among other works, Choron and Fayolle's *Dictionnaire historique des musiciens* (Paris, 1810–11) and Sainsbury's *Dictionary of Musicians* (London, 1824) and he compiled and published his *Tonkünstler-Lexicon*, a biographical dictionary of musicians (1790–92 and its amplified version, *Tonkünstler-Lexikon* 1812–14).

Further reading
J.P. Larsen, *Die Haydn-Überlieferung* (Copenhagen, 1939). O. Wessely, ed., *Ernst Ludwig Gerber: Ergänzungen-Berichtigungen und Nachträge zu Ernst Ludwig Gerbers Tonkünstler-Lexika* (Graz, 1969, 2/1977).

Gesellschaft der Musikfreunde (Society of the Friends of Music)
A Viennese society dedicated to the 'advancement of music in all its forms' founded, largely due to the efforts of Joseph Sonnleithner, in 1812, which in turn led to the founding of a music conservatory, the *Conservatorium der Gesellschaft der Musikfreunde*. But in its capacity as a kind of national library, it also housed some extremely important music-collections, being the result of generous donations by such figures as Baron van Swieten (early church music), Aloys *Fuchs (from 1820 including autographs and transcriptions of *J.S. Bach, *Handel, *Gluck, *W.A. Mozart and *Beethoven), *Czerny, *Archduke Rudolph (including a collection of Beethoven's letters), *Gerber (books and music from the seventeenth and eighteenth centuries), *Johann Strauss, Köchel (Mozart's cataloguer and originator of the K numbers for his compositions), Ferdinand, brother of Franz *Schubert (a large number of the composer's autographs) and *Brahms.

Giga (see *gigue)

Gigue (Fr.; Eng. jig; It. *giga*)
A dance with its origins in Ireland, Scotland and Great Britain. French,

German and Italian usage suggests its derivation from a medieval word for fiddle, which survives in the modern German *Geige* (violin). The English word, imported from the Continent is more likely to have come from the French *giguer* (to jump or gambol) and in early usage the dance seems associated with licentiousness. By the beginning of the eighteenth century, two types had emerged, the Italian *giga*, very fast and usually in 12/8 and the French, moderate or fast, in 6/4, 6/8 or 3/8, although compound time-signatures are almost always found, 6/8 becoming almost standard. It was common in small ensemble-pieces and particularly popular as a movement for keyboard and in the keyboard *suite where, in the *Baroque period, it became one of the four 'permanent' movements, along with the *Allemande, *Courante and *Sarabande.

Gilbert and Sullivan

Musico-literary partnership of the comic writer Sir W[illiam] S[chwenck] Gilbert (1836–1911) and the composer Sir Arthur (Seymour) Sullivan (1842–1900), the greatest products of which are the 'Savoy Operas'. These were written for the Impresario Richard D'Oyly Carte, who formed a special opera company, leased the Opéra Comique (London) and later built the Savoy Theatre for them. The operas abound in topical social as well as musical satire and the musical style is eclectic, drawing from as wide a sweep as Purcell, *Handel, *Felix Mendelssohn and balladry. The partnership – professional only – spanned twenty years, surviving a breach, and the operas include *Trial by Jury* (the first for D'Oyly Carte, perf. 1875), *HMS Pinafore* (perf. 1878), *Patience* (perf. 1881), *Iolanthe* (perf. 1882), *The Mikado* (perf. 1885) and the last and only failure of the series, *The Grand Duke* (perf. 1896).

Girl I Left Behind Me, The [*Brighton Camp*]

Traditional song associated with the British Army at times of withdrawal. Words and music can be traced to the end of the eighteenth century.

Giustini, Lodovico (Maria)

Italian composer, keyboard performer (b. 12 Dec 1685, Pistoia; d. 7 Feb 1743, Pistoia).

His father was organist in Pistoia, and he succeeded him in 1725, remaining in the post until his death. Giustini is famous for having been the first composer to write pieces specifically for the piano, his op. 1, 12 *Sonate da Cimbalo di piano e forte detto volgarmente di martellati* ('12 Sonatas for keyboard with soft and loud commonly called with hammers') (pub. Florence, 1732 and in facsimile, Cambridge, 1933, and in Florence, 1982). The particular dynamic markings applying to the piano are *più piano* ('softer', implying a *decrescendo*) and *più forte* ('louder', implying a *crescendo*). Example given in Carew/MUSE (Pl. 4).

Glass harmonica (see *Armonica)

Glee (Anglo-Saxon and Old English *gliv* or *gléo*, 'entertainment', especially 'musical entertainment')

Name given to a kind of unaccompanied partsong in England which flourished from the seventeenth to the nineteenth centuries and was particularly prevalent between 1750 and 1835. Although beginning as a male genre – which it largely remained – with words celebrating male bonding, alcoholic drink and lechery, it became more of a mixed social entertainment which was reflected in the more seemly sentiments expressed. This was especially true when ladies' nights were instigated in the many glee clubs which grew up in most urban centres. Indeed, glees began to include a soprano part as well as the expected alto, tenor and bass parts. They contained passages of simple counterpoint as well as chordal settings, with each phrase of the poem set separately and a penchant for *word-painting. The glee lived on in the American barbershop quartet and the operatic ensembles of *Gilbert and Sullivan.

Glockenspiel (see **Carillon*)

Gluck, Christoph Willibald, Ritter von German composer (b. 2 Jul 1714, Erasbach nr Berching, Upper Palatine; d. Vienna, 15 Nov 1787).

Son of a forester and huntsman, Gluck was practically self-taught in music apart from some lessons in singing, violin and possibly cello by local teachers during childhood. The family moved to Reichstadt (now Liberec) in northern Bohemia and his father, having bettered himself through several posts and moves, retired to his own large estate at Hammer bei Brüx. He tried to discourage his son from a musical career, so the boy ran away from home at around the age of thirteen and appeared in Prague about a year later with a letter of recommendation from a clergyman friend. After several years, he was reconciled with his father, which resulted in financial help from him and, possibly, from Count *Lobkowitz. He nevertheless received no secondary schooling and although he matriculated in the faculties of logic and mathematics at Prague University, he did not complete his course. He was influenced in his earlier years by the operatic theories of J.A.

Scheibe and Algarotti, the Enlightenment outlook enshrined in the ideas of Diderot and the **Encyclopédie*, by the philosophies of *Rousseau and Winckelmann and the ideas on dance of Cahusac.

In 1734 or 1735 he left Prague for Vienna, where he stayed for two years before being offered a post in the orchestra of an Italian prince, moving to Milan in 1737. In 1741 his first opera, *Artaserse* (to a libretto by Metastasio) was produced in Milan and, after initial indifference, became a great success, leading to a string of operatic commissions and resulting in a further seven operas over the following three years. Early in 1745 Gluck went to England and had two operas – much of the music culled from earlier works of his – but the visit was no great success except, perhaps for his performances on musical glasses. Between 1746 and 1752 Gluck travelled in Europe, although little is known of these years, except that he was associated with, and possibly a member of, an opera company which performed in Dresden and that he received a commission for an opera, *Semiramide riconosciuta*, for Vienna, where he arrived in early 1748 for rehearsals; the opera was a musical and financial success.

In 1750, after more travelling, Gluck settled in Vienna, marrying the daughter of a rich merchant. In spite of his comfortable means, he looked for a post and was appointed *Konzertmeister*, then **Kapellmeister*, to the Prince of Saxe-Hildburghausen, remaining from *c*.1753 to 1761, when the Prince's orchestra was disbanded. His post, however, introduced him to the Viennese aristocracy, among whom was Count Durazzo, who was manager of both of the Viennese theatres. At his invitation, Gluck was commissioned to alter and, occasionally replace, some of the music in French operatic works which Durazzo had introduced to Vienna. Thus Gluck laid the foundations of his later operatic reforms.

Italian opera was revived in Vienna in 1760 and Durazzo's desire to incorporate French elements (especially ballet-scenes) into Italian opera was supported by Raniero Calzabigi. He began a collaboration with Gluck as librettist and their first work (together with the choreographer Angiolini), a ballet-pantomime *Don Juan, ou Le festin de pierre* (1761), was a huge success. Gluck obviously thought highly of the work, since he plundered it for a number of later operas. Apart from a few trips to Italy and Paris, Gluck remained in Vienna producing stage works receiving varying public receptions, but he nevertheless became quite rich through commissions. Having no children of his own, he adopted his dead sister's daughter and she developed into a good singer. He now set his sights on Paris, intending to reform French *tragédie lyrique*, and set a libretto based on Racine's *Iphigénie en Aulide*, hoping to impress the French and attract the patronage of the dauphin's wife, Marie Antoinette, who was already familiar with his works. Gluck and his family left for Paris, arriving in November of 1773. The opera, performed in the presence of the dauphin and his wife was a great success and he began to adapt his *Orfeo*, using a French text, as *Orphée et Euridice*, which was an even greater success. He received an annual pension of 6,000 livres from the newly-crowned Louis XVI and on his return to Vienna in October 1784, he was appointed *Hofcompositeur*. Various trips to Paris ensued, but the invitation of Piccinni to the city as a rival to Gluck gave rise to the famous 'war' between the composers' supporters. He died in Vienna in 1787 after a series of strokes

Gluck's later operas struck a new equilibrium between music and drama and he strove to impart a simpler, more natural expressiveness (exemplified above all in *Orfeo*'s famous aria 'Che farò senza Euridice'), to dispense with the formalism of the Metastasian libretto and the rigidity of the musical succession of recitative-and-aria as well as the succession of aria-types, and to curb the virtuosic liberties of singers. His music impacted on *W.A. Mozart in general and, in particular, his *Singspiel, Die Entführung aus dem Serail* (perf. 1782), which was influenced considerably by Gluck's *La rencontre imprévu* (perf. 1764) and to the German translation of his *Iphigénie en Tauride* (perf. 1781). He also influenced the young Salieri, who thought of him as his master, although there was no formal tuition. Gluck revitalized the *tragédie lyrique* and influenced the efforts of *Cherubini, Spontini and *Méhul in this area. Wagner and especially *Berlioz owe much to Gluck and he was a pioneer in the relationship between composer and librettist and especially the tailoring of a libretto to a particular composer.

Works

Ballets: *Don Juan* (Vienna, 1761), *Semiramis* (pantomime) and *Iphigénie* (both Vienna, 1765); Operas: *Orfeo e Euridice* (1762, French version: 1774), *La rencontre imprévue* (Vienna, 1764, Paris, 1776, German version: 1772), *Alceste* (Vienna, 1767, French version: Paris 1776), *Paride ed Elena* (Vienna, 1770), *Iphigénie en Aulide* (Paris, 1774), *Armide* (Paris, 1777), *Iphigénie en Tauride* (Paris, 1779, German version: Vienna, 1781).

Further reading

P. Howard, *Gluck and the Birth of Modern Opera* (London, 1963). K. Hortschansky,

Parodie und Entlehnung im Schaffen Christoph Willibald Glucks (Cologne, 1973); many more specific articles and studies.

'God Save the King/Queen'
British National Anthem (although Wales and the Isle of Man have their own, often used in conjunction with it). It is the oldest national anthem and the model or inspiration for a number, such as *J. Haydn's for Austria (*'Gott erhalte Franz den Kaiser'). Words and music are anonymous, and attempts have been made to attribute it to James Oswald, Henry Carey, Thomas *Arne and John Bull; however, a seventeenth-century origin seems most plausible. Its first appearance in print was in a collection of miscellaneous songs, *Harmonia Anglica*, issued by John Simpson in 1744. The earliest performances appear to have been at Drury Lane and Covent Garden Theatres, London, where it was sung on several consecutive nights in September 1745 after the defeat of Sir John Cope's army at Prestonpans by the Jacobite army led by Prince Charles Edward Stewart ('Bonnie Prince Charlie'). It was used, in the past, as a national anthem for several countries – Denmark, Switzerland, Sweden and Russia among them – and still serves for that of Liechtenstein. The German Empire adopted it, with words by Heinrich Harries, from 1871 to 1922. Many composers have used it in larger works and as the basis for variation-sets.

'Goldberg' Variations (*Aria mit [30] verschiedenen Veraenderungen*: 'Air with [30] different Variations')
A set of thirty variations on an original theme (called 'Aria') by *J.S. Bach (BWV988 in G major) published in 1741–

42 as the fourth part of his *Clavier-Übung*, a compilation of keyboard pieces which also includes the *'Italian Concerto'. The set includes variations in the form of a *fughetta* (see *fugue) and an *ouverture* and in addition, each third variation is a two-part *canon, the interval ascending by *step from unison to ninth – that at the fifth is by inversion – culminating in a final *quodlibet*. The name derives from that of a harpsichordist to whom Bach gave a copy, but it is unlikely that he commissioned them.

'Gott erhalte Franz den Kaiser' **[*Kaiserhymne*]**
Composed by *J. Haydn in 1797 to words by Lorenz Leopold Haschka as the Austrian national anthem after hearing the English *God Save The King* during his first London Visit (1791–92); it remained in use until the beginning of the Second World War. In 1922 it was adopted by Germany with words by August Heinrich Hoffmann von Fallersleben (beginning 'Deutschland, Deutschland über alles'). The Federal Republic replaced the first verse with Fallersleben's third verse (beginning 'Einigkeit und Recht und Freiheit') from 1950.

Gottschalk, Louis Moreau
American pianist and composer (b. 8 May 1829, New Orleans; d. Tijuca, Brazil, 18 Dec 1869).

Son of an English merchant educated in Germany and a Haitian mother of French ancestry, Gottschalk made such musical progress that his teacher, the organist of St Louis Cathedral in New Orleans, recommended that he be sent to Paris for further training. He was refused audition for the Conservatoire by the head of piano studies, Zimmermann, because of anti-American prejudice and took lessons elsewhere, studying piano with Charles Hallé and Carl Stamaty and composition with Pierre Maleden. He gave a hugely successful recital at the Salle *Pleyel at the age of 15, which drew plaudits from *Chopin, among others, and after his formal debut at the same venue four years later, critics compared their playing to the younger man's credit.

Between these recitals, he had established himself as a widely-admired composer of salon music in an American idiom. Highly successful tours of Switzerland, provincial France and Spain, where he enriched his compositional output with pieces in Spanish style, prompted him to return to America, and he gave his first concert in New York in 1853, which was only moderately successful. The death of his father in October of the same year placed the welfare of his six younger siblings in his care and he needed to give more recitals and to pander rather more to public taste. He toured for three years including a long sojourn in Cuba and visits to Canada, before departing for the Antilles and South America for five years, which included a period of withdrawal in Guadeloupe.

Financial exigency caused him to return to the United States and he was contracted to a punishing 3-year tour of the country during which he is estimated to have given 1,100 recitals and travelled 95,000 miles. Untrue reports of an amorous affair with a student at the Female Seminary at Oakdale caused a national scandal and he escaped to South America, where he remained until his death, in spite of his friends' successful attempt to clear his name. He continued to push himself in spite of illness, organizing 'monster concerts' and giving his own, until his death, apparently of yellow fever, in Brazil.

Gottschalk was the first major American virtuoso performer-composer to acquire international status and one of the first to include native American flavour in his works, in his case Creole music; he left a body of salon piano pieces in this and other exotic styles.

In his use of musical quotation within works, he could be said to prefigure Ives and there are uncanny pre-echoes of jazz and ragtime in some of the works from his Antilles period.

Works
Piano: the 'Louisiana trilogy' (*Bamboula* op. 2 (?1846–48), *La savane* op. 3 and *Le bananier* op. 5 (both ?c.1848)); *Le mancenillier* op. 11 (?1849–50); *La scintilla* (*L'étincelle*) op. 20 (1848–53); *Danse ossianique* op. 12 (?1850); *Souvenirs d'Andalousie* op. 22 (1851); *The Last Hope* op. 16 (1854); *Le Banjo* op. 15 (?1854–55); *Souvenir de Porto Rico* op. 31 (?1860); *The Maiden's Blush* (?1863–64); *The Dying Poet* (?1863); and many others. There are some instrumental works and operas, and a lost piano concerto.

Further reading
V. Loggins, *Where the Word Ends: the Life of Louis Moreau Gottschalk* (Baton Rouge, LA, 1958). R. Offergeld, 'The Gottschalk Legend: Grand Fantasy for a Great Many Pianos' in V. B. Lawrence, ed., *The Piano Works of Louis Moreau Gottschalk* (New York, 1969). J.G. Doyle, *The Piano Music of Louis Moreau Gottschalk, 1829–1869* (diss., New York U., 1960); *Louis Moreau Gottschalk 1829–1869: a Bibliographical Study and a Catalog of Works* (Detroit, MI, 1983). W.T. Marrocco, 'America's First Nationalist Composer: Louis Moreau Gottschalk', *Scritti in onore di Luigi*

Ronga (Milan and Naples, 1973). W.E. Korf, *The Orchestral Music of Louis Moreau Gottschalk* (Henryville, PA, 1983).

Gounod, Charles (François)

French composer (b. 17 Jun 1818, Paris; d. St Cloud, 18 Oct 1893).

His father was a successful painter who died when he was five, and his mother a pianist who gave him his earliest music-lessons; he was then taught by *Reicha. He entered the Paris Conservatoire at 18 to study counterpoint with Halévy, composition with Le Sueur and piano with Zimmermann, winning the Second *Prix de Rome* after a year, and the *Grand Prix* itself two years later in 1839. He duly set off for Rome in December. He was much impressed by the sixteenth-century music which he heard at the Sistine Chapel (especially that of Palestrina) and became friendly with Ingres, who was the director of the Villa Medici, home of the *Prix de Rome* scholars in which Gounod stayed. Ingres knew Gounod's father and was impressed with the young man's artistic ability, such that he suggested that he revisit him in Rome as an art scholar.

Gounod met Fanny *Mendelssohn, who introduced him to *J.S. Bach, *Beethoven and *Felix Mendelssohn, and the influence of the last two can be clearly discerned, especially, in his two symphonies. His friendship with the singer Pauline Viardot, whose husband was the director of the Théâtre Italien, eased his way in the musico-theatrical world. He went to Vienna in 1842, where he had two masses commissioned, then on to visit the Hensels in Berlin and Mendelssohn in Leipzig. He returned to Paris with a wide knowledge and experience of music of all ages (within the ken of the period).

Now a church organist, Gounod lived with his mother in Paris and was drawn to the company of priests, prompting him to begin a course of study for Holy Orders as an external student, which he abandoned after two years. He immediately changed direction as a composer of church music and was inveigled to write his first opera, *Sapho*, by Pauline Viardot because of her promise to sing the title role. In spite of this – and in spite of *Berlioz's praise for the music – the work was not a success; Gounod's next venture, a grand opera *à la* *Meyerbeer, shared the same fate. The success of some choruses which he wrote for a drama at the Comédie-Française led to his appointment as conductor of a prominent male-voice choir in 1852 and he married Anna Zimmermann, daughter of the head of piano at the Conservatoire. Several ecclesiastical works were well-received, notably the *Messe solenelle de Sainte Cécile* (1855) and he began writing stage works for the Théâtre-Lyrique, directed by Léon Carvalho; it was these works – including *Faust*, his first great operatic success, and *Roméo et Juliette* – which earned him his place in musical history.

At the first hostilities of the Franco-Prussian War of 1870–71, Gounod and his family fled to friends living just south of London. *Faust* was very popular there – in fact it was Queen Victoria's favourite opera – and he was appointed first conductor of the newly-formed (1871) Royal Albert Hall Choral Society. He was also aware of the Victorian penchant for sentimental over-sweet pious songs, some of which he had already written, including the famous *Ave Maria* (1852), and on which he would continue to capitalize, producing such chestnuts as *There is a Green Hill far Away* (1871) and *Prière du Soir* (1872). He was much occupied with a semi-amorous affair with an amateur (married) singer well-connected socially, Georgina Weldon, to whose various musical ventures he lent his support, moving in to the house occupied by her and her estranged husband. This whole affair was to cause him great problems personally, socially and professionally and, after Gounod's return to France in the middle of 1874, there was much acrimony.

Nevertheless, he continued to write, even in England, where he remained popular, and the remainder of his life produced 12 mass settings, each in a simple, formulaic style which can tend to tedium. At its best his music is of a simple piety and purity and, at worst, platitudinous sentimentality, but with great technical facility. He greatly influenced the succeeding generation of French composers, for example, Bizet, in his *Les pêcheurs de perles* and parts of *Carmen*, and Massenet so much that he was nicknamed 'la fille de Gounod'. Auric and Poulenc held him in high regard and Ravel, perhaps surprisingly, thought him the founder of French song. His stamp on the English choral tradition was also marked, his sentimentality and piety appealing to Victorian – and *Biedermeyer* – sensibilities.

Works
Stage works include *Le médecin malgré lui* (Paris, perf. 1858), *Faust* (Paris, pef. 1859), *Roméo et Juliette* (Paris, perf. 1867), *Jeanne d'Arc* (Paris, perf. 1873). Masses: (dates are first performances): *Messe solenelle de Sainte Cécile* (perf. 1874), *Messe brève pour les morts* (*Requiem*) (London, perf. 1873), *Requiem* (Paris, 1895). There are also seven oratorios, vocal/choral pieces in Latin, much part-music and songs, including *Jésus de Nazareth* (1856), *Ave Maria* (after Bach), *There is a green hill far away* (1871), *Thy will be done* (1873), *My beloved spake* (1873), *L'Eucharistie* (1895). His instrumental music includes two symphomies (in D, 1855 and E♭ major, perf. 1856), various marches, *Méditation sur Faust* (piano, harmonium, violin/cello), *Petite symphonie* (winds, 1895) and piano pieces.

Further reading
H. Büsser, *Charles Gounod* (Lyons, 1961). J. and J. de Lassus Saint-Geniès, *Gounod et son temps* (Fontenay-le-Comte, 1965). F. Noske (tr. R, Benton), *French Song from Berlioz to Duparc* (London and New York, 1970). J. Harding, *Gounod* (London, 1973).

Gradus ad Parnassum [Steps to Parnassus]
Textbook on counterpoint and strict composition by the Austrian theorist and composer Johann Joseph Fux (1660–1741). Written in Latin in the form of a dialogue, it also discussed free composition and enjoyed enormous influence as a primer for the Viennese Classics and later composers, also furnishing the basis for many later theoretical works on counterpoint – those of Albrechtsberger, *Cherubini and Schenker included. The work was partially translated in English in 1943 as *Steps to Parnassus: the Study of Counterpoint*, which was issued in a revised form in 1965 as *The Study of Counterpoint*.

Graf, Conrad
German (Austrian nationalized) piano-maker (b. 17 Nov 1782, Riedlingen, Württemberg; d. 18 Mar 1851, Vienna).

He moved from Württemberg to Vienna in about 1799 and after military service, was trained as a cabinet-maker in the piano-workshop of Jakob Schelkle. He married his employer's widow in 1804 and set up in business on his own as a piano-maker in the fashionable 'Mondscheinhaus'. He was appointed Royal Court Piano and Keyboard Instrument Maker in 1824 and won the gold medal for his pianos in the first Viennese exhibition of industrial products in 1835.

A consolidator rather than an innovator, Graf built in the *'Viennese' piano tradition of practically all-wood construction with slightly heavier action and three to five pedals. He built pianos – often very decorated – for *Beethoven and for the *Schumanns' wedding; he supplied *Chopin with an instrument for his Viennese concert in 1829 and *Liszt probably had a Graf piano, since he is depicted playing one in the famous Dannhauser painting (1840). Graf's pianos survive in instruments in museums in Vienna, Bonn, Halle, Nuremberg, Stockholm, Trondheim (Norway) and Copenhagen.

Further reading
F.J. Hirt, *Meisterwerke des Klavierbaues* (Olten, 1955). W.S. Newman, 'Beethoven's Pianos Versus His Piano Ideals', *JAMS*, xxiii (1970). D. Wythe, *Conrad Graf (1782–1851): Imperial Royal Court Fortepiano Maker in Vienna* (diss., New York U., 1990).

Gravicembalo (see *Harpsichord)

'Gretchen am Spinnrade' ('Gretchen at the Spinning-wheel')
Song by Franz *Schubert (D118), published as 'op. 2', composed in 1814 to words from Goethe's Faust, the discovery of which prompted its composition. The piano-part, suggestive of the continual motion of the girl's spinning-wheel, is more than mere accompaniment and becomes an indispensable element in the song, in which the abandoned Gretchen remembers her lover, Faust.

Grétry, André-Ernest-Modeste
Flemish (French naturalized) composer (b. 8 Feb 1741, Liège; d. 24 Sep 1813, Montmorency, Seine-et-Oise).

Son of a violinist at the Collegiate Church of St Denis at Liège, his father sent him to local musicians for musical training. He also learned more practical skills from a visiting company of Italian singers who helped him greatly with his soprano voice, which was much admired locally. André himself soon became a second violinist in the orchestra, sang in the choir and became a solo boy soprano. His early compositions, some symphonies and a mass, gained him a scholarship to the Collège de Liège in Rome where he stayed from early 1760 to early 1766. He found the quality of tuition disappointing, apart from G.B. Casali, but certainly learned from his attendances at Pergolesi's *opere buffe*. Many works from this period are lost. After becoming a singing-teacher in Geneva, he met Voltaire who advised him to try his luck in Paris as an opera composer, and Grétry arrived there in the autumn of 1767. After the failure of his first attempt, his success was assured with *Le huron* (1768, on a drama by Voltaire); many commissions followed and he began a collaboration with the writer and critic *Marmontel; their work became well-known on continental Europe. A cooling of their relationship was responsible for his collaboration with 'd'Hèle' (an obscure English writer, Hales, who had settled in Paris) who wrote the libretti for his greatest successes, *Le jugement de*

Midas and *Les fausses apparences* (both 1778), and *Les événemens imprévus* (1779). D'Hèle died suddenly and Grétry looked to Sedaine for libretti.

His career henceforth was somewhat hit-and-miss, though some of the hits were big: his *opéra-ballet La caravane du Caire* delighted the Court at Fontainebleau in 1873 and its transfer to the Opéra early the following year was one of the greatest of operatic triumphs ever. His *Panurge dans les îles des lanternes* (1783), despite being criticized in principle for being a comedy (and therefore inappropriate for the Opéra) was a huge success also and this was cause enough for the pension which Grétry was already paid by the Opéra to be doubled. He was, in addition, inspector of the *Comédie Italienne* and Royal Censor for Music as well as holding the titular Director of the Queen's Private Music to Marie-Antoinette after her accession in 1774 and he was friendly with all the great cultural figures of the period, as well as enjoying the admiration of Robespierre, no doubt because of his espousal of Revolutionary themes and attitudes.

Many critics consider *Richard Coeur-de-lion* (1784) his best work and it was publicly acclaimed when it was reissued with an altered ending at the end of 1785. It is also generally agreed that his output declined in quality thereafter. This was partly due to personal circumstances – three of his much-loved daughters died of tuberculosis – and political ones, particularly those associated with the Revolution, which, in spite of the honour of a Napoleonic pension, caused a diminution in ardour for Grétry and his work, to put it mildly. In the face of larger, more appropriate pieces by *Méhul, *Cherubini and others, he turned to writing his *Mémoires* (1789)

and his last years, after the death of his wife in 1807, were devoted to producing the eight volumes of his *Réfléxions d'un solitaire (Reflections of a Solitary*, pub. 1919).

Grétry raised French comic opera to new heights, largely due to his almost Gluckian infusion of truth and realism and reduction of vocal and other excesses. His ability to fuse disparate elements – Italian song forms but without their over-vocalizations, French *folk-types and vaudeville, comedy and tragedy – delighted audiences of all kinds and social levels, and he was a true child of the Enlightenment and the *Encyclopédistes* in his true-to-life and affecting character-portrayals.

Works

Le huron (perf. Paris, 1768); *Zémir et Azor* (perf., Fontainebleau, 1771); *Le jugement de Midas* and *Les fausses apparences* (both perf. Paris, 1778), and *Les événemens imprévus* (perf. Paris, 1779); *Colinette à la cour* (perf. Paris, 1782); *La caravane du Caire* (perf. Fontainbleau, 1783); *Richard Coeur-de-lion* (perf. Paris, 1784); *Panurge dans les îles des lanternes* (perf. Paris, 1785); *Raoul Barbe-bleu* (perf. Paris, 1789); *Guillaume Tell* (perf. Paris, 1791). Writings: *Mémoires, ou Essais sur la musique* (1789, enlarged 2/1797); *Méthode simple pour apprendre à préluder* (Paris 1803); *Réfléxions d'un solitaire* (8 volumes, 1801–13, pub. Brussels 1919–22), ed. M. Brix and Y. Lenoir (Naumur, 1993).

Further reading

L. Jongen, 'André-Ernest-Modeste Grétry, curieux et habile homme', *Académie Royale de Belgique: bulletin de la classe des beaux-arts*, xlii (1960). G. de Froidcourt, ed., *La correspondence général de Grétry* (Brussels, 1962). J. Quitin, 'Les compositions de musique religieuses d'André-Modeste Grétry', *RBM*, xviii (1964). R.D. Jobe, *The Operas of André-Ernest-Modeste Grétry* (diss., U. of Michigan, 1965). K. Pendle, 'The Opéras Comiques of Grétry and Marmontel', *MQ*, lxii (1976). D. Charlton, *Grétry and the Growth of Opéra-Comique* (Cambridge, 1986).

Groves of Blarney, The (see *'Last Rose of Summer, The')

'Guitar cello' (see *Arpeggione*)

Gyrowetz [Gyrowez, Girowetz], **Adalbert** [Jírovec, Vojtěch, Matyáš] Bohemian composer and conductor (b. 19/20 Feb 1763, Česke, Budějovice; d. Vienna, 19 Mar 1850).

Son of a choirmaster who taught him the piano, the violin and composition, he was composing ambitious works during his schooldays. He studied philosophy and law in Prague and was a skilled linguist. He went to Vienna 1785–86 and had some works performed in a concert given by *W.A. Mozart, whose attention he caught and got to know *J. Haydn, *Dittersdorf and Albrechtsberger. He became music master and secretary to Prince Ruspoli and travelled to Italy with him and his family (1767–68), where he meet Nardini (Florence) and Goethe, who was in Rome at the time; the set of six string quartets which he wrote there was his first publication. He left the Prince's service and studied composition with Nicola Sala in Naples.

1789 saw him in Paris, but he quickly sailed for England, meeting Haydn in London and becoming his assistant. He was welcomed into the highest company and performed for the Prince of Wales

several times, also sharing the platform with Haydn. Several of his compositions were published in London, but his main project, an opera – *Semiramis* – commissioned for the Pantheon had to be abandoned when the theatre burnt down, complete with the MS. After a visit to Bohemia, he spent the rest of his life in Vienna and was appointed composer and conductor of the Vienna Court Theatre, 1804–31, with the stipulation that he write at least an opera and a ballet *per annum*. He spent his last years in comparative poverty, but was helped by young musicians, especially *Meyerbeer, as he himself had helped them. *Chopin began his career playing a concerto by Gyrowetz in 1818.

Gyrowetz's manuscripts were often attributed to Haydn, He supported the cause of Czech nationalism and wrote Czech songs, but most of his music was destined for the Viennese *salons*. He was a pallbearer to *Beethoven in 1827.

Works
Some 50 stage works; about 40 symphonies, mostly without op. nos, two piano concertos, opp. 26 (pub. 1796) and 49 (1800), three concertantes [*sinfonie concertantes*]; much chamber music including sets of six string quartets opp. 1, 2 and 3, sets of three opp. 5, 9, 13, 16, 21, 29 and 42; some 46 piano trios (some substituting flute for violin); songs, including 14 Italian ariettas, 33 German songs; also 11 masses, two settings of vespers, *Te Deum*, *Tantum Ergo*, etc.

Further reading
K. Mey, 'Adalbert Gyrowetz und seine neu aufgefundene Hans Sachs-Oper', *Die Musik*, ii (1902–1903). F. Bartoš (ed. and tr.), *Vlastniživotopis Vojtěcha, Jirovce* [*Gyrowetz's Biography*] (Prague,

1940). H.C.R Landon, *The Symphonies of*   E. Doernberg, 'Adalbert Growetz', *ML*,
Joseph Haydn (*passim*) (London, 1955).   xliv (1963).

H

Habanera (Sp.-American; Fr. *havanaise*, from the Cuban capital city, Havana)
Afro-Cuban dance and song in a slow tempo and in 2/4 time with the first quaver dotted, in the same *metre as the tango. It became very popular in America in the early nineteenth century and then spread to Europe where it was equally popular. The dance was a particular favourite with later French composers, such as Bizet (who famously included an example in *Carmen*), Debussy, Chabrier and Ravel as well as Spaniards such as Albéniz and Falla.

Habeneck, François-Antoine
French violinist, conductor, composer (b. 22 Jan 1781, Mézières; d. 8 Feb 1849, Paris).

Son of a German military bandsman serving in France, he studied the violin with his father and later at the Paris Conservatoire under Baillot, winning the *Premier Prix* in 1804. In the same year he joined the Opéra orchestra. He was promoted to first violin, succeeding *Kreutzer in 1817, and became director from 1824–31, raising the standard of the orchestra immeasurably and conducting the premières of *Meyerbeer's *Robert le diable* and *Les Huguenots*, Halévy's *La juive*, *Rossini's *Guillaime Tell* and *Berlioz's *Benvenuto Cellini*.

Habeneck is best remembered for his founding of the *Société des Concerts du Conservatiore* which gave its first performance in 1828 including a performance of *Beethoven's Third Symphony. This was by no means the first Beethoven symphonic work to have an airing in Paris: Habeneck's other great achievement was to introduce the composer to the city with first-rate performances, although he was not above rewriting the odd passage. Habeneck also taught the violin at the Conservatoire from 1825 to the year before his death in 1849.

Works
Mostly including the violin, two concertos for the instrument and an *Air varié* and *Grand *polonaise*, both with orchestra, as well as works for two and three violins and his theoretical work *Méthode théorique et pratique de violon* (Theoretical and Practical Method for Violin, pub. *c*.1835).

Further reading
L. Schrade, *Beethoven in France* (New Haven, CT, 1942). A. Carse, *The Orchestra from Beethoven to Berlioz* (Cambridge, 1948). H.C. Schoenberg, *The Great Conductors* (New York, 1967). J. Cooper, *The Rise of Instrumental Music and Concert Series in Paris 1828–1871* (Ann Arbor, MI, 1983). *Fétis/BIOGRAPHIE. MGG.*

Hackbrett (see *Dulcimer)

Haigh, Thomas
English composer, violinist and pianist (bap. 30 Jan 1769, Wakefield; d. London, ?Apr 1808).

There is little available information. He met *J. Haydn during the latter's first London visit (1791–92) and studied with him, dedicating his violin sonatas opp. 8 and 10 to him; he also arranged a good deal of Haydn's works for piano. Haigh lived in Manchester, 1793–1801, then returned to London, where he remained until his death, which may be later than the 1808 suggested, as some works of his seem to have been published in and up to 1819. He left a body of good quality work, much of it in the homegrown style of Boyce and *Arne, though there are traces of Haydn's influence also.

Works
A symphony and six harpsichord/piano concertos, op. 1 (*c.*1783); many sonatas (piano, piano with another instrument), 28 piano sonatinas (*c.*1795), many rondos and variation-sets.

Further reading
J.D. Brown and S.S. Stratton, *British Musical Biography* (Birmingham, 1897). Fétis/*BIOGRAPHIE. MGG.*

'Halle' Bach (see *Wilhelm Friedemann Bach)

'Halo'
A name given to the effect produced when the damper pedal on an early piano is kept raised, so that the harmonies mingle and the overtones accumulate.

**'*Hammerklavier' Sonata*
Name (meaning 'pianoforte') given to *Beethoven's longest and most difficult piano sonata, no. 29 op. 106 in B♭ major (1817–18, dedicated to the Archduke *Rudolph). It is meaningless as a title, since all Beethoven's piano sonatas were written '*fur das Hammerklavier*') except the early ones which were advertised as for 'piano or harpsichord'. The name, however, has stuck.

Handel [Händel, Hendel]**, George Frideric** [Georg Friederich]
German (naturalized English) composer (b. 23 Feb 1685, Halle; d. London, 14 Apr 1759).

Handel was the son of a barber-surgeon of 63 years of age and his second wife, daughter of a pastor. His musical pursuits were opposed by his father who wished him to enter the legal profession; however, the boy smuggled a small clavichord into the house, practising in the attic. A visit to the court of Saxe-Weissenfels, where his half-brother – who was 36 years older – was a valet resulted in the Duke's hearing the boy play the organ and urged his father to allow him to study music. This he did with F.W. Zachow, organist at the Liebfraukirche in Halle, who gave the boy a thorough grounding and made him familiar with many musical styles and nationalities, teaching the boy organ and violin as well as harpsichord, composition, harmony and counterpoint. After a year at Halle University (probably studying law), during which he was appointed probationary organist at the Calvinist Cathedral, Handel left for Hamburg.

The city supported a regular opera company, unique in Germany, where the form was confined to the many courts and its musical kingpin was the opera's director, Reinhard Keiser. The latter's temperament often put him at odds with other musicians, Handel not least, as he played in the second violins and, later, harpsichord at the opera. His friendship with *Mattheson, dating from this time, was interrupted by their duel, but soon resumed. Handel's first two operas were produced, *Almira* (a great hit) and *Nero* (a failure). Keiser's sentiments can be gauged by the fact that, within the following year and a half he chose the same texts to set.

Following his meeting with Prince Ferdinando de' Medici, son of the Grand Duke of Tuscany, Handel was invited to visit Italy, which – wishing to gain experience of Italian opera – he did in 1710 and he visited Florence and Rome becoming acquainted with and having works commissioned by prominent patrons of the arts, including Cardinals Ottoboni and Colonna and The Marquis (later Prince) Ruspoli. The latter appointed him household musician (1707–1709) and he composed many works, of which the cantata *La Ressurezione* (April 1708) – in reality an opera – was a huge success, requiring a new theatre to be constructed with special scenery and a greatly augmented orchestra led by Corelli; its second performance was attended by the Pope with the soprano part being sung by a *castrato*, since he objected to women in opera.

Handel met the main musicians of the time – the *Scarlattis, Caldara, Lotti, Pasquini, Gasparini, Vivaldi, Albinoni and Perti. He also met the Duke of Manchester, the English ambassador, who urged him to visit England, and the Master of the Horse to the Elector of Hanover (probably meeting the latter's brother, Prince August Ernst, also) and this last encounter may have resulted in his return to Germany in 1710, refusing the offer of a post at Innsbruck in favour of that of *Kapellmeister* to the Elector of Hanover at a very good salary. However, a condition in the contract was that Handel should have a year's leave of absence – immediately effective – to visit London. This was granted, no doubt partly because the Elector was heir to the English throne. He arrived in London in September 1710.

During his eight months' stay he had a great impact on the city and was well received at Queen Anne's court. His first opera for the city in Italian (written in two weeks) was *Rinaldo*, produced with elaborate scenery and machines, and augmented orchestra and large cast and was an enormous success. Much of the music was re-used from earlier works, a practice which had already started and

which would continue throughout his life. A set of songs from the opera was published – Handel's first approved publication – beginning his association with the firm of John Walsh with great mutual benefit. He moved in a wide social circle which included the ten-year-old Mary Granville, later to become the artist Mary Delany. His return to Hanover divorced him from opera (the city had no company) in favour of instrumental and orchestral music. He began taking English lessons and received permission from the Elector for a further London visit provided he returned within a 'reasonable time'.

He was back in London in late 1712 and stayed with Lord Burlington for three years (1713–16) at his house in Piccadilly and produced operas with mixed success. His operas were now beginning to be heard in Germany also. A commission from the English Queen (resulting in a pension of £200) to write church music added a further important string to Handel's bow and he produced several works, all of which show a strong Purcellian influence. He had long outstayed his 'reasonable time' in England and, when the Queen died in August 1714, she was succeeded by Handel's old employer the Elector of Hanover, as George I. There are various stories of a reconciliation between them though it is most likely that this was unnecessary; in any case, the new King doubled his pension and his wife, Queen Caroline raised it further to £600 when Handel began to teach her daughters.

Returning to London after a visit to Hanover in 1716, Handel was a year later in the service of the Earl of Carnarvon – three years later to become 1st Duke of Chandos – as composer-in-residence. The Earl had a resident orchestra and singers and Handel composed the famous *Chandos Anthems* (eleven in all) for his private chapel, completed in 1720, and the masque *Acis and Galatea*. It would not be long, however, before opera beckoned again, this time in the form of 'The Royal Academy of Music'. This is not to be confused with the educational institution founded over a century later (1822) but was a collection of noblemen, under the patronage of George I, dedicated to establishing Italian opera in London by subscription. Handel was its musical director and his first task was to collect 'the best singers in Europe', to which end he left London in May 1719. He narrowly missed the chance to meet *J.S. Bach in Halle – in fact, strangely, for such a cosmopolitan composer as Handel, who met most of his contemporaries, they never did meet.

By 1820 the enterprise was finally up and running and for almost a decade made London the operatic hub of the continent attracting the finest singers, instrumentalists and composers, although relationships within the company were frequently strained to breaking-point and beyond. Inevitable factions sprung up among the supporters of particular singers and composers, and the greed of the singers caused financial problems for the Academy, which was forced to rely more and more on its subscribers. Audience behaviour – never good in London – deteriorated and the two *prime donne* came to blows on stage during a performance of a Bononcini opera in the presence of the Princess of Wales. The bickering infected the directors also and the whole venture fell apart in 1728. Undaunted, Handel decided to 'go it alone' and leased the King's Theatre from the directors, gaining the patronage of the new King, George II. The pattern was soon much as the first Royal Academy and the new Prince of Wales set up a rival company (in opposition to his father as well as Handel) called the Opera of the Nobility which managed to secure the services of the well-known *castrato* Farinelli.

The very successful revival of his oratorio *Esther* (the first oratorio heard in London) prompted Handel to write more and he also composed organ concertos which he himself played with the orchestra between the acts of oratorios. In spite of some successes, Handel's position was not secure and certainly not helped by illness and a stroke. Indeed, it was rumoured that he was to leave England for Germany. However, the intervention of the Lord Lieutenant of Ireland overturned the situation completely, inviting him to Dublin, where he enjoyed one of his most triumphal periods, culminating in the composition (in just over three weeks) and hugely successful performance (13 April) of the *Messiah*, expressly for the benefit of Dublin charities. He intended to return a year later for another season, but was tempted to abandon the plan when, back in London (1743), he revised (for the London company) and revived his oratorio *Samson* to great accolade. Again, his fortunes began to wane, and he endured factions among audiences, bankruptcy, ill-health and, later, the onset of blindness, before another swing of the pendulum brought him back in favour, first with *Judas Maccabeus* (1747, containing the chorus 'Hail, the Conquering Hero' for the Duke of Cumberland returning victorious from Culloden). Handel died in 1759, in his house in Brook Street, London, which still stands. He expressed the hope, in his will, of being buried in Westminster Abbey 'in a private manner'. He was granted the first part, but the funeral was attended by about 3,000 people.

One of the greatest of *Baroque composers, he transformed oratorio and opera, although his reputation in other fields has been slower in being recognized. Among many other achievements he invented the English oratorio and the organ concerto. His dramatic works show a tremendous understanding of human character and emotion.

Works

Operas etc.: *Rinaldo* (perf. London, 1711), *Amadigi di Gaula* (perf. London, 1715), *Radamisto* (perf. London, 1720), *Giulio Cesare in Egitto* (perf. London, 1724), *Rodelinda* (perf. London, 1725), *Scipione* (perf. London, 1726), *Orlando* (perf. London, 1733), *Ariodante* and *Alcina* (both perf. London, 1735), *Serse* (perf. London, 1738); Oratorios: *Acis and Galatea, Esther* (Cannons, 1718), *Deborah* (perf. London, 1733), *Athalia* (perf. Oxford, 1733), *Alexander's Feast* (perf. London, 1736), *Saul, Israel in Egypt, Ode for St Cecilia's Day* (perf. London, 1739), *Messiah* (perf. Dublin, 1742), *Samson* (perf. London, 1743), *Semele* (perf. London, 1744), *Judas Maccabeus* (perf. London, 1747), *Solomon* (perf. London 1749), *Jephtha* (perf. London, 1752); many vocal works (inc. 'Chandos' anthems, Cannons 1711–18, solo and duo cantatas and songs); instrumental: 6 Concerti Grossi op. 3 (1734, rev. *c.*1734 and 1741), 12 Concerti Grossi op. 6 (1740), 6 Organ Concertos op. 4 (1738) (no. 4 also for harp and orchestra), A Second Set of 6 Organ Concertos (no op., 1740), A Third Set op. 7 (1761), Orchestral Suites *Water Music* (1717) and *Music for the Royal Fireworks* (1749), overtures, dances, etc. trio sonatas, solo sonatas and suites and dances for harpsichord.

Further reading

From an enormous body of literature: P.H. Lang, *George Frideric Handel* (New York, 1966). C. Hogwood, *Handel* (London, 1985). J. Keates, *Handel: the Man and his Music* (London, 1985). D. Burrows, *Handel* (Oxford, 1994).

Hand stop (see *Stop)

Harding, Rosamond E(velyn) M(ary)
English writer, musicologist (b. 6 Apr 1898, Doddington, Cambridgeshire; d. St Cloud, 18 Oct 1993).

Her PhD dissertation at Newnham College, Cambridge, became the basis for her book *The Piano-forte: its History Traced to the Great Exhibition of 1851* (Cambridge, 1933, rev. 2/1978), which is still the standard work on its subject and for which she drew many of the technical illustrations. She was awarded a LittD in 1941 in recognition of this and other literary works.

Works
The Piano-forte: its History Traced to the Great Exhibition of 1851 (Cambridge, 1933, rev. 2/1978); *Towards a Law of Creative Thought* (London, 1936); *The Origins of Musical Time and Expression* (London, 1938); *An Anatomy of Inspiration* (Cambridge, 1940); ed., [facs edn] *L. Giustini: Twelve Piano-forte Sonatas* (Cambridge, 1933).

Harmonic
(1) To do with harmony.

(2) See *Overtones.

Harmonica (see *Armonica)

Harmonicon, The
A London musical periodical whose full title was *The Harmonicon: A Journal of Music*. It was edited by William *Ayrton and published from 1823–33, one volume

per year, each in two parts, text and music.

Harmonies poétiques et religieuses
A collection of poetry by Lamartine, which inspired *Liszt's piano-pieces of the same name.

'Harmonious Blacksmith'
A nickname given (after his death) to the air and variations from *Handel's Harpsichord Suite No.5

Harmonium
A wind keyboard instrument modified and so named by A.F. Debain (1809–77) in Paris after 1840. It was intended to be a domestic instrument analogous to the upright piano, although it was, and still often is, used in churches. The principle is that of vibrating brass reeds excited by the air pumped from two foot-pedals, the tone of which is altered by the shapes of the cavities in which they sound and by different sizes of reed. The sound is modified by drawstops (see *stop) named after the instruments to whose sounds they approximate: Flute, *Cor anglais*, *Clarinette*, *Basson*, *Fifre*, *Musette*, *Hautbois* and *Clarion*, for example. The *Grand jeu* stop brings all the others into play and there is usually an additional Tremolo stop. Dynamics can be controlled by the feet's speed of pumping. A later version, the American Organ, or Cabinet Organ, is larger, more versatile and more ornate.

Harpsichord (Dutch *klavecimbel*; Fr. *clavecin*; Ger. *Cembalo*, *Kielflugel*; It. *cembalo*, *clavicembalo*; Lat. *clavicymbalum*; Sp. *clavicordo*)
A keyboard instrument shaped like a grand *piano in which the strings (running at right angles to the keyboard) are plucked by *plectrums of leather, quill or plastic set into *jacks – small slips of wood or plastic fixed to the keys. When the key is released, the jack falls back and a spring mechanism ensures that the string is not re-plucked; a piece of stiff cloth, also fixed to the jack, silences the string when the jack comes to rest. Noticeable gradation of sound is impossible on the instrument, although the tone can be altered and the volume increased or decreased by the addition of extra banks of strings, either of the same pitch or an octave higher and/or lower, which have their own sets of jacks which can be *coupled in various combinations. Some harpsichords have two manuals, or keyboards, with their own mechanisms and sets of strings which can also be coupled. Thus the description of the instrument as having *'terraced dynamics' (like the organ without the use of a *swell-box) as opposed to the gradual dynamics of the *clavichord and *piano. On early instruments the adding or subtracting of strings was achieved by drawing *stops close to the keyboard, while on later instruments pedals were substituted.

The earliest reference to a harpsichord is from 1397 when it was supposed to have been invented by Hermann Pohl. Its two most common variants in shape and smaller size are the virginals (a term used in English to refer to a type in which the strings are at an acute angle to the keyboard) and the spinet (in which they are parallel); the latter term was occasionally (and even less occasionally is still) applied to the square *piano. The harpsichord remained in use as the most common and widespread keyboard instrument until the early nineteenth century when it fell out of favour because of the piano. However, interest revived in the last two decades of that century and instruments were restored – occasionally very unauthentically – and new copies made, leading to the proliferation of recitals and recordings of, especially, *Baroque keyboard music. The process was greatly aided by the pioneering concert-giving and championing of Arnold Dolmetsch and, during the next generation, Wanda Landowska, the first modern virtuoso on the instrument with an international following. The harpsichord's popularity as a domestic instrument increased greatly with the possibility of buying copies of historic instruments in kit form at reasonable prices.

Further reading
C. Hoover, *Harpsichords and Clavichords* (Washington, DC, 1969). W.J. Zuckerman, *The Modern Harpsichord* (New York, 1969). H. Schott, 'The Harpsichord Revival', *Early Music*, ii (1974). M. Campbell, *Dolmetsch, the Man and His Work* (London, 1975). E.M. Ripin, ed., *Keyboard Instruments: Studies in Keyboard Organology* (Edinburgh, 1971). The New Grove. The New Grove Dictionary of Instruments. Boalch/HARPSICHORD. Hubbard/HARPSICHORD. Russell/HARPSICHORD.

Haschka, Georg
Austrian piano-maker (b. *c.*1772, Moravia (then Austrian); d. early 1828, Vienna).

Little else is known of Haschka except that he occupied premises 'Am Neubau 232' in 1818 and 'Am Neubau Holzplazl. 140' in 1820.

Hässler, Johann Wilhelm
German pianist, composer and organist (b. 29 Mar 1747, Erfurt; d. 29 Mar 1822, Moscow).

The nephew of the organist J.C. Kittel with whom he studied keyboard and composition, Häsler was appointed organist in his home town about 1762 and wrote his first keyboard works during the following decade and toured as a pianist, meeting *C.P.E. Bach in Hamburg. He married a singer in 1779 and gave recitals with her while continuing to tour, meeting *W.A. Mozart in Dresden in 1789. He was in London, teaching and performing, 1790–92 until he went to St Petersburg in 1792, without his family and was appointed pianist to Grand Duke Alexander a year later. He stayed the rest of his life in Russia and was an important link between Western composers and their Russian counterparts, upon whom he had much influence.

Works
Many lost, but survivors include a great body of sonatas for piano (five sets of *6 leichte Sonaten* (1780–90) and several for three hands, organ pieces (*48 kleine Orgelstücke* (1789)), many freer pieces (fantasies, capriccios, variations) including a very popular *Grande gigue* op. 31; a 'Grand concert' for piano op. 50 and some chamber music and songs as well as his autobiography (1787).

Further reading
H. Strobel, *Johann Wilhelm Hässlers Leben und Werken* (diss., U of Munich, 1922). R.A. Mooser, *Annales de la musique et des musiciens en Russie*, ii (Geneva, 1951). E. Stöckl, *Musikgeschichte der Russlanddeutschen* (Dülmen, 1993). *MGG*.

Hawkins, Sir **John**
English historian of music, antiquarian (b. 29 Mar 1719, London; d. 21 May 1789, London).

Son of a carpenter, he studied architecture for a year around 1736 and was articled to a solicitor in the City of London, setting up his own practice in 1742, after a very demanding period of study, and moving to Lombard Street in 1751. He published essays and became interested in music as an amateur. Befriended by the composer and organist John Stanley, he provided the words for 11 of his solo cantatas and he was on good terms with William Boyce, who also set some of Hawkins's poems. Through various club connections he became friendly with *Handel, Pepusch, Samuel Johnson, Burke, Goldsmith and Joshua Reynolds. He married in 1753 and several of the couple's children became writers; their home in Broad Street, London became a popular musical venue. A legacy enabled Hawkins to give up work and the family moved to Twickenham, outside of London where their neighbours included Walpole and Garrick. An irascible man, he had a tendency to antagonize friends and neighbours with petty lawsuits although as a magistrate (which he was appointed in 1763) he had a reputation for severity and fairness. He applied for, and was granted, a knighthood in 1772.

His *General History of the Science and Practice of Music*, on which he had been working for some 16 years, was published in 1776 in five quarto volumes. The first volume of his rival *Burney's history of music had been published half a year before and, although Hawkins's work was well received, Burney anonymously began a campaign of vilification of Hawkins's work in the press, a main *leitmotif* of which was his rebutting of Hawkins's elevation of sixteenth and seventeenth-century music at the expense of modern works, especially opera; Burney even circulated a satirical poem

against Hawkins; inevitably, the sales of the History declined.

Hawkins was appointed as Johnson's executor and asked to write his biography; this was also much criticized. The Hawkins family moved to Westminster and in 1785 a fire destroyed much of the library. Hawkins died in 1789 and was buried in the cloisters of Westminster Abbey.

Hawkins's *History of Music* and Burney's similar publication were the first of their kind in Britain.

Works
General History of the Science and Practice of Music (5 vols, with the last including an *Account of the Institution and Progress of the Academy of Ancient Music*) (London, 1776).

Further reading
P.A. Scholes, *The Life and Activities of Sir John Hawkins* (London, 1953). A.H. King, *Some British Collectors of Music* (Cambridge, 1963). B.H. Davis, *A Proof of Eminence: the Life of Sir John Hawkins* (Bloomington, IN and London, 1973). K.S. Grant, *Dr. Charles Burney as Critic and Historian of Music* (Ann Arbor, MI, 1983).

Hawkins, John Isaac
British piano-maker and inventor (b. 14 Mar 1772 nr Taunton; d. 24 Jun 1854, Elizabeth, NJ).

Little is known; he spent most of his life in the United States. He patented his 'portable grand' *piano (actually an upright in our modern sense rather than a grand turned on its end) in Philadelphia and London in 1800; *Matthias Müller independently invented the upright in Vienna at around the same date. Hawkins also invented and applied the first example of a metal *compensation frame and also a bowed keyboard instrument (the *'claviola') which was played in a public concert in Philadelphia in 1802 and in London in 1813, achieving some popularity there. His pianos, however, were never very popular and were considered not to have a very good tone. Hawkins also covered his leather hammers with cloth.

Further reading
W.E. Mann, *Piano Making in Philadelphia before 1825* (diss., U. of Iowa, 1977). Harding/PIANO-FORTE. Loesser/MEN. Cole/PIANOFORTE.

Haydn, (Franz) Joseph
Austrian composer (b. 31 Mar 1732, Rohrau (Lower Austria); d. 31 May 1809, Vienna).

One of 12 children, another of whom (*Michael Haydn) also became a composer. Their father, Mathias, was a wheelwright and a self-taught musician who learnt the harp and sang; he involved all his children in the family concerts which were to remain in Haydn's memory throughout his life. The details of most of Haydn's life before the late (London and Vienna) years are very hazy and only four sources are available: an autobiographical letter which the composer himself wrote in 1776, and three biographical booklets published after his death by, respectively, the painter Albert Christoph Dies, the poet Giuseppe Carpani and the writer and diplomat Georg August Griesinger – the most reliable – whose *Biographische Notizen über Joseph Haydn*, published, after appearing in serial form, in 1810, was based on his conversations with Haydn after the two became friends from 1799.

His fine voice suggested a musical education – though his parents, apparently, wanted him to take holy orders – and he was sent, at the age of six, to live with a distant relative, a strict schoolmaster, in Hainburg, where he learnt several instruments. As a choirboy, he was well-trained and when Georg Reutter, the *Kapellmeister* at St Stephen's Cathedral in Vienna, arrived on a journey to recruit young boys with good voices, Haydn was accepted (with the consent of his father) as soon as he would reach eight years of age. He arrived in Vienna in the late spring of 1740 and lodged, like all the choristers, in Reutter's house.

It seems that Haydn's training during his eight – or ten, depending on the source – years as a chorister was almost exclusively musical and almost exclusively vocal at that. However, he must have received some wider instruction, as, when he left the choir school (*c.*1749) after his voice broke, he was able to earn a meagre living as a teacher of keyboard and performing violin and organ in church, while devoting the rest of his time to his musical self-education; he said he learnt mostly from *C.P.E. Bach's *Versuch über die wahre Art das Clavier zu spielen*. Other than this meagre education, he was self-taught in music. Haydn took the attic rooms in the Michaelerhaus, a large Viennese apartment-house whose residents included, on the first floor, the dowager duchess *Esterházy – the family by whom Haydn would be employed for 30 years – and on the third, the court poet Pietro Metastasio, through whom he was to be introduced to new pupils and through whom he met Nicola Porpora, a prominent Viennese composer and singing-teacher, to whom he was accompanist and valet. This was an important contact for the young man, as, apart from lessons in composition and Italian, he was introduced, and exposed, to many members of the Viennese musical and social aristocracy, including *Gluck and Wagenseil. He is known to have written a number of didactic keyboard works for cheap sale to his pupils as well as small chamber works, the music for some stage pieces and string quartets which were published in 1764–66 as opp. 1 and 2, with six in each.

In 1759 Haydn secured his first appointment, as *Kapellmeister to Count Morzin, who spent the winter in Vienna and the summer on his country estate in Bohemia. The composer married Maria Anna Keller, a wigmaker's daughter, in 1760, but the union was unhappy and childless. In the same year he was appointed Vice-*Kapellmeister to Prince Paul Anton Esterházy due, it is suggested, to Count Morzin's disbanding of his orchestra for financial reasons. The 'vice' in the title was in consideration for the existing incumbent in the Esterházy household at Eisenstadt (Werner), who was too old to continue the actual work associated with the title, except that, according to Haydn's contract, he was to defer to the older man whenever choral music was involved. Haydn's responsibilities were to compose whatever the Prince required and to care for the music and the instruments; he was forbidden to give away any copies of his music or to accept commissions from elsewhere without special dispensation. However, Prince Paul Anton died in 1862 and was succeeded by his brother, Prince Nikolaus – nicknamed 'Nikolaus the Magnificent' because of his love of lavish festivities – who reigned for almost thirty years, and whose personal musical tastes Haydn occasionally found restricting. Nevertheless, the post, with one of the richest and most important Hungarian noble Electoral families, was quite a coup for a 29-year-old freelance musician

and he entered a musical establishment which had strong traditions, an excellent orchestra and a newly-built theatre. To this was shortly added a magnificent palace, *'Eszterháza', on the site of a summer hunting lodge, in which the court settled for most of the year. When Werner died in 1766, Haydn had sole responsibility for all things musical. A possible result of this was what has been called his 'romantic crisis' or *'Sturm und Drang period': a series of works, in several genres and in predominantly minor keys, of passionate intensity, the symphonies being the most striking and original. He could also, for the first time in half a decade, write church music, including a series of masses and smaller pieces and he also wrote many pieces for the Prince's favourite instrument the baryton, an instrument similar to a six-stringed cello with nine extra sympathetic strings behind the neck which could also be plucked.

Given the quality and assuredness of his works up until 1790, it is difficult to believe that Haydn was not in the habit of meeting and conversing with composers of all sorts and ranks, and hearing their music – and vice versa. Yet it seems that most of his life was spent in Eszterháza with much shorter sojourns to Eisenstadt and a few trips to Vienna and Pressburg. However, his name was certainly becoming known, through dissemination of his works (mostly stolen, or pirated and mostly in smaller genres), through some concerts which occurred during his visits elsewhere and through the visit of various VIPs to Prince Nikolaus at Eszterháza, including the Empress Maria Theresia and the Archduke Ferdinand (a great patron of *Beethoven). From 1775 much of his time was taken up with opera: composing his own and inserts for others, arranging the works of others and supervising the musical productions and conducting them. This also applies to Eszterháza's marionette theatre.

1779 stands out among these years as of particular importance in a number of ways. Firstly, he became a client of the very prominent Viennese publisher *Artaria, and it is interesting that when Haydn's contract of employment with the Esterházys was renewed that same year, it did not contain the clause forbidding any use of his compositions without the express consent of the Prince, who had hitherto held exclusive rights to them. The other event in 1779 was a personal one: a passionate affair with the nineteen-year-old soprano, Luigia Polzelli, who was engaged (with her husband) for the Eszterháza opera. The attachment lasted a long time and the composer was very generous in his provision for her and her two sons into the next century. Haydn met *W.A. Mozart during visits to Vienna in the second half of the 1780s and it is clear that they became friends, although there is very little evidence. Despite his attachment to Luigia, he also formed a close friendship (and perhaps a little more) with Maria Anna (Marianne) von Genzinger, the wife of the prince's physician, and their correspondence gives much information unavailable from other sources.

In early 1790 Prince Nikolaus' wife died and he followed her in September; he was succeeded by Prince Anton Esterházy, who had little interest in music and disbanded the orchestras, keeping only the wind band for ceremonial occasions. Haydn, however, was kept on with full salary but without specific duties and decided to move to Vienna. However, his peaceful retirement was not to be. As soon as he heard of the Prince's death, the

German impresario and violinist Johann Peter *Salomon, domiciled in London and a concert-manager there, rushed to Vienna and bluntly put the proposition to Haydn that he should accompany him to London. Salomon was successful – others had tried and failed during the 1780s – and an agreement was reached that the composer would write an opera, six symphonies and some twenty other works, as well as conduct them in 20 concerts; the fee was a substantial one.

In the event, there were two London visits (New Year's Day 1791 – June 1792 and February 1794–August 1795), another six symphonies and another love-affair. The visits produced, among other works, the great set of 12 'London' Symphonies, and Haydn resisted all blandishments to stay in the English capital, even the offer of private apartments by the King and Queen and returned to Vienna. Prince Paul Anton had died in 1794 and his successor, Nikolaus II wrote to Haydn asking that he should re-establish the orchestra.

Haydn managed to fulfil his – much lighter – duties to the Prince while continuing to live in Vienna and we owe the existence of the great late masses of Haydn to his employer's love of church music, which required an annual input on the composer's part. He also composed the oratorios *The Creation* and *The Seasons* (to an English libretto) and continued to write string quartets – all of these works showing no waning in his creative powers. He died at home on 31 May 1809, was given a great memorial service, including the performance of Mozart's Requiem and is buried in Eisenstadt.

Haydn was one of the main founders (with Mozart and possibly *Clementi) of the *Classical style and contributed music of the highest quality in all genres; his subsequent influence was enormous. He taught *Beethoven but the relationship was fractious and short-lived; his influence on the younger man is apparent, however. He also taught, among others, *Ignace Pleyel and the young *Hummel, whose career he furthered.

Works
Instrumental Some 107 symphonies including nos 6–8 ('Le matin', 'Le midi' and 'Le soir'), no. 26 in D minor ('Lamentatione'), no. 44 in E minor ('Trauersinfonie'), no. 45 in F♯ minor ('Farewell'), nos. 82–7 (the 'Paris' symphonies, including nos 82, 'L'ours' ('The Bear'), 83, 'La poule' ('The Hen') and 85, 'La reine' ('The Queen')), nos. 93–104 (the 'London' symphonies (including nos. 94, the 'Surprise', 100, the 'Military', 101, 'The Clock', 103 the 'Drumroll' and 104 the 'London' or 'Salomon')) as well as the *Sinfonia Concertante (for violin, cello, oboe, bassoon and orchestra) no. 105. Some concertos for keyboard and for violin. 68 string quartets (of which the last consists of the inner two movements only). These include the 10 Divertimentos opp. 1 and 2, the quartets (six each) of opp. 9, 17, 20 (the 'Sun' quartets), 33 (the 'Russian' quartets including no. 2 'The Joke' and no. 3 'The Bird'), 50 (the 'Prussian' quartets), 64 (the 'Tost' quartets including no. 5 'The Lark'), 76 (the 'Erdödy' quartets, including no. 2, 'Fifths', no. 3, 'Emperor' and no. 4 'Sunrise'). Baryton trios (*c.*120), keyboard trios (29), keyboard sonatas (47) and some variation-sets.

Vocal 14 masses, including the '*Nelson*' ('*Nelsonmesse*', '*Missa in angustiis*'), '*Theresienmesse*', '*Schöpfungsmesse*' ('*Creation Mass*') and '*Harmoniemesse*', and many other sacred and secular works, including '*Stabat Mater*', '*Applausus*'

Cantata, *Die Sieben letzten Worte ... (The Seven last Words ...), Die Schöpfung (The Creation)* and *Die Jahreszeiten (The Seasons)*.

Many operas (about 25) including *Lo speziale* (or *Der Apotheker*), *Le pescatrici* (or *Die Fischerinnen*), *L'infideltà delusa, L'incontro improvviso, Il mondo della luna, La vera constanza* and *La fedeltà premiata*. Many works for voice(s) and keyboard, including over 400 settings of English, Irish, Scottish and Welsh *folksongs.

There are also hundreds of works attributed to Haydn and he made many arrangements of other composers' works.

Further reading (from a long list)
K. Geiringer, *Joseph Haydn* (Potsdam, 1932, 2/1959); *Haydn: a Creative Life in Music* (New York, 1946, enlarged 3/1982). R. Hughes, *Haydn* (London, 1950, 6/1989). B. Redfern, *Haydn: a Biography, wih a Survey of Books, Editions and Recordings* (London, 1970). H.C.R. Landon, *Haydn: Chronicle and Works* (5 vols, London, 1972); and D.W. Jones, *Haydn: his Life and Music* (London, 1988).

Haydn, (Johann) Michael

Austrian composer, younger brother of *Joseph Haydn (bap. 14 Sep 1737, Rohrau, Lower Austria; d. 10 Aug 1806, Salzburg).

His father was a self-taught musician who liked to involve the family in 'concerts' and Michael's fine voice earned him a place in the choir in St Stephen's Cathedral in Vienna where he studied Fux's *Gradus ad parnassum*. After his voice broke, he became freelance in the city before becoming *Kapellmeister to the Bishop of Grosswardein (in Hungary, now in Romania), where he stayed for five years. He then moved to an important position in Salzburg, that of *Konzertmeister* to Archbishop Schrattenbach, and met the young *W.A. Mozart, with whom he became friendly – in fact Mozart helped out the older man by writing works for him when he was unable to fulfil some of his compositional commissions. The Empress Maria Theresia sang the solo soprano part in a performance of his *Missa sotto il titulo di Teresia* in 1801 and she was much taken with the work. Prince Nikolaus II offered him the post of Vice-*Kapellmeister* in *Eszterháza (working under his brother Joseph) but he preferred to remain at Salzburg, where, in failing health, he died in 1806.

Haydn taught *C.M. von Weber, *Anton Diabelli and Sigismund Neukomm, and was admired by *Schubert and by W.A. Mozart, whose Requiem shows clear resemblances to Haydn's in C minor, written two decades before.

Works
Some 35 masses including two Requiems and other sacred and secular vocal works and stage works as well as over 40 symphonies, 12 concertos and many other instrumental works (divertimentos, dances, marches and a dozen string quartets).

Further reading
C.H. Sherman, *The Masses of Michael Haydn: a Critical Survey of Sources* (diss., U of Michigan, 1967). G. Croll and K. Vössing, *Johann Michael Haydn, sein Leben, sein Schaffen, seine Zeit: eine Bildbiographie* (Vienna, 1987).

Hebenstreit [Hebestreitt], Pantaleon
German pantaleon-player, violinist, dancing-master and composer (b. 27 Nov

1668, Kleinheringen, nr Naumburg; d. 15 Nov 1750, Dresden).

Little is known about his early life except that he appears to have been a student in Leipzig and then a tutor to a pastor's children in Merseburg, where he had fled to escape his debtors. His enjoyment of a primitive dulcimer in the local inn gave him the idea of developing it into something more refined and he was aided by the pastor, a craftsman, in producing an acceptable instrument. He and his dulcimer apparently attracted the attention of a passing courtier from Dresden, who arranged for a visit to the court. After this he was back in Leipzig, where Johann Kuhnau heard him, describing him as a '*maître de danse*'. After a period of practising in Berlin, he was appointed dancing-master to the court of Weissenfels. A visit to Paris in 1705 included a performance for Louis XIV who was so taken with the instrument and its player that he ordered it to be called the *'Pantaleon'; the name 'Pantalon' is occasionally used.

He was appointed dancing-master to the children at the court at Eisenach in 1706, where he expanded the musical facilities and was praised on several musical levels by Telemann, who became musical director two years later. When Telemann was appointed *Kapellmeister* over him, Hebenstreit left the court and embarked on a number of concert-tours with great success. He became chamber musician and pantaleon-player at the court of Dresden, soon becoming Vice-*Kapellmeister*, in which post he was largely responsible for *W.F. Bach being appointment as organist at the Sophienkirche in 1733.

Hebenstreit's declining eyesight caused a cessation in his playing and several small appointments provided for his old age. He took out a writ against *Gottfried Silbermann in 1727 as the latter was making many more pantaleons than Hebenstreit had commissioned from him. The popularity of the instrument faded with the piano's development, to which it contributed in no small measure. He taught J.C. Richter.

Works
Little known except for 10 orchestral suites; he probably made many arrangements for the pantaleon.

Further reading
F. Rollberg, 'Aus einer Thüringer Hofkapelle der Barockzeit: P. Hebenstreit, fürstliche Tanzmeister und Musikus G. Ph. Telemanns Eisenache Jahre', *Thüringer Fähnlein*, vi (1937). A. Egerland, 'Das Pantaleon', *Die Musikforschung*, xxiii (1970). C. Ahrens, 'Pantalon Hebenstreit und die Frühgeschichte des Hammerklaviers', *Beiträge zur Musikwissenschaft*, xxix/1 (1987). Fétis/*BIOGRAPHIE*. *MGG*.

Heilman, Matthäus
German keyboard-tuner, piano-maker (b. 10 May 1744, Hofheim am Taunus; d. 1798 or 1817, Mainz).

Little information is available. He worked in Mainz, of which he was made a freeman and a member of the Goldsmith's Guild. He established his piano-making and repair workshop and was appointed court tuner (and, by implication, repairer).

Heller, Stephen [István]
Hungarian (French naturalized) pianist, composer (b. 15 May 1813, Pest; d. 14 Jan 1888, Paris).

As a child, Heller studied piano with Franz Bauer and composition with an organist in Pest. He moved to Vienna to study with Carl *Czerny but, because of the high fees, he changed to Anton Halm through whom he met *Beethoven and *Schubert. His very successful debut in 1828 resulted in his father taking him on a two-year long concert tour encompassing Transylvania, Hungary, Poland and Germany and caused the 15-year-old boy to suffer a nervous breakdown. After his recuperation in Augsburg, he decided to stay there, living in the family home of one of his first pupils; he was encouraged by a local Count to study composition, which he did with the *Kapellmeister*, Hippolyte Chelard. His early Lieder were enthusiastically reviewed by *R. Schumann in the *Neue Zeitschrift für Musik*, and invited him to become the Augsburg correspondent. Heller settled in Paris in 1838 where he taught piano and was music critic of the *Gazette musicale*. His *L'art de phraser* (The Art of Phrasing, op. 16, 1840) and the concert-study *La chasse* (1844) made him famous as a composer of high-quality studies which, however, resulted in a degree of typecasting. His poor health and failing eyesight came to the attention of his friend, Charles Hallé and, in 1883, together with Robert Browning and Lord Leighton he set up a trust fund to support Heller. The latter was appointed a *Chevalier* of the Légion d'Honneur not long before his death.

Heller was adopted by Schumann under the *nom-de-plume* 'Jeanquirit' as one of the 'Davidsbündler', the fictional group of compositional 'good guys' after a favourable review by the older composer, and he foresaw a great career for Heller. His music was performed by *Liszt around Europe. Together with Liszt's own, his transcriptions of *Schubert's songs made the latter well-known in France. His very idiomatic and imaginative writing for piano influenced mainly later French composers, such as Massenet and Bizet, who admired him very much, and later Russian composers (Rakhmaninov and Medtner).

Works
Almost exclusively for piano, they include his set of studies *L'art de phraser* (The Art of Phrasing, op. 16, 1840), *La chasse* op. 29 (a concert-study, 1844), *25 études faciles* (Easy Studies) op. 45, *30 études progressives* op. 46 (both also 1844) and others, including a set of *21 technischen Studien als Vorbeitung zu den Werken Chopin*s (Technical Studies as Preparation for *Chopin's Works, 1879). There are many character-pieces, including *4 arabesques* op. 49, *Scènes pastorales* op. 50 (both 1844), *Spaziergänge eines Einsamer* op. 78 (Wanderings of a Solitary Man, 1851), three sets of pieces entitled *Im Walde* (In the Forest, 1854 onwards) and the *Blumen-, Frucht-, und Dormenstücke* op. 82 (Flower-, fruit- and Village-Pieces, 1853) as well as smaller dance-pieces, variations and arrangements.

Further reading
R. Booth, *The Life and Music of Stephen Heller* (diss., U of Iowa, 1969). J.-J. Eigeldinger, *Lettres d'un musicien romantique à Paris* (Paris, 1981). U. Müller-Kesten, *Stephen Heller, ein Klaviermeister der Romantik: biographische und stilkritische Studien* (Frankfurt, 1986). Fétis/*BIOGRAPHIE*. Marmontel/*PIANISTES*. Newman/SSB.

Henderson, J.
British piano-maker. All that is known of him is that he had a workshop at 56 Castle Street, East Oxford Street, London

and that he finished his trade there in 1835.

Hensel-Mendelssohn, Fanny (Cäcilie); [Mendelssohn (-Bartholdy)]
German composer, pianist (b. 14 Nov 1805, Hamburg; d. 14 May 1847, Berlin).
Sister of *Felix Mendelssohn, she came from a close-knit (though large) and wealthy family which gave them both a secure home, although political events caused some upheaval; her grandfather was the philosopher Moses Mendelssohn and the other grandfather, a banker, was financial adviser to Friedrich II. Her mother, one in a long line of independent cultured women, was the young girl's first teacher; she said that Fanny had 'Bach-fugue fingers' at her birth and she apparently could play *J.S. Bach's *Wohltemperirtes Clavier* from memory at the age of 13. She also studied piano with Ludwig *Berger and composition with Friedrich *Zelter, correspondent of Goethe. Pressure from the French forces to uphold a potentially ruinous trade blockade with England caused the family to flee to Berlin. During a family visit to Paris, she studied piano with Marie Bigot, of whom *J. Haydn and *Beethoven thought well; she also attended lectures on the science of geography (Humboldt) and physics (Holtei).
She married the court painter William Hensel in 1829, and a visit to Italy with him ten years later was a major cultural event in her life. She became the Mendelssohn family's cultural centre after her mother's death in 1842 and took charge of their series of Sunday-morning concerts in Berlin. Although these were nominally semi-private, they were large and frequently contained large choral and orchestral works including symphonies and concertos. In fact it was during the

rehearsals for one of these concerts, at which Felix' oratorio *Die erste Walpurgisnacht* was to be performed, that she died.

Fanny is an invaluable source of information on her brother, Felix and on concert-life in Germany. She was also a gifted composer and pianist, and six of her songs were published under his name (with his consent), since there was strong – though not acrimonious – family opposition to her becoming a jobbing musician of any kind. The Sunday concerts, in the running of which she first assisted her mother, and then took over, were important points of social congregation for cultured friends, many of whom went far beyond the family's musical circle and included Humboldt, Hegel and Ingres.

Works
Many (mostly vocal) remain unpublished; those which were include sets of songs (six were published in Felix's opp. 8 and 9 under his name) opp. 1, 9 and 10, the *Gartenlieder* (choral songs) op. 3, three sets of *Lieder onhe Worte* (Songs Without Words) opp. 2, 6 and 8, a piano trio op. 11 and other works for piano among them *Die Jahr* (The Year, a kind of musical diary written during her visit to Italy in 1939–40) and a Piano Sonata in G minor.

Further reading
V.R Sirota, *The Life and Works of Fanny Mendelssohn Hensel* (diss., Boston U., 1981). F. Tillard, *Fanny Mendelssohn* (Paris, 1992); Eng. tr., Portland, OR, 1996). Fétis/*BIOGRAPHIE*.

Henselt, (Georg Martin) Adolf (von)
German pianist, composer (b. 9 May 1814, Schwabach, Bavaria; d. 10 Oct 1889, Bad Warmbrunn, Silesia [now Cieplice Slaskie-Zdroj, Poland]).

After his studies with *Hummel in Weimar (with help from King Ludwig I) and *Sechter in Vienna and several German concert-tours, he settled in St Petersburg in 1838, becoming court pianist and imperial music-inspector. He visited England twice (1852 and 1867) but only played in private; during the second of these his playing of *Chopin was praised by Hipkins, remarking that the composer was 'difficult for Germans to interpret'. An important pianistic link between Hummel and *Liszt, he achieved a *legato* style and beautiful piano sonorities with minimum use of pedals and was hailed as one of the great pianists of his time by *R. Schumann, Liszt and others.

Works
Best known for two sets of musically-written studies, opp. 2 and 5 (12 each), the Piano Concerto in F minor op. 16, the Trio in A minor and a Duo for horn and piano as well as smaller salon pieces (*Wiegenlied, La Gondola*) and transcriptions, particularly of some of Weber's works.

Further reading
R.B. Davis, 'Henselt, Balakirev and the Piano, *MR*, xxviii (1967). G. Puchelt, *Verlorene Klage: Studien zu deutschen Klaviermusik 1830–80* (Berlin, 1969). A. Ho, *A Stylistic Analysis of the Piano Music of Adolph von Henselt* (diss., U. of Hawaii, Manoa, 1980).

Herder, Johann Gottfried
German Theologian, philosopher, writer (b. 25 Aug 1744, Mohrungen (East Prussia); d. 18 Dec 1803, Weimar).

Son of a teacher and Lutheran Kantor, he studied theology at Königsberg

University, where he knew Kant and became friends with Hamann, whose help gained him a teaching post at Riga, where he was ordained a Lutheran minister in 1767. He travelled to Paris in 1769 and met many of the leading minds in the city. On his return, he met Müthel, Lessing and Goethe (1770) and became tutor and travelling-companion of the Prince of Holstein-Gottorp during which period he got to know Latvian *folksong. As Chief Pastor at the court of Bückberg from (1771–76) he produced the texts for cantatas by *J.C.F. Bach. He moved to Weimar as general superintendent of the Lutheran Church and died there in 1803.

Herder coined the term *Volkslied (Folksong), seeing it as the true indicator of the soul of a people and collected, translated and wrote about it. Affected by the empiricism of Locke and the ideas of Hamann and Jean-Jacques *Rousseau he believed in the equal value of all nations (and regional identities) and considered primitive cultures to be superior to modern ones – because their sensory responses were less modified by rationality. He was at odds with Winckelmann's ideas of ancient Greek art as an ideal to be imitated, claiming, in a remarkably 'modern' way, that it was the product of its cultural environment and therefore not superior to any other such. His pantheistic ideas were espoused by Goethe, Schelling and Hegel, and Schleiermacher and the *Romantics in general were influenced in his attitude to The People and folk-song and folk-poetry.

Works
Tr. J.H. Moran and A. Gode, 'Essay on the Origin of Language', *On the Origin of Language* (Chicago, IL, 1966). Tr. T.O. Churchill, *Outlines of a Philosophy of the History of Man* (New York, 1966). Ed. and tr. Maria Bunge, *Against Pure Reason: Writings on Religion, Language, and History* (Minneapolis, MN, 1993).

Further reading
R.R. Ergang, *Herder and the Foundations of German Nationalism* (New York, 1966). W. Koepke, *Johann Gottfried Herder* (Boston, MA, 1987); ed., *Johann Gottfried Herder: Innovator throughout the Ages* (Bonn, 1982). H.B. Nisbet, *Herder and the Philosophy and History of Science* (Cambridge, 1970). R.E. Norton, *Herder's Aesthetics and the European Enlightenment* (Ithaca, NY, 1991).

Herold [Hérold], (Louis Joseph) Ferdinand

French composer (b. 28 Jan 1791, Paris; d. 19 Jan 1833, Paris).

He was taught by his father, a pianist, teacher and composer who had studied with *C.P.E. Bach. The young Hérold studied at the Paris Conservatoire – piano (Louis Adam), violin (Rodolphe Kreutzer), harmony (Catel) and composition (*Méhul) – winning the *premier prix* for piano in 1811 and the *Prix de Rome* (composition) in 1812, the same year in which he played his piano concerto in public. However, his inherited tuberculosis (which was to kill him) caused him to leave Rome and settle in Naples, where he taught at the court of the King of Naples. The success of his first opera there was the beginning of his lifelong interest in the genre. He spent two months in Vienna, meeting Salieri and *Hummel, and arrived back in Paris in 1815 to become accompanist at the Théatre Italien. His operatic career was bedevilled by the difficulty of finding good libretti and his works alternated between success and failure – among the former were *Les rosières* (*The Rose-Gatherers*) and *La clochette* (*The Little Bell*, both perf. 1817). In 1821 he was dispatched to Italy to find singers and returned with the soprano Pasta and the bass Galli as well as the score of *Rossini's *Mosè in Egitto* whose Parisian premiere he would direct the following year. He was at last fortunate in finding a good libretto and *Marie* was produced with great acclaim, having 100 performances within a year. In 1826 he became principal singing coach at the Opéra and wrote a number of ballets. In spite of the political situation – the 1830 revolution and the Parisian riots of 1832 – he wrote his masterpieces, *Zampa* (perf. with great success 1831) and *Le pré aux clercs*, which was given to tumultuous applause in 1832. Already terminally ill, his unfinished opera *Ludovic* was completed by Halévy.

Works

The operas *Les rosières* and *La clochette* (both 1817), *Le muletier* (1823), *Marie* (perf. 1826), *Zampa, ou la fiancée de marbre* (1831) and *Le pré aux clercs* (perf. 1832). Ballets include *La somnambule* (1827), *La fille mal gardée* (1828) and *La belle aux bois dormant* (1829). He also wrote four piano concertos, two symphonies, some chamber music and much for solo piano including sonatas, variations and operatic fantasies.

Further reading

I. Guest, *The Romantic Ballet in Paris* (London, 1966). A. de Place, *Le pianoforte à Paris entre 1760 et 1822* (Paris, 1986).

Herschel, Sir William [Friedrich Wilhelm]

German (English naturalized) musician, astronomer (b. 15 Nov 1738, Hanover; d. 25 Aug 1822, Slough).

Son of a military bandsman, Herschel at the age of 14, became oboist and violinist in the garrison's band. The family moved to England when Herschel senior was posted there at the outbreak of the Seven Years War (1756–63), but the regiment returned soon after its commencement and the young man left the army. He travelled to London, where he became a music copyist, and in 1760 moved to Sunderland to instruct the Durham military band and became acquainted with Charles Avison and other musical notaries in the North. He also studied languages and mathematics and wrote 18 symphonies. A performance for the Duke of York (with Avison) brought him into contact with the English royal family. After five years in Bath as organist at the Octagon, he returned *via* Paris to Hanover in 1772 and brought his sister, Caroline, back to Bath, to help him with astronomy (which was beginning to occupy more and more of his time); he helped her as a soprano vocalist. Herschel was made a member of the Bath Literary and Philosophical Society in 1780 and delivered many lectures to it. In 1781 he discovered a new planet – now called Uranus – for which the Royal Society gave him a medal and made him a member. He also discovered several planetary moons, over 2,000 nebulae and over 800 double stars as well as infra-red solar rays (in 1800). A year later (1782), in an audience with George III at Windsor, he accepted the post of Astronomer Royal and was granted a modest pension which allowed him to devote his time to scientific research and amateur music-making. As well as scientific luminaries, visitors to the Herschel home included *J. Haydn and *Burney, and he took British citizenship in 1793. After much travelling, he had interviews with Napoleon and Laplace in France, was knighted in 1817 and appointed first President of the Royal Astronomical Society.

Works (musical)
Larger works (24 symphonies, about 12 concertos, mostly for wind) – very influenced by the *empfindsamer Stil* – and smaller works (trios, accompanied sonatas, and many keyboard (mostly organ) pieces) couched in the *galant* style of *J.C. Bach. Also sacred vocal music (anthems).

Further reading
A.J. Turner, *Science and Music in Eighteenth-century Bath* (Bath, 1977). J.B. Sedgwick, *William Herschel, Explorer of the Heavens* (London, 1954). I. Woodfield, *The Celebrated Quarrell between Thomas Linley (senior) and William Herschel: an Episode in the Musical Life of Eighteenth-century Bath* (Bath, 1977). F. Brown, *William Herschel: Musician and Composer* (Bath, 1990).

Herz, Henri [Heinrich]
German pianist, composer, teacher (b. 6 Jan 1803, Vienna; d. 5 Jan 1888, Paris).
As a child he studied the piano with his father and with the father of the pianist-composer *Hünten, and later, from the age of thirteen, with Pradher and *Reicha at the Paris Conservatoire, where he was made professor of piano after his studies in 1842. He toured widely in various European countries – including Spain and Russia – as well as South America (1845) and traversed the United States three times between 1845 and 1851, where he gave over 400 concerts. His interest in the piano extended to the construction of the instrument and he became a shareholder in a piano-making business which failed, embroiling him in debt. However, he

established his own factory in 1851 with much greater success and his instruments won first prize in the Paris Exhibition of 1855, placing them in the league of *Erard and *Pleyel. He also founded, with his brother, the Ecole spéciale de piano in Paris through the doors of which many distinguished pupils of the next generation passed.
Herz's style in playing and composing was of a similar cut to that of *Hummel, *Field and *Moscheles of the previous generation, but, in spite of its elegance, it was often criticized – by *R. Schumann among others – for emptiness and for courting virtuosity for its own sake.

Works
Many pieces which are for, or include, piano: variations, fantasies, concertos and his travel journal *Mes voyages en Amérique* (Paris, 1866; Eng. tr. 1963).

Further reading
D. Garvelmann, Introduction to *H. Herz, Variations on Non più mesta* (New York, 1970). Fétis/*BIOGRAPHIE*. Marmontel/*PIANISTES. MGG*.

Heterophony (from Gk. *heteros*, 'different' and *phone*, 'voice')
Simultaneous sounding of a given part and its variation(s). It is common practice in many ethnic art-musics and widespread in *folk music, especially when appearing as simultaneous but differently-*decorated instrumental and vocal part(s), as in Irish folk music and Gaelic (Scottish Highland) psalm-singing.

Further reading
T. Knudsen, 'Ornamental Hymns/Psalms Singing in Denmark, the Faroe Islands and the Hebrides', *DFS Information*, 68/2 (1968). *MGG*.

Hoffmann, E(rnst) T(heodor)
A(madeus) [Ernst Theodor Wilhelm]
German writer composer, artist (b. 24 Jan
1776, Königsberg [now Kaliningrad]; d.
25 Jun 1822, Berlin).

His father, a high-ranking lawyer, was
separated from his wife, Hoffmann's
mother, with whom he lived in his
grandmother's home. Both of the women
were recluses and the boy's well-being
and education was undertaken by an
intelligent but uninspiring uncle, whose
quarters he shared. He enrolled in the
faculty of law in Königsberg University
in early 1792, although he continued to
study music – piano with Carl Gottlieb
Richter and theory with C.W. Podbielski
– and painting as well. He had written a
three-volume novel by the age of 19 and
had begun work on another; both are lost.
On completion of his legal studies he was
appointed junior lawyer but a failed love-
affair forced him to move to Glogau to
stay with another maternal uncle, with
whom he moved to Berlin in 1798 and
who successfully recommended him for
a position in the Supreme Court. He got
to know B.A. Weber and had composition
lessons with J.F. *Reichardt and his first
public outing as a composer took place
on New Years' Eve, 1800 with a cantata
for the new century. In 1802 he married
and was appointed *Regierungsrat*
(Administrative Adviser) but this was
annulled when he was discovered to have
been drawing unflattering caricatures of
the town worthies and he was exiled to
southern Prussia, where several attempts
to have his music published failed.

He was transferred to Warsaw in 1804
and found the musical life so congenial
and encouraging that he could afford to
give up his legal work. He had an opera
produced and his conductorship of a local
orchestral society allowed him to try

out works in public. Political events in
the wake of French occupation began to
hamper Hoffmann in a number of ways
and he moved to Bamberg to take up the
post of theatre director, only to find that
the management had changed and the
post given elsewhere. He remained on
the fringes of theatrical life as a semi-
salaried theatre composer, the meagre
recompense from which he supplemented
by teaching singing and *piano. Most of
the short incidental works he wrote for the
theatre at this time have been lost. It was
about this time that he dropped his third
name Wilhelm in favour of Amadeus, in
homage to *W.A. Mozart.

His literary career, however, was
taking off. His first publication, a
story ('Ritter Gluck') led to his being
commissioned for musical criticisms in the
Allgemeine musikalische Zeitung and his
groundbreaking review of *Beethoven's
Fifth Symphony appeared in 1810. He
remained as a regular contributor to
the magazine for another five years.
A literary contract produced several
works including the first two volumes
of his *Fantasiestücke in Callots Manier*
(*Fantasias after Callot*, Easter 1814),
but musical fame eluded him. In April
1813 he moved to Leipzig for another
theatrical post, but this lasted less than
a year and the out-of-work 38-year-old
finally resigned himself to recommencing
his first career. As a brilliant lawyer, he
was appointed supreme court judge
in 1814 and could set himself to his
creative tasks with an easier mind. His
long-cherished desire to stage his opera
Undine was finally realized (though he
was not involved in its presentation) and
it was a great success. He also earned a
good deal of money for his folk-inspired
stories. He died in 1822 of an unknown
illness, involving paralysis.

A leading figure of German literary *Romanticism, he admired *The Monk* (Matthew Lewis) and the work of Laurence Sterne and championed the fantastic and the supernatural in his writings, often through the medium of folk-like narrative. Works of his formed the basis of Offenbach's operetta *Tales of Hoffmann*, Tchaikovsky's *Nutcracker* ballet and *R. Schumann's *Kreisleriana*. A gifted composer, especially of *Singspiel*, his opera *Undine* exerted great influence on the early-nineteenth-century *Singspiel* tradition, especially *C.M. von Weber's contribution, and an analysis of his dark, horrific story 'Der Sandmann' is the basis of Sigmund Freud's essay 'Des Unheimlichs' ('The Uncanny', 1919). This story is also the basis of the ballet *Coppélia* (Delibes) and the opera *La poupée de Nuremberg* (A. Adam). His music reviews set the tone for nineteenth-century criticism, distinguishing between form and content and helped, in his Beethoven criticisms, to justify the composer's genius and place him in a historical perspective – and in the *Canon.

Works

Literary Several collections of stories and shorter pieces (*Fantasiestücke in Callots Manier* (*Fantasias after Callot*, 1813–15)), *Nachtstücke* (*Night Pieces*, 1815), *Die Serapions-Brüder* (*The Brotherhood of Serapion*, 1819–21) *The Golden Pot and Other Tales* (tr. R. Robertson (Oxford, 1992)); some novels (*Die Elixiere des Teufels* (*The Devil's Elixir*, 1815–16), *Lebensansichten des Kater Murrs*, 1820–21 (tr. A. Boli as *Life and Opinions of the Tomcat* (London, 1999)).

Musical Many *Singspiel*, including *Die lustigen Musikanten* [*The Happy Minstrels*,

1799]; *Der Trank der Unsterblichkeit* [*The Drink of Immortality*, 1808]; *Aurora* (1812); *Undine* (1816) and other vocal works. Some chamber (a Piano trio in E major, 1809) and orchestral (a Symphony in E♭ major, 1805–1806) works and some for piano (Sonatas in F minor and F major (both ?1807) and in C♯ minor (1808)). Many lost works (not included in these titles).

Further reading
H.W. Hewett-Thayer, *Hoffmann, Author of the 'Tales'* (Princeton, NJ, 1948). R. Taylor, *Hoffmann, a Study of Romanticism* (London, 1963). R. Murray Schafer, *E.T.A. Hoffmann and Music* (Toronto, 1975). D. Kremer, *E.T.A. Hoffmann. Erzählungen und Romane* (Berlin, 1999). F. Schnapp, ed., *Der Musiker E.T.A. Hoffmann. Selbtzeugnisse, Dokumente und zeitgenössische Urteile* (Hildesheim, 1981). D. Charlton, ed., *E.T.A. Hoffmann's Musical Writings* (Cambridge, 1989).

Holmes, Edward
English critic, organist and teacher (b. 10 Nov 1799, Hoxton; d. 28 Aug 1859, London)

Son of a tradesman, Holmes was influenced by the literary scholar Charles Cowden-Clarke at whose father's school he was educated and became friendly with Keats there also. After an apprenticeship to a London bookseller, he went to live as a musical apprentice in the London home of Vincent Novello where he got to know, among others, Shelley, Leigh Hunt, Hazlitt, the Lambs, *Attwood, *Hummel, S.S. Wesley, *J.B. Cramer, *Felix Mendelssohn and *Liszt. Holmes became music critic of the *Atlas* on its foundation in 1826 and the following year he toured Europe, the outcome of which was the famous *A Ramble among the Musicians* *of Germany* (published in 1828, under the pseudonym of 'a music professor'). He also wrote for *Frazer's Magazine* and *The Spectator* and began a biography of *W.A. Mozart, for whose music he had a passion; this appeared in print in 1845, and had occasioned another Continental tour. He became organist at a church in Poplar, East London in 1833 and taught the piano. In 1845 he joined the staff of the *Musical Times*, recently founded by Novello, and visited America in 1749–50. He married the daughter of the composer Samuel Webbe in 1857 and died two years later.

Due to Holmes's wide educational and, especially, musical background, his music criticism gave respectability and authority to the genre in English and his first-hand accounts of musical life in Europe as well as detailed information on some of its greatest composers. His life of Mozart was the fullest account in English and a model for his successors.

Works
A Ramble among the Musicians of Germany ... [by a Music Professor] (London, 1828); *The Life of Mozart* (London 1845, rev. 4/1991); articles on *Berlioz, Purcell, and various aspects of Mozart's music.

Further reading
E. Newman, Preface to E. Holmes, *The Life of Mozart* (London, 1912). E.D. Mackerness, 'Edward Holmes (1797–1859)', *ML*, xlv (1964). L. Langley, *The English Musical Journal in the early nineteenth Century* (diss., U. of North Carolina, 1983).

Home, sweet Home
Song by Sir Henry *Bishop to words by J.H. Payne (1791–1852) composed in 1821 as a '*Sicilian Air*' for a book of national songs and incorporated into Bishop's opera *Clari* (1823). One of the archetypal drawing-room ballads (see *Ballad (3)), it was used by Donizetti in his opera *Anna Bolena* in a varied form.

Homophony
A musical texture in which one of a series of parts or 'voices' – though they may be purely instrumental – is discernibly melodic and the others accompanimental, usually chordal. (Compare *monody and *polyphony.)

Hornpipe
(1) A wind instrument consisting of one (or more commonly two joined) simple pipe(s) made from wood or bone whose sound is produced by a vibrating cane reed. A bell of cowhorn is normally fixed to the open end. It occurred throughout the ancient world and in modern Europe including England, Scotland, Wales and Cornwall and is associated with shepherds.

(2) A dance common in Britain and Ireland with affinities to the *jig in 3/2, 2/2 or 4/4 time; it does not appear to have any connection with the instrumental definition of the term ((1) above) but with the fiddle, *bagpipe and harp. It is known as a *folk dance for hundreds of years and as a dance in *suites – by Purcell, Holborne, Byrd, *Arne, *Handel et al. – from the sixteenth century, where it lost its triple-*metre form. Characteristically a solo dance, with minimum (if any) movement of hands, arms and upper body, it also existed as a couple-dance and as a group-dance in sets of *country dances. Its particular association with seamen seems to have no real basis in fact, although *Handel's *Water Music* contains some examples and the myth

is perpetuated in *Gilbert and Sullivan's nautical operettas. The famous 'Sailor's Hornpipe' (properly called the 'College Hornpipe') is not a typical hornpipe.

Further reading
E. Sherman, 'Music in Thomas Hardy's Life and Work', *MQ, xxvi* (1940). D. O'Sullivan, *Irish Folk-music and Song* (Dublin 1952). L. Blake, *Welsh Folk Dances and Costume* (Llangollen, 1954). J.F. Flett, T.M. Flett and F. Rhodes, *Traditional Dancing in Scotland* (London, 1964). G. Emmerson, 'The Hornpipe', *Folk Music Journal*, ii/1 (1970).

'How dear to me the hour'
A song from Thomas *Moore's *Irish Melodies* ['*Moore's Melodies*'].

Hüllmandel [Hullmandel], **Nicolas-Joseph** [Jean Nicolas, James Nicolas] Alsatian composer, performer (b. 23 May 1756, Strasbourg; d. 19 Dec 1823, London).

Both parents were musicians and he also studied, when a chorister at Strasbourg cathedral, with Joseph Garnier and/or F.X. Richter and possibly later with *C.P.E. Bach. Moved from Strasbourg to Paris about 1776 and moved with ease and success in higher social circles, dedicating his op. 1 to Marie-Antoinette. Hüllmandel is reputed to have been in the service of the Duc de Guines, French ambassador to London (and patron of *W.A. Mozart), which must have facilitated his flight, with his wife (niece of the Receiver-General) to London after the beginning of the Revolution in 1789. He appeared to cease composition after his op. 12 (1796), devoting himself to teaching and performing on the piano and *glass harmonica. He died at the age of 72 in London.

One of the earliest devotees of the piano, he wrote well and sensitively for the instrument and, in spite of many of his accompanied sonatas heavily favouring the keyboard, his op. 6/3 violin sonata (1782) has the instruments immediately on an equal footing, with several instances of the violin leading. He wrote the article 'Clavecin' for the *Encyclopédie méthodique* of Diderot and d'Alembert but his projected entry on 'Piano' was cut short by his flight to London. His op. 12 *Principles of Music* ... (London 1996), together with his espousal of the *piano as opposed to the *harpsichord, influenced many following. His pupils included Jadin, Onslow, Auber and Gounod's mother.

Works
His output of 12 opus numbers divides almost equally between pieces written for solo harpsichord or piano – though his penchant was for the latter – and for those instruments with violin *ad lib* or occasionally *obbligato*.

Further reading
R. Benton, *N.-J. Hüllmandel and French Instrumental Music in the Second Half of the 18th Century* (diss., U of Iowa, 1961); 'N.-J. Hüllmandel (1756–1823), quelques aspects de sa vie et de ses œuvres', *Revue de Musicologie*, xlvii (1961). Fétis/ *BIOGRAPHIE*. Newman/SCE.

Hummel, Johann Nepomuk
Austrian composer, pianist, teacher, conductor (b. 14 Nov 1778, Pressburg [now Bratislava]; d. 17 Oct 1837, Weimar).

Son of a practising musician who gave him his early grounding in music, Johann was a prodigy, reading music and playing piano and violin by the age of six. The family moved to Vienna when he was eight, so that his father could take up the post of music director at the Theater auf der Wieden. Almost immediately, Johann became a pupil of *W.A. Mozart, apparently without fee, living in his home for two years. In 1788 he suggested that Hummel's father take the boy on a European tour which was destined to last four years. Their first stop was Prague, meeting *J.L. Dussek, and their next Dresden, where the boy played in his first concert, including a set of his own variations. Their success spurred them on to visit Berlin (where Mozart was in the audience), Magdeburg, Göttingen, Brunswick, Kassel, Weissenstein (where Johann suffered from smallpox), Hanover, Celle, Hamburg, Kiel, Lübeck and Copenhagen, among others.

They arrived to great acclaim in Edinburgh in the spring of 1790 and settled – both of them – to teaching, which allowed them to retrench financially and to improve their English. They travelled south towards London in the summer, giving concerts in Durham and Cambridge and arrived in London in the autumn, where they got to know the visiting *J. Haydn. The young prodigy's first concert was probably May 1792 in the Hanover Square Rooms, in which he played a Mozart piano concerto and some pieces of his own. The subscription list for his op. 2 (three sets of variations on British tunes) attests to his great success, with 92 subscribers from Vienna and 159 from London. Projected tours in France and Spain had to be abandoned because of the Revolutionary wars and they headed for Holland, spending two months in The Hague (where the boy played every Sunday for the Prince of Orange). Napoleon's advance finally caused their moving on through Amsterdam, Cologne,

Bonn, Mainz, Frankfurt am Main and Linz, arriving home in Vienna in early 1793.

Hummel spent the next ten years on study, composition and teaching, learning counterpoint from Albrechtsberger, vocal compositions and musical philosophy and aesthetics from Salieri. Haydn, whom he knew from their London visit, gave him organ lessons on his return from England in 1795. The appearance of *Beethoven in Vienna daunted Hummel as it did all the other aspiring young composer-performers, but the two became friends – on and off.

Haydn recommended Hummel for his own post with the *Esterházy family at Eisenstadt and he became *Konzertmeister* to Prince Nikolaus; he was, in fact, *Kapellmeister* in all but name, since Haydn retained that title. All his sacred and most of his theatrical compositions were written for his Esterházy appointment. Hummel had more than one eye on Viennese audiences, since he composed a good deal of music for venues in the capital. He was facilitated in this by his father's appointment as director of the *Apollosaal, the public dance-halls for the opening of which Hummel junior wrote the music and for which he supplied a steady stream of dances. He was dismissed from his post at the end of 1808 but, probably because of his connection with Haydn, was reinstated until May 1811, when the contract was ended and he returned to Vienna. Here he composed a number of instrumental and dramatic works and married the famous singer, Elisabeth Röckl in 1813. He took part in a performance (playing percussion) of Beethoven's *'Battle' Symphony, conducted by the composer, and received the great man's equivalent of a 'thank-you' note. At the same time he was persuaded by his wife to return to the stage as a pianist, and he made a great impression – and many valuable contacts – with the foreign visitors and dignitaries visiting Vienna for the *Congress of Vienna. He toured Germany with great success in 1816, but realized that a man with a young family – two sons – to support needed something more stable. He was appointed *Kapellmeister in Stuttgart but the terms were very uncongenial, especially in that leave for concert tours was very grudged, and he resigned after less than two years. The immediate reason was his appointment as grand-ducal *Kapellmeister at Weimar, and his new contract included a three-month annual leave for concert-tours; in addition, he was excused any involvement with the sacred music, since the court was Protestant and Hummel was a Catholic. His main preoccupation was with the opera, and he had a great deal of freedom in this. Goethe was also attached to the Weimar court and through him he met the intelligentsia of Europe. Composition continued unabated, mostly for his own use on his tours and centring on the piano, but also vocal music for the court and the Masonic lodge, and arrangements of his own and others' works as well as a busy teaching schedule. His main recreation during these years was gardening. His tours traversed much of mainland Europe, especially Paris, meeting *Field in Russia (1822) and *Chopin in Poland (1828). On hearing of the impending death of Beethoven, he and his wife (with his pupil Ferdinand Hiller) rushed to Vienna, a meeting to which Beethoven evidently looked forward. Hummel was a pallbearer at his funeral and, following Beethoven's wish, improvised on his works at the memorial concert. He also met *Schubert, with whom he got on well,

and he dedicated his last three sonatas to Hummel; however, by the time they were published, both composers were dead and the works were published with a dedication to *R. Schumann.

Hummel's tour of 1830 was a momentous one, as he had two years' worth of leave to combine (six months in all) and it included his first visit to Britain since his childhood 40 years earlier. Two further tours were less successful, partly because of the coincidental presence of *Paganini. His last tour, to Vienna in 1834 was only moderately successful and he died in 1837, honoured by a performance of Mozart's *Requiem*.

Hummel was considered to be one of the greatest composers and pianists of his time, and was possibly the greatest improviser beside Beethoven. His classical elegance and neatness as a pianist and his superb tone was constantly praised. His preference was for the Viennese piano and he is considered one of the main transmitters of the high Classical style of Mozart and Haydn to the nineteenth century. He was admired and emulated by many composers, including *Chopin (who mentions him as being on a par with Haydn and Mozart), Schubert, Schumann, *Brahms and *Felix Mendelssohn. His fluency and clarity as a pianist was much envied, and his *Piano School*, although late in coming, was greatly respected.

Works
Instrumental Many for solo piano, including variations (*Adagio, Variations and Rondo on 'The Pretty Polly'* op. 75 (*c*.1817)), potpourris, caprices, fantasies (in E♭ major op. 18 (*c*.1805) *Rondo quasi una fantasia* op. 19 (*c*.1806), *Recollections of Paganini* (?1831)), dances (*La bella capricciosa, polonaise* (*c*.1811–15)), six

sonatas (including no. 3 in F minor, op. 20 (*c*.1807), no. 5 in F♯ minor op. 81 (1819) and no. 6 in D major (1824)), two sonatas and other pieces for piano duet. Chamber music: including flute/violin sonatas op. 50 in D major (*c*.1810–14), op. 64 in A major (*c*.1814–15), a cello sonata in A major op. 104 (1824); piano trios, *Adagio, Variations and Rondo on 'Schöne Minka'* in A major op. 78 (piano, flute and cello, *c*.1818); three string quartets (C, G, E♭, majors (bef. 1804)) the Piano Quintet in E♭ minor op. 87 (violin, viola, cello, double bass and piano, 1802); septets in D minor op. 74 (piano, flute, oboe, bassoon, viola, cello and double bass, *c*.1816) and C major op. 114 ('*Militaire*', piano, flute, violin, clarinet, cello, trumpet and double bass – also arranged for the same instruments as op. 87 – both 1829). Various pieces for piano and orchestra (including concertos in C major op. 34a and op. 36 (c.1811) in A minor op. 85 (c.1816), in B minor op. 89 (1819)); *Variations in B flat on a theme from the Berlin Singspiel 'Das Fest der Handwerker'* op. 115 (1830), *Oberons Zauberhorn*, fantasy (1829), *Gesellschafts Rondo* in D major op. 117 (1829); Trumpet Concerto, E♭ major S49 (1803), Concerto for Piano and Violin in G major op. 17 (*c*.1805); many sets of dances for orchestra.

Vocal   Some 20 operas (inc. *Pimmalione* S22 (?*c*.1805–15), *Mathilde von Guise* op. 100 (perf. 1810), *Die Eselshaut, oder Die blaue Insel* S101 (perf. 1814), *Attila* S163 (*c*.1825–27)), ballets and pantomimes and incidental music. Sacred: five masses (B♭, E♭, and D majors and D minor and *Missa Solemnis* in C major (1806)) and other works; songs and partsongs. His *Ausführlich theoretisch-practische Anweisung zum Piano-forte Spiel* ['*Piano*

School'] was written *c*.1822–25 and published in 1828.

Further reading
K. Benyovszky, *J.N. Hummel: der Mensch und Künstler* (Bratislava, 1934) and *Hummel und seine vateratadt* (Bratislava, 1937). F.H. Mitchell, *The Piano Concertos of Johann Nepomuk Hummel* (diss., Northwestern U., 1957). R. Davis, 'The Music of J.N. Hummel, its Derivation and Development', *MR*, xxvi (1965). D. Zimmerschied, *Die Kammermusik Johann Nepomuk Hummels* (diss., U. of Mainz, 1966). J. Sachs, 'Hummel and the Pirates: the Struggle for Musical Copyright', *MQ*, lix (1973); *Kapellmeister Hummel in England and France* (Detroit, MI, 1977). D.G. Brock, 'The Church Music of Hummel', *MR*, xxxi (1970). D. Carew, *The Composer/Performer Relationship in the Works for and including Piano of J.N. Hummel* (diss., U. of Leicester, 1984) and 'Hummel's Op. 81, a paradigm for Brahm's Op. 2?', *Ad Parnassum*, vol. 3(6), October 2005. K. Thomas, *Johann Nepomuk Hummel und Weimar* (Weimar, 1987). H. Schmid, ed., *Johann Nepomuk Hummel, ein Komponist zur Zeit der Wiener Klassik: Eisenstadt 1987* (Eisenstadt, 1989).

Hünten, Franz
German composer, piano teacher (b. 26 Dec 1793, Koblenz; d. 22 Feb 1878, Koblenz).

   Son of the court organist of Koblenz who also taught the piano, the young boy was discouraged by his father in his desire to be a musician, although showing promise in composition. Nevertheless, he enrolled at the Paris Conservatoire in 1819, studying with Pradher for piano and with *Reicha and *Cherubini for composition. He settled in Paris two years later where he made a name for himself as a *salon* composer and became fashionable as a piano teacher. He retired to Koblenz in 1848, remaining there until his death thirty years later.

Works
Hunten wrote technically-undemanding music, mostly for amateurs and mostly for piano: many variation-sets, rondos, fantasias, dances and character-pieces for solo piano and for piano duet; four Piano Trios and various character pieces for violin and piano as well as some songs.

Further reading
W. Georgii, *Klaviermusik* (Zurich, 1941, 5/1976). G. Zöllner, *Franz Hünten: sein Leben und sein Werk* (Cologne, 1959). *MGG*.

Hurdy-gurdy (Fr. *Vielle* [*à roue*], *chifonie*; Ger. *Leier, Radleier*; It. *ghironda, lyra tedesca, sambuca*; Lat. *symphonia, organistrum*)
A stringed keyboard instrument shaped vaguely like a viol, lute or guitar consisting of a set of two melody strings and two sets of two string drones, all bowed by a wooden resined wheel turned by one of the player's hands or by a second player. Melody-notes are produced by a keyboard of some one to two octaves (usually chromatic) to which tangents are attached which, when depressed, push the strings against the rotating wheel and stopping them at pre-ordained points. Various sound-effects can be achieved by articulation of the keys and the speed and motion of the bow-wheel. It is played on the lap or suspended under the chest by a neck-strap. Originating in the Orient, it was widespread in Europe in the Gothic period and the Middle Ages used by the Church and the laity. It was widespread as a *folk instrument but particularly popular in France where, having died out in the rest of Europe, it is still used in the *Massif Centrale*.

The fashion for Louis XIV's court for all things *pastoral caused the hurdy-gurdy to be taken up by the French aristocracy in their *fêtes champetres* (outdoor pastoral entertainments where they dressed as peasants) and several composers have written pieces and *suites for the instrument in its various forms including Boismortier, Naudot and Chédeville. Vivaldi included it in some of his set of sonatas published in *c.*1737 as *Il pastor fido* [*The Faithful Shepherd*] and *W.A. Mozart in his German Dances K602 (1791), and the 'lira organizzata' for which *J. Haydn wrote concertos (?1786–87) to the King of Naples's commission was probably for a close relative, the *Geigenwerk*. Donizetti also used it as an accompanying instrument in his opera *Linda di Chamounix* (perf. 1842).

Further reading
F. Ll. Harrison and J. Rimmer, *European Musical Instruments* (London, 1964). F.W. Galpin, *Old English Instruments of Music* (London, rev.4/1965). A. Buchner, *Folkmusic Instruments of the World* (London, 1971).

I

Idée fixe (Fr.: 'fixed idea', 'obsession')
A term coined by *Berlioz to characterize
a recurring theme in his *Symphonie
fantastique* (1830). The symphony
represents aspects of his love-affair with
the Irish Shakespearian actress, Harriett
Smithson and she is represented by the
theme, which undergoes modifications
according to the different emotional
contexts of the five movements. It was
recalled in his monodrama *Lélio* (1831–
32). His symophony *Harold en Italie* also
has a (different) *idée fixe*. The term was
used by Balzac at about the same time
and passed into psychiatry.

Impromptu, impromptu **performance**
(see *Improvisation)

Improvisation (NB only musical
improvisation is dealt with here)
(1) The almost simultaneous creation and
performance of music: the virtual lack
of preparation and lack of notated score
before and after the event is understood.

Always considered as a prime
attribute of highly creative musicians,
it was prized in the *Baroque and
*Classical periods and had something
of a heyday in the public performances
of the virtuoso-composers (especially
pianists) in the early nineteenth century,
after which it died out apart from in the
province of organists. It is basic to many
non-Western art-musics, ethnic musics,
jazz and some forms of popular and pop
music and surfaced in a very free, and
often collective, form in the second half
of the twentieth century.

(2) The technique is 'built into' other
musical activities, such as *figured bass

and *preluding and is called into play in
musical *decoration and interpretation.

(3) The word and its derivatives have
been used to suggest music of a free or
improvisational nature, occasionally
appearing in titles (such as Rubbra's
*Improvisations on Virginal Pieces by
Giles Farnaby* (1939)).

Incendie par l'orage, L' (Fr.: 'The Fire
after the Storm')
Title given to *Field's Piano Concerto
No. 5 in C major, because of its storm
interlude.

[International] Standard Pitch
Historically, pitching of scales has
varied considerably between countries,
areas, institutions, musical venues and
individual instruments, often by as much
as a tone and a half. This was due to many
factors, such as changes in temperature,
wear and tear of instrumental parts
– organ-pipes, for example – and the
need/desirability for greater brilliance in
larger public venues. The agreed standard
of pitching for musical performances on
conventional (that is, non-electronic)
instruments is, at present, a' = 440 Hz
[Herz], arrived at after an international
conference in 1885 in Vienna. This
discussed, among other related matters,
the temperature at which an orchestra
should tune and its agreement was
endorsed by British Standards Institution
Conference in 1938, accepted by the
International Standardising Organisation
(ISO) in London (May, 1939) and
reaffirmed by them in 1953. The standard
is not to everyone's satisfaction.

Inversion
(1) A melodic procedure by which a
given melody is turned upside down, so

that each movement (whether by *step or leap) is reproduced in the opposite direction. Thus, a move of a 5th upward from C to G would be inverted to become a move of a 5th downward from C to F. Inversion can be exact, or strict, in that each interval is exactly reproduced, e.g. the upward movement from E to F (a semitone) is inverted to become a move of E down to E♭ (also a semitone). Inversion may also be free, a minor 3rd in one direction (say, F to D) becoming a major 3rd in the other (F to A).

(2) The complement of an interval with respect to the octave, found by reversing the notes (C to D; D to C). This can be reckoned as a subtraction from nine (as the note in common between the intervals is counted twice), so that a 3rd becomes a 6th, a 4th inverts to a 5th, etc. The type of interval also changes, for example, major inverts to minor (and *vice versa*), diminished to augmented (and *vice versa*), while perfect intervals (unison, octave, 4ths and 5ths) remain perfect. Thus a major 2nd (A up to B) inverts to become a minor 7th (B up to A). Invertible *counterpoint is an extension of this principle in which either the given part or its inversion may act as a bass line.

(3) Changing the position of a chord so that one of its notes other than the root (or fundamental note) appears as the bass. Thus the chord of C-E-G (the chord of C major) has C in the bass in its root position but its first and second inversions have, respectively, E and G in the bass. The positions of the upper two notes is immaterial for theoretical purposes; it is the note on the bottom which determines the inversion.

Ionian mode (see *Modes)

Irish Melodies (see *Moore)

'Italian' Concerto (*Concerto nach italienischen Gusto*, 'Concerto after the Italian Style')
A piece in F major (BWV 971) which, in spite of its name, was written for solo harpsichord by *J.S. Bach in 1735. The concerto element derives from its use of different *registration on the two *manuals of the instrument, indicated by the simultaneous markings of *piano* and *forte* in the score and giving the impression of a *tutti/solo alternation. The three movements are i. [no tempo indication] 2/4 in F major; ii. Andante 3/4 in D minor; iii. Presto, ℂ, F major.

Italian Symphony
Title given by *Mendelssohn to his Fourth Symphony in A major op. 90 (1830–32) which he began in Rome during his Italian sojourn of the same dates. The four movements are: i. Allegro vivace, A major, 6/8; ii. Andante con moto D minor 4/4; iii. Con moto moderato A major 3/4; iv. Saltarello, Presto A minor 4/4.

J

Jack

The part of a harpsichord's mechanism to which is attached the *plectrum, which plucks the string, causing it to sound.

Jackson, George K(nowil)

English (naturalized American) composer, teacher and editor (bap. 15 Apr 1757, Oxford; d. 18 Nov 1822, Boston, MA).

Little is known about his early life; he lived in Oxford and London, studying, apparently, under Nares at the Chapel Royal and gaining his honorary DMus at St Andrews University in 1791. He was in the United States (New Brunswick, New Jersey) by 1797 and became known for his private academy and his concert-series. He lived in New York, 1801–12 where he continued with his concerts and teaching and when he moved to Boston in 1812, he played a key role in its musical life, becoming a consultant for the new *Handel and *[J.] Haydn Societies there.

Works

Various sacred vocal works, including *David's Psalms* (Boston, MA, 1804), Masonic Songs and instrumental works, including piano works. He also edited collections of music, such as *The Choral Companion* (Boston, MA, 1814) and *A Choice Collection of Chants in 4 Voices* (Boston, MA, 1816) and published *A Treatise on Practical Thoroughbass ... Composition and Modulation* (London, 1785) and *Instruction Book to the Piano Forte* (New York, 1825).

Further reading

H.E. Johnson, 'George K. Jackson, Doctor of Music (1745–1822)', *MQ*, xix (1943). C.H. Kaufman, *George K. Jackson:*

American Musician of the Federal Period (diss., New York U., 1968).

Janissary Music (see *Turkish music)

Jansen [Janson Jansson; Bartolozzi], Therese (née Jansen)

German (naturalized British) pianist (b. *c*.1770, ?Aachen; d. 1843, Calais).

Daughter of a dancing-master in Aachen she was much in demand as a piano teacher at her home in London, where she lived with her brother, also a teacher (and composer) until her marriage to the picture dealer Gaetano Bartolozzi (son of the engraver Francesco). A pupil of *Clementi, she met *J. Haydn during his London visits and so impressed him with her pianistic brilliance that he dedicated several works to her, including his last three piano sonatas. Haydn was, in fact, one of the witnesses at her wedding. Gaetano, a talented violin and viola player, did so well in business that he could afford to buy an estate outside Venice. The couple had a daughter in 1797, who would become the celebrated dancer Madame Vestris. Soon after they went to France where mother and daughter were left for a year or so with the Spanish ambassador to England, a friend of the Jansen family, before joining Gaetano in Vienna. A visit to the Venetian estate coincided with its seizure by Napoleon's troops and the Bartolozzis were forced to return to London where, in early January 1800, we find Bartolozzi advertising for drawing pupils.

Therese was the dedicatee of Haydn's last three piano sonatas nos 60–62, Hob. XVI:50–52 (London, 1774–(?)75) (in C, D and E♭ majors) and the last three Piano Trios nos 43–5 Hob. XV:27–29 (in C, E and E♭ majors, 1796(?)) and possibly also of the Piano Trio no. 41 in E♭ minor,

Hob.XV:31 (1795). *Clementi, her teacher, dedicated his three piano sonatas op. 33 – the last of which also exists as a piano concerto – and J.L. *Dussek his op. 13 violin sonatas and his Grand Sonata op. 43 (1800).

Further reading
O. Strunk, 'Notes on a Haydn Autograph', *MQ*, xx (1934). J.C. Graue, 'Haydn and the London Pianoforte School', *Haydn Studies* (Washington, DC, 1975).

Jeunesse Musicale, La
One of several series of published pieces by *Czerny aimed at children published in 1841 by D'Almaine & Co. of London. As the subtitle – *a selection of Popular National and other Airs arranged as Rondos for Pianoforte* – tells us, they are character-pieces in the form of *rondos (with the French title *Rondeau*), and are typified as *élégant*, *sentimental*, *brillant*, *militaire*, *ecossaise*, *allemand*, and even *maritime* and *chinoise*.

Jig (see *Gigue)

Joachim, Joseph
Austro-Hungarian violinist, composer, conductor and teacher (b. 28 Jun 1831, Kitsee, nr Pressburg [now Bratislava]; d. 15 Aug 1907, Berlin).

The family moved to Pest when Joseph was two and he was a pupil of the leading violinist there, Serwaczyński; he gave his first public performance in a double concerto at the age of 8. The same year (1839) he was sent to Vienna to study violin with Hauser and George Hellmesberger (senior) and Joseph Böhm, and joined the Leipzig Conservatory in 1843, coming into close contact with *Felix Mendelssohn, who recommended composition lessons with Hauptmann

and F. David. His Leipzig début was in a concert with Pauline Viardot, *Clara Schumann and Mendelssohn. He visited London in 1844, becoming a favourite of audiences there and in 1850 he became *Konzertmeister* in Weimar under *Liszt, from whose guidance he benefited. However, Joachim's more *Classical leanings led to friction and he took up the post of violinist to King George V in Hanover where, in a letter to *Liszt, he dissociated himself from the *'New German School' of the younger man and his followers. It was at Hanover that he composed the finest of his compositions.

At the same time he became closer to the Schumanns and became an advisor and friend to the young *Brahms and their admiration for each others' music drew them into an anti-New-German-School alliance. The friendship was threatened, however, when Brahms took the part of Joachim's wife when he divorced her in 1863. Joachim moved to Berlin in 1868 as head of the new Hochschule für Ausübende Tonkunst, where he remained for the rest of his life, apart from concert-tours. In spite of their rift, he never wavered in his admiration for, and promotion of, Brahms's music, especially in England, to which he began regular yearly visits from 1862. He conducted the British première of the younger man's First Symphony in Cambridge in 1877. It was Joachim who established *Beethoven's Violin Concerto in the repertory and, in an age of virtuosity, placed greater importance on beauty of tone and musical integrity. He influenced the young Brahms, especially in orchestration.

Works
Orchestral works include various overtures and several works for violin – the *Konzert in einem Satze* (*Concerto

in *One Movement*) in G minor, op. 3 (*c.*1855), *Konzert in ungarischer Weise* (*Concerto in the Hungarian Style*) op. 11 (1861) and the Concerto in G major (1899). There are various lighter chamber works (inc. *Hebräische Melodien* (*Hebrew Melodies*) after Byron for viola and piano op. 9 (1855)) and cadenzas for Violin Concertos by Beethoven, Mozart, Viotti and Brahms, as well some songs and arrangements of other composers' works.

Further reading
Y.A. Breitburg, *Joseph Joachim: pedagog i ispolntel'* [*Pedagogue and interpreter*] (Moscow, 1966). B. Stoll. *Joseph Joachim, Violinist, Pedagogue and Composer* (diss., U. of Iowa, 1978). R.T. Oliver, 'Brahms, Joachim and the Classical Tradition', *International Brahms Congress, Detroit 1980*. B. Schwartz, 'Joachim and the Genesis of Brahms's Violin Concerto', *International Brahms Congress, Detroit 1980*. B. Borchard, *Stimme und Geige: Amalie und Joseph Joachim, ein Beitrag zur Künstlersozial- und Interpretationsgeschichte des 19. Jahrhunderts* (Frankfurt, 2000).

Jullien, Louis (and some thirty odd other Christian names)
French conductor, composer (b. 23 Apr 1812, Sisteron; d. 14 Mar 1860, Paris).
Son of a violinist and bandmaster, he served in the army before enrolling in the Paris Conservatoire in 1831 or 1833, spent three or five years there, but, being more drawn to dance-music than to serious study, left prematurely in 1836 and ran a dance-band whose concerts were as popular as those of *Musard. He left for England in 1838 and gave his first concert in Drury Lane two years later. His avowed aim in his concerts – some

of which, because of the number of musicians involved, were called 'Monster Concerts' – was to blend the popular with the sublime for less-affluent audiences. There was a strong emphasis on popular dances, especially the *quadrille, often tied to a topical event (see *Works*). Not all his ventures were successes, however: a publishing business went bankrupt and a 'grand opera' of his was withdrawn after only five performances. After a series of farewell concerts, he returned to Paris in 1859 where various grandiose plans were abandoned because of his mental problems. He died after a month in a lunatic asylum.

Jullien pioneered the promenade concert – which, later under Sir Henry Wood, were to become a mainstay of British concert life – and the popular concert in general, aimed at ordinary people and combining simple dance music and musical classics in the same programme. He was also important in his championing of conducting with the baton and, indeed, of the cult of the conductor, and he introduced many first-class Continental musicians to Britain.

Works
Mainly light music, such as the *Swiss Quadrille* (1847), the *Great Exhibition Quadrille* (1851), the *British Navy Quadrille* (1845) and the hugely successful *British Army Quadrilles* written for a full orchestra and four military bands (1846), as well as an opera, *Pietro il grande* (*Peter The Great*, perf. 1852). Many of his major scores were lost in a fire at Covent Garden in 1856.

Further reading
Anon., 'A Sketch of the Life of Louis Jullien', *Musical World* (1853), May–

July. H. Davison, ed., *Music during the Victorian Era, from Mendelssohn to Wagner: being the Memoirs of J.W.* Davison (London, 1912). A. Carse, *The Life of Jullien* (Cambridge, 1951). Fétis/*BIOGRAPHIE*.

K

Kaiserhymne (scc **Gott erhalte Franz den Kaiser*)

Kaiserquartett (see **'Emperor'* (1))

Kalkbrenner, Frédéric [Friderich Wilhelm Michael]
German (naturalized French) pianist, composer, teacher (b. Nov 1785; d. 10 Jun 1849, Enghien-les-Bains).

Born while his parents were travelling in Germany, he attended the Paris Conservatoire 1799–1801 learning piano from Nicodami and harmony from Catel, for both subjects of which he won the *Premier prix*. He was in Vienna 1803–1804 and met, and was advised by, *J. Haydn and *Clementi. On his way back to Paris he played, to great effect at Stuttgart, Frankfurt am Main and Munich. In Paris he was influenced by the young *Chopin. He is known only as a composer until 1814, when he began a ten-year sojourn in England, first Bath then London, where he remained for the rest of his stay. Here he built up a formidable reputation as a pianist, composer and teacher and made a great deal of money.

In 1823 he embarked on a tour of Germany, Austria, Ireland and Scotland, playing to great acclaim and in 1824 settled in Paris, where he remained for the rest of his life. The decade from 1825 contained his greatest achievements; he joined the piano-making firm of *Pleyel and married a general's daughter, as well as gaining many official European honours, including Légion d'honneur (1828) and the Order of the Red Eagle of Prussia (1833). On Chopin's arrival in Paris, Kalkbrenner suggested that he should join his training course for teachers, but, in spite of his admiration for the older man, Chopin declined the offer and the two remained on good terms, Chopin dedicating his op. 11 concerto in E minor to him. In turn, he helped arrange Chopin's first Paris concert (26 February 1832). Ill-health (nervous trouble and gout) forced his retiral from performing in 1839 and he died during a cholera epidemic in 1849.

Kalkbrenner's playing developed from the late Classical style to the early *Romanticism of *Hummel and *Field, although his was more virtuosic and foreshadowed Chopin and, to a lesser extent, *Liszt. He developed a mechanical aid to piano-practice, the *guide-mains*. He taught Marie Pleyel, Osborne and Camille Stamaty, who used the *guide-mains* to teach, among others, Saint-Saëns.

Works
Piano: 13 piano sonatas (including those in G minor op. 13 (pub. 1813), in F major op. 56 (pub. 1821) and in A♭ major op. 177 (pub. 1845)) an *Elégie harmonique 'Les regrets'* op. 36 (pub. 1817), *Grande fantaisie 'Effusio musica'* op. 68 (pub. 1823) and a *Scène dramatique 'Le fou'* op. 136 (pub. 1837) as well as many rondos, fantasias, variation-sets and dances; some piano duet music and a Grand duo in D major op. 128 (pub. 1835) for two pianos; four piano concertos (D minor op. 61 (pub. 1823), E minor op. 80 [op. 86] (pub. 1826), A minor op. 107 (pub. 1829) and A♭ major op. 125 [op. 127] (pub. 1835)) and a concerto for 2 pianos in C major op. 125. Chamber music includes duo-sonatas for flute and for violin, five piano trios and two quartets, two quintets, two sextets and two septets, all including piano. There are also didactic works, sets of *préludes* and *études* and the *Méthode*

pour apprendre le piano-forte à l'aide du guide-mains op. 108 (pub. 1831).

Further reading
C.E. and M. Hallé, eds, *Life and letters of Sir Charles Hallé* (London, 1896; abridged by M. Kennedy as *The Autobiography of Charles Hallé* (1972)). R. Benton, 'London Music in 1815, as seen by Camille Pleyel', *ML*, xlvii (1966). Marmontel/*PIANISTES*.

Kammermusicus (Ger.: chamber-musician)
A musician appointed to play chamber music, usually at a court.

Kaňka, Jan (Nepomuk) [Kaňka, Johann Nepomuk]
Czech composer, pianist (b. 10 Nov 1772, Prague; d. 15 Apr 1863, Prague).

Member of a Czech musical lineage with a famous architect for a grandfather and a lawyer for a father, an excellent amateur cellist who arranged many home concerts and was a close friend and correspondent of *Beethoven, whom he helped financially. The young Kaňka was also a lawyer, studying the subject at Prague University before being appointed *Hofrat* (Court Counsellor) to the Elector of Hesse (1812), becoming dean of law in Prague University (1815) and its rector in 1829. He became a close friend, and financial helper, of Beethoven, was a fine pianist and a good composer and founded several of Prague's important musical institutions.

Works
Two piano concertos (in E♭ and D majors (both *c.*1804)) a symphony in E♭ major, piano pieces, chamber music and cantatas as well as Austrian patriotic songs which became popular and well-known.

Further reading
J. Klapková, *Jan Nepomuk Kaňka* (diss., Prague U., 1954). E. Forbes, *Thayer's Life of Beethoven* (Princeton, NJ, 1964, 2/1967).

Kapellmeister
The director of music in a *Kapelle*, or 'chapel' in its broadest sense. Although originally a religious body of musicians, secular music was also performed, and during the seventeenth and eighteenth centuries the term *Kapelle* was also applied to all the musicians in a court and, indeed, any organized and more-or-less permanent group of musicians, sacred or secular. In line with this, the meaning of *Kapellmeister* was similarly widened and loosened to mean the music director of any such body. Up to the nineteenth century, compositional duties were understood to be part of the post, but the *Kapellmeister* became more of a musical supervisor and administrator when the status of the composer rose.

Key (Fr. *clef*; Ger. *Tonart*; It. *tonalità*)
(1) In music of the *tonal or 'common practice' period, the basic 'home' scale (major or minor) to which a musical work, movement or passage adheres; this is centred around the key-note, or tonic. It is common for this to be temporarily suspended for other keys during modulation, before being reinstated towards the end.

(2) One of a set of levers, usually oblong in shape which activates the sound-producing mechanism on a *keyboard instrument. Traditionally wooden, keys are usually covered in plastic, ivory or bone, in white or black, depending on the function of the note produced.

(3) The term is used in the same way in mouth-blown instruments to describe the finger-operated devices to cover and uncover holes too far or difficult for the fingers to access directly. Several of these operations may be coupled under a single key and the keys, when at rest, may be open or closed.

Keyboard (Fr. *clavier*; Ger. *Klaviatur*, *Tastatur*; It. *tastiera*, *tastatura*)

A set of *keys which activate the mechanism to produce sound on keyboard instruments such as the *piano, *clavichord, *harpsichord, *hurdygurdy, *organ, etc. It has traditionally been designed in the key of C major, with each white key assigned to a note of the *diatonic scale, the black notes giving extraneous chromatic accidentals which, of course, take their place as regular notes in other scales apart from C.

Key-dip

The amount of space the *key of a *keyboard instrument moves downwards before it is checked. The key-dip on a 'Viennese' fortepiano is in the close region of 5 millimetres and that of a British piano of the same period, 9, whereas that of a modern piano is 13. (See also *Touch.)

Kiesewetter, Raphael Georg

Austrian musicologist (b. 29 Aug 1773, Holleschau [now Holešov, Czech Republic]; d. 1 Jan 1850, Baden).

Son of a doctor and medical author, he was taught piano and singing as a child and later learnt to play the flute, adding proficiency on bassoon and guitar in adulthood. He studied philosophy at Olomouc and law at Vienna, without completing the latter course. He worked in the chancellery of the imperial army and became a councillor in the war office

in Vienna in 1807, studying music theory with, among others, Albrechtsberger, and took part in many public and private concerts as a bass singer. He was ennobled in 1843 and retired with a pension two years later and returned to Baden in 1848, where he died in 1850.

A pioneer of musicology, not only in Western, but also non-European (Arabic) and *Classical (Ancient Greek) musics, Kiesewetter's interest in early music (sixteenth and seventeenth centuries) led to series of concerts in his home in Vienna and he amassed an important collection of scores of this music, donating them to the Austrian National Library. This became an important collection for subsequent research. He received many musical honours during his lifetime.

Works

Geschichte der europäisch-abendländlischen oder unserer heutigen Musik (Leipzig 1834, 2/1846; Eng tr. 1848). *Ueber die Musik der neuern Griechen nebst freien Gedanken über altaegyptische und altgriechische Musik* (Leipzig, 1838). *Die Musik der Araber* (Leipzig, 1842). *Gallerie der alten Contrapunctisten: eine Auswahl aus ihren Werken in verständlichen Partituren* (Vienna, 1847). *Über die Octave des Pythagoras* (Vienna, 1848).

Further reading

H. Kier, 'Kiesewetters historische Hauskonzerte: Zur Geschichte der kirchenmusikalischen Restauration in Wien', *Kirchenmusikalisches Jahrbuch*, lii (1968); *Raphael Georg Kiesewetter (1773–1850): Wegbreiter des musikalischen Historismus* (Regensburg, 1968). P. Bohlman, 'R.G. Kiesewetter's "Die Music der Araber": a Pioneering Ethnomusicological Study of Arabic

Writings on Music', *Asian Music*, xviii/1 (1968).

Kirckman [Kirchmann, Kirkman], **Jacob** [Jakob]
Alsatian (British naturalized) keyboard instrument maker (b. 1710, Bischweiler, nr Strasbourg; d. (buried) 9 June 1792, Greenwich (nr London))

He came to London in his early twenties and became an apprentice to the Flemish harpsichord maker Hermann Tabel, marrying his widow and setting up their business near to another of Tabel's apprentices, Burkat *Shudi; their friendly rivalry guaranteed instruments of high quality and, indeed, Kirckman's harpsichords were considered among the finest – if not *the* finest – of the period (see Carew/MUSE, Pl. 27). Many of his instruments from the mid-1760s were provided with a pedal-operated lid *swell.

Further reading
Boalch/HARPSICHORD.
Russell/HARPSICHORD.
Hubbard/HARPSICHORD.

Knee-lever (Fr. *genouillère*; Ger. *Kniehebel*)
A lever, moving vertically or horizontally placed under the *keyboard of a *harpsichord or *piano or *harmonium) and operated by one of the player's knees, resulting in modification of the sound produced, such as damping, muffling and so son. Knee-levers were invented to replace the earlier *stops which required the player to break off playing briefly to operate them, although many instruments had both. In turn they were both superseded by pedals and, again, there are instruments which have all three.

Knee-pedal (see *Knee-lever)

Koch, Heinrich Christoph
German theorist, violinist (b. 10 Oct 1749, Rudolstadt; d. 19 Mar 1816, Rudolstadt).

He studied violin and composition in his home town, then at Berlin, Dresden and Hamburg. Koch gave up his post as a court musician and later *Konzertmeister* in Rudolstadt to pursue his theoretical writing. His three-volume *Versuch einer Anleitung zur Composition* (1782–93) deals with aesthetics as well as musical form and composition, from first principles to symphonic forms. The examples use more up-to-date *galant* pieces and procedures rather than the modally-based counterpoint of Fux's teaching, and his sections on melodic construction and phraseology are still relevant. The *Musikalisches Lexikon*, although a dictionary, is a comprehensive reference work on contemporary theoretical and aesthetical ideas. All the subsequent theorists of the nineteenth century drew from Koch's works, including *Reicha, Choron, *Czerny, Marx, Prout and Riemann.

Works
Versuch einer Anleitung zur Composition (Rudolstadt and Leipzig, 1782–93; partial Eng. tr., by N.K. Baker as *Introductory Essay on Composition: the mechanical Rules of Melody, Sections 3 and 4* (1983)). *Musikalisches Lexikon ...* (Frankfurt am Main, 1802, R/1817). *Handbuch bey dem Studium der Harmonie* (Leipzig, 1811). 'Über den technischen Ausdruck: Tempo rubato', *AmZ*, x (1808).

Further reading
C. Dahlhaus, 'Der rhetorische Formbegriff H. Chr. J. Kochs und die Theorie der Sonatenform', *Archiv für Musikwissenchaft*, xxxv (1978). J. Lester, *Compositional Theory in the*

Eighteenth Century (Cambridge, MA, 1992). N.K. Baker and T. Christensen, tr. and eds, *Aesthetics and the Art of Musical Composition in the German Enlightenment: Selected Writings of Johann G. Sulzer and Heinrich C. Koch* (London, 1995).

Koczwara, Frantîsek [Franz; Kotžwara, Francis]

Bohemian composer, instrumentalist (b. *c.*1750, ?Prague; d. 2 Sep 1791, London).

Something of a shadowy figure, little is known for certain about Koczwara and there are conflicting accounts even from reputable musical chroniclers. *Fétis, as a child, remembers meeting and playing for him in his (Fétis's) father's house. According to him, Koczwara played viola and double bass (which he was known to have played in London) but also a variety of other instruments including the violin, cello, flute, oboe, bassoon, piano and cittern. He seems to have spent much of his life in Britain and most of his music was published there, particularly in London, from *c.*1775. He is listed among the performers in the great *Handel Commemoration in May 1971, played in the *Concerts of Ancient Music and was reputed to be in the double bass section of the King's Theatre at the time of his death in 1791. He was famous for his hugely successful piano-piece, **The Battle of Prague*, first published in Dublin *c.*1788. He was also a consummate and convincing forger of other composers' styles (in particular *J. Haydn and *Pleyel) and supplemented his income thereby. Besides the *Battle*, Koczwara's other claim to notoriety was the manner of his death, widely reported, by accidental hanging in a brothel.

Works

Include a potpourri, *The Agreeable Surprise* op. 33 (*c.*1791) for solo piano; three sonatinas op. 36 (pub. *c.*1790) and smaller pieces. Various violin sonatas, piano/harpsichord trios and string quartets. *The Battle of Prague* op. 23 for piano/harpsichord trio with *ad lib* accompaniment of drum (pub. *c.*1788), also arranged for solo piano and two pianos and pub. under various opus numbers. There are also some orchestral overtures and songs.

Further reading

W.T. Parke, *Musical Memoirs* (London, 1830). H.E. Johnson, *Musical Interludes in Boston: 1795–1830* (New York 1943). L.P. Pruett, 'Napoleonic Battles in Keyboard Music of the Nineteenth Century', *Early Keyboard Journal*, vi–vii (1988–89). Fétis/*BIOGRAPHIE*. Loesser/ MEN. Newman/SCE.

Kollmann, George Augustus

English composer, pianist, inventor (b. 30 Jan 1789, London; d. 19 Mar 1845, London).

Born into a musical family, Kollmann was taught by his father (Augustus Frederic Christopher), a composer, organist and musical theorist who moved to London in 1782 to become organist-schoolmaster at the Royal German Chapel in St James's Palace. He was a passionate advocate of the work of *J.S. Bach. Young Augustus was his father's pupil and premiered his father's piano concerto at his début at the age of 15. After a tour of Ireland accompanying a singer he was elected to the Royal Society of Musicians in 1811 and he became more and more involved with the organization throughout his life. He was an Associate of the *Philharmonic Society from 1816 and took over his father's post as organist, clerk and chapel-keeper of the Royal German Chapel in St James's Palace in 1829.

He was much interested in engineering, being granted patents for inventions in the sphere of locomotion, especially the railway, and this interest extended to the mechanism and development of the piano. An instrument with a *down-striking action, an extended soundboard and improved tuning mechanism which he invented was patented in 1825 and he built several for sale. A series of concerts which he gave in London in 1838–39 was intended to show off these models but, although they were received favourably, he was made bankrupt in 1840 and died five years later.

Works

Three Piano sonatas op. 1 (one with violin accompaniment), an Air with variations for piano (both 1808) and a set of waltzes also for piano (1812).

Further reading

'The Late George Augustus Kollmann', *Dramatic and Musical Review*, iv (1845). E.R. Jacobi, 'Augustus Frederic Kollmann als Theoretiker', *Archiv für Musikwissenschaft*, xiii (1956).

Konzertstück [Concertstück] (Ger.: 'concert-piece'; It. *concertino*)

A piece of music written for a solo instrument or instruments and orchestra, it is generally smaller than a *concerto and often in a single movement – hence its often being called a *concertino – although there are usually fairly clearly-differentiated sections within it. The first use of the term is thought to have been by *C.M. von Weber for his *programmatic *Konzertstück* for piano and orchestra in F minor J282 (1821).

The genre was particularly popular with French composers.

Koželuch [Kotzeluch, Kozeluh], **Leopold** [Jan Antonín, Ioannes Antonius]

Bohemian composer, pianist, teacher, publisher (b. 26 Jun 1747, Velvary; d. 7 may 1818, Vienna).

Although christened Jan Antonín, like his older cousin, a professional musician, he changed his name to Leopold and, in fact, studied music with that cousin in Prague although he was at first destined for law. He also studied with F.X. Dussek (piano and composition) and the successes in the 1770s of his first stage pieces encouraged him to devote all his energies to music. He settled in Vienna in 1778 and established himself as a respected pianist, teacher and composer, to the extent that he refused the proffered post of court organist to the Archbishop of Salzburg vacated by *W.A. Mozart. In 1785 he set up his own publishing house, soon managed by his brother, and made useful contacts with publishers abroad, notably in England, which brought him to the attention of George *Thomson, who commissioned him (among others) to arrange British *folksongs. He was commissioned to write as cantata for the coronation of Leopold II as King of Bohemia in 1791 and the following year appointed Kammer *Kapellmeister* and imperial Court Composer on the accession of the Emperor Franz II, which posts he held until his death in 1818.

One of the earliest champions of the piano, he forged an idiomatic style which foreshadowed *Romanticism, as did some of his compositions, and some of the smaller pieces are an early step in the development of the *character-piece.

Works

About 50 piano sonatas with another half-a-dozen for four hands and many dances and smaller works for piano including the forward-looking *Trois caprices* (*c*.1797). There are 60-odd piano trios (some of which allow for substitution of flute for violin) and 30-odd duos, mostly for violin and piano, many of them arranged as, or from, piano pieces. In addition, some 11 symphonies and many concertos: two for clarinet and 22 for harpsichord/piano, with a *Concerto en rondo* in C major (pub. 1793) and, also for pf, a *Rondo Concerto* in E♭ major and a *Fantasia Concertante* in D minor. There is quite a body of vocal music – cantatas, oratorios and songs – as well as his arrangements of British folksongs for *Thomson.

Further reading

G. Löbl, *Die Klaviersonate bei Leopold Koželuch* (diss., U. of Vienna, 1937). O.E. Duetsch, 'Koželuch ritrovato', *ML*, xxvi (1945). K. Pfannhauser, 'Wer war Mozarts Amtsnachfolger?', *Acta Mozartiana*, iii (1956). M. Poštolka, *Leopold Kozeluh: život a dílo* [Life and Works] (Prague, 1964) [with thematic catalogue, bibliography; Eng. and Ger. summary]. C. Flamm, *Leopold Koželuch: Biographie und stilkritische Untersuchung der Sonaten für Klavier, Violine und Violoncello* (diss., U of Vienna, 1968); 'Ein Verlegerbriefwechsel zur Beethovenzeit', in E. Schenck, ed., *Beethoven-Studien* (Vienna, 1970). R. Hickman, 'Leopold Koželuch and the Viennese quatuor concertant', *College Music Symposium*, xxvi (1986).

Krause, Christian Gottfried

German lawyer, aesthetician, composer (bap. 17 Apr 1719, Winzig [now Winsko], Silesia; d. 4 May 1770, Berlin).

Son of a town musician who taught him violin, keyboard and timpani, he decided, in spite of this, upon a career in law, studying at the University of Frankfurt an der Oder from 1740 to 1745. He then became legal secretary to Count Rothenburg in Berlin 1745 and lawyer to the municipal council in 1753. His new post and its high status enabled him to have a large house in Potsdam where he ran a very popular *salon* which attracted many of the intellectual and musical luminaries of the time. He became *Justizrat* of the High Prussian Court (*c*.1762) and remained in post until his death eight years later.

Krause is remembered for his theoretical writings, his *Von der musikalischen Poesie* (1747) was one of the first works to discuss musical setting of words and was an important source for the first *Berlin Lied School on its publication in 1752. In it he called for a return to the 'purity' of *folk music, holding up French folksong as a model (no doubt in deference to the Francophile culture at *Frederick the Great's court at Potsdam). He and an associate collected, edited and published 31 lieder and, although the composers were deliberately not named, they are known to include *C.P.E. Bach, *Agricola and *Quantz as well as Krause himself and the poets included Hagedorn, Lessing and Kleist. His influence on the Berlin Lied School and subsequent composers of *Lieder* and *chansons* was significant.

Works

Hundreds of lieder, and some dozen cantatas (including *Der Tod Jesu* (*c*.1758)), eight of which are lost, some stage works, four symphonies and a small number of chamber and keyboard works.

Further reading
J. Beaujean, *Christian Gottfried Krause: sein Leben und seine Persöhnlichkeit ... als Ästhetiker und Musiker* (Dillingen an der Donau, 1930). P.F. Marks, 'The Rhetorical Element in Musical *Sturm und Drang*: Christian Gottfried Krause's *Von der musikalischen Poesie*', *MR*, xxxiii (1972). J.H. Mallard, *A Translation of Christian Gottfried Krause's Von der musikalischen Poesie, with a Critical Essay on his Sources and the Aesthetic Views of his Time* (diss., U. of Texas, Austin, 1978). *MGG*.

'Kreisler, Capellmeister' (see *Böhner)

Kreutzer [Kreuzer], **Conradin** [Conrad, Konradin]
German composer, conductor (b. 22 Nov 1780, Messkirch; d. 14 Dec 1849, Riga).

His father was a burgher and the child was taught music theory and several instruments including the *organ. He studied law but devoted himself entirely to music after the death of his father in 1800. It is thought that he was in Switzerland from 1800 until 1804 and in that year he went to Vienna; he met *J. Haydn and it is likely that he would have studied with Albrechtsberger, very much the right pedigree for an up-and-coming musician. He was on tour in Germany and Switzerland in 1810 and his operas *Konradin von Schwaben* and *Feodora* were performed to acclaim. He was appointed Hofkapellmeister in the middle of 1812 and married that autumn. His friendship with the poet Uhland was formed during this time and continued even though the composer left Stuttgart in 1816. In 1818 Kreutzer was appointed *Kapellmeister* to the court of Donaueschingen and, after four years, was made *Kapellmeister* at the Kärntnertortheater in Vienna in which post he remained until 1827 and, after a two-year sojourn in Paris, reclaimed from 1829–32. The following year he was at the Theater in der Josephstadt and the next two years were his must successful, with productions of his *Das Nachtlager in Granada* and *Der Verschwender*. In 1840 he accompanied one of his daughters (a singer) on a German concert tour and on their return he became music director to the city of Cologne (1840–42). He moved to Riga in 1848 and died of a stroke within days of a disastrous performance by his younger daughter (also a singer) in 1832.

His choral pieces (mostly settings of Uhland) continue to be popular in the German-speaking lands.

Works
Many stage works including the operas *Konradin von Schwaben*, *Feodora* (both perf. 1812), *Die Alpenhütte* (pub. 1815), *Das Nachtlager in Granada* and *Der Verschwender* (both perf. 1834), incidental music, as well as part-songs and some 150 lieder. His chamber music usually includes wind instruments – including a Septet in E♭ major op.62 (*c.*1823) – and some with piano. There are also a number of piano pieces and three piano concertos (in B♭ major, op. 42 (?1819), in C major op. 50 (?1822) and in E♭ major op. 65 (?1825).

Further reading
A. Bauer, *Opern un Operetten in Wien* (Graz and Cologne, 1955); *Das Theater in der Josephstadt zu Wien* (Vienna, 1957). H.Lester, *Conradin Kreutzers Lieder für Männerchor* (diss., U. of Mainz, 1963). R. Heinemann, 'Kreutzer, Konrad', *Rheinischer Musiker*, iv, ed. K.G. Fellerer (Cologne, 1966). L.E. Peake, 'Kreutzer's Wanderlieder: the

other Winterreise', *MQ*, lxv (1979). K.-P. Brecht, *Conradin Kreutzer: Biographie und Werkverzeichnis* (Messkirch, 1980).

'Kreutzer' Sonata

The name given to the sonata for violin and piano in A major op. 47 by Beethoven, composed in Vienna in 1802–1803 and published in Bonn and London, 1805. He wrote it for a performance by himself with the British violinist George Bridgetower which took place in the Augarten in Vienna on 24 May 1803 and was a great success. The dedication to the French violinist Rodolphe Kreutzer was partly due to Beethoven's later falling out with Bridgetower and partly to help ease the way for his proposed visit to Paris, which never took place.

Kuhlau, Friedrich [Frederik] (Daniel Rudolph)

German (Danish naturalized) pianist, composer (b. 11 Sep 1786, Uelzen, nr Hanover; d. 12 Mar 1832, Copenhagen).

Son of a military bandsman, he studied theory and composition in Hamburg, where he had some music published and gave piano recitals. When French troops took over in 1810, he escaped to Copenhagen and settled there, giving a concert at the Royal Theatre. He played his Piano Concerto in C major on this occasion and afterwards dedicated it to the Danish composer C.E.F. Weyse, who was to remain a lifelong friend. In 1813 he was appointed chamber musician to the court and chorus-master of he Royal Theatre 1816–17. From these years date his first operatic successes and he built up a great reputation in northern Europe as a pianist and teacher and was the piano-teacher of choice for the nobility of these countries. He visited Vienna a few times, on the second of which he spent some happy times with *Beethoven, exchanging *impromptu* canons. Kuhlau died of a respiratory disease brought on by a fire in his house which also destroyed all his unpublished manuscripts.

His piano music and that for flute(s) is particularly admired, although he could not actually play the flute. His early interest in *folk music remained and can be seen in much of his later music, especially Danish works such as the incidental music to Heiberg's play *Elverhøj* (*The Elf's Hill*) with its strongly nationalistic bent. It ends with the Danish national hymn *Kong Christian* which finds its official form here. His adeptness in writing canons was much admired. He taught many of the next generation of Scandinavian composers.

Works

Stage works include the *Singspiel Røverborgen* (*The Robbers' Castle*, 1814) and several operas – *Trylleharpen* (*The Magic Harp*, 1816), *Lulu*, whose libretto stems from the same fairytale as that of Mozart's/Schikaneder's *Die Zauberflöte* (1824) – and incidental music, such as that to Boye's *William Shakespeare* (1826) and *Elverhøj* (*The Elf's Hill*, 1828). Orchestral music: a Piano Concerto in C major op. 7 (1810) – a second one was destroyed in a fire at his home – and a Concertino in F minor for two horns and orchestra (1821). Apart from three piano quartets (no. 1 in C minor (1820), no. 2 in A major (1822) and no. 3 in G minor (1833)), four violin sonatas and a string quartet (1841), the rest is for, or includes, flute, and many of these are for from one to four unaccompanied flutes. Other instruments are occasionally admitted, including the piano, and – rather nicely subverting the usual state of affairs in accompanied sonatas of the period – there are three Fantasias op. 95 (1829) for flute with piano *ad lib.*

Further reading
K. Graupner, *Friedrich Kuhlau* (Remscheid, 1930). J.-L. Beimfohr, *Das C-Dur Klavierkonzert opus 7 und die Klaviersonaten von Friedrich Kuhlau* (Hamburg, 1971). D. Fog, ed., *Kompositionen von Fridr. Kuhlau: thematisch-bibliographischer Katalog* (Copenhagen, 1977). G. Busk, *Friedrich Kuhlau: hans liv og værk* (Copenhagen, 1986). *MGG.*

Kuhnau, Johann (see * *'Biblical Sonatas'*)

Kuhreigen (see *Ranz des vaches*)

Kuhreihen (see *Ranz des vaches*)

Kujaviak [*Kujawy*]
A Polish *folk couple-dance called after its region of origin Kujawy. It is in triple time and moderately fast and has been considered as a slower version of the *mazurka. Examples often alternate medium-paced with slower sections and there is often an air of melancholy about the dance.

Kullak, Theodor
German pianist, teacher (b. 12 Sep 1818, Krotoschin [now Krotoszyn, Poland]; d. 1 Mar 1882, Berlin).
A child prodigy, he played his first concerto for the King of Prussia in Berlin at 11 and continued to study music as well as medicine in Berlin. After a year of music study with *Czerny, *Sechter and Nicolai in Vienna, he returned to Berlin teaching the upper classes and royalty and was appointed court pianist in 1846. He and a few others founded the conservatory

(to become the Stern Conservatory) and left it, in 1855, to found another institution dedicated to the training of pianists, the (private) Neue Akademie der Tonkunst. This went from strength to strength and at the time of his death in 1882, it had 1,100 students taught by 100 teachers, making it the largest private institution in Germany.
One of the best piano teachers of the nineteenth century, his methods were encapsulated in the Akademie which he founded and where he taught, among other famous pupils, both Xaver and Philipp Scharwenka, Moszkowski and Bischoff.

Works
Many piano pieces including two *Etudes de concert* op. 2 (c.1840), Grande sonate in F# minor op. 7 (*c*.1845), *Symphonie de piano* op. 27 (*c*.1848), *Ballade* op. 54 (*c*.1849), *Ballade 'Leonore'* op. 81 (*c*.1853) and *Deutsche Volksweisen* op. 111 (*c*.1862). There is also a small amount of chamber music (including an *Andante* for piano and violin op. 70 (*c*.1850) and Piano Trio in E minor op. 77 (pub. 1853)), some songs and the Piano Concerto in C minor op. 55 (*c*.1850). His pedagogical works include the still useful *Schule des Oktavenspiels* (*Method for Octave-playing*) op. 48 (1848 3/1877) and the *Schule der Fingerübungen* (*Method for Finger-practice*) op. 61 (*c*.1850).

Further reading
O. Reinsdorf, *Theodor Kullak und seine Neue Akademie der Tonkunst* (Neusalz, 1870). H. Bischoff, *Zur Erinnerungen an Theodor Kullak* (Berlin, 1883).

Kurpiński, Karol Kazimierz
Polish composer, conductor, teacher (b. 6 Mar 1785, Włoszakowice, Wielkopolska; d. 18 Sep 1857, Warsaw).

Son of an organist who gave him his first lessons; he himself, at the age of 12, became organist at the church where his uncle was parish priest. Another uncle, a cellist, took him to the estate of a wealthy amateur musician and Karol became one of the second violins. In 1808 he was a resident music master to a family and moved to Warsaw in 1810, where he became a protégé of *Elsner, through whom he became deputy and (in 1824) principal conductor of the Warsaw Opera. He founded, and taught at, music and drama schools and was honoured with membership of many European musical societies, including the Warsaw Society of Friends and Learning and the Société des Enfants d'Apollon in Paris and was presented with a medal in recognition of his musical services in 1819. The same year saw his appointment as *Kapellmeister at the Polish royal chapel. He founded the first musical periodical in Poland, published weekly, and married a singer in the Warsaw Opera.

Kurpiński was central in Warsaw musical life, conducting *Chopin's first concerts in public. As a composer, he was one of the main forerunners of Chopin, who undoubtedly knew his work, and his innovations in Polish opera were long-lasting. His interest in, and use of, native Polish *folksong was also a great influence.

Works

Most of his stage works are lost or preserved incomplete, but such operas as *Zamek na Czorsztnie* (*The Castle of Czorsztn*, perf. 1819) and *Jadwiga królowa Polska* (*Jadwiga, Queen of Poland*, perf. 1814) are still popular; his ballets include *Mars i Flora* (*Mars and Flora*, perf. 1820) and *Trzy gracje* (*The Three Graces*, perf. 1822). Vocal works include six masses, cantatas – one on Napoleon's coronation dates from 1810 – and songs. He wrote a *Potpourri, or Variations on national themes* (1822) for piano and orchestra and a clarinet concerto. There is a small amount of chamber music and a body of piano music, including fantasies and *polonaises.

Further reading

A. Hedley, ed., *Selected Correspondence of Fryderyk Chopin* (London, 1962). T. Przyblski, *Karol Kurpiński, 1785–1857* (Warsaw, 1975, enlarged 2/1980).

L

Ladurner, Josef Alois

Austrian composer (b. 7 Mar 1769, Algund, nr Merano; d. 20 Feb 1851, Brixen [Bressanone]).

Of Tyrolean descent he was sent to study with his uncle at the monastery of Benediktbeuren, becoming organist at Algund in 1784 and studying theology and philosophy (but also piano, counterpoint and composition) in Munich until 1798. A year later he was ordained priest and held various administratively-oriented posts – including court chaplain – within the Catholic Church locally. He took a full and active part in the local musical life, conducting choirs, giving lessons and composing. His compositions were well-respected during his lifetime.

Works
Some religious vocal works and pieces for piano, many of which remain in manuscript, as well as a *piano *method (*Grundlichees Lehrbuch*).

Further reading
G.W. Fink, 'Joseph Aloys Ladurner', *AmZ*, xxxvii (1835). Fétis/*BIOGRAPHIE*. *MGG*.

Ländler

A generally slowish *folk dance in triple (usually 3/4) time very widespread in Austria, southern Germany and in German Switzerland. It was carried far afield by Germanic settlers (for example in Transylvania and Carpathia). The name comes from 'Land ob der Enns', an old name for upper Austria; it could also be related to Ländle (Swabia). The dance exists in many variants – *Dreher*, *Schleifer*, *Scheiben*, *Spinner*, *Steirer*, *Weller*, *Wickler* – and was Frenchified to 'Tyrolienne' or 'Styrienne' when it appeared in opera or the ballroom. *W.A. Mozart wrote sets of *Teutsche* as part of his employment in the last years of his life.

As an outdoor dance, it was vigorous, with hopping and stamping of hob-nailed boots, the female often being passed underarms or thrown over the male's shoulder. In its later, more refined, indoor form, it quickened in tempo and became more gliding and twisting, becoming the *waltz, which soon took over. It survived into the waltz period, with Lanner still calling his early waltzes '*Ländler*' and '*Deutsche*'.

The foot-pattern of the dance is left-right-left with all beats stressed and frequently is accompanied by hand-clapping in two strains of 8 or 16 bars, both repeated. Melodically and harmonically it is *diatonic and often contains arpeggiated figures – a reminder of its debt to Alpine folksong, and indeed it is sung as well as danced or played. (In *Hummel's 'New Vienna Waltz, with three trios' which appeared in the British musical periodical *The *Harmonicon* (1824), the third trio is sung, ideally by two tenors and a bass (see Carew/*MUSE*, Pl. 51).) Many other composers have written or incorporated *Ländlers* or *ländler*-like passages in their works, notably the Austrian symphonists, *J. Haydn, W.A. Mozart, Bruckner, Mahler and also in *C.M. von Weber, *Brahms and Berg, in whose Violin Concerto, the 'Carpathian tune' is a *Ländler* melody.

Further reading
H. Dondl, *Der Ländler* (Munich, 1912). R. Zoder, 'Die melodische-stychische Anordnung von Ländlermelodien', *Das deutsche Volkslied*, xvi (1914).

H. Gielge, 'Der geradtaktige Ländler: ein musikalischer Eigenbrötler', *Das deutsche Volkslied*, xlii (1940). P. Nettl, *The Story of Dance Music* (New York, 1947/R1961). E. Hamza, *Der Ländler* (Vienna, 1957).

Lanner, Josef (Franz Karl)
Austrian composer, violinist (b. 11 Apr 1801, Vienna; d. 14 Apr 1843, Oberdöbling, nr Vienna).

Musically self-taught, he was the son of a glovemaker and joined Michael Pamer's dance-orchestra at the age of 12, becoming friendly with *Johann Strauss I who was also a member. In 1818 Lanner left to form his own trio of two violins and guitar, to be joined by Strauss (viola) in 1819 and a cellist the following year. It is most likely that *Schubert, among others, would have been familiar with the group, which became larger until it was finally a full-sized orchestra. It played in all the main venues in Vienna, including the city's amusement park, the Prater, instigating a long tradition of open-air concerts there. Their great popularity resulted in the orchestra being split – the other under Strauss. However, quarrels arose and the orchestras split, a fact which Lanner 'documented' in his *Trennungs-Walzer* (*Separation-Walzer*) op. 19 (*c.*1828). Lanner toured the main cities of the Austrian empire and was in Milan at the coronation of Ferdinand II. He died, prematurely, of typhus. His son August was also a conductor and band master but died of tuberculosis at the age of 21. His daughter Katti became a famous ballet-dancer; she was dubbed the 'Taglioni of the North'.

Lanner created the classic waltz-set of an introduction (often pictorial), some five waltzes and a coda which usually recalled all or some of the waltzes. The idea came from Weber's *Aufforderung zum Tanze* (*Invitation to the Dance*) op. 65 (1819). Many have violinistic characteristics and he combined a Viennese melodiousness and finely contoured melodic line with *Romantic harmony.

Works
Many sets of *waltzes, *galops, and some *ländler, marches and *mazurkas, all published for piano and most for orchestra and in chamber arrangements.

Further reading
F. Lange, *Josef Lanner und Johann Strauss* (Vienna, 1904, 2/1919). M. Carner, *The Waltz* (London, 1948). A. Weinmann, *Verzeichnis der im Druck erschienen Werke von Joseph Lanner* (Vienna, 1948). H. Krenn. '*Lenz-Blüthen': Joseph Lanner – sein Leben, sein Werk* (Cologne, 1994).

Lass of Richmond Hill, The
Popular English song; music by James Hook, words by L. McNally. The Richmond in question is that in Yorkshire.

'Last Rose of Summer, The' ['Tis the Last Rose of Summer']
Irish air originally entitled 'Castle Hyde', also known as the 'The Groves of Blarney' (*c.*1790). Thomas *Moore wrote his own words to it and included it (under its best-known title) in his *Irish Melodies* ('*Moore's Melodies*'), 1813. It was very popular throughout Europe and America in the nineteenth century, and was set by, among others, *Beethoven (for flute and piano op. 107/5 (*c.*1818)), *Felix Mendelssohn (*Fantasia*, op. 15 (1827)) *Thalberg (*Air irlandais varié* op. 73) and Flotow (Act 2 of *Martha* (perf. 1847)).

The first verse gives the flavour of the whole song:

> 'Tis the last rose of summer,
> Left blooming alone;
> All her lovely companions
> Are faded and gone;
> No flower of her kindred,
> No rosebud is nigh,
> To reflect back her blushes
> Or give sigh for sigh.

Latrobe [La Trobe], Christian Ignatius

English composer (b. 12 Feb 1758, Fulneck, Leeds; d. 6 May 1836, Fairfield, [now Manchester]).

Son of a family of Huguenot line, his father was a minister of the Moravian Church and Superintendent of Moravian Brethren in England, which allowed him access to the highest circles. Self-taught in music, his first compositions were instrumental, but, having 'discovered' the vocal music of *J. Haydn and Graun with whom he subsequently became friendly, he turned in that direction. He edited several collections of Moravian Church hymns as well as the *Anthems for One or More Voices Sung in the Church of the United Brethren* (pub. 1811), but also wrote Anglican music, writing in the style of Haydn's late masses. His six-volume *Selection of Sacred Music* (pub. 1806–26) introduced a (largely Anglican) Britain to European Catholic Church music in the works of such composers as Pergolesi, Graun, Hasse, Haydn and *W.A. Mozart.

Works

Editions: *The Hymn-tunes of the Church of the Brethren* (London 1790); *A Selection of Sacred Music from the Work of Some of the Most Eminent Composers of Germany and Italy* (pub. 1806–26);

Anthems for One or More Voices Sung in the Church of the United Brethren (including 12 of his own compositions, pub. 1811). Original compositions: Many Anthems, two cantatas (*The Dawn of Glory* (1893) and *In Memory of a Beloved Sister* (1826)); three Piano Sonatas op. 3 (*c.*1790).

Further reading

C.E. Stephens, *The Musical Works of Christian Ignatius Latrobe* (diss., U of North Carolina, 1971).

Leduc, Alphonse

French composer, instrumentalist, music-publisher (b. 11 Mar 1804, Nantes; d. 17 Jun 1868, Paris).

Little is known of his life except that he played flute, bassoon and guitar and studied harmony with *Reicha at the Paris Conservatoire. He founded a music-publishing firm *c.*1841 which passed to his son (also called Alphonse Leduc (1844–92)). It was very prominent in the provision of didactic material and had a huge instrumental list.

Works

He wrote much for his three instruments, flute, bassoon and especially piano, for which he left almost a thousand pieces, many of them dances, and a very popular piano *method, op. 130.

Further reading

C. Hopkinson, *A Dictionary of Parisian Music Publishers 1700–1950* (London, 1954). Fétis/*BIOGRAPHIE*.

Lemière [Le Mière, Le Mierre, Lemierre] de Corvey, Jean-Frédéric-Auguste

French military man, composer (b. 3 Aug 1771, Rennes; d. 24 Apr 1832, Paris).

He is reputed to have begun composing before receiving musical training and his early opera, *Constance*, is said to have been performed at Rennes when he was 20. In 1792 he moved to Paris and studied harmony with Berton, writing a good number of *opéra comiques* between 1792 and 1798, when his military career claimed him. He was involved in many campaigns under Napoleon, including the battle of Waterloo (1815). In 1817 he returned to Paris writing more comic operas with limited success. His military pension proved insufficient to keep him and his family in comfort and he earned money by music proofreading. He died of cholera in meagre circumstances in 1832.

Works
Many *opéras comiques* including *Constance* (1790), *Le poëme volé* (1793), *La reprise de Toulon par les français* (perf. 1794), *Andros et Almona, ou le français à Bassora* (1793–94), *Les suspects* (perf. 1795) and *Les rencontres* (perf. 1828). Other works include the programmatic pieces *La bataille de Jéna gagnée sur les prussiens* op. 36 (*c.*1806) for orchestra (also arranged for piano) and *La Révolution du 10 Aoust 1792* (1792) for piano, as well as chamber works (several including harp) and military band-music.

Further reading
F. Clément and P. Larousse, *Dictionnaire lyrique, ou Histoire des opéras* (Paris 1867–69, 3/1905/R1969). H. Gougelot, *La romance française sous la Révolution et l'Empire*, i (Melun, 1938).

Lichnowsky Family
Austro-Hungarian aristocratic family who patronized the arts.

Prince Karl [Carl] von Lichnowsky spent most of his time in Vienna and married the Countess Thun, who was a pupil of *J. Haydn and a friend of *W.A. Mozart, as indeed was the Prince himself, who belonged to the same Masonic Lodge in Vienna. They befriended the young *Beethoven when Haydn introduced them to him on his arrival in 1792 and he lived in their house for a time. The Lichnowskys held evening concerts at which the social and cultural elite of the city met and at their regular Friday-morning concerts Beethoven's early chamber works were given their first performances. The Prince supported Beethoven financially also.

His sister, **Countess Henriette**, was also a friend of the composer and when, on her marriage to a French aristocrat, she went to live in Paris, she also moved in musical circles, including that of *Chopin. Their brother, **Count Moritz von Lichnowsky**, was himself a talented composer and pianist and patronized (and was friendly with) Mozart and *Beethoven, never losing an opportunity to further the career of the latter. He lobbied to get him appointed court composer, gave financial advice and helped in the arrangements for the premiere of the Ninth Symphony. He also befriended *Chopin later in his life. A later member of the family, Prince Karl's grandson, **Prince Felix**, corresponded on friendly terms with *Liszt.

Lid swell (see *swell)

Lied (Ger.: 'song'; *Gesang* also used but more rarely; Fr. *chanson*; It. *canzona*)
The generally-accepted term for the song in German, not exactly translated into the other languages mentioned. It originated as a polyphonic form in the fourteenth century, but in the *Baroque period (and just before) it became a solo song with

basso continuo accompaniment. It is in this form that it is seen at its most typical, reflecting general changes in musical style and becoming centred on Berlin in the second half of the eighteenth century with the First and Second *Berlin Lieder Schools and a less-productive offshoot in Vienna. In the nineteenth century the literature of the lied burgeoned with the works of *Schubert, *Loewe, the *Mendelssohns, *R. Schumann, Wolf and *Brahms, and it grew in stature, many examples being mini-dramas. Poets (especially German-speaking poets from Goethe onwards) wrote poetry specifically with musical setting in mind.

Liederjahr [Ger.: 'Year of Song[s]'] (see *Schumann, R.)

Liederkreis [Ger.: *'Song-cycle']
Though a general term it is particularly applied to *R. Schumann's two song-cycles opp. 24 and 39.

Lied ohne Worte [pl. *Lieder ohne Worte*] (see *Song Without Words)

Leitmotiv (from Ger. *Leitmotiv*, 'leading motif' or 'motive'; Fr. *idée fixe*)
In music, the recurrent use (with or without modification) of a theme or similar musical idea to give unity to a work. It is generally considered to be recognizably longer than a motif, which is usually five or less notes, and is often used in operas, associated with particular characters, ideas or states of mind, frequently being modified or developed to reflect their development or emotional state. Wagner's use in his music-dramas was as a comprehensive musical sub-text, at times paralleling the dramtic movement and certainly underpinning it, although *C.M. von Weber had used the technique

in a less rigorous way before him. Indeed, it was in a book (by F.W. Jähns) on the latter's works that the term was invented.

Liszt, Franz [Ferenc]
Hungarian composer, pianist, teacher (b. 22 Oct 1811, Raiding (Doborján); d. 31 Jul 1886, Bayreuth).

Born on the *Esterházy estates, his father was an official and a good amateur cellist in the court orchestra, as well as playing the piano, which he taught Franz. He may have played in public at the age of six and was composing by eight, but, after concerts in Sopron and Poszony in late 1820 (when he was nine), local aristocrats banded together to subsidize his musical education and the family moved to Vienna (1821). He studied piano with *Czerny and composition with Salieri, meeting *Beethoven (who, Liszt later said, kissed his forehead) and *Schubert and his first public concert the following year was a great success. Although not yet 12 he was asked to contribute a variation to the set being compiled by the composer-publisher Anton *Diabelli, who wrote a waltz as the theme. All composers living or visiting the city at the time were asked to supply one, and among those who responded were Schubert, *Czerny, *Hummel and *Moscheles; Beethoven wrote a whole set of 33 and fugue as his contribution (his *'*Diabelli Variations*' op. 120). The Liszt family moved to Paris in 1823, giving concerts en route. He was refused admission to the Conservatoire (on the grounds of being a foreigner) but studied theory with *Reicha and composition with Paer. His first concert in the French capital on 7 March 1824 was a sensation, leading to other engagements and invitations to all the best houses. Later that year he played his London début in the Argyll rooms as 'Master Liszt' playing Hummel's very difficult piano concerto in A minor on an *Erard piano. He had already written bravura pieces on themes by popular opera composers, such as Spontini and *Rossini, but the composition of his *Etude en douze exercices* (*Study in Twelve Exercises*) of 1826 was the start of his serious composition. This piece was the original version of the *Transcendental Studies*.

The constant tours which Liszt was undertaking were beginning to take a toll on his health and he went with his father to Boulogne to rest, where the latter contracted typhoid fever and died suddenly. Liszt, still in his mid-teens, returned to Paris and moved in with his mother and became a piano-teacher. Forced to break off a romantic attachment to one of his pupils, he became ill again and suffered bouts of depression and religious doubts in spite of his strong Catholicism; he was discouraged by his mother in his desire to join the Church.

A number of events conspired to revive his spirits – the July Revolution (1830), his meeting with *Berlioz and the premiere of the latter's *Symphonie fantastique*, and his first hearing *Paganini on 9 March 1831. The result of this was that Liszt redefined piano technique in a series of dazzling works, the six *Études d'exécution transcencdente d'après Paganini* (1838–40, rev. 1851). However, the other, more spiritual, side of his personality was also finding its authentic voice; with this and his growing friendship with *Chopin came the *Harmonies poétiques et religieuses* (*Religious and Poetic Harmonies*) after, and dedicated to, Lamartine and the three *Apparitions* (both 1834). Liszt also became friendly with Delacroix, Lammenais, Hugo, Lamartine, Heine, and was especially influenced by Berlioz and

Paganini, whose brilliant violin-playing staggered him – as it did most musicians of the period. He was introduced to the ideas of the Saint-Simonians by Urhan and read much at this time to compensate for his lack of more general education.

Yet another friendship, and a vital one, was his introduction, by George Sand, to Countess Marie d'Agoult (1834), with whom he was soon having a love-affair. The following year the Countess left husband and family to join Liszt in Geneva, where Liszt was teaching at the new Conservatory. He wrote a piano *method which, unfortunately, has been lost. For the next four years the couple, and their baby daughter, travelled through Switzerland and Italy, and Liszt chronicled the journeys (inwardly as well as outwardly) in *Album d'un voyageur* (*Traveller's Notebook*) of 1835–36, later revised as the first of the three books of *Années de pèlerinage* (*Years of Pilgrimage*), the other two of which were composed 1837–49 and 1867–77 respectively. On one of their visits to Paris, the celebrated pianistic duel between Liszt and *Thalberg, who was threatening the Hungarian's position, did not produce an overall victor. He spent the next year or so with the Countess in Italy and another daughter and a son were born. The relationship was becoming strained, however, and a convenient forced separation offered itself when Liszt decided to go on concert-tours again. The immediate stimulus was the fact that the proposed Beethoven monument in Bonn was running short of sponsors and he offered to donate the remainder himself. He gave six concerts in Vienna and visited his native Hungary for the first time since the family left it; he was everywhere received with great acclaim. He proposed the foundation of a national conservatory in Budapest and renewed his acquaintance with gypsy music. He continued to tour and the decade 1838–47 is often referred to as his 'Glanzeit' ('golden age'); Heine coined the term *Lisztomanie* ('Lisztomania') to describe the sometimes hysterical reception which he was given almost everywhere except, perhaps, England, where things were a little muted, no doubt because the news of his liaison with the Countess and perhaps his other mistresses had reached Queen Victoria. Nevertheless, from small villages in the south of Ireland to the dazzling European capitals and many points north and south, he played to audiences of all types and sizes. While playing in Kiev in February 1847, he met the Countess Carolyne Sayn-Wittgenstein, who would be his greatest influence for most of the rest of his life. She dissuaded him from touring and encouraged him to spend more of his time on composition. Liszt decided (February 1848) to take up the offer, already made for some time, of the post of *Kapellmeister* to the Grand Duke Carl Friedrich (and his successor Carl Alexander) at the court of Weimar, a prestigious court whose previous incumbents included *Herder, Goethe, Schiller, Wieland and Hummel. Here, he created a centre for contemporary music, both his own (of which he composed a huge amount) and others, including Wagner (the premiere of whose *Lohengrin* Liszt conducted), Schubert, Schumann, Berlioz, Verdi, Donizetti and Peter Cornelius; it was the bad reception of an opera by the latter that prompted Liszt's resignation in 1859. It did not help that a protest appearing in the Berlin *Echo* against the 'New German School' of composers (led by Liszt and Wagner) was signed by *Brahms, Grimm, *Joachim and Scholz.

There were other reasons also: his open living with Countess Carolyne did not please the staid burghers and his championship of Wagner (then a political refugee) was not approved of. Also, in 1859, his only son Daniel, died in Berlin at the age of 20 and Liszt wrote *Les Morts*, for orchestra, in his memory. The Countess visited Rome for an audience with the Pope in the hope of getting her marriage annulled to marry Liszt. With high hopes of an impending marriage, he joined her in Rome in 1861, on the day before his fiftieth birthday. The marriage was forbidden. His eldest daughter died in 1862.

Liszt spent the next eight years in Rome composing religious music; he became a friend of Pope Pius IX and entered the Catholic Church, taking minor orders of the priesthood in 1865. He was invited back to Weimar in 1869 to give piano masterclasses, and to Budapest, for the same reason, two years later; the rest of his life was spent travelling between these centres and Rome and was visited by many composers – Rubinstein, Albéniz, Saint-Saëns, Fauré, Debussy and Borodin among them – and taught many of the next generation of pianists (see below). A rift with Wagner (occasioned by Liszt's only surviving child, his daughter Cosima, having an affair with the composer and bearing two illegitimate children) was healed when he attended the Bayreuth Festival in 1872. He undertook a last concert-tour (including London) which was very successful and visited Bayreuth again for the wedding of his granddaughter, but was diagnosed with dropsy. This developed into fatal pneumonia and he died; Carolyne died a year later.

Considered the greatest pianist of his time – of all time, by many – Liszt expanded the technique of piano-playing immeasurably and this is enshrined in most of his music. As a harmonist, his original use of the whole-tone and gypsy scales, and chromatic chords without recourse to harmonic syntax fixes him as one of the founders of several strands in twentieth-century music, while his compositional techniques eschew the more fixed forms of sonata-form etc. for a freer, improvisatory transformation of themes. A great supporter of other composers, he championed many, not least Wagner, and introduced their music to many in his recitals. He invented the *Symphonic Poem (Sinfonische Dichtung), an orchestral work of free construction based on pictorial or literary ideas. His enigmatic personality made an immediate and lasting impression on all who met him, or saw him play.

Liszt's influence was enormous on subsequent harmony, compositional and pianistic techniques. He taught many of the next generation of great pianists, among them *Amy Fay, Frederic Lamond, Moritz Rosenthal, Eugen d'Albert, Sophie Mentor, Emil von Sauer, José Vianna da Motta and Felix Weingartner

Works

Piano: *Harmonies poétiques et religieuses* (*Religious and Poetic Harmonies*) S154/R13, *Apparitions* S155/R11 (both 1834); three *Années de pèlerinage* (*Years of Pilgrimage*), (S160/R10a, 1848–54; S161/R10b, 1837–49 and S163/R10e, 1867–77); six *Consolations* S172/R12 (1849–50); two *Légendes* S175/R17 (1863); *Nuages gris* S199/R78 (*Grey Clouds*, 1881); *La lugubre gondola* S199/R81 (*The Sad Gondola*, 1882); *Études d'exécution transcencdente d'après Paganini* S140/R3a (*Transcendental Studies after Paganini*, 1838–40, rev.

1851); *Études d'exécution transcencdente* S139/R2b (*Transcendental Studies*, 1851); Piano Sonata in B minor S178/R21 (1852–53) and hundreds of dance-pieces, works based on national themes, operatic transcriptions and paraphrases, and smaller works; also many arrangements of his own and others' works. For piano and orchestra there are the two piano concertos, no. 1 in E♭ major S124/R455 (1849, rev. 1853 and 1856), and no. 2 in A major S125/R456 (1839, rev. 1849–61), *Malédiction* S121/R452 (piano and orchestra, *c.*1840), *Fantasie über Motive aus Beethovens Ruinen von Athen* S122/R454 (*Fantasy on a Motif from Beethoven's 'The Ruins of Athens'*, ?1848–52) and *Totentanz* S126/R457 (*Dance of Death*, 1849, rev. 1853 and 1859). Among the orchestral works are the *symphonic poems including *Tasso: lamento e trionfo* S96/R412 (*Tasso: Lament and Triumph*, 1849, rev. 1850–51 and 1854), *Orpheus* S98/R415 (1853–54), *Prometheus* S99/R416 (1850, rev.1855), *Mazeppa* S100/R417 (1851, rev. bef. 1854), *Hungaria* S103/R420 (1854), *Hamlet* S104/R421 (1858), and *Hunnenschlacht* S105/R422 (*The War Against the Huns*, 1857) and the *Faust* and *Dante* Symphonies (S108//R425 (1854–57) and S109/R426 (1855–56)). There is a huge body of sacred and secular choral works, including the oratorio *Christus* S3/R478 (1862–67), a Missa solemnis S9/R484 (1855, rev. 1857–58), a Missa choralis S10/R486 (1965), Requiem for male voices S12/R488 (1867–8), Psalms, choruses, hymns, etc. and many songs.

Further reading

A large body of material on various aspects of the composer's life and works, from which the following have been selected: H. Searle, *The Music of Liszt*

(London, 1954, rev. 2/1966). A. Walker, *Franz Liszt* (3 vols, Ithaca, NY, 1987–97). F. Liszt (tr. and annotated C. Suttoni), *An Artist's Journey: Lettres d'un bachelier ès musique* (Chicago, IL, 1989).

Lobkowitz [Lobkowicz, Lobkovic] Bohemian aristocratic family, noted patrons of the arts, many of whose members played, or were interested in, music.

Prince **Ferdinand Philipp Joseph** took *Gluck to London in 1745, but the best-remembered is **Joseph Franz Maximilian** [Josef František Maximilián]. He played the violin and cello and was a bass singer, one of the group of aristocrats in charge of directing the Viennese court theatres and, later with sole responsibility for opera. Having been a patron to *J. Haydn – commissioning his op. 77 string quartets and helping to sponsor *The Creation* and *The Seasons*, in both of which he performed – he joined Prince Kinsky and *Archduke Rudolph in funding an annuity for *Beethoven to ensure his remaining in Austria. The composer dedicated some of his finest works to him, including the 'Eroica' (whose first performance was at one of his private concerts) as well as the Fifth and Sixth Symphonies, the six string quartets op. 18, the triple Concerto and the song-cycle *An die ferne Geliebte*.

Further reading
A.W. Thayer, 'The Lobkowitz Family', *Musical World*, lvii (1879). S. Ley, 'Beethoven und Fürst Lobkowitz', *Atlantis*, ix (1937).

Loewe, (Johann) Carl (Gottfried) German composer, singer (b. 30 Nov 1796, Loebjuen, nr Halle; d. 20 Apr 1869, Kiel).

Youngest of a schoolmaster's twelve children, and first by his father, he became a choirboy and was already composing – with some publications – when he went to high school at 12 and studied composition and piano with *Türk. Jérôme Buonaparte was so impressed with his fine voice that he granted him an annuity until he was deposed in 1813. A devout Catholic, he read theology at Halle University and 1819–20 he toured the German cities and met Goethe, *C.M. von Weber and *Hummel. Loewe was appointed Kantor and professor at the Gymnasium and seminary in Stettin, spending the rest of his life there and being promoted to Musikdirektor and organist of St Jacobus's Cathedral in 1821. The same year he married his first wife who died two years later and, in 1826, his second wife Auguste Lange who was a well-known singer who often gave his songs in public. His oratorio *Die Zerstörung Jerusalems* (*The Destruction of Jerusalem*) was acclaimed on its premiere in 1832. He received a gold medal and was elected a member of the Berlin Academy in 1837. His music was by now well-known and loved in Germany, and he was called the 'north German *Schubert'. He toured Austria, England and Scandinavia and on his return in 1864, suffered a stroke which rendered him unconscious for three weeks. On his recovery, he had to resign his post in 1865 and died four years later after another stroke.

Works
Some solo piano works, including a *Grande sonate élegique* (Grand Elegiac Sonata) in F minor op. 32 (1819–25, rev.1834), the *tone-poem *Mazeppa* op. 27 (1830) and a *Ziguener-Sonate* (Gypsy-Sonata) op. 107b (1842). A small number

of dramatic works include the *Romantic opera *Emmy* (1842) and there are some 15 *oratorios and a sizeable body of secular works. There are hundreds of songs, including four sets of *Hebraïsche Gesänge* (*Hebrew Songs*, with texts by Byron and from the Bible), and settings of Goethe's *Erlkönig* (1823) and some from Chamisso's *Frauenliebe* (1836) which hold their own very well against Schubert's and Schumann's settings respectively.

Further reading
H. Engel, *Carl Loewe: Überblick und Würdigung seines Schaffens* (Greifswald, 1934). W. Serauky, 'Zu C. Loewe's Biographie und musikalischem Schaffen', *Festschrift Arnold Schering* (Berlin, 1937). R. Sietz, *Carl Loewe: ein Gedenkbuch zum 150 Geburtstag* (Cologne, 1948). M.J.E. Brown, 'Carl Loewe, 1796–1869', *MT*, cx (1969). J. Smeed, *German Song and its Poetry 1740–1900* (London, 1987).

'London' Bach (see *Johann Christian Bach)

London Piano School
Portmanteau name given to the piano-composers who lived in, or visited, London during the first half of the nineteenth century. This grouping of composers – from a number of countries, and many on short visits to the capital – seems too arbitrary for the name to imply any shared stylistic or pianistic traits and therefore seems pointless. Similarly, there were comparatively few native British piano-composers at work in London during the period, and none of international importance, to justify considering them as group under the name. The British ('English', but not 'London') piano cannot really be seen as any kind of link, as composers were quite capable of playing on non-British pianos and many of them only used it while in London.

Louis Ferdinand [Friedrich Christian Ludwig] **Prince** of Prussia
German composer, pianist (b. 18 Nov 1772, Friedrichsfelde, nr Berlin; d. 13 Oct 1806, Saalfeld).

Although educated for a military career, he showed great aptitude for the piano as a child and had his early compositions tried out by his uncle's orchestra and met many of the visiting French intelligentsia and cultural figures at his home. He joined the army at 19 and took part in the Silesian campaign in 1790 and the Franco-Prussian War (1792–95), narrowly escaping death on many occasions. He was decorated for bravery by the Austrian government. Louis came into contact with the Schlegel brothers, Wackenroder, Schleiermacher, Fichte, Tieck, Dorothea Veit and others, and met *Beethoven, who admired his playing. He studied with *J.L. Dussek and made him his *Kapellmeister, remaining his patron. He commanded the Prussian advance guard during Napoleon's invasion in 1806 and was killed at the battle of Saalfeld the same year, at the age of 33. His music was much played and admired by musicians of many kinds, and Beethoven – who said he played the piano less like a prince than a 'right good piano-player' – dedicated his Third Piano Concerto to him.

Works
There are some songs but most are for, or incorporating, the piano including three Piano Trios, a fine Piano Quartet in F minor op. 6 (1806) and two quintets (op. 1 in C minor (pub. 1803) and op. 5 in

Eb major (1806)), some works for larger ensembles and two rondos for piano and orchestra, in Bb major op. 9 (1808) and in Eb major op. 13 (pub. 1823).

Further reading
B. Nadolny, *Louis Ferdinand* (Dusseldorf, 1967). E. Klessman, *Louis Ferdinand von* *Preussen, 1772–1806* (Munich, 1972). B.H. McMurtry, *The Music of Prince Louis Ferdinand* (diss., U. of Illinois, 1972).

Lute stop (see *Stop (5))

Lydian mode (see *Mode)

M

Macfarren, Sir **George (Alexander)**
British composer (b. 2 Mar 1813, London;
d. 31 Oct 1887, London).

Son of a London dancing-master
and dramatist from whom he had his
first lessons, he also had lessons with
Charles Lucas, a conductor and composer
prominent in London musical life, and
attended the *Royal Academy of Music
in 1829. He studied composition with
Cipriani *Potter and helped in the founding
of the Society of British Musicians
(1834) and the Handel Society (1844)
and began to be noticed as a composer.
Macfarren was appointed professor at
the RAM in 1837, resigning ten years
later because of a dispute with the other
staff over teaching material; however, he
was recalled by Potter in 1851. He had
become conductor at Covent Garden
theatre in early 1845 and his opera *King
Charles II* was produced in the Princess's
Theatre with great success – one of his
few theatrical successes. His eyesight,
always weak, failed and he became blind
in 1860, although he continued to write,
lecture, teach and compose to the end of
his life. Many honours were conferred
on him; appointed professor of music
at Cambridge University (succeeding
Sterndale *Bennett) and principal of the
RAM; knighted in 1883 and had honorary
degrees conferred on him from the
great British musical centres of Oxford,
Cambridge and Dublin.

Macfarren, an ardent admirer of *W.A.
Mozart, was a dogmatic man who found
any kind of innovation distasteful almost
on principle and whose rigid ideas put
him hopelessly out of touch with his times
towards the end of his life. Wagner, who
conducted – and enjoyed – Macfarren's
overture *Chevy Chace* in London in
1855, described him as 'a popmpous
melancholy Scotsman' and *Felix
Mendelssohn, conducting the same work
in Leipzig some twelve years earlier, had
no praise for it in spite of its popularity.
He never had consistent success, but kept
on persevering; this is especially evident
in his stubborn persistence in continuing
to write symphonies in spite of public
indifference.

Works
Stage works include *Genevieve, or The
Maid of Switzerland* (perf. 1834); *The
Devil's Opera* (perf. 1838); *An Adventure
of Don Quixote* (perf. 1846); *King
Charles II* (perf. 1849); *Robin Hood*
(perf. 1860); *Kenilworth* (perf. 1880).
There are some 13 works for choir and
orchestra, among them the cantatas
Songs in a Cornfield (to poems by C.
Rossetti, perf. 1868), *The Lady of the
Lake* (perf. 1877) and *Around the Hearth*
(perf. 1887). Nine symphonies survive,
concertos for flute in G major (1863),
violin in G minor (1871–74) and piano
in C minor (perf. 1835) as well as a cello
concertino in A major (1836) and some
overtures – including *The Merchant of
Venice* (c.1834), *Romeo and Juliet* and
Chevy Chace (both 1836). Chamber
music includes five string quartets, a
string quintet (with double bass) and
instrumental sonatas, and there are three
piano sonatas – no. 2 is 'Ma cousine' in
A major (1845) – an organ sonata in C
major (1869) and smaller piano pieces.
His writings include *A Sketch for the
Life of Handel* (London, 1859), *The
Rudiments of Harmony, with Progressive
Exercises* (London, 1860), *Six Lectures
on harmony, delivered at the Royal
Institution* (London, 1867) and *On the
Structure of a Sonata* (London, 1871).

Further reading
H.C. Banister, *George Alexander Macfarren* (London, 1891). W. Macfarren, 'George Alexander Macfarren', *R.A.M. Magazine*, no. 1 (1900). G.B. Shaw, *Music in London 1890–94* (London, 1932). N. Temperley, 'The English Romantic Opera', *Victorian Studies*, ix (1966).

Macfarren, Walter (Cecil)

British pianist, composer; brother of *George Macfarren (b. 28 Aug 1826, London; d. 2 Sep 1905, London).

He was a chorister at Westminster Abbey from 1836 to 1841 and the following year studied at the *Royal Academy of Music with W.H. Holmes, for piano and for composition with his brother *George Macfarren and with *Potter. Macfarren became professor of piano and lectured at the RAM (1846–1903), conducting many of the orchestral concerts. He was well respected as a teacher and pianist, involved in the *Philharmonic Society, of which he was treasurer 1877–80 and music critic of *The Queen* from 1862 until 1905, the year of his death.

Macfarren taught Henry Wood, Stewart Macpherson and Tobias Matthay and edited *W.A. Mozart's and *Beethoven's piano music.

Works
Mostly for piano – sonatas, preludes, studies and smaller pieces including *L'Amitié. Caprice for the Piano Forte* (pub. 1848) and a *Scale and Arpeggio Manual* (pub. 1882) – but also a symphony in B♭ major, concert overtures and much vocal music, including partsongs and songs.

Further reading
W. Macfarren, *Memories: an Autobiography* (London, 1905). 'Mr Walter Macfarren', *MT*, xxxix (1898).

Machine stop (see *Stop (10))

Maestro e lo scolare, Il (It.: 'The Master and the Student')
The subtitle of a didactic *Divertimento by *J. Haydn for piano duet, the main title of which is *Sonata a quattro mani* (It.: 'Sonata for four Hands', 1768–70). A set of variations, the student's part becomes progressively more difficult, though it remains at beginner's level. The piece is one of the composer's only two known pieces for piano duet.

Magazin der Musik
A periodical edited and published by Carl Friedrich Cramer, German linguist, writer on music and publisher, which ran from 1783 for three years and was then issued from 1789 in Copenhagen under the title *Musik*. It contained essays on various aspects of music, including theory, criticisms of concerts, and information about concert programme-listings in various parts of Europe as well as lists (by genre) of published music as it appeared.

Malibran [née Garcia], **Maria(-Felicia)**
Spanish mezzo-soprano, eldest daughter of tenor Manuel Garcia and sister to Pauline Viardot (b. 24 Mar 1808, Paris; d. 23 Sep 1836, Manchester).

Her father, a famous tenor, was very hard on the young singer, who made her London debut at the age of 17 in the King's Theatre in Rossini's *Il barbiere di Siviglia*, and later the same year – with her father also taking part – in the same work in the Park Theatre, New York. Her first marriage, as a means of escaping from her father, to Eugène Malibran, lasted very little time, and she was back in Europe alone in 1827. She had a varied and successful career for the next nine years, singing in London, Paris, and the important Italian opera centres. Her first marriage was annulled and in 1836, she married the violinist Charles de *Bériot. A riding accident the same year (during her pregnancy) resulted in an illness while participating in the Manchester Festival, and she died a few months later. Having a powerful flexible voice with large compass (g – e''') – much due to her father's training – Malibran sang all the major contemporary soprano title-roles.

Further reading
P. Larionoff and F. Pestellini, *Maria Malibran e i suoi tempi* (Florence, 1935). D. Bielli, *Maria Malibran* (Castelbordino, 1936). S. Desternes and H. Chandet, *La Malibran et Pauline Viardot* (Paris, 1969). A. Fitzlyon, *Maria Malibran* (London, 1987).

Mandolin (Fr. *mandoline*; Ger. *Mandoline*; It. *mandolino*; Sp. *bandolin*, *mandolino*)
A string instrument of the lute family with a similarly-[half-pear]shaped body and from (most commonly) four to six strings. In most cases these are tuned in unison pairs, for example, the four-string version has eight strings (usually steel) tuned in pairs a fourth apart (*g—d'—a'—e''*). It is played held across the body, either stroked as with the lute and guitar, or played *tremolando* with finger-tips, nails or a *plectrum. The instrument was – and remains – popular in Italian (and latterly other) *folk music. There are a number of types – Milanese, Genoese and so on – differing in tuning and other ways. It was popular in the eighteenth century both as a solo and ensemble instrument, but also appeared in opera (the serenade from *W.A. Mozart's *Don Giovanni* (1787), for example) and *Beethoven and

*Hummel wrote pieces for it, the latter a concerto.

'Mannheim *Bebung' orchestral device (see *Mannheim orchestra)

Mannheim orchestra
Specifically, the orchestra associated with the Palatine court of Mannheim during the reign of the Elector Carl Theodor. He was well-known as an ardent patron of the arts, especially music and played several instruments himself. He built up a large body of musicians and an orchestra, under the virtuoso violinist and composer Johann *Stamitz, which was the envy of Europe. In *Burneys's famous words (1772), 'There are more solo players [i.e. as opposed to being 'just' orchestral players] and good composers in this than perhaps in any other orchestra in Europe; it is an army of generals, equally fit to plan a battle as to fight it.' The orchestra exhibited an unusual precision of attack, fine dynamic shading, uniform bowing. As the composer Daniel *Schubart wrote 'Its *forte* is a thunderclap, its crescendo a cataract, its diminuendo a crystal stream babbling away in the distance, its *piano* a breath of spring.'

The orchestra specialized in a number of musical devices featured in the music written for it by, mainly, the incumbent composers, such as the *Stamitz family, Cannabich, Toeschi, the Cramer brothers and the Eck brothers. These devices were already recognized in the eighteenth century as part of the 'Mannheim Style' (called Mannheim *Manieren* [figures] by the historian Hugo Riemann, but referred to by, for example, *W.A. Mozart's father *Leopold, as '*vermanierten* Mannheimer goût'). These figures include the 'Mannheim rocket', a rising arpeggiaic melody with a flourish at the top (examples are to be found in *Beethoven's first piano sonata op. 2/1/i in F minor and the finale of Mozart's late G minor symphony, no. 40, K550/iv); the 'Mannheim roller' or 'Mannheim steamroller' (*Walzer* in German), a crescendo, originating not in Mannheim, but earlier in Italy, in which a (usually rising) melodic line over a pedal-point, is accompanied by *tremolando* figures which crescendo through it; the 'Mannheim sigh', an expressive appoggiatura associated with an anticipatory note; and the 'Mannheim *Bebung*', a fast turn.

'Mannheim rocket' orchestral device (see *Mannheim orchestra)

'Mannheim roller' or **'steamroller'** orchestral device (see *Mannheim orchestra)

'Mannheim sigh' orchestral device (see *Mannheim orchestra)

Manual

A *keyboard played by the hands, as opposed to one played by the feet. It is usually used in the case of an instrument with more than one keyboard (such as the *harpsichord or organ) or has a *pedal-board (as in the *organ or *pedal piano).

Marius, Jean

French instrument-maker, inventor (d. 6 Apr 1720).

On a quest to produce a keyboard instrument with dynamic gradation, Marius submitted four versions of possible actions for *clavecins à maillets* (keyboards with hammers) to the Académie des Sciences in Paris in 1716, and received a royal privilege for 20 years. The fourth design was a harpsichord with a register of hammers as well as the normal jacks;

each was independent, and they could also be combined. He also invented a *clavecin brisé*, a harpsichord in three hinged sections which could be folded up and carried around.

Further reading

P. James, *Early Keyboard Instruments* (London, 1930, rev.1967). H.K. Lange, 'Das Clavecin brisé von Jean Marius in der Berliner Sammlung und die Schlick-Stimmung', *Die Musikforschung*, xxxi (1978). G. Juramie, *Histoire du piano* (Paris 1948). Boalch/HARPSICHORD. Harding/PIANO-FORTE.

Marmontel, Antoine François

French pianist, teacher, composer (b. 18 Jul 1816, Clermont-Ferrand; d. 16 Jan 1898, Paris).

He studied at the Paris Conservatoire with Zimmermann (piano) and Le Sueur (composition) winning the *Premier prix* in 1832 and then taught *solfège* there until 1887. He was appointed to teach piano after his piano-teacher, Zimmermann, retired in 1848 and he remained in this post until he died in 1898. A brilliant teacher, Marmontel's pupils included Dubois, Bizet, d'Indy, Albéniz and Wieniawski. His book, *Les pinaistes célèbres* (pub. 1878), is a valuable source on nineteenth-century pianists and pianism.

Works

Many piano works (sonatas, studies, smaller pieces). Also wrote *L'art classique et moderne du piano* [*The Classic and Modern art of the Piano*] (Paris, 1876); *Les pianistes célèbres* [*The Great Pianists*] (Paris, 1878, abbreviated here as Marmontel/*PIANISTES*); *Symphonistes et virtuoses* (Paris, 1881); *Virtuoses contemporains* (Paris, 1882); *Elémens d'aesthétique musicale* [*Elements of a musical aesthetic*] (Paris, 1884); *Histoire du piano et ses origines* [*History and Origins of the Piano*] (Paris, 1885).

Further reading
C. Pierre, *Le Conservatoire national* (Paris, 1900). W. Dean, *Georges Bizet* (London, 1965). A. Rousselin-Lacombe, 'Piano et pianistes', in J.-M. Bailbé and others, eds, *La Musique en France à l'époque romantique* (Paris, 1991).

Marquetry
A design or pattern, usually in wood veneer, but can be metal, bone, ivory or (later) plastic, which is glued onto the *case of a *keyboard instrument.

Marschner, Heinrich August
German composer (b. 16 Aug 1795, Zittau; d. 14 Dec 1861, Hanover).

Born into a musical family of Bohemian artisans, he sang in the choir at school but was self-taught in music until the age of 14, when, having already composed songs and a ballet, he took composition lessons with the music-director of the seminary. He studied law in Leipzig and music (part-time), meeting *Tomášek, and was encouraged by the Thomaskantor, Schicht, to familiarize himself with the works of Kirnberger, *Türk, Righini and the symphonies of *Beethoven, whom he met in Vienna. In 1816 Marschner became music-teacher in the home of a count in Pressburg (now Bratislava) and met *C.M. von Weber in Dresden – as he had agreed to produce Marschner's opera *Heinrich IV* – and settled in the city in 1821. He got to know Tieck and Kind and received commissions for incidental stage-music. He publicly declared his belief in national German opera and wrote *Der Holzdieb* [*The Wood-Thief*] in 1823. He was appointed music-director

in Dresden under Weber (but against his wishes). Marschner married a singer, met *Felix Mendelssohn in Berlin and accepted a post at the Stadttheater in Leipzig and, after his German operas *Der Vampyr* [*The Vampire*] (1827) and *Der Templer und die Jüdin* [*The Templar and the Jewess*] (1829) had spread his name throughout Germany, he was appointed conductor at the Hoftheater in Hanover in 1830. *Hans Heiling* (1831–32) was also a great success and works were performed at various music festivals. However, his position in Hanover was not comfortable, especially in that his views on German opera went counter to the prevailing taste for Italian works and his life appointment was not forthcoming until 1852. He was given the post of *Generalmusikdirektor* – which was in the nature of a pension – in 1859 but still decided to remain in Hanover despite offers from elsewhere. His fourth marriage comforted him, but his works were falling out of favour, especially with the advent of Wagner and *Meyerbeer.

Marschner can be seen as an operatic link between C.M. von Weber and Wagner in terms of his plots and the forms used. He laid great store by psychological depiction of character, particularly in cases of dual personality, and was adept in the use of *leitmotiv* technique and characterful accompaniments. He was also much lauded for his use of *folk elements in his stage works and his influence was noticeable on subsequent composers of German music, especially Wagner.

Works
25 stage works including the operas *Heinrich IV und d'Aubigné* (1817–18), *Der Vampyr* [*The Vampire*] (1827), *Der Templer und die Jüdin* [*The Templar and*

the Jewess] (perf. 1829), *Hans Heiling* (1831–32), and the *Singspiel Der Holzdieb* [*The Wood-Thief*] (1823). Various piano works (seven sonatas, character-pieces, variations, rondos, etc.) and works for guitar, part-songs and choruses and many songs.

Further reading
J.F.A. Bickel, *Heinrich Marschner in seinen Opern* (diss., U. of Erlangen, 1929). G. Hausswald, *Heinrich Marschner* (Dresden, 1938). K. Günzel, 'Heinrich Marschner, ein Zittauer Musiker', *Sächsische Heimatblätter*, viii (1962). V. Köhler, 'Heinrich Marschner', *Hannoverische Geschichtsblätter*, new series, xvi (1962). A.D. Palmer, *Heinrich August Marschner, 1795–1861: his Life and Stage Works* (Ann Arbor, MI, 1980).

Mattheson, Johann
German composer, theorist, writer on music (b. 28 Sep 1681, Hamburg; d. 17 Apr 1764, Hamburg).

Son of a tax collector, he received an excellent and broad education, being taught general music by the local Kantor, with additional lessons in drawing and dancing, in riding and fencing, as well as French, Italian, English and arithmetic. He had four years' tuition with Hanff in keyboard and composition as well as singing, flute, oboe, violin, gamba, organ and lute; he also studied law. Because of his fine voice, he was invited to join the Hamburg opera company while still a young teenager. Having finished at the Johanneum in 1693 he decided to make the opera company his career. He met *Handel in 1703 and they worked well together, until a quarrel led to a duel, in which Handel was protected from a sword-thrust by a large coat-button. They were, however, reconciled.

Mattheson declined a number of offers (mainly for organ posts) and in 1704 became the tutor to the son of the English ambassador in Hamburg; he did so well that he was made the ambassador's secretary in 1706, which post he retained for most of his life, remaining when the son became ambassador. The same year he was made music director of Hamburg cathedral and he composed much music while in post. However, approaching deafness caused his resignation in 1728 and he was completely deaf by 1735. In addition to his music composition, he also wrote important treatises and translated a quantity of books, articles and pamphlets from English into German and wrote many articles himself also. He donated most of his fortune to St Michael's Church, Hamburg, to restore the great organ which had been burnt, on condition that he and his already deceased wife would be buried in the crypt. Telemann conducted an ode which Mattheson had written for his own funeral.

The most important Baroque writer on music, Mattheson charted the progress from *Baroque to *Classical styles and wrote on all the aspects of music in his time. His influence on subsequent music-history writers was immense. Most of his own music was lost during the bombing of the Second World War.

Works
Because of bombing during the Second World War, only some keyboard collections, chamber music and one opera (from 8) and one oratorio – *Das Lied des Lammes* [*The Song of the Lamb* (1723)] – from over 24 survive. His writings on music include *Das neu-eröffente Orchestre* (pub. 1713); *Exemplarische Organisten- Probe in Artikel vom general-*

Bass (pub. 1719); *Critica Musica* (pub. 1722); *Der volkommene Capellmeister* (pub. 1739); *George Friedrich Händels Lebensbeschreibung* (pub. 1761).

Further reading
B.C. Cannon, *Johann Mattheson, Spectator in Music* (New Haven, CT, 1947). W. Braun, *Johann Mattheson und die Aufklärung* (diss., U. of Halle, 1952). H. Lenneberg, 'Johann Mattheson on Affect and Rhetoric in Music', *JMT*, ii (1958). F. Feldmann, 'Der Hamburger Johann Mattheson und die Musik Mittel- und Ostdeutschlands', *Hamburger Mittel- und Ostdeutsche Forschungen*, v (1966). H.J. Marx, ed., *Johann Mattheson (1681–1764): Lebensbeschreibung des Hamburger Musikers, Schriftstellers und Diplomaten* (Hamburg, 1892).

Mayer, Charles
German pianist, teacher (b. 21 Mar 1799, Königsberg [now Kaliningrad]; d. 2 Jul 1862, Dresden).

Born into a musical family which moved to Russia when he was a baby, settling in Moscow, he studied with his mother, then with *Field, but they were forced to flee to St Petersburg when Moscow was burnt in 1812. Charles toured Poland, Germany, France and Holland in 1814, with great success, and he became a well-respected teacher in St Petersburg. When *Henselt began to gain in popularity in Russia, Mayer moved to Dresden, where he died in 1862. His style was very similar to Field's and he was praised by *R. Schumann. He had some 800 pupils, including Glinka, whom he influenced a good deal.

Works
Up to 351 opus numbers, including *Six études*, mazurkas, etc.

Further reading
Loesser/MEN.

Mazourka (see *Mazurka)

Mazur
An alternative name for *mazurka.

Mazurek
An alternative name for *mazurka.

Mazurka (Pol. *mazur*)
A Polish country dance taking its name from the people (Mazurs) who occupied the area around Warsaw where it originated, Mazovia. A modern version of the earlier song-dance, the *polska* ['Polish dance'], 'mazurka' is a generic term for three similar dances, the medium-paced mazurka itself (also called *mazur* and *mazurek*), the slower *kujawiak* (from the nearby Kujavy area) and the faster *oberek* (or *obertas*). However, apart from the difference in pace, they all share their main characteristics: triple time, syncopation and a tendency to subdivide the beat into duplet or triplet groups. The shape is episodic, two (occasionally four) six- or eight-bar phrase, each repeated. Appearing in the sixteenth century, the mazurka spread through Poland's neighbouring countries and became particularly fashionable in Paris, then in London in the early nineteenth century and thence to the United States. The most famous mazurkas are those of *Chopin – some 50 for piano – but they were also written by, among others, Borodin, Glinka and Szymanowski.

Further reading
Z. and J. Stezewski, 'Zur Genese und Chronologie des Mazurkarythmus in Polen', *Chopin Congress* (Warsaw, 1960). A. Thomas, 'Beyond the Dance', in

J. Samson, ed., *The Cambridge Companion to Chopin* (Cambridge, 1992).

Méhul, Etienne-Nicolas

French composer (b. 22 Jun 1763, Givet, Ardennes; d. 18 Oct 1817, Paris).

Son of a *maître d'hôtel*, later wine-merchant, he was apprenticed to an old blind local organist until he was 10 and attended the school of the orgnist Hanser from the ages of 12 to 15 or 16, when the family moved to Paris (in 1778 or 1779). He lived in the house of Mme Silly under her patronage, publishing his first book of keyboard sonatas in 1783 and teaching keyboard, which he shortly gave up to concentrate on composition with Edelmann. He began a musico-dramatic partnership with the librettist François-Benoît Hoffman and their first work, *Euphrosine* (perf. 1790), was a great success, as was *Adrien* (perf. 1799), and several of Méhul's airs from these works were sung throughout France. The political situation, however, was very unstable and did not favour public forms such as opera, especially if royalty was portrayed, as it frequently was.

In 1793 the Institut National de Musique was founded, several composers were appointed to the staff, including Gossec, Le Sueur and also Méhul, and his first republican hymn, the *Hymne à la raison* [*Hymn to Reason*], was sung in the (now-converted) church of St Roch. The republican opera *Horatio Coclès* was performed in 1794 and several others followed, and he was greatly honoured (for someone so young) by being granted a pension by the Comédie-Italienne; he was also one of the five inspectors of the newly-formed Paris Conservatoire in 1795. The same year he was the sole musical appointee of the French Institute and in 1804, one of the earliest members

of the Légion d'honneur. He declined Napoleon's invitation to join his Egyptian campaign along with the other artists and scholars, but remained on cordial terms with him. On the victory at Marengo, Napoleon commissioned a work from Méhul in celebration of this and of the fall of the Bastille; the result was the *Chant national du 14 juillet 1800*. It was a large work which was carefully tailored to the acoustical properties of its first-performance venue, Les Invalides, and foreshadows *Berlioz's Requiem, written with the same building in mind.

A general Italianate interest (including *W.A. Mozart's Italian operas), promulgated by, among others, Napoleon, was not shared by Méhul and it may have been part of the reason for the waning of public interest in his stage works. His overtures, however, remained popular and he soon turned to the symphony, writing seven, of which the one in G minor ('no. 1', but in fact his third, 1809) was given in a performance by *Felix Mendelssohn and admired by *R. Schumann.

Méhul's health was beginning to decline and his tuberculosis was advancing. Although he withdrew from public life, he continued to teach at the Conservatoire and to compose – mostly patriotic cantatas, but his opera, *Les Amazones* (perf. 1811) failed and the demise of the First Empire did not help his position, neither did the closure of the Conservatoire by the Bourbons, which was then downgraded to a music-school. He died in 1817 and his estranged wife outlived him by 40 years.

Méhul's operas have a great sense of atmosphere, rendered appropriate to their geographical setting through melodic awareness and first-class orchestration, a trait which was absorbed by *Berlioz. He uses *leitmotiv* techniques and had a symphonic sense of motivic and thematic development. These features can be seen compressed and intensified in his overtures while his harmony is often forward-looking in its chromatic intensity, as is his use of large forces.

He influenced *Berlioz and *C.M. von Weber in orchestration and the use of reminiscence-motifs (a forerunner of leitmotivic processes) and on *Beethoven, *Boieldieu and *Hérold and Wagner particularly admired *Joseph* (perf. 1807).

Works
His *opéras comiques* include *Euphrosione, ou Le tyran corrigé* rev. as *Euphrosine et Coradin* with 3, instead of 4, acts; *Stratonice* (perf. 1792); *Le jeune Henri* (perf. 1797); *L'Irato, ou L'emporté* (perf. 1801); *Uthal* (perf. 1806); *Joseph* (perf. 1807) as well as four ballets and incidental music. There are many patriotic choral *Hymnes*, *Chants* and cantatas and many songs. Seven symphonies (some lost and/or unpub.), three sonatas, harpsichord/piano op. 1 (1781), three more with violin *ad lib* and keyboard arrangements.

Further reading
R. Brancour, *Méhul* (Paris, 1912). H. Rasdiguer, 'E-N Méhul', *EMDC*, I/iii (1921). W. Dean, 'Opera under the French Revolution', *PRMA*, xciv (1967–68). C. Godfrey, 'Gros and Méhul', *Burlington Magazine*, cxiv (1972). B. Deane, 'The French operatic Overture from Grétry to Berlioz', *PRMA*, xcix (1972–73). D. Charlton, *French Opera 1730–1830: Meaning and Media* (Aldershot, 1999).

Melodrama (from Gk. *melos*, ['melody'] and Fr. *drame* ['drama']; Fr. *mélodrame*; Ger. *Melodram*; It. *melogo*)

(1) A genre, or part of a larger work, in which a speaking voice declaims against a background of music. Occasionally, the usage is antiphonal, with the speech – usually heightened – in pauses between the musical phrases, but the music can also accompany the speech. It appeared in a drama by Eberlin (*Sigismund*, perf. 1753, Salzburg) but it is *J.J. Rousseau who is credited as the deviser of the first complete example, his radically experimental spoken monodrama *Pygmalion* (text, *c.*1762, music (himself and H. Coignet), and first performance, 1770, Lyons). It was enormously influential on dramatists and composers alike and, with the slightly later *Ariadne auf Naxos* (1774, perf. 1775, pub. 1781) by *Georg Benda, had several prominent imitators, including a very impressed *W.A. Mozart (two examples in the unfinished Singspiel, *Zaide* (1779–80)), *Beethoven (in *Fidelio*, 1804–14) and *C.M. von Weber (in *Der Freischütz*, 1817–21) as well as later composers.

(2) The term is also applied to early-nineteenth-century stage plays interspersed with music and songs. It soon after denoted – a usage which has survived to the present time – any play with romantic sensational (often violent) themes and a happy ending, of which there are many in the Victorian and Edwardian periods

Further reading
J. van der Veen, *Le mélodrame musical de Rousseau au romantisme: ses aspects historiques et stylistiques* (The Hague, 1955). J.L. Smith, *Melodrama* (London, 1973). E.F. Kravitt, 'The Joining of Words and Music in Late Romantic Melodrama', *MQ*, lxii (1976). E.N. Olin, *Le ton et la parole: Melodrama in France 1871–1913* (diss., Northwestern U., 1991).

Mendelssohn(-Bartholdy) [Hensel],
Fanny (Cäcilie)

German pianist, composer, sister of *Felix
Mendelssohn (b. 14 Nov 1805, Hamburg;
d. 14 May 1847, Berlin).

She was granddaughter of the
philosopher Moses Mendelssohn and
the family were prosperous bankers.
Her father converted from Judaism
to Christianity and they moved to
Berlin when she was six because of the
French occupation. She was musically
precocious, learning from her mother,
then studying piano with *Berger and
composition with *Zelter, also from
Marie Bigot; she reputedly could play
*J.S. Bach's *Wohltemperirtes Clavier*
from memory at 13. She also attended
lectures by Humboldt (geography) and
Holtei (physics). In 1829, after waiting
several years in deference to her father's
wishes, she married William Hensel, the
court painter and had a son by him. They
visited Italy 1839–40 and Fanny kept a
diary, and a musical one also in the set
of pieces, *Das Jahr*, which is a month-
by-month record of the journey. When
her mother Lea died in 1842, she became
the family matriarch and led their famous
Sunday morning concerts in their home
in Berlin, where the intellectual figures
of the city – and farther afield – would
gather to hear music ranging from solo
pieces to concertos and large choral
pieces. In fact, it was during the rehearsal
for one of these, her brother Felix's
Die erste Walpurgisnacht, that she died
in 1847.

As talented as her brother Felix, she
had some of her songs included in a
published set under his name; most of her
works were not printed or published due
to opposition from her father and brother.
Under her direction the Sunday morning
concerts attracted the cream of European
artists and intellectuals. Her diaries are a
valuable source of family information.

Works

A concerto for piano, the Piano Trio in
G minor op. 11 and pieces, such as the
Lieder ohne Worte opp. 2, 6 and 8) as well
as songs (*6 Gartenlieder* op. 3 for choir
and solo songs, some published under her
brother *Felix's name).

Further reading

J. Werner, 'Felix and Fanny Mendelssohn',
ML, xxviii (1947). F. Schnapp, 'Felix
Mendelssohn-Bartholdys Brief an seine
Schwester Fanny Hensel', *SMZ*, xcix
(1959). V.R. Sirota, *The Life and Works of
Fanny Mendelssohn Hensel* (diss., Boston
U., 1981). F. Tillard, *Fanny Mendelssohn*
(Paris, 1992); Eng. tr. (Portland, OR,
1996). Fétis/*BIOGRAPHIE*.

**Mendelssohn(-Bartholdy), (Jakob
Ludwig) Felix**

German composer, pianist (b. 3 Feb 1809,
Hamburg; d. 4 Nov 1847, Leipzig).

From a wealthy banking family with a
strong intellectual tradition, music had a
prominent presence in family life. Felix's
grandfather was the philosopher Moses
Mendelssohn, who was a great champion
of Jewish emancipation. The boy was
taught by his parents (music from his
mother) and had some lessons from Marie
Bigot in Paris during a visit. In 1819 his
education was undertaken by C.W.L.
Heyse (general subjects), L. *Berger
(piano) and C.F. *Zelter (composition,
with special emphasis on *J.S. Bach
and *W.A. Mozart); he also had lessons
from C.W. Henning (violin) and J.G.S.
Rösel (painting, at which Felix was very
skilled). Felix's father, and the children,
converted from Judaism to Christianity.
They had to fly from Hamburg to Berlin

in 1811 because of French occupation and the father became a town councillor, thus establishing his social position. Felix made his performing début (in private) at the age of nine, playing a *Dussek Concerto; he was also drawing, writing poetry and composing small pieces and two *Singspiels*. When his composition teacher Zelter took him to meet Goethe in Weimar, the two got on extremely well, and it was to be the first of half-a-dozen extended visits. The German poet was a lasting influence and stimulated his interest in literature and all things *Classical; however, his attempts to interest Goethe in *Beethoven's music came to nothing. He also met *Hummel and the music-critic Rellstab and began to write larger pieces, including the early concertos for piano (A minor) and violin (D minor), piano and violin, and two violins, some of the string symphonies and a few chamber works. Later he knew *Kalkbrenner, *Moscheles, Rode, Baillot, *Rossini, Boucher, *Meyerbeer and Thibaut, who fired his interest in early music. He attended the University of Berlin in 1827.

In 1825 the Mendelssohns moved into a large house and grounds in Berlin and quickly established the foremost artistic *salon* in the city, with the Sunday morning concerts – the *Sonntagsmusiken*, ranging from solo pieces to concertos and large orchestral and choral works – literary readings and theatrical performances. Visitors to the salon included Hegel, Humboldt, A.B. Marx, the actor Devrient, F. David, Ingres, *Paganini, *C.M. von Weber, *Liszt and *E.T.A. Hoffmann. His first great work, the String Octet op. 20, written in 1825 at the age of 16, shows an astonishing musical maturity, in advance of *W.A. Mozart's works of the same age.

His interest in the music of the past came to fruition in his arranging and conducting a ground-breaking performance of *J.S. Bach's *St Matthew Passion* in the Berlin *Singakademie* in 1829, when he was 20. The next five or six years were devoted to travel, a kind of Grand Tour, during which time he visited London, where a diplomat friend together with the piano virtuoso-composer *Moscheles and his wife took him under their wing and introduced him to London musical society. He also played in a number of concerts – Beethoven's *'Emperor' concerto, and his own double piano concerto with Moscheles. He then travelled to Edinburgh and the highlands, calling in on Sir Walter Scott *en route* and storing away ideas for a 'Scottish' symphony. A stormy steamship crossing to the island of Staffa inspired the Overture *Die Hebriden* (*The Hebrides*) op. 26 (1829) and a knee injury in the homeward coach afforded an opportunity to stay with Thomas *Attwood, a former pupil of Mozart, and he arrived home in Berlin in early December of 1829.

He was offered the chair in music at Berlin University, but, instead recommended his friend A.B. Marx; after an attack of measles, he was off on his travels again, this time to Italy, at Goethe's suggestion. He stayed in the principal Italian cities, finishing the *Hebrides Overture* in Rome and beginning the *Italian Symphony*, and continued through Switzerland and back to Germany, completing (and performing, in Munich) his G minor piano concerto, and spending the winter in Paris where he met Baillot, *Cherubini and Heine again, and *Chopin for the first time.

He was deeply moved by the deaths of both Zelter and Goethe and, after a visit to London in early 1832, he applied for Zelter's post at the Berlin *Singakademie*, for which he was passed over in favour of Zelter's deputee. In 1833 he was invited, by the Philharmonic Society of London, to conduct his *Italian Symphony* at one of their concerts, and was also invited to conduct the Lower Rhine Music Festival in Düsseldorf. Here, he included performances of some of *Handel's oratorios in his own arrangements, an important contribution to the older composer's popularity in the German-speaking lands. He would continue this work over the two years of his contract, and also composed and presented his own oratorio in Handelian style, *St Paul*.

Mendelssohn accepted the conductorship of the Leipzig Gewandhaus orchestra and took up the post in 1835, where his care in training the orchestra laid the foundations of what was to become one of Germany's greatest orchestras; he also made a point of formulating programmes which would include great variety of material, from historical to contemporary, in which he also performed himself. A brief visit to Frankfurt resulted in his marriage (1837) and, after directing the Birmingham festival the same year, the couple moved to Leipzig and had three sons and two daughters. His time at the Gewandhaus allowed the Leipzigers to hear a vast quantity of all kinds of music from a huge number of composers of all periods. Contemporary (or near-contemporary) works included pieces by *R. Schumann, Niels Gade, Ferdinand David, Justus Rietz and Ferdinand Hiller. He also encouraged performers, including *Clara Schumann, Dreyschock, *Thalberg, Anton Rubinstein, *Joachim, Vieuxtemps, Jenny Lind and Clara Novello.

With the accession of Friedrich Wilhelm IV King of Prussia, a new dawn for the arts was promised, especially music, and the King offered Mendelssohn the responsibility of organizing it, at a salary three times that at Leipzig. As his correspondence with the King shows, he was required to be available in Berlin for a year so as to be on hand when required. He kept his Leipzig position, putting in a deputy conductor. He was to work with Ludwig Tieck (who was to translate Greek tragedies into German) and to provide incidental music for the performances; the first venture was Sophocles' *Antigone* and it was a marvellous success, ushering in a new age of Classical tragedy in German. Unfortunately, his scope for purely musical performances, including those of his own works, was very curtailed and he was becoming deeply disillusioned. He completed his *Scottish Symphony* in 1842 and it was performed in London the same year to great acclaim; the composer paid two visits to Queen Victoria – to whom he dedicated the work – and the Prince Consort. Back in Berlin, he resolved to resign but, heeding his mother's advice, he offered to take a drop in salary to half, and he was instead appointed director of sacred music with no specified duties. At the end of the year (1842) his mother died. The performance of his revised cantata, *Die erste Walpurgisnacht*, was a great success and the audience included *Berlioz whose German tour was not being successful; Mendelssohn helped the young Frenchman and also the Danish composer Niels Gade.

In 1840 Mendelssohn, hearing of a bequest for a cultural and educational establishment whose administration was entrusted to the Saxon King, Friedrich August II, suggested a music academy to be built in Leipzig. This proved successful and the institute was opened in 1843, with Mendelssohn in charge. He set about attracting the best musicians for the lead posts – Moritz Hauptmann for harmony and counterpoint, Ferdinand David (violin), C.F. Becker (organ, history and theory) and *R. Schumann (piano, composition and score-reading) and, a little later, Schumann's wife, *Clara, Ferdinand Hiller, Gade and *Moscheles; the latter took over the leadership after Mendelssohn's death in 1847.

In the meantime, matters improved in Leipzig and a concert-series was instigated as well as a male-voice choir. The dramatic productions (requiring incidental music) also resumed, and Mendelssohn decided on Shakespeare's *A Midsummer Night's Dream*, using material from the Overture he had written to the same play 17 years previously. It was a huge success, and Mendelssohn moved to Berlin with his family the same year (1843). He visited England for the eighth time in 1844, conducting six of the Philharmonic concerts and, on his return to Germany during a holiday with his family, he composed the Violin Concerto op. 64. This was performed in the Gewandhaus in March 1845 with David as soloist conducted by Gade. However, matters again became difficult for him in Berlin and, after further compromises, he finally resigned later in the same year.

The Mendelssohns moved back to Leipzig and he resumed his post of concert-director at the Gewandhaus but ill-health forced him to share his duties with Gade, now his deputy. A punishing schedule followed, involving him in travelling (Liège, Cologne, Birmingham, London – where the first performance of the oratorio *Elijah* elicited a very complimentary letter from Prince Albert – Frankfurt am Main), composing to commission and conducting (the Lower Rhine Festival again, Corpus Christi in Liège, Schiller festival in Cologne,

etc.). His last compositions remained unfinished, but a tenth (and last) visit to England brought him enormous success. During his homeward journey he learnt the terrible news of his beloved sister *Fanny's recent death and he travelled during the summer to help his recovery, composing his last great work, the F minor string quartet op. 80 as a requiem for her. He himself died four months after her and was buried near her grave. Memorial concerts were held in several cities.

Mendelssohn found his natural creative niche in earlier music, especially Bachian counterpoint, Handelian choral writing and *W.A. Mozart in general, together with *Beethoven's instrumentation; consequently, he was a neo-classicist. There are *Romantic traits, however, in his extramusical stimulations by poetry, landscape – he was a very talented artist himself – and history. This is also evident in his natural flair for drama, shown not only in avowedly dramatic works but also in his music generally and in the incidental music in particular, in which his ability to capture mood, scene and character as well as psychological motivation, is uncanny. The family theatrical productions and readings during his childhood, as well as his closeness to Goethe played a large part in this. As a composer of oratorios, the English have appropriated him almost as much as they have Handel.

Mendelssohn almost single-handedly instigated the J.S. Bach revival, primarily in his editing and conducting of the performance of his *St Matthew Passion* in the Berlin *Singakademie* at the age of 20 (1819) and secondarily in his use of Bachian traits and techniques in his compositions. He encouraged, and actively helped the careers of, many musicians, both performers – *Clara

Schumann, *Thalberg, the Dreyschock brothers, A. Rubinstein, *Joachim, Vieuxtemps, Jenny Lind, Clara Novello and *Moscheles – and composers – F. David, F. Hiller, *Berlioz, Gade, Joachim, Rietz and (posthumously, in premiering his C major symphony) *Schubert. His influence waned in the later nineteenth century, due to various reasons (anti-Semitism being prominent), and this also caused the proscription of his works in German-speaking lands and the destruction of his monument in Leipzig in the 1930s and 40s.

Works
Overtures: *Meeresstille und glückliches Fährt* (*Calm sea and Pleasant Voyage* (1828)), *Die Hebriden* (*The Hebrides* ['*Fingal's Cave*'], 1830). Incidental music: *Ruy Blas* (Hugo, 1839); *A Midsummer Night's Dream* (Shakespeare) op. 81 (1842); *Oedipus at Colonnos* (Sophocles) op. 93 (1845). The oratorios *Die erste Walpurgisnacht* (1832, rev 1843), *St Paul* op. 36 (1836), *Elijah* op. 70 (1846). Other orchestral including 12 String Symphonies and five symphonies, no. 1 in C minor op. 11 (1824), no. 5 ('Reformation') in D major op. 107 (1832), no. 4 (*Italian*) in A major op. 90 (1833), no. 2 (choral symphony, 'Lobgesang') in B♭ major op. 52 (1840) and no. 3 ('Scottish') in A minor op. 56 (1842). Concertos for violin in D minor (1822) and E minor op. 64 (1844), for violin and piano in D minor (1823), for piano no. 1 in G minor op. 25 (1831), no. 2 in D minor op. 40 (1837), for two pianos in E major (1823) and in A♭ major (1824), and the Capriccio brillant in B minor op. 22 (?1825–6) and the Rondo brillant in E♭ major op. 29 (1834) both for piano and orchestra. Chamber music includes sonatas (with piano accompaniment) for violin (2), clarinet and cello (2), two piano trios (in D minor op. 49 (1839) and C minor op. 66 (1845)), three piano quartets (his opp. 1, 2 and 3), six string quartets, and several smaller pieces, two string quintets, a piano sextet, the String octet in E♭ major op. 20 (1825). Piano: includes eight books of *Lieder ohne Worte* (*Songs Without Words*), several piano sonatas, variation-sets (including the *Variations sérieuses* in D minor op. 54 (1841)) and many smaller pieces, pieces for piano duet and organ works. There are many choral pieces – psalms, cantatas, secular cantatas, choral songs – and many solo songs and duets, together with transcriptions of works by (mainly) *J.S. Bach and *Handel.

Further reading
Much literature of which a few are: M. Hurd, *Mendelssohn* (London, 1970). H. Kupferberg, *The Mendelssohns: Three Generations of Genius* (New York, 1972). P. Ranft, *Felix Mendelssohn Bartholdy: eine Lebenschronik* (Leipzig, 1972). Y. Tiénot, *Mendelssohn: musicien complet* (Paris, 1972). R. Elvers, ed., *Felix Mendelssohn: A Life in Letters* (New York, 1986). W. Konuld, *Felix Mendelssohn-Bartholdy und seine Zeit* (Laaber, 1984). Larry R. Todd, *Mendelssohn and his World* (Princeton, NJ, 1991).

Meno (It,: 'less')
'Less', as in Meno mosso ('less movement', that is, 'slower').

Mercadante, (Giuseppe) Saverio (Raffaele)
Italian composer, teacher (bap. 17 Sep 1795, Altamura, nr Bari; d. 17 Dec 1870, Naples).

An illegitimate child, his father took him with him to Naples when securing a post with the customs service there and the boy, showing musical talent, attended the Collegio di San Sebastiano (1808–20) where he studied flute, violin, *solfeggio and figured bass and harmony (with Furno), counterpoint (with Tritto) and had composition lessons with Zingarelli, the director, from 1816. He wrote some orchestral and band compositions and was put in charge of the orchestra. He also wrote music for several ballets at the San Carlo Theatre and, the director, *Rossini, and others encouraged him to devote his time to vocal music and opera; his first opera, L'apoteosi d'Ercole was well received, but real success came with Elisa e Claudio at La Scala in 1821, when he was 26, securing his European reputation. He directed the Viennese performances and wrote three operas for the Kärntnerthor-Theater which were not successful. Back in Italy, his Caritea, regina di Spagnia (or Donna Caritea) was very well received in Venice in 1826. He spent the next five years in the Iberian Peninsula but negotiations for commissions and a post in Madrid came to nothing firm and he was back in an Italy which was in the thrall of *Bellini and would soon be of Donizetti. In 1832, the year of his marriage to a young widow, he had great success with I normanni a Parigi in Turin and the next year he accepted the post of maestro di cappella at Novara cathedral, where he remained for seven years, during which his operatic career continued unabated. A commission from Rossini to write an opera for the Théâtre Italien in Paris failed, because the original libretto did not arrive in time, and he had to rush ahead with an inferior one. He was impressed with *Meyerbeer's work while in Paris and the influence can be heard in Il giuramento (perf. 1837, Milan). He refused Rossini's offer of a post for that

of head of the conservatory at Naples in 1840 and he remained in post for the rest of his 30 years of life; one result of this was an inevitable slowing-down of his operatic output, but he continued to have successes, and a tumultuous one with Orazi e Curiazi (perf. 1846, San Carlo).

Having already lost the sight of an eye, he became completely blind in 1862 and dictated his compositions from then on.

A vital operatic link between the early (Rossini, Bellini, Donizetti) and the later (Verdi) nineteenth century, Mercadante's harmony was more characteristic of the latter periods than that of his contemporaries, while his recitatives were powerful and his orchestration telling. He was praised by *Liszt, Rossini and Verdi, who learnt much from him: there are literal echoes of Mercadante in his works, especially Aida. His music fell into disuse after his death but has been revived since the 1940s.

Works

Some 60 operas, including L'apoteosi d'Ercole (1819), Elisa e Claudio, ossia L'amore protetto dall'amicizia (Elisa and Clausio, or Love protected through Friendship, 1821), Caritea, regina di Spagnia (Donna Caritea) ossia La morte di Don Alfonso re di Portogallo (Caritea, Queen of Spain, or the Death of Don Alfonso, King of Portugal, perf. 1826) Il giuramento (The Judgment, perf. 1837), Orazi e Curiazi (perf. 1846). There are also four ballets, cantatas, hymns with orchestra, concertos (horn, clarinet, six for flute) and quite a number of symphonies, many programmatic, and some chamber music.

Further reading

F. Walker, 'Mercadante and Verdi', ML, xxxiii (1952) and xxxiv (1953).

E. Brizio, 'Saverio Mercadante: cause e rimedi di una ingiustizia', *Altamura: bolletino dell'archiivo* (Jan 1967). F. Lippmann, 'Vincenzo Bellini und die Italienische opera Seria seiner Zeit', *Analecta Musicologica*, vi (1969). M. Rinaldi, 'Significato di Mercadante', *Ritratti e fantasie musicali* (Rome 1970). S. Palermo, *Saverio Mercadante: biografia – epistolario* (Fasano, 1985). G.-L. Petrucci, *Saverio Mercadante: l'ultimo dei cinque re* (Rome, 1995). Fétis/*BIOGRAPHIE.*

Merlin, John Joseph

Flemish (naturalized British) instrument-maker, inventor (b. 6 Sep 1735, Huys, nr Liège; d. 4 May 1803, Paddington, London).

Merlin spent the years 1754–60 in Paris before arriving in England in 1760 as part of the entourage of the Spanish ambassador and spent a short while at a goldsmith's before being employed as a mechanic at a museum. He went into business on his own as a maker of mathematical instruments, but he contributed to many branches, inventing important improvements for the invalid chair and roller-skates, which remain today. He took out patents for a combined harpsichord and piano ('compound harpsichord') and a piano with *down-striking action, both in 1774. The patent averred that any harpsichord could be thus adapted, but an instrument of this kind (1780) in the Deutsches Museum, Munich is very complicated, having various banks of strings for both 'instruments' and a device which records the music played by pricking a roll of paper. He made a piano for *Burney (to his specifications) in 1777 and he also extended the compass in both directions to give six octaves.

Further reading
Boalch/HARPSICHORD.
Russell/HARPSICHORD.
Hubbard/HARPSICHORD.
Harding/PIANO-FORTE.

Méthode des méthodes ('Method of Methods')

A treatise on piano-playing written in 1840 by Ignaz *Moscheles and François-Joseph *Fétis for which *Chopin wrote his *Trois nouvelles études* (1839).

'Method'

Another name for the 'School' as in Pianoforte School, a textbook for students and teachers. Piano schools or methods were more than the title would suggest – although subtitles were usually more informative – in that, in most cases, they provided complete general musical instruction for beginners and dealt with such matters as musical aesthetics, taste and, to some extent, history. Most of the great early-nineteenth-century pianist/composers wrote one, and some (such as *Czerny) several of different types and emphases.

Metre

(1) *Music* The number of beats (rhythmically important notes) in a bar of music, of which the first is the most heavily stressed, although there are secondary stresses also. It is commonly referred to as 'time' and shown by a *'time-signature' appearing at the beginning of a piece of music.

(2) *Poetry* In traditional poetry, the sound patterns (called 'feet', equivalent to a bar in music) which, when repeated, give the rhythm. They are expressed in groups of stressed (shown by the sign '‾') and unstressed (shown by '˘') syllables (in

music, the beats). The most common are the iambus (ˇ ¯), trochee (¯ ˇ), anapaest (ˇ ˇ ¯) and dactyl (¯ ˇ ˇ). The number of feet per line give rise to the traditional metres, viz. dimeter (two per line) trimeter (three per line) – these two correspond to music's time-signatures – pentameter (five feet per line) and hexameter (six).

Metronome (from Gk. *metron*, 'measure', *nomos*, 'law'; Fr. *métronome*; Ger. *Metronom, Taktmesser*)
An instrument for giving and maintaining the speed of performance of music. It was first made by Johann Nepomuk Maelzel, having copied the principle from a compound pendulum invented by Winkel which he saw in Amsterdam. A resultant lawsuit gave the credit to Winkel, but Maelzel had already set up a factory and was selling metronomes happily. The metronome is set to tick at an adjustable rate giving a predetermined number of ticks per minute, shown by a note and a figure – in the form ♩ = 60, i.e. sixty crotchets per minute – printed above the stave after the tempo indication. The number of beats per minute ranges from 40 to 200. Composers used it as a kind of absolute tempo-indicator, of which the first major figure was *Beethoven. Unfortunately because of bad memory, miswriting and changing his mind, his indicators do not provide a reliable guide. Modern metronomes have the option of an accompanying flashing light and the possibility of silencing the tick.

Meyerbeer [Beer], **Giacomo** [Jakob Liebmann Meyer]
German composer (b. 5 Sep 1791, Vogelsdorf, nr Berlin; d. 2 May 1864, Paris).
   Born of a wealthy family, his father was a highly respected elder of the community. Their home was frequented by the cultured élite of Berlin, including the King-to-be, Friedrich Wilhelm IV, Humboldt and Iffland. After piano lessons in Berlin with Franz Lasuka, who also taught the royal princes, he had his first public concert appearance at the age of 11 and composition lessons with *Zelter and B.A. Weber, who recommended him to his own former teacher Abbé Vogler with whom he studied in Darmstadt for two years. His fellow pupils included *C.M. von Weber, Gottfried Weber, Dusch and Gänsbacher. He decided to try his luck as a freelance opera composer and in spite of several failures in Munich and Stuttgart, he arrived in Linz to discover that Vogler had recommended him for the post of court composer to the Grand Duke of Hesse. He was making headway as a pianist, however, and was highly praised by *Moscheles and Gänsbacher. He decided that a trip to Paris was a necessity for any composer hoping to make a name for themselves in opera and arrived there in late 1814. Since no commissions presented themselves, he travelled to London at the end of the following year and heard *J.B. Cramer play, also meeting *Ries and *Kalkbrenner and becoming infected with the *folksong 'bug'.
   This he put to good use in his next venture, his first trip to Italy, collecting folksongs during a stay in Palermo. He decided to remain in Italy and at last gained success as an opera composer – so much so that he was mentioned in the same breath as *Rossini and several of these works remain in the repertory, such as *Il crociato in Egitto* (1824). This was performed in the King's Theatre in London very successfully but in Paris, at the Théâtre Italien in the presence of Friedrich Wilhelm III, it was a sensation.

He met Scribe, the brightest star in the French theatrical firmament, on this occasion, an encounter which would prove very productive at a later date. He realized that only a first-class libretto would do as the basis of a French opera but he began by adapting an already-composed work for French audiences, his Italian opera *Margherita d'Anjou*, which ran for 37 performances in 1826. He decided to re-work *Il crociato* as a grand opera for the Paris Opéra with a new overture, ballet-music and several other new numbers, but abandoned the project in favour of a new opera, which had already been agreed with Scribe, who was to provide the libretto. The result, the grand opera *Robert le diable*, produced in November 1831, was the greatest triumph the Opéra had ever had and placed Meyerbeer on the pinnacle of European opera; Rossini gave up opera-writing and *Fétis's review of *Robert* in the *Revue musicale* was a veritable eulogy. The opera then swept the Continent and, ten years later, the 28-year-old Wagner was unstinting in his praise. The opera spawned an industry of arrangements, fantasias and variations by *Chopin, *Liszt, *Kalkbrenner, *Thalberg, Adam and *J. Strauss, and Meyerbeer was showered with honours – Chevalier of the Légion d'honneur (1832), member of the senate of the Prussian Academy of Arts (1834) and a member of the French Institute.

It was important to capitalize on the success of *Robert*, but several projects fell through for various reasons. Eventually Scribe and Meyerbeer signed a contract with Véron, the director of the Opéra, for *La Barthélemy*. Its gestation was beset by problems of all sorts – illnesses, changes and additions to the text, censorship, quarrels – until finally the work, having changed names several times, was premiered on February 29 1836 as *Les Huguenots*, one of the most remarkable in the history of opera.

He met Wagner in 1839 and responded to his request for help – financial and professional; in particular the speedy presentation of *Rienzi* and *Der fliegende Holländer* was largely due to Meyerbeer. He withdrew his support, however, when he realized that Wagner had been insulting him in private. Plans got under way for a new opera with Scribe and several ideas loomed, including *Le prophète* and *L'africaine* but, again, delays intervened. Meyerbeer was offered the post of Prussian *Generalmusikdirektor* after the death of Friedrich Wilhelm III and the dismissal of the incumbent, Spontini. Meyerbeer accepted in 1842 and *Les Huguenots* (which the King had refused to have performed) was given with huge success and the composer was the first to receive the Order of Peace, newly created. Things did not go smoothly, due to wranglings over status, and Meyerbeer resigned, remaining as, effectively, court composer, which was not onerous. He turned his attention to Paris again, as his new operas were long overdue. He had already completed the score of *Le prophète* in 1840, but many changes were necessary because of changes in the cast – including the arrival of the contralto Pauline Viardot-Garcia – and eventually a complete revision. The work was received with enormous enthusiasm and swept Europe. Meyerbeer became the first German musician to be awarded the title of Commandeur of the Légion d'honneur. His *L'étoile du nord* (with Scribe) was a great success on its premiere in 1854 with the Emperor and Empress in attendance and another success followed five years later with *Le pardon de Ploërmel*. Meyerbeer also wrote an overture for the

World Exhibition in London in 1862, but Cambridge University's offer of a MusD was declined, due to his taking a cure. Plans for *L'africaine* dragged on, not helped by Scribe's death in early 1861, but finally rehearsals began in 1864, with the composer faithfully in attendance. He himself died after a brief illness during the night of 2 May 1864.

A great experimentalist in orchestration, Meyerbeer tried out new instruments (bass clarinet, saxophone) and placing of instruments and groupings. Wagner was very much influenced by his instrumentation and his use of **leitmotiv* in *L'étoile du nord* (perf. 1854); Meyerbeer also influenced Verdi, d'Albert, Brüll, Korngold, Schreker and French opera in general. He took great care in researching for the basic ideas and background of his operas, using, almost for the first time in opera, real historical events instead of the regular round of Classical and other favourite stories and scenarios. He paid meticulous attention to local colour and to his singers' characteristics and musical needs. His works were banned in Germany from the 1920s until after the Second World War.

Works
Operas: include *Margherita d'Anjou* (perf. 1820), *Il crociato in Egitto* (perf. 1824), *Robert le diable* (perf. 1831), *Les Huguenots* (perf. 1836), *Le prophète* (perf. 1849), *L'étoile du nord* (perf. 1854), *Le pardon de Ploërmel* (perf. 1859). There are also many festive pieces for particular occasions, sacred music, hundreds of songs and instrumental works including ceremonial music, a symphony in E♭ major and a piano concerto (both 1811) as well as a concerto for piano and violin (1812) and smaller piano pieces.

Further reading
C. Frese, *Dramaturgie der grossen Opern Giacomo Meyerbeers* (Berlin, 1970). S. Segalini, *Diable ou prophète? Meyerbeer* (Paris, 1985). H. John and G. Stephan, eds, *Giacomo Meyerbeer: Dresden 1991* (Dresden, 1992). A. Gerhard, *The Urbanization of Opera: Music Theater in Paris in the Nineteenth Century* (Chicago, IL, 1998).

Middle C
The note C which is nearest to the middle of the **keyboard on a keyboard instrument.

Military Style
The importation of musical traits from military usage into pieces of music not designed for military use. This can be on the level of motifs, phrases, melodies or passages, rarely whole movements or pieces, and usually involve the use of fanfares (arpeggios), tattoos (often rhythmic) and/or instruments with a particularly military association such as brass generally, piccolo, E♭ clarinet and occasionally those not normally found in the symphony orchestra (saxophone, cornet and certain percussion).

Minuet (Fr. *menuet*; Ger. *Menuett*; It. *minuetto*; Sp. *minuete, minué*)
French dance in triple (usually 3/4) **metre, slow or moderately slow. It was the most popular social dance in aristocratic ballrooms from the mid-seventeenth century into the early nineteenth. Its steps, and the dancers' floor-patterns were complex, but executed in a relaxed, dignified and elegant manner; it was recognized as being the most elegant of the dances. The minuet was usually danced by one couple at a time, their order strictly controlled by

social precedence, using the full extent of the floor and climaxing with the presentation of both hands to each other and paying homage to the highest social orders present. There were many varying choreographies, which may explain the dance's long life and even when it was ousted by later, more popular dances, such as the *waltz or *contredanse with their national and regional variants, minuet steps and patterns were often incorporated into these.

As an instrumental piece, the minuet (occasionally several) was very common in the *Baroque instrumental *suite, especially for keyboard, but also instrumental ensembles, and they were also composed as free-standing pieces, by such composers as Lebègue, Chambonnières, Marchand, *F. Couperin, Rameau, Leclair, Boismortier and Hotteterre. *J.S. Bach and *Handel wrote many.

In the suite, the minuet soon took on a binary (or ternary) form, two sections with related melodic material, each repeated and followed by a (usually unrelated) trio of similar shape and the minuet again without repeats. The Italian version of the minuet was usually faster (often 3/8) and many composers wrote both kinds of minuet. A particular type of serious French minuet was called the 'motto'-type because of its use of a 'motto-rhythm' of crotchet-4 quavers. This type found great favour in London, especially with the influx of fleeing French aristocrats seeking a safe haven after the French Revolution.

Mixolydian mode (see *modes)

Mode (adj., **modal**)
Broadly speaking, referring to a system of music used before the eighteenth century using a variety of modes in place of the two modes of later periods (our major and minor). The history of the modes ranges backwards in time from ancient Greece through the Middle Ages and the Renaissance and sideways through various cultures – art and folk – and is outside the scope of a reference book of this kind. The basic features of the modes in their Medieval and Renaissance use (as well as Western *folk music) can be appreciated by visualizing them as on a piano keyboard. By taking the various notes of the C major scale of (C, D, E, etc.) and playing the *steps between it and its octave using only the white notes, we arrive at the later forms of the various modes: D-D (Dorian), E-E (Phrygian), F-F (Lydian), G-G (Mixolydian), A-A (Aeolian) B-B (the rare Locrean), while our present major scale , C-C was the Ionian mode. As soon as musicians and composers began to sharpen or flatten particular notes to avoid certain 'awkward' or stylistically unacceptable intervals, the modes began to lose their individual characters and their number was reduced. Thus, flattening the B in the Lydian mode (to avoid the tritone between F and B) turned it into a *transposed Ionian mode (our major, as I have said), and so on. The modal system found its full flowering in the Church music of the Middle Ages (*plainsong) and the art music of the great *polyphonic composers of the Renaissance (Victoria, Palestrina, etc.) and remains a still-vital presence in non-Western cultures and Western folk music. It has also been drawn on by Western composers for particular effects such as the use of the Phrygian mode in the slow movement of *Brahms's Fourth Symphony in E minor (1884–85) and enjoyed a brief revival in the work of the so-called English pastoral school of, for example, Vaughan Williams and

colleagues who were influenced by the folk-collecting revival and by English music of the Renaissance, of which Vaughan Williams's own *Fantasia on a Theme of Thomas Tallis* (1910) for strings is a prime example.

Moderator
A *stop, *knee-lever or *pedal which places a strip of soft cloth between the hammers and the strings to give a softer, veiled sound. It is distinct from the modern 'soft' pedal and from the *una corda*, each of which produce their related effects by different methods.

Mondonville, Jean-Joseph Cassanéa de
French composer, violinist, conductor (bap. 25 Dec 1711, Narbonne; d. 8 Oct 1772, Belleville).

He studied with his father, an organist, and was in Paris in the early 1830s where his op. 1, *Sonates* for violin and *basso continuo* were published in 1833 and where he played in an Easter *Concert Spirituel. He spent some time in Lille and was back in Paris in 1739, where he was a violinist of the royal chapel and chamber and, according to the *Mercure de France*, he was already known as a fine player and composer, having had motets performed at the Concerts Spirituels and played in many other parts of France also. His position near the top of Parisian concert life was now assured. He was *sous-maître* at the royal chapel in 1740 and four years later was promoted to intendent. He was also associated with the Académie Royale de Musique, producing operas and motets and playing as well. In 1748 he married a wealthy harpsichord-player and they had a son. Mondonville took the French part in the 'Querelle des Buffons' and his opera *Titon et l'Aurore* was, with Rameau's *Castor et Pollux*, held up as a prime example of the French style. He used Gascon dialect in his libretto for his own opera *Daphnis et Alcimadure*, a 'pastorale languedociennc' (perf. 1754).

Mondonville's virtuosity as a player is shown in his published compositions, where he uses harmonics and prefaces his op. 4 violin sonatas with valuable information on their use – the first we have – though virtuosity is never used for its own sake. His elegant and lively style was taken as typical of the French style in the 'Querelle des Buffons'.

Works
Some five operas including *Titon et l'Aurore* (perf. 1753) and *Daphnis et Alcimadure*, a 'pastorale languedocienne' (perf. 1754), several ballets, e.g. *Les fêtes de Paphos* (perf. 1758) and 17 Grand motets. His instrumental music includes the *Sonates* op. 1 (violin and basso continuo, pub. 1733) the *Sonates en trio* op. 2 (two violins/flutes and basso continuo, pub. 1734) and *Les sons harmoniques, sonates* op. 4 (violin and basso continuo, pub. 1738).

Further reading
E. Borroff, *The Instrumental Works of Jean-Joseph Cassanéa de Mondonville* (diss., U of Michigan, 1958); 'The Instrumental Style of Jean-Joseph Cassanéa de Mondonville', *Recherches sur la musique française classique*, vii (1967). C. Pierre, *Histoire du Concert spirituel 1725–1790* (Paris, 1975). R. Machard, *Jean-Joseph Cassanéa de Mondonvilke: virtuose, compositeur et chef d'orchestre* (Béziers, 1980). Fétis/*BIOGRAPHIE*.

Monferrina (monfrina, monfreda, manfredina)
A country dance from Piedmont in compound (usually 6/8) time, it was

popular in Britain in the early nineteenth century. *Clementi wrote two sets of 12 each (op. 49, 1821) and six others (WO15-20) and *Hummel wrote a set of *Variazioni alla Monferrina* op. 54 for cello and piano (pub. *c.*1810–15).

Monochord

(1) In stringed *keyboard instruments, the use of a single string for a note as opposed to two (*bichord) or three (*trichord) – or, occasionally, more – tuned in unison.

(2) In early (pre-seventeenth-century) usage, the *clavichord.

(3) An ancient one-stringed instrument used mainly for didactic purposes to show the relationship between string lengths and the tension, the pitch and the *timbre of the note produced.

Monodic (see *monophonic)

Monophonic, monodic

Music written in a single unaccompanied melodic line, as opposed to *homophony and *polyphony. It can also be applied to music in which the melodic line is doubled in a more-or-less consistent way (for example in octaves, thirds and so on); a significant exception is the application of the term 'monody' to a body of Italian (mostly secular) song for solo voice and *basso continuo* during the period *c.* 1600–1650.

'Moonlight' Sonata

Name given to *Beethoven's piano sonata no. 14, op. 27/2 in C# minor (1801, dedicated to Countess Giulietta Guicciardi). It was so designated in a review by the German poet Rellstab, as the first movement reminded him of an aquatic moonscape. The sonata is one of

two in op. 27 each of which Beethoven called 'Sonata quasi una fantasia'.

'Moore's Melodies' (see *Moore)

Moore, Thomas

Irish poet, musician, historian, journalist, Classicist (b. 28 May 1779, Dublin; d. 26 Feb 1852, Sloperton Cottage, nr Devizes).

Son of a grocer and wine merchant, he described himself as a 'slow child' but nevertheless taught himself music, later studying with his sister's teacher, and learnt French and Italian. He published his first verses at the age of 14 and attended Trinity College, Dublin in 1794 – it had been opened to Catholics, of which Moore was one, in the previous year – graduating in 1798. Nicknamed 'Anacreontic Moore' because of his translations of Anacreon while still a student, he undertook law studies in London in the Middle Temple (1799) and was made registrar of Bermuda in 1803, which he handed over to a deputy and returned to England. A failed duel with Francis (later Lord) Jeffrey, editor of the *Edinburgh Review*, resulted in their becoming close friends. His singing and his verses made him popular and he wrote the libretto for Michael Kelly's opera *The Gipsey Prince* (1801), becoming famous through publication of his poetry and songs. Moore became friendly with Robert Emmett, Francis Jeffrey, Canning, Peel, the Shelleys and Leigh Hunt. The publisher William Power, wishing to emulate the success of George *Thomson's collection of British *folksongs, suggested a similar publication of Irish songs. Moore used material from *Bunting's collection and wrote words of his own, publishing the *Irish Melodies* in ten numbers and a supplement between 1808 and 1834, with piano accompaniments by Sir John *Stevenson. He married an Irish actress in 1811 and met and became close friends with Byron the same year.

A comic opera of his failed, but he could command an advance fee of £3,000 for his oriental story with interpolated poems, *Lalla Rookh* (1817), which spread his reputation throughout Europe. In 1818 he learned that his deputy in Bermuda had embezzled £6,000 for which Moore was liable. He fled to Italy to escape debtors' prison but returned once the debt was paid. His four-volume *History of Ireland* (1835–46) was not a success, and although happily married with many friends – who arranged a literary pension for him in 1835 – he was depressed; all his five children had died by 1846 and his mind began to fail. He was awarded and civil list pension in 1850 and died two years later.

A man of many contradictions, he was friendly with the Irish revolutionary Robert Emmett, after whose execution he wrote a eulogy, yet he lived the greater part of his adult life in England, much of it in the company of the ruling classes. His poetry divided critics: although most of the poets and critics of the time liked his work, there were a few dissenters (Coleridge and Hazlitt among them). He had a huge following in his time and his *Irish Melodies* – '*Moore's Melodies*', as they were popularly known – had a global impact; sung and played throughout the known world, they became part of, for example, American as well as European culture and indispensable in any middle- or lower-middle-class drawing room. His *The Letters and Journals of Lord Byron, with Notices of his Life* (1830) is an invaluable insight on the great poet.

Moore influenced the young Keats and Byron. Moore's verses were set by many composers (besides himself), among others, *Berlioz, *C.M. von Weber, *R. Schumann, *Felix Mendelssohn, A. Mackenzie, Cornelius, Jensen, Taneyev, Parry, Walker, Duparc, Hindemith, Warlock and Ireland.

Works
Include the libretto for *The Gipsey Prince* (by M. Kelly, 1801); *Irish Melodies* (10 numbers and a supplement, 1808–34); *Sacred Songs* (1816, 1824); *Lalla Rookh* (1817); *The Fudge Family in Paris* (1817); *The Letters and Journals of Lord Byron, with Notices of his Life* (1830); *History of Ireland* (4 vols, 1835–46).

Further reading
P. Quennell, ed., *The Journal of Thomas Moore* (London, 1964). H.H. Jordan, *Bolt Upright: The Life of Thomas Moore* (2 vols, Salzburg, 1975). T. de V. White, *Tom Moore: The Irish Poet* (London, 1977). L. Davis, 'Irish Bands and English Consumers: Thomas Moore's Irish Melodies and the Colonized Nation', *Ariel*, no. 24 (1993). J.W. Vail, *The Literary relationship of Lord Byron and Thomas Moore* (Baltimore, MD, 2001). M.O Súilleabháin, 'All our Central Fire: Music, Meditation and the Irish Psyche', *Irish Journal of Psychology*, xv/2–3 (1994).

Mordent (from It. *mordente*, from *mordere*, 'to bite'; Fr. *mordant*; Ger. *Mordent*)
A musical *ornament first codified in the *Baroque period in which a principal note was sounded, followed by the note below it and itself again, in quick succession, shown by the sign ᴧ above or below the note. There was also a double version:

note—note above (or below)—note—note above (or below)—note, which was called the double mordent (shown ✦✦). Any chromatic alteration to the extra note(s) was left to the performer's discretion in the period, but signified in later times. Later usage also divided the mordent into upper (sometimes called 'inverted mordent') and lower types, using the note(s) above and below (respectively) as the decorations. There is, however, some looseness about the application of the terminology.

Moscheles, Ignaz (Isaac)
Czech (naturalized German) composer, pianist, conductor (b. 23 May 1794, Prague; d. 10 Mar 1870, Leipzig).

He was taught piano by B.D. Weber, director of the Prague Conservatory from 1804 to 1808 on a diet of *J.S. Bach, *W.A. Mozart and *Clementi, though the boy also played *Beethoven. He moved to Vienna in 1808, he studied counterpoint with Albrechtsberger and composition with Salieri and soon became one of the city's most sought-after players. He was commissioned to prepare a piano reduction of *Beethoven's *Fidelio*, and his piece for piano and orchestra *La marche d'Alexandre* op. 32 (1815) became a great favourite. In the decade 1815–25 he travelled on recital-tours in Germany, Paris, Prague and London, where he gained much praise from *J.B. Cramer and Clementi, with both of whom he became friends. He married a Hamburg girl in 1825 and the couple settled in London, where Moscheles was appointed to the *Royal Academy of Music as a piano-teacher, where he gathered pupils of great talent around him. The *Philharmonic Society – where he was co-director 1832–41) appointed him conductor and he conducted Beethoven's

Ninth Symphony (1837 and 1838) and also the first London performance of his *Missa Solemnis* in 1832. His interest in music of the past prompted him to organize a series of 'historical soirées' which included performances of J.S. Bach and *D. Scarlatti on the harpsichord. Moscheles was of enormous help to *Felix Mendelssohn during his early visits to London, giving him lodgings and social and professional *entrées* and the two played together often (including performances of Mozart's Two-piano concerto and Moscheles' own). Moscheles also played with *Chopin in Paris and visited Leipzig, appearing with Mendelssohn in the Gewandhaus concerts (1835). When Felix Mendelssohn was looking for the best teachers to staff his newly-founded Leipzig Conservatory, he offered Moscheles the post of principal professor of piano, which he accepted, moving to Leipzig for good on taking up the post in 1846. Mendelssohn's death the following year at the early age of 38 was a deep shock.

Moscheles's playing was noted for its clarity and precision. His interest in, and interpretations of, earlier music were much admired and his 'historical soirées' or 'classical chamber concerts' stimulated much interest in this kind of music. *R. Schumann rated him highly as a sonata composer and he taught many in London and Leipzig, including the young Felix Mendelssohn, *Thalberg and Litolff.

Works
Orchestral works include a Symphony in C major op. 81 (1829), eight Piano Concertos (no. 6 in B♭ major op. 90 ('Fantastique', 1833) and no. 7 in C minor op. 93 ('Pathétique', 1835–6)) and eight other pieces for piano with orchestra

(including *La marche d'Alexandre* op. 32 (1815), *Souvenirs d'Irlande* op. 69 (1826) and *Anklänge aus Schottland* op. 75 (1826)). Many pieces for piano including six sonatas (inc. two for piano duet, and the solo piano *Sonate mélancolique* in F♯ minor op. 49 (1814)). There are also the *Charakteristische Studien* op. 95 (each with its own title and character, 1836) and smaller pieces, together with chamber music (mostly with piano), songs and many arrangements. He also collaborated with *Fétis on a Piano School, the *Méthode des méthodes* (1840).

Further reading
C. Moscheles, ed., *Aus Moscheles' Leben* (Leipzig, 1782; Eng. tr. 1873). I. Heussner, *Ignaz Moscheles in seinen Klaviersonaten, Kammermusicwerken und -Konzerten* (diss., U. of Marpurg, 1963). J. Roche, 'Ignaz Moscheles 1794–1870', *MT*, cxi (1970). C.D. Gresham, *Ignaz Moscheles: an Illustrious Musician in the Nineteenth Century* (diss., U. of Rochester, NY, 1980). E. Smidak, *Isaak-Ignaz Moscheles: das Leben des Komponisten und seine Begegnungen mit Beethoven, Liszt, Chopin, Mendelssohn* (Vienna, 1988; Eng. tr., 1989). Newman/SSB.

Motivische Arbeit (Ger.: 'motivic working-out')
A developmental technique by which musical material (particularly melodic) is broken down into small motifs and these are manipulated in various ways – extended, compressed, varied, with different harmonization, texture or tessitura, etc. It is one of the greatest characteristics of improvisation, in which it comes into its own.

Moto perpetuo (see *Perpetuum mobile*)

Mozart, Franz Xaver Wolfgang
['Wolfgang Amadeus']
Austrian composer, pianist, son of *Wolfgang Amadeus (b. 26 Jul 1791, Vienna; d. 29 Jul 1844, Carlsbad).

Taught piano by Niemetschek and F.X. Dussek (where he lived in) in Prague and with Neukomm, A Streicher, *Hummel, Salieri, Vogler and Albrechtsberger in Vienna and, later, counterpoint with Mederitsch, his first compositions, including the Piano Quartet op. 1, were published in 1802 when he was 11. In 1807 he spent three years as tutor to the family of Count Viktor Baworowski and then two years as music teacher in the house of Janiszewski, the imperial chamberlain, after which he went freelance in Lemberg. In 1819 he was on a two-year concert-tour, playing in Russia, Poland, Germany, Austria, Italy and Denmark. He settled in Vienna in 1838 and was made honorary *Kapellmeister of the Dom-Musik-Verein and the Mozarteum in Salzburg, seeing the unveiling of the Mozart memorial in 1842 and playing his father's D minor piano concerto at the festival concert. His piano music shows the influence of Hummel's brilliant figuration, but also foreshadows *Chopin and *Liszt.

Works
Include two piano concertos, a symphony (unpub.), some chamber music, a piano sonata, sets of *Polonaises and variations, some choral works and *Lieder*.

Further reading
W. Hummel, *W.A. Mozarts Söhne* (Kassel, 1956); 'W.A. Mozart-Sohn in Banne der Romantik', *Mitteilungen der Internationalen Stiftung Mozarteum*, xi/3–4 (1963). R. Angermüller, *Franz Xaver Wolfgang Mozart: Reisetagebuch 1819–1821* (Bad Honnef, 1994).

Mozart, (Johann Georg) Leopold

Austrian composer, violinist, theorist (b. 14 Nov 1719, Augsburg; d. 28 May 1787, Salzburg).

He attended the Augsburg Gymnasium (1727–35) and the Lyceum (1735–36). Destined to be a career clerk, he moved to Salzburg to attend the Benedictine University in 1737 but was expelled for poor attendance after two years; he may have been taught composition by J.E. Eberlin, *Kapellmeister* of the Salzburg court. Mozart became valet-musician to the Count of Thurn-Valassina and Taxis in Salzburg, dedicating his op. 1 (six trio sonatas) to him. In 1743 he joined the orchestra of the prince-archbishop of Salzburg and taught violin to the choirboys at the oratory from the following year. He was promoted to the post of court and chamber composer in 1757, by which time he had married (1747) and had, amongst other children who didn't survive into adulthood, a daughter, *Maria Anna ('Nannerl') and a son, *Wolfgang Amadeus; he was soon to give up his teaching and his composition to devote his time outside work to these children, both musical prodigies. From this point on, his life becomes inextricably entwined with that of his son Wolfgang Amadeus, to whose musical and other welfare he dedicated his life. His *Violinschule* of 1826 is the last in an important trio of such works in the eighteenth century, the others being by *Quantz on the flute ((1752)) and *C.P.E. Bach on the keyboard (his *'*Versuch*' (1753))

Works

A sizeable body of compositions, especially allowing for the fact that he gave up composing to dedicate more time to Wolfgang. It includes church music (masses, litanies and cantatas), many symphonies (of which a quantity is lost), some of which are topical – 'burlesca', 'pasrorella', 'da caccia' – a few surviving concertos (trumpet in D major (1762), two horns in E♭ major (1752)), some chamber music (trio sonatas, violin duos), some keyboard music and the *Versuch einer gründlichen Violinschule* ('Violin-school' 1756).

Further reading

L. Wegele, ed., *Leopold Mozart, 1719–1787: Bild einer Persönlichkeit* (Augsburg, 1969). A. Layer, *Ein Jugend in Augsburg: Leopold Mozart 1719–1787* (Augsburg, 1975). F. Lanegger, *Mozart Vater und Sohn: eine psychologische Untersuchung* (Zürich, 1978). R. Halliwell, *The Mozart Family* (Oxford, 1998).

Mozart, Maria Anna (Walburga Ignatia) ['Nannerl']

Austrian pianist; daughter of *Leopold Mozart and older sister of *Wolfgang Amadeus Mozart (b. 30 or 31 Jul 1751, Salzburg; d. 29 Oct 1829, Salzburg).

A child prodigy like her brother, she learnt music from her father *Leopold and she accompanied and played with him and *Wolfgang on their first tours in 1763. However, from 1767, she was only performing for the family. She also composed, and her brother thought highly of her works, but none have survived. She married a magistrate, had three children by him and taught the piano after his death in 1801. She died in sad circumstances, being blind and poor. Her written reminiscences, diaries and letters are an important source for Mozart study and she appears in several Mozart-family portraits.

Further reading

W. Hummel, *Nannerl: Wolfgang Amadeus Mozarts Schwester* (Vienna,

1952). D.-R. de Lerma, 'The Nannerl Notebook', *MR*, xix (1958). E. Rieger, *Nannerl Mozart: Leben einer Künstlerin im 18. Jahrhundert* (Frankfurt, 1990). R. Halliwell, *The Mozart Family* (Oxford, 1998).

Mozart, (Johann [Joannes] **Chrysostom** [Chrysostomus]) **Wolfgang** [Wolfgangus] **Amadeus (Amadè, Amadé, Amadeo, Gottlieb)** [Theophilus]
Austrian composer, pianist; son of *Leopold Mozart (b. 27 Jan 1756, Salzburg; d. 5 Dec 1791, Vienna).

Seemingly without any formal schooling, Wolfgang was a prodigy, showing enormous musicality from an extremely early age. He received his musical and general training from his father, *Leopold, an excellent musician, who set aside his own career as a composer and teacher to devote himself to his children's education, while keeping his post as violinist in the orchestra of the Prince-Archbishop Colloredo in Salzburg. Much of the boy's childhood was spent travelling around Europe with Leopold and his sister, *Maria Anna ('Nannerl') to display their talents. In January 1762 Wolfgang played the harpsichord for the Elector of Bavaria and he played several times before the Empress Maria Thereia at Schönbrunn the same year; she sent them a set of clothes for court and ordered their portraits to be painted. A newspaper report of the next year gives an insight into the boy's talents: playing like a seasoned artist, improvising in a variety of styles, playing at sight, playing with a cloth covering the keyboard, adding a bass to a given theme and identifying any note given to him.

The next step for Leopold was to take the young genius to the other great European cities, Paris and London (and points in between), and he invested a good deal of capital in the trip, with his own coach and servant. They performed at Munich, Augsburg, Ludwigsburg (meeting Jommelli and Nardini), Schwetzingen, near Mannheim (playing before the Elector Palatine Carl Theodor), Mainz, Frankfurt, Koblenz, Aachen (playing before the Princess Anna Amalia of Russia), Brussels and finally Paris, on 18 November, where they stayed five months. Here, Wolfgang played before Louis XV and they met the composer-performers *Schobert and Eckard, and Baron Grimm, the writer. Mozart published his first works in Paris (four violin sonatas) and they left for London, arriving in the early summer of 1764, when the boy was ten.

During their 15 months in the English capital, Mozart played before George III – who gave him some tough tests – three times and in Ranelagh Pleasure Gardens and elsewhere, as well as private engagements; Leopold kept 'open house' for music-lovers and they became friendly with *J.C. Bach whose music influenced him a great deal. The philosopher Daines *Barrington examined and tested the boy and made a report to the Royal Society. Mozart probably composed his first symphonies while Leopold was recuperating from illness in Chelsea.

The family embarked for France on 1 August 1765 and had to remain at Lille for a month while Mozart recovered from his illness. They visited Ghent, Antwerp and The Hague, where both the children were ill. Moving on through Amsterdam, Utrecht, Antwerp and Brussels, they arrived again in Paris, staying for two months, after which they travelled back to Salzburg – again stopping to give concerts at several points – laden with their accumulated gifts of gold rings, jewelled snuffboxes and watches.

After a 'rest' of nine months, during which Mozart wrote his first dramatic works, the Latin comedy *Apollo et Hyacinthus* and the first part of an oratorio *Die Schudldigkeit des ersten Gebotes* – the other two parts being written by *M. Haydn and Adlgasser – they set off on a 15-month stay in Vienna. They gave several concerts, but a projected opera production was thwarted by court intrigues, although another dramatic work was performed privately, and met Franz Anton Mesmer, discoverer of Mesmerism. Arriving back in Salzburg in January 1769, Mozart wrote a mass and sets of dance-music and by late October young Mozart was appointed honorary *Kapellmeister* to the court and by December the Mozarts, this time only father and son, were on the road again, southward-bound to Italy.

Again, every possible opportunity for performing was taken and the young genius's talents shown off and tested. They spent a short time in Milan, meeting Sammartini and Piccinni and on an overnight stop at an inn near Lodi, Mozart completed his first string quartet. In Bologna they met Padre Martini and the *castratos* Farinelli and Manzuoli as well as the young Thomas *Attwood, of an age with Mozart, and the two soon became friends; Attwood was to have lessons from Mozart later. The Mozarts spent Holy Week in Rome then visited Naples and, on returning to Rome, Wolfgang was given an audience with the Pope and was invested as a Knight of the Order of the Golden Spur. On the way northwards, he passed the tests for admittance to the Accademia Filarmonica in Bologna and also that in Verona and they settled for a little time in Milan, so that Wolfgang could write the opera *Mitridate, rè di Ponto*. In spite of intrigues and problems, it was a great success and had 22 performances directed by Mozart.

After a mere five months at home, father and son again visited Italy – one of several planned while they were there the first time – and Mozart wrote and directed *Ascanio in Alba*. As soon as they arrived back in Salzburg, their employer, the prince-archbishop Count Schrattenbach, died and his successor, Hieronymus, Count Colloredo, was invested and Wolfgang composed a serenata, *Il sogno di Scipione*, for the festivities and, after having been honorary for three years, he was formally appointed *Konzertmeister* on 9 July 1772 at a salary of 150 florins. Their last Italian journey began three months later, Leopold constantly seeking a better situation for his son, as he had done on all the previous visits, since he was sceptical about Wolfgang's chances in Salzburg. He decided that it was time to try closer to home, in Vienna, and they arrived there in July 1773, spending some ten weeks in the city. Here, Mozart was able to hear and read the latest music, including that of *J. Haydn, and the result was a marked maturity in style, and the composition of his first really great works, exemplified in the 'little' G minor symphony K183/173dB (his first in a minor key), which breathes different air from the previous ones, in its urgent, *Sturm und Drang*-inspired syncopations and dynamic contrasts, and in the A major, K201/186a.

Mozart was 18 when he received, and fulfilled, a commission for an opera buffa (*La finta giardiniera*) for the Munich carnival, and wrote his first piano sonatas while visiting the city. Salzburg seemed provincial now, with an unstimulating employer and establishment and leave becoming more rationed, but there was a commission for an operatic work, *Il rè pastore*, to be performed either in concert or semi-staged, for the visit of the Archduke Maximilian Franz and Mozart also wrote his five violin concertos and a number for keyboard as well; the visit of the French keyboard virtuosa, Mlle Jeunehomme, in early 1777, elicited the E♭ major concerto K271, named after her.

Later that year, Mozart wrote to his employer asking for his release; the result was that both Mozarts were 'released', but Leopold reinstated soon after. Mozart was accompanied by his mother on his next journey, through Munich and Augsburg (where he was most impressed when he visited the piano workshop of *J.A. Stein) to Mannheim (October 1777), from where his letters home to his father give a full picture of the court, its famous orchestra and its musical activities. He met Cannabich, Holzbauer and Wendling and fell in love with the sixteen-year-old Aloysia Weber, which caused him to postpone his moving on to Paris. This whole business infuriated Leopold who finally ordered him on, and son and mother arrived in March 1778. Mozart was not content in Paris; he disliked French music and taste in general and was not prepared to kowtow to high-rankers who might have been a source of employment – however temporary – but his music had success. His mother became ill and died of a fever. Mozart stayed with Baron Grimm, who wrote to Leopold that if his son had half his talent and twice as much shrewdness, he'd have done much better.

Leopold urged him to return to Salzburg with news of an offer from Colloredo by which he would remain *Konzertmeister* but also be court organist, with a better salary and more generous conditions of leave, which, having singularly failed to obtain any employment or even prospect of employment, he was in no position to refuse. On the way he stopped again at Mannheim – where his high hopes of an electoral appointment were dashed – and having heard one of *Georg Benda's *melodramas, he wished to write one himself; the resultant work (*Semiramis*) is lost, if it were ever written. He stopped off at Munich and was coolly received by his love and he arrived home miserable. His journeys, however, had an effect on his subsequent music; apart from ongoing maturity, the sonic possibilities of the Mannheim orchestra can be heard, and not only in orchestral music, and, in spite of his feelings, a French brilliance also becomes part of his stylistic armoury.

During the summer of 1780 Mozart was delighted to receive a commission for an opera for Munich and began work immediately, as he knew a number of the principal singers; his letters home from Munich are a very valuable insight into his methods. The opera, *Idomeneo, rè di Creta* was a great success. On his way home, he was summoned by Colloredo to Vienna, for the accession of the Emperor, Joseph II. His three-month stay brought home the lowliness of his position in the house of a traditional potentate, below the valets but above the cooks. He was refused permission to play, depriving him of a considerable amount of money, as the city was full of nobility and there were many concerts and social occasions. He had an angry audience with Colloredo who, according to Mozart's letter, abused him verbally and he again asked for release from his contract and was at first refused. However, a month later he got his wish – in fact he was thrown out 'with a kick on my arse', as he wrote to Leopold, whose letters of reply do not survive, but whose content can easily be guessed as full of consternation. Mozart went to stay with the Webers, whose daughter Aloysia, his erstwhile love, had meantime married, and it appears he became interested in the third of the four girls, Constanze. His letters to Leopold, who had heard rumours, are full of denial, especially about marriage, to which Leopold was passionately opposed.

Mozart now had some pupils and played in private concerts, during one of which, at court, he had his famous 'duel' with *Clementi. It appears that Mozart was the 'winner' and he was scathing about his rival – and continued to be so for some years – whereas the latter was more measured and complimentary about Mozart. The relationship with Constanze deepened, and it seems that, through her family's scheming, he was placed in a position which required that he marry her, which he did, on 4 August in St Stephen's Cathedral; Leopold's consent (given with bad grace) arrived the next day. The Mozarts' legendary money problems began within weeks of their wedding, but the marriage was happy.

Mozart's interest in *Baroque music (especially that of *J.S. Bach and *Handel) was stimulated by Baron Gottfried van Swieten, whom he visited on a regular basis. The significance of this can be exaggerated, but, certainly, traces of it remain in the studied archaism of the C minor Mass (unfinished). A more important musical encounter was that with *J. Haydn, which dated from 1781, the year of publication of the older composer's set of six great string quartets op. 33. There is little doubt that Mozart's own set of six (pub. 1784) sought to emulate Haydn's and they were dedicated to him in an affectionate preface, causing them to be called the 'Haydn' Quartets.

He also wrote piano concertos for his own use.

Mozart became a freemason at the end of 1784, entering the lodge 'Zur Wohlthätigkeit', although he attended others as well. Masonry attracted a wide range of people at the time, nobles and intellectuals – members included J. Haydn and the scientist Ignaz von Born – and was not a particularly secret or anti-religious organization, but with ideas of the brotherhood of Man rooted in Enlightenment ideals. Mozart wrote music for their ceremonies and masonic features can be discerned in a number of works of the period and later. He continued to teach and his lessons with *Attwood survive and are a fascinating insight on Mozart's methods; he also taught the young *Hummel, who 'lived in' with the Mozarts for two years. He may also have given some lessons to the young *Beethoven, on the latter's first short visit to Vienna (1787).

He still had a great desire to write operas, and opportunities presented themselves and his meeting with the poet Lorenzo da Ponte provided him with his best libretti for which he wrote his operatic masterpieces Le nozze di Figaro, enthusiastically received, and Don Giovanni, more muted, although highly successful in Prague. Leopold Mozart died in May 1787 and Wolfgang's debts were mounting; a series of begging letters survive, and he was lent money on several occasions by a fellow-mason Michael Puchberg. Later the same year he was appointed court Kammermusicus after *Gluck died and his duties were simply to write music for the court balls; his salary was less than half of Gluck's. In spite of his perilous financial situation, works continued to flow – string quintets, piano quartets, trios and concertos, the

'Prague' Symphony and the miraculous composition of his last three symphonies within three months in the summer of 1788. None of his ventures, however, whether in composition, performance or publication, seemed to provide the remuneration which he could reasonably expect and his letters to Puchberg grow increasingly desperate. He saw Haydn off on his first London trip in December 1790 and had a premonition – fulfilled, in the event – that he would never see him again.

But he had a commission from an old acquaintance, the actor-manager Emanuel Schikaneder whose theatrical troupe put on *Singspiels* at the Theater auf der Wieden in the suburbs, and they collaborated on *Die Zauberflöte* which was performed on 30 September to a cautious audience; however, the opera increased in popularity over the next few performances, at one of which Salieri had a 'bravo' or a 'bello' to describe each number. Another commission was for the fateful Requiem, from a Count Walsegg-Stuppach, who wanted it composed in secrecy and anonymously, so that he could pretend it was his own tribute to his dead wife. Before he could finish it, Mozart died, most likely of rheumatic inflammatory fever, after a brief illness. There is no evidence to suggest any foul play, especially not poisoning by Salieri. His burial in a mass grave with few, or no, mourners is consistent with contemporary Viennese burial customs. Responsible for a body of work and many masterpieces in every medium extant in his time, Mozart can be seen as the most versatile composer in Western music history.

Works

Sacred works include Missa solemnis in C minor K139 (1768), unfinished Mass in C minor K427 (1782), unfinished Requiem in D minor K626 (1791), Motets 'Exsultate, jubilate' K165 (1773) and *Ave verum corpus* K618 (1791), *Vesperae solennes de confessore* K399 (1780). Operatic works include *Idomeneo* (1780, rev. 1786), *Die Entführung aus dem Serail* (1782), *Le nozze di Figaro* (1876, rev. 1789), *Don Giovanni* (1878, rev. 1788), *Così fan tutte* (1790) and *La clemenza di Tito* and *Die Zauberflöte* (both 1791). There are five violin concertos, a clarinet concerto, a bassoon concerto, four horn concertos and 27 piano concertos, including no. 9 in E♭ major ('Jeunehomme') K271 (1777), no. 17 in G major K453, nos 20 in D minor K466 and 21 in C major K467 (both 1785), nos 23 in A major K488 and 24 in C minor K491 (both 1786) and no. 27 in B♭ major K595 (1791). Chamber music includes the six string quartets dedicated to Haydn (1782–85), K387, K421 in D minor, K428, K458 'Hunt' and K465 'Dissonant'; the piano quartet in G minor K478 (1785), piano trios, violin sonatas, the Clarinet Quintet in A major K581 (1789) and the string quintets in G minor K515 and C major K516 (both 1787). There are 41 numbered symphonies including nos 25 in G minor K183 (1773), 29 in A major K201 (1774), 31 in D major 'Paris' K297 (1778), 36 in C major 'Linz' K425 (1783), 38 in D major 'Prague' K504 (1786), 39 in E♭ major K543, 40 in G minor K550, and 41 in C major 'Jupiter' K551 (all 1788) as well as serenades, divertimenti and dances.

Further reading

From a huge literature: H.C. Robbins Landon (ed., *The Mozart Compendium* (London, 1990). G. Gruber, *Mozart and Posterity* (London, 1991). R. Halliwell, *The Mozart Family* (Oxford, 1998).

M. Solomon, *Mozart: a Life* (New York, 1995). C. Eisen, *The New Grove Mozart* (London, 2001). *MGG*.

Müller, Matthias

German (Austriian naturalized) piano-maker (b. 24 Feb 1770, Wernborn, nr Frankfurt; d. 28 Dec 1844, Vienna).

He was recognized as a citizen and master craftsman of Vienna in 1795 and in 1804 he was granted a privilege to build instruments. He was also president of an association of Viennese piano-makers. Various inventions and patents included a cast, or wrought, iron frame (patented in 1829 in Vienna) and he was also one of the first two makers to invent the true upright *piano (as opposed to a vertical grand; the other was Isaac *Hawkins of Philadelphia).

Further reading

H. Ottner, *Der Wiener Instrumentenbau 1815–1833* (Tutzing, 1977). Harding/ PIANO-FORTE. Cole/PIANOFORTE. Maunder/KEYBOARD.

Müller, Wilhelm

German poet (b. 7 Oct 1794, Dessau; d. 30 Sep 1827, Dessau).

He studied classical philology in Berlin (1812–17), fought in the War of Liberation and then lived in Berlin and Dresden. Greek lyrics were an important influence on his poetry, as was *folk poetry. He knew Tieck, Arnim, Brentano and *C.M. von Weber and strongly influenced Heine. Müller travelled in Italy, after which he returned to Dessau (1819) becoming librarian to the duke and writing criticisms until his early death in 1827. His poetry is based on folk models in simple, direct language which were very susceptible to musical setting. His poetry-cycles *Die schöne Müllerin*

and *Winterreise* were set by *Schubert and his work was also set by *Brahms and Goetz.

Works

77 *Gedichte aus den hinterlassenen Papieren eines reisenden Waldhornisten* (1821 and 1824) in which *Die schöne Müllerin* and *Winterreise* (dedicated to his friend *C.M. von Weber) appear

Further reading

B. Hake, *Wilhelm Müller: seinen Leben und Dichten* (diss., U of Berlin, 1907). C. Baumann, *Wilhelm Müller: the Poet of the Schubert Song Cycles* (University Park, PA, 1981). S. Youens, *Schubert, Müller, and Die schöne Müllerin* (Cambridge, 1997).

Musard, Philippe

French composer, conductor (b. 8 Nov 1792, Tours; d. 31 Mar 1859, Auteuil).

Born of a poor family, he learnt horn and violin and earned money by playing for local dances. Visited London *c*.1817 and possibly studied with *Reicha in the late 1820s. He directed masked balls at the Théâtre des Variétés in Paris in 1830 and was asked to conduct dances and popular concerts on the Champs-Elysées. His *Concerts-Musard* became very fashionable, and he also continued to conduct the masked balls at the Opéra-Comique and the Salle Ventadour, coinciding with the rage of the *galop and using spectacular effects such as pistol-shots. He went to England in 1840 to conduct the promenade concerts at the theatre in Drury Lane, and the following year at the Lyceum. He remained popular until 1852, but dropped completely out of view on his retirement to Auteuil the same year.

Works
Many *waltzes and *quadrilles, some based on operatic airs. He also wrote three string quartets (*c.*1831) and began a *Nouvelle méthode de composition musicale* which he dedicated to *Reicha.

Further reading
A. Carse, *The Life of Jullien* (Cambridge, 1951). A. Martin-Fougier, *La vie élégante ou la formation du Tout-Paris, 1815–1848* (Paris, 1990). Fétis/*BIOGRAPHIE*.

Musical Glasses (See *Armonica)

Musical Magazine, The
A British music periodical published in London, in English, with a music supplement. Published monthly, only one volume appeared, that of the year 1835.

Musical Offering (see **musikalischer Opfer, Das*)

musikalischer Opfer, Das
A group of 13 pieces written by *J.S. Bach upon a theme given to him for extemporization by *Frederick the Great of Prussia during Bach's visit to Potsdam in 1747 while he was trying out the King's new *Silbermann pianos. Bach was so taken with the theme and its possibilities that he wrote a series of ricecars and *canons on it, had the work engraved and presented it to Frederick. Some of the pieces are written on two staves and lie within the compass of the hands on a keyboard, others suggest an ensemble of up to three instruments.

Mute (Fr. *sourdine*; Ger. *Dämpfer*; It. *sordino*)
(1) A device used to muffle the tone of a musical instrument; it can be either applied, or built in. One usual result is a reduction in volume. In the violin family it takes the form of a (metal, ivory, wood or plastic) clamp placed onto the strings at the bridge and in brass instruments it is a cone inserted into the bell. On the early piano and harpsichord the word is occasionally used to refer to the *moderator *stop or pedal (see *Stop (3) and *Pedal (4)); used thus, the French form (*sourdine*) or Italian (*sordino*) forms are more common than the English 'mute'.

(2) In this connection the direction '*con sodrdino*' is used in musical scores – almost exclusively in the Italian – to instruct the player to apply the mute to their instrument; it is cancelled by '*senza sordino*' (without mute'). The plural is *sordini*.

Myrthen
A song-cycle of 26 numbers by *Robert Schumann, his op. 25, written and published in 1840. It was written and specially bound as a wedding present for *Clara, whom he had married the same year, and he wrote to her that he 'wept for joy' while writing them. The songs, setting poems by various writers, are as follows:
1. 'Widmung' (Rückert); 2. 'Freisinn' (Goethe); 3. 'Der Nussbaum' (Mosen); 4. 'Jemand' (*Burns, tr. Gerhard); 5. 'Lieder aus dem Schenkenbuch im Divan I' (Goethe); 6. 'Lieder aus dem Schenkenbuch im Divan II' (Goethe); 7. 'Die Lotosblume' (Heine); 8. 'Talismane' (Goethe); 9. 'Lied der Suleika' (Goethe, attrib. Marianne von Willener); 10. 'Die Hochländer-Witwe' (Burns, tr. Gerhard); 11. 'Lieder der Braut aus dem Liebesfrühling I' (Rückert); 12. 'Lieder der Braut aus dem Liebesfrühling II' (Rückert); 13. 'Die Hochländers Abschied' (Burns, tr. Gerhard); 14. 'Die

Hochländisches Wiegenlied' (Burns, tr. Gerhard); 15. 'Aus den hebräischen Gesängen' (Byron, tr. J Körner); 16. 'Rätsel' (C. Fanshawe, tr. K Kannegiesser); 17. 'Zwei Venetianischer Lieder I' (*Moore, tr. Freiligrath); 18. 'Zwei Venetianischer Lieder II' (Moore, tr. Freiligrath); 19. 'Hauptmanns Weib' (Burns, tr. Gerhard); 20. 'Weit, weit' (Burns, tr. Gerhard); 21. 'Was will die einsame Träne?' (Burns, tr. Gerhard); 22. 'Niemand' (Burns, tr. Gerhard); 23. 'Im Westen' (Burns, tr. Gerhard); 24. 'Du bist wie eine Blume' (Heine); 25. 'Aus den östlichen Rosen' (Rückert); 26. 'Zum schluss' (Rückert).

N

Nag's head swell (see *Swell)

Nameboard, nameplate
A piece of (usually) wood, ivory, bone or plastic placed in full view above the *keyboard of a keyboard instrument on which the name of the maker or his/her company appears, occasionally with an address and relevant title, such as 'Maker(s) to His Majesty King George' or similar.

'Nannerl' Mozart (see Mozart, *Maria Anna)

'Nannerl Notenbuch' ['*Nannerl Notebook']
A music manuscript book purporting to contain the earliest compositions of *W.A. Mozart between the ages of six and eight. They are mostly written in the hand of his father, *Leopold Mozart and contain the earliest keyboard pieces and the violin sonatas K6–9. The pieces, which are derivative of similar ones in circulation at the time, are likely to represent the kind of compositions the young Mozart was composing or improvising at the time, though with the emendations and suggestions of his father.

Napier, William
Scottish musician, music publisher (b. ?1740–41; d. 1812, Somerston [?Somers Town, London]).
Earliest records find him playing the violin in Edinburgh in the Canongate Playhouse orchestra and in 1765 he was in London and a member of the Royal Society of Musicians. He played for a time in George III's private band and the Professional Concerts and led the violas in the *Handel Commemoration of 1784. In the same year he set up a circulating music library, having gone into publishing in 1772, and both the publisher George Smart (father of *Sir George Smart) and the caricaturist James Gillray were sometime employees of his. He published the music of, among others, *J.C. Bach, *J.S. Schroeter and Shield as well as popular ballads. He had financial difficulties; a concert was given by *J.B. Cramer in 1788 for the benefit of his surviving children (11 of them) and he went bankrupt in 1791. The same year *J. Haydn, newly arrived in London, helped his rehabilitation by contributing accompaniments to the second volume of his well-known collection of Scottish *folk and popular songs *A Selection of Original Scots Songs in Three Parts. The Harmony by Haydn* which appeared in 1792; the first volume, *A Selection of the Most Favourite Scots Songs* had been issued in 1791, and the third in 1795. These sold so well that Napier repaid Haydn as well as commissioning more work from him for the third volume.

Further reading
C. Humphries and W.C. Smith, *Music Publishing in the British Isles* (London, 1954, 2/1970). C. Hopkinson and C.B. Oldman, 'Haydn's settings of Scottish Songs in the Collections of Napier and Whyte', *Edinburgh Bibliographical Society Transactions*, iii (1954). O. Neighbour and A. Tyson, *English Music Publishers' Plate Numbers in the First Half of the Nineteenth Century* (London, 1965).

Neefe, Christian Gottlob
German composer (b. 5 Feb 1748, Chemnitz; d. 26 Jan 1798, Dessau).
He was taught by the Chemnitz city organist and C.G. Tag, and was partly

self-educated (using works by Marpurg and *C.P.E. Bach); he began composing at the age of 12. After law studies in Leipzig, he had lessons from J.A. Hiller and took the latter's post as music director of a theatre troupe in 1776. Three years later he was in Bonn with another troupe and taught the young *Beethoven. From 1782 he was court organist, with Beethoven occasionally deputizing and he himself deputized for the *Kapellmeister 1783–84. The theatre he worked for was closed, however, on the death of the Elector Max Friedrich in 1784 and his organist salary was reduced, whereupon he took pupils. The court was disbanded in 1794 and, although he became music director at a theatre in Dessau in 1796, he died of an illness two years later. Neefe taught the young Beethoven piano, organ, thoroughbass and composition and drew his attention to *J.S. Bach's Das *wohltemperirte Clavier and C.P.E. Bach's Gellert-Lieder. He helped to popularize Mozart's operas by preparing vocal scores of them and his later songs foreshadow those of *Schubert and the *Romantic period.

Works

Dramatic works include Die Apotheke (comic opera, perf. 1771), Die Ziguener (perf. 1777), Sophonisbe (monodrama, perf. 1776) and Adelheit von Veltheim (perf. 1780). There are also songs, including Freimaurerlieder (Masonic Songs, pub. 1774) and the Klopstock Odes, and 12 Klaviersonaten (pub. 1773) a Piano Sonata (pub. 1780) and smaller pieces as well as some chamber pieces and a harpsichord concerto (pub. 1782).

Further reading

A. Becker, Christian Gottlob Neefe und die Bonner Illuminaten (Bonn, 1969).

J.B. Neely, Christian Gottlob Neefe's Early Vocal Style as Reflected in 'Oden von Klopstock' (1776) and 'Serenaten beym Klavier zu singen' (1777) (DMA diss., Indiana U., 1977).

Neue Zeitschrift für Musik (abbrev. NZfM)

German periodical founded in 1834 by *Robert Schumann with Friedrich Wieck, Ludwig Schunke and Julius Knorr. Schumann, who edited it for ten years, saw it as a *Romantic standard-bearer and wanted to move music away from the mere show of virtuosity, as he saw it, to enshrining the poetry of art again. It was aimed at the professional and knowledgeable, not the dilettante. In the hands of his successor, Franz Brendel, who edited it from 1845 until his death in 1868, it became a mouthpiece for the 'new German school' (*Liszt and Wagner primarily); as such it was opposed by composers like *Brahms, *Joachim and others. In 1887 it became allied to the Allgemeiner Musikverein and after that vacillated under various managements until 1975, when it joined with Melos, when it was published as Melos/NZ Neue Zeitschrift für Musik and from 1979 it dropped the 'Melos'.

'New German School'

Name given to a group of Germanic composers around the middle of the nineteenth century led by *Liszt and Wagner, whose ideas were opposed (in various public letters, etc.) by *Brahms, *Joachim, Grimm and Scholz.

New Studio (see *Studio per il pianoforte)

Nocturne (Eng., Fr.; Ger. Nachtstuck; It. notturno)

(1) During the eighteenth century, a name given to serenade-like pieces which were intended for evenings and, often, outdoors; *J. Haydn and *W.A. Mozart wrote a number of them

(2) The better-known usage dates from the early nineteenth century as the designation for a dreamy solo-piano piece of slower tempo in which a melodic line was embellished over a regular (and usually arpeggiaic) accompaniment. The Irish composer John *Field is credited as being the first to issue pieces of this type, calling them 'Nocturnes' later, and the idea was continued with great success by *Chopin.

O

Oberek, obertas (see *mazurka)

Octave *coupler
A device (usually a pedal or stop) used on the *harpsichord to allow two or more registers of strings which are tuned one or more octaves apart to sound simultaneously by pressing a single key. The device is occasionally found on some early *pianos or *combination-instruments involving piano or harpsichord actions, or both.

Oden mit Melodien
Title of a collection of anonymous song-settings published in 1753 in Berlin by Christian Gottfried *Krause and a local Berlin poet, Ramler, both members of the first *Berlin Lied School. The composers are now known to include *Franz Benda and *C.P.E. Bach. This collection was an illustration of Krause's ideas on song-writing (published the year before), showing a new, simpler approach to the lied.

Ogiński, Michał Kazimierz
Polish prince, musician, poet (b. 1728, Warsaw; d. 31 May 1800, Warsaw).

He lived mostly in France in his youth, at Lunéville, then Paris, learning the violin (from Viotti), also the harp and clarinet. He improved the pedal system on the harp, which was adopted by the *Erard firm in Paris. At his court in Lithuania, from 1771, he kept two theatres, a ballet troupe, opera company and orchestra with a wide repertory and founded a school for the local children on his estates.

Works
Some eight operas, for which the music is lost; over two dozen songs with texts by himself, about half of which are unaccompanied, and the rest accompanied by two violins and bass; *polonaises and mazurkas.

Further reading
A. Ciechanowiecki, *Michał Kazimierz Ogiński und sein Musenhof zu Slonim* (Cologne, 1961).

Oratorio
In its use of solo voices, chorus and narrative, oratorio can be seen as sacred opera but without action, scenery or costume. The musical setting of an extended sacred text, usually on a biblical theme, it flourished from the seventeenth until the first half of the nineteenth centuries (and especially in the eighteenth) but is still occasionally found today. Examples are *J.S. Bach's Passions (*St Matthew*, *St John*) and *The Christmas Oratorio*, *Handel's *Messiah* and, later, Walton's *Belshazzar's Feast* and Tippett's *A Child of Our Time*.

Further reading
F. Raugel, *L'oratorio* (Paris, 1948). H.E. Smither, *A History of the Oratorio* (Chapel Hill, NC, 1977). G. Massenkeil, ed., *Das Oratorium Das Musikwerk*, xxxvii (1970; Eng. tr., 1970). K. Pahlen, *The World of Oratorio* (Portland, OR, 1990).

'Orchestra in the drawing Room'
Name given to the early *piano in the early years of the nineteenth century because of its ability to reproduce orchestral scores in the breadth of its pitch-range and because of its colouristic and polyphonic possibilities. The name also refers to the number of arrangements and 'piano-reductions' of music from other media – including, of course, the orchestra.

Ordre (see *Suite)

Organ (from Gk. *organon* via Lat. *organum*; Fr. *orgue(s)*; Dutch, Ger. *Orgel*; It. *organo*)
A wind-operated *keyboard instrument by which an air current – usually bellows-generated by means of human, mechanical or electrical energy – is directed through rows ('*registers' or 'ranks') of tuned pipes to produce the sound. The instrument very often has several keyboards and may have a *pedal-board, which can be *coupled together in various ways, and to each of which several ranks of pipes may be assigned, by the use of drawstops (see *stop). It is of considerable antiquity, and is known from the Hellenistic period in the third century BC. During the Dark Ages it became associated with the (Catholic and Byzantine) Church and was to be found mostly in churches, an association which persists even today. In spite of the fact that it possesses basically *terraced dynamics – although a kind of artificial grading of dynamics has been incorporated into it in the form of the *swell-box – it has remained popular with composers throughout history and a huge and growing body of work exists for it. Many historic organs in churches are of great beauty in terms of design.
   The organ exists in several forms as well as the large church type. The small personal regal, the portative, which was capable of being played while being carried, strapped around the player's neck, and the positive (which was also portable but had to be set down to be played) were all much-used in the Middle Ages and Renaissance and many Elizabethan and later houses had organs built into reception-halls (sometimes in 'minstrels' galleries') or music-rooms.

Later, the more homely *harmonium was used in homes and small churches and chapels, and the large theatre and cinema organs. The cinema organ was developed by the Wurlitzer Company in the United States at the end of the nineteenth century and came into its own in the late 1920s accompanying silent films. The advent of the 'talkies' from 1928 onwards put an end to this, but the tradition lived on in the large theatres and playhouses, in Blackpool, Lancashire and elsewhere with their recitals of popular music of the early twentieth century such as those by Reginald Dixon.

Further reading
O. Ochse, *The History of the Organ in the United States* (Bloomington, IN and London, 1975). P. Williams, *A New History of the Organ: from the Greeks to the Present Day* (London, 1980); *The Organ in Western Culture, 750–1250* (Cambridge, 1993). B. Sonnaillon, *King of Instruments: a History of the Organ* (New York, 1985).

'Organised piano' (see *combination instruments)

Ornament, -ation (see *decoration)

Ouverture (see *Overture)

Overspun string
In the piano, a technique in which a string (in this case called the 'core') is covered by a wire wound uniformly around its length. The core is usually of iron or steel and the overwinding copper or brass. It is rarely used outside the bass and middle registers and, although modern *harpsichord-makers use the technique, it is not traditional for that instrument.

Overstringing [Cross-stringing]
A device used in the piano by which the bass and the rest of the strings are divided into two closely-aligned levels, or planes, with one set crossing over the other at an acute angle. It was patented by Henri *Pape in France in 1828 for some of his upright pianos, but it was soon taken up in the United States and Europe. The advantages were twofold: first, it allowed for smaller instruments since the full length of the bass strings (longer than the others because of their lower pitch) did not stretch for their full length from the keyboard backwards in grand pianos, or from the floor upwards in uprights (an important consideration when hoping to interest the less opulent of the middle classes with less space and money); and, secondly, it distributed the tension more evenly around the frame, thus lessening the danger of cracking or warping.

Overtones [partials, harmonics]
The basic pitch of a sound, which is usually that which we are most aware of, is the *fundamental tone*, the strongest frequency at which the source (string, pipe) vibrates and at which the excited medium (usually air) is caused to vibrate, carrying the sound to our eardrums. This fundamental tone is, in practice, accompanied by sympathetic vibrations at different pitches above the fundamental which help to give the sound its quality; these are *overtones* or *partials*. The large number (and their strength) in, for example, the tone of some bells often makes it difficult to recognize the fundamental pitch. In the case of musical instruments, whether strings or wind, the overtones or partials generated have a mathematical relationship with the frequency of the fundamental. This represents a series of pitches which vibrate at whole-number multiples of the

fundamental's frequency. For example, those at twice, four times, eight times, etc. the fundamental's frequency give the higher octaves; thus the fundamental A below middle C, vibrating at 110 Hertz (Hz), will give octaves at 220Hz, 440Hz, 880Hz, etc.

However, others also sound and, together with the octaves, these *harmonics* give the *Harmonic Series*, moving from the fundamental (A) upwards to give the upper octave (A), then compound 5th (E above, 330Hz), octave again (A), major 3rd (C♯, 550Hz), 5th again (E, 660Hz), minor 7th (G, 770Hz), octave (A) and so on. Some of the higher ones are not true, and some are dissonant with the fundamental and/or other harmonics. However, they are usually much softer than the fundamental (and quite difficult to separate from the sound as a whole) and they get even softer as they get higher. These harmonics are what give the sound its quality and the construction of particular instruments favour some and not others; also, the harmonics present frequently differ in strength. The clarinet's timbre, for example, is the result of the complete lack of the even-numbered harmonics. Individual harmonics, or passages of them, are occasionally called for in compositions because of their strange ethereal purity. Vocal harmonics are used in *falsetto.

Overture (Fr. *ouverture*; Ger. *Ouvertüre*; It. *sinfonia*)
(1) From the French *ouverture* ('opening'), the term described the introduction or, more commonly, introductory movement in two or more sections to an opera, oratorio or ballet in the seventeenth century.

(2) In the *Baroque period, it was also used to describe the whole of an orchestral

or keyboard *suite, as well as the first (opening) movement.

(3) The French O[u]verture was a particular form which was used in the seventeenth and eighteenth centuries, derived from French composers, such as Lully. This was a two-part movement, the first of which was slow – usually marked *grave* – and occasionally pompous, with dotted rhythms which, in keeping with performance practice of the period, was double-dotted. This was followed by a faster section (*allegro*) which was usually imitative and often fugal or containing fugato writing (see *fugue).

(4) The Italian Overture, from the same period as the French, was tripartite, with two fast sections surrounding a slower one. It was also called 'sinfonia' and, in fact, developed into the symphony when the sections became longer and separated from each other.

(5) In the later eighteenth century the overture, as used in dramatic music, began to foreshadow – either in mood or with actual musical references – some of the music of the following dramatic work. It could occasionally lead directly into the first number without a break as, for example *Gluck's overture to his opera *Iphigénie en Tauride* (*Iphigenia in Tauris*) where the overture depicts the storm which is the setting for the opening number. Later nineteenth-century overtures often use

material from the subsequent work (usually an opera) and in many cases, particularly in the comic genre, the overture is more of a medley of the 'big tunes' to follow. This can be seen in the Savoy Operas (operettas) of *Gilbert and Sullivan and the comic operas of Offenbach and Auber as well as the twentieth- and twenty-first-century stage musicals.

(6) In some cases in the nineteenth century, the 'overture' can be less of a movement, and more of a short introduction, or scene-setter. Examples of this kind of 'Prelude' ('Vorspiel') are found in Wagner in, for example, the music-dramas in the *Ring* and in *Tristan und Isolde*.

(7) The nineteenth-century Concert Overture is an overture which stands independent from any musical dramatic work and can either be part of a suite of pieces of incidental music (to a play, for example, as in that which *Felix Mendelssohn wrote for Shakespeare's *A Midsummer Night's Dream*), or free-standing, with some programmatic intent. Examples of this type also often refer to items of literature – as in *Beethoven's *Coriolan* (*Coriolanus*) op. 62 (1807) to Collin's play of the same name – or to historical events – Tchaikovsky's *1812* (1880) – or places, such as Mendelssohn's *Die Hebriden* (*Fingals Höhle*) (*The Hebrides* (*Fingal's Cave*)) (1829–30). This type can be seen as a kind of shorter *tone-poem.

P

Paganini, Nicolò

Italian violinist, composer (b. 27 Oct 1782, Genoa; d. 27 May 1840, Nice).

Son of a poor, but musical, shipping clerk, he taught himself to play the mandolin at the age of five, before changing to the violin, being taught by his father, and was made to practise all day long; the boy also composed. Paganini then studied with a violinist in the theatre orchestra, Antonio Cervetto, and had harmony lessons from a young opera composer, Francesco Gnecco, who suggested that he go to Giacomo Costa, one of the city's best virtuosi. The boy was acclaimed in a church performance at the age of 12. A visiting, rather showy Polish virtuoso, Duranowski, impressed Paganini because of his violinistic tricks, which he tried to emulate, and he later ascribed his own 'tricks' to the experience. He then went to Parma, studying with Paer (composition) and Ghiretti (counterpoint). Back in Genoa he met *Kreutzer, learnt the guitar and discovered Locatelli's *L'arte del violino* (1733).

The family moved to Livorno when he was 18 because of the French invasion, and was appointed leader of the orchestra; he also taught. In 1805 Napoleon's sister Elisa set up court at Lucca and, after spending two years in her small orchestra, he was made court solo violinist, and stayed on with his brother (also a violinist) when the establishment was reduced to a string quartet. Apart from playing in that, his only other duties were to teach the Princess. He left the post in 1809 to go freelance.

The next three or so years were spent travelling and performing, perfecting the showmanship for which he later became so famous. In Milan, he hired the Teatro alla Scala and premiered his concerto-like *Le streghe* (*The Witches*) op. 8 in October 1813 with great success and followed it with another 11 concerts, which made him famous nationally. However, in spite of his evident superiority when playing with the great French violinist Lafont, he did not feel ready for the more musically-sophisticated public in Paris or Vienna, who expected a virtuoso to play his or her own compositions, and so he set about creating a repertory for himself. When, in 1820, his first works (concertos, and the 24 solo violin *Caprices* op. 1) were published, violinists declared them unplayable – which Paganini very soon showed was not the case. He had already played an Italian tour but illnesses – which resulted in the cadaverous thinness which became his trademark – dogged him for the next four or five years. Finally, he arrived in Vienna in March 1828, giving 14 concerts in less than four months and was a sensation. He separated from his mistress of four years and was awarded custody of their child, to whom he was a very good father. Later that year he was in Prague, where his success was only moderate and he lost all his teeth. He fared much better in Germany, however, both artistically and financially, and he met Goethe in Weimar (who was impressed despite himself) and the violin virtuoso-composer *Spohr (who was not). He also met and got on with *Hummel, and they collaborated on a guitar concerto, now lost. But he was admired by Heine, *R. Schumann and H.W. Ernst.

His Paris sojourn in the first four months of 1831 was a mixture, triumph at first – even though the French were very proud and protective of their violin school – but then vilification in the press because of his apparent refusal to play in a benefit concert. In London, in May of the same year, he also faced a greed campaign in the press, led by *The Times*, because of the expensive tickets for his first concert; this was postponed and the prices reduced, and the press was completely won over – not least *The Times*, which expressed its praise in very un-English superlatives. That same year, apart from his Paris concerts, he gave an amazing 113 in tours of England, Ireland and Scotland.

The next two years were spent travelling between Paris and England giving concerts; the press had turned on him again and, in spite of his charity concerts, was still calling him a miser. After a *Berlioz concert, he commissioned a viola concerto from the young composer and *Harold en Italie* was the outcome. By now he was beginning to lose his talents and his public, due to a hand injury, mainly, and peoples' lack of interest in his new love, the viola. He went back to Italy at the end of 1834.

Here, his powers seemed to revive; his concerts were a great success again and he settled in Parma, where he was put in charge of the music at the court of Marie-Louise of Austria, who was settled there. He was very happy at first, but administrative intrigues caused his resignation in 1836 and he was soon back in France and back on form; his son was now legitimized by the courts. In the following year he was backer to a Casino (the Casino Paganini) in Paris, where music and gambling were combined. He became dangerously ill and the casino, being, apparently, contrary to the law, was closed after two months leaving him with large debts which his fellow-businessmen made no attempt to alleviate. Nevertheless,

he made Berlioz a present of 20,000 francs after a concert at the end of 1868. His last two years were accompanied by insomnia and a constant cough, which gravely restricted his eating, talking and writing. He refused to see a priest and the Church gave up on him. When he died in May 1840, he was refused permission for burial and his coffin remained in a cellar for five years until the Grand Duchess of Parma buried him in her villa, and finally, in 1876, his remains were transferred to the cemetery in Parma.

Paganini's virtuosity was legendary, and, combined with his cadaverous appearance, was often ascribed to diabolical influence. He was also possessed of great magnetism and had an aura of mystique which was noticed by everyone. More than anyone else except, perhaps, *Liszt (who fell under his spell), he enshrined virtuosity as a positive, and very *Romantic, aspect of music and music-performance. However, his non-virtuoso playing in slow movements was also admired, by no less a personage as Friedrich Wieck, *Clara Schumann's father. His *24 Caprices* op. 1 for solo violin opened a new world not only in violin technique but in virtuosity generally and as a creative component in music. His concertos are excellent examples of their type and of their (Romantic) period and his influence was enormous, on virtuosos of all kinds, and not only violinists, but (especially) pianists also, including *Berlioz, *R. Schumann, *Chopin, *Liszt, *Hummel, *Moscheles and *Brahms.

Works

For violin solo including *24 Caprices* op. 1 (*c.*1805); over 100 solo works for guitar; chamber works including 30 sonatas for violin and guitar, 21 guitar quartets, string quartets and others. Works with orchestra include *Sonate Napoleone* in E♭ (1807); *Le streghe, variations on a theme from Süssmayr's 'Il noce di Benevento'* op. 8 (1813) *St Patrick's Day, variations on the Irish folktune* (1831), *Balletto campestre*. Some vocal works.

Further reading
G.I.C. de Courcy, *Paganini the Genoese* (Norman, OK, 1957). L. Sheppard and H.R. Axelrod, *Paganini* (Neptune, NJ, 1979). P. Barri, *Paganini: La vita e le opere* (Milan, 1982). A. Kendal, *Paganini: a Biography* (London, 1983). E. Neill, *Paganini* (Genoa, 1994).

Paisiello, Giovanni
Italian composer (b. 9 May 1740, Roccaforzata, nr Taranto; d. 5 Jun 1816, Naples).

After the Jesuit school in Taranto and the Conservatorio di S Onofrio in Naples, he spent two years in northern Italy composing operas and in 1766, settled in Naples, becoming one of the principal composers of comic opera there. He was appointed *maestro de cappella* to Catherine II of Russia in 1776 and his duties included all the opera-composition for the court and the direction of the orchestra. Although he got on well with the Empress, there were tensions with some court officials and in 1783 he was offered a year's paid leave to go back to Italy because, he said, of his wife's health, but he never returned to Russia. In fact, he had been nominated *compositore della musica de' drammi* to Ferdinand IV of Naples, which he took up in late 1784. The following year the King awarded him a life pension and in 1787, made him *maestro della real camera*; both salaries were high. In January 1799 Naples fell to republican forces and after the King fled, Paisiello remained, becoming *maestro di cappella nazionale* to the new republic. By June the same year, the king was back in power and Paisiello was officially investigated because of his apparent collusion with the republicans; however, he was pardoned and fully reinstated by July 1801.

Napoleon, whose taste was for Italian rather than French music, greatly admired Paisiello and negotiated to bring him 'on loan' to Paris and in April 1802 he was installed as the emperor's director of chapel music, which he was for two years before returning to Naples. He was awarded the Légion d'honneur in 1806 and a member of the Institut français three years later.

In 1806 Napoleon's brother Joseph drove the King out of Naples and Paisiello became director of music at the new court as well as being one of the three directors of the newly-founded state college of music. In 1815 Naples reverted to the control of King Ferdinand and Paisiello, in disgrace, only retained the post of *masestro della real cappella* and in addition lost his French pension; he died in the following year. His very original comic operas with sharp characterization and winsome melodies greatly influenced *W.A. Mozart, especially in *Le nozze di Figaro* and *Don Giovanni*.

Works
Many operas, including *L'idolo cinese* (perf. 1767); *Artaserse* (perf. 1771); *Motezuma* (perf. 1772); *Il tamburo* (perf. 1773); *Demofoonte* (1775); *Il barbiere di Siviglia* (perf. 1782) and the famous *intermezzo La serva padrona* (perf. 1781). There is a great deal of sacred music and some instrumental, including string quartets, flute quartets, violin sonatas and six piano concertos.

Further reading
A. Ghislanzoni. *Giovanni Paisiello: valutazione critiche retificate* (Rome, 1969). M. Robinson, *Naples and Neapolitan Opera* (Oxford, 1972). J.L. Hunt, 'The Keyboard Works of Giovanni Paisiello', *MQ*, lxi (1975); *Giovanni Paisiello: his Life as an Opera Composer* (New York, 1975).

Pantaleon [Pantalon]

A large hammered *dulcimer. The name is taken from that of its inventor, Pantaleon *Hebenstreit, a renowned virtuoso throughout Europe on the instrument, after the decree of a very impressed Louis XIV before whom Hebenstreit played in Paris in 1705. It was developed from the gut-stringed peasant dulcimer (*Hackbrett*) used to accompany dancing in a village inn frequented by Hebenstreit while he was a tutor to a local pastor's children. The keyboard-instrument-maker Gottfried *Silbermann built a number of *Pantalons*, until a dispute with the inventor caused a cessation. Some German writers applied the name to the square *piano in the second half of the eighteenth century.

Pantalon stop (Ger. *Pantalonzug*; *Pantaleonzug*)

A mechanism for keeping the strings of a clavichord sounding after the key is released and the *tangent falls a way from it; the effect is similar to that obtained by raising the dampers when playing on a piano.

Pape, Jean Henri [Johann Heinrich]

German (French naturalized) piano-maker (b. 1 Jul 1789, Sarstedt, nr Hanover; d. 2 Feb 1875, Asnières, nr Paris).

Little is known of him; he arrived in Paris in 1811 and worked in the factory of *Ignace Pleyel, setting up his own in 1815. He is responsible for many patents and different types of piano for different locations. Although prosperous during most of his life, employing a workforce of some 300, he died poor, possibly through the unpopularity of some of his more radical designs.

Pape designed pianos of all types – round, hexagonal, etc. which did not sell. He also invented a piano with *down-striking action which, because of the low placement of the strings, did not need bracing. He experimented with felt coverings on his hammers, with tempered steel wire strings, and with cross-stringing, all of which became standard much later. He also invented the 'pianino' (see *piano (6)), which he patented in 1828. This was a small cheap domestic instrument which used *overstringing to reduce the size, making it ideal for the smaller middle-class drawing-room and which practically became a fixture there towards the middle of the nineteenth century and after. He was called the 'Broadwood of the French capital' and his instruments were bought by *Moscheles, *Boieldieu, Auber and *Cherubini, who used his to compose upon.

Further reading
F.J. Hirt, *Meisterwerke des Klavierbaus* (Olten, 1955; tr. Eng., 1968). C. Michaud-Pradelles, *Jean-Henri pape: un facteur de pianos allemand à Paris (1789–1875)* (diss., Paris Conservatoire, 1975). Harding/PIANO-FORTE. Ehrlich/PIANO.

Paradies, [Paradisi] (Pietro) Domenico

Italian composer, teacher (b. 1707, Naples; d. 25 Aug 1791, Venice).

Not a great deal is known of his life, but he is supposed to have studied with Porpora. His early operas were not successful and he emigrated to London c.1746 and although an opera failed there also, he did have some arias published by Walsh and sung often by Signora Galli. From 1753–56 he and a friend leased the King's Theatre in the Haymarket, providing insertion arias when necessary. He was, however, well known as a teacher of singing and harpsichord, and he may have lived in the Bath area at some stage. His set of 12 two-movement *Sonate di gravicembalo* (pub. 1754) were popular. They look forward to *C.P.E. Bach in their use of thematic contrast in their sonata-form construction and enjoyed great popularity and many reprintings. They were praised by *W.A. Mozart, *Clementi and *Cramer. He taught the future Mme Mara and the elder Thomas Linley.

Works
Dramatic works include *Il decreto del fato* (perf. 1740), *Fetonte* (perf. 1747) and *La forza d'amore* (perf. 1751). Other works include 12 *Sonate di gravicembalo* (pub. 1754) and other keyboard works, as well as *A Favourite Concerto* for organ or harpsichord (pub. c.1768).

Further reading
G. Giachin, 'Contributo alla conoscenza di Paradisi', *Nuova rivista musicale italiana*, ix (1975). D.C. Sanders, *The Keyboard Sonatas of Giustini, Paradisi, and Rutini: Formal and Stylistic Innovation in Mid-Eighteenth-Century Italian Keyboard Music* (diss., U. of Kansas, 1983).

Passing-note
A note which passes by linear *stepwise motion (i.e. through a semitone or a tone) between two other notes, such as the movement F—E—D , G—A♭—A♮,

me—ray—doh, where the middle note in each case is the passing-note. It may be chromatic or *diatonic and accented (on the strong beat) or unaccented.

Pastorale [pastoral]
The use, or evocation of, scenes or characters from rural life in literature, painting, drama or music. It may refer to *Classical antiquity and its idealized existence of amorous nymphs and shepherds and mythical beasts, or to contemporary country life, and may simply be confined to single movements or other divisions, or to episodes within them. As a topic in the eighteenth and nineteenth centuries, its use was characterized by being cast in certain keys, of which F and B♭ majors were common, but also D major, largely *diatonic in harmony with *folk-like melodies and rhythms (occasionally using the lilting rhythm of crotchet-quaver units in 3/8 (or 6/8) and long stretches of the same harmony as well as a penchant for the subdominant. Orchestral evocations usually highlight flute(s) and oboe(s), to suggest birdsong and the presence of the Classical god Pan and occasionally clarinet(s), as well as French horn(s) to suggest hunting with oscillating strings to suggest running water. Depictions of storms in contrasting episodes are also very common, with imitations of rain, wind, thunder and lightning. Titles of such pieces sometimes refer to the Classical poetry of antiquity, such as *Eclogue* [*Eglogue*], *Dithyramb* and, within this specialized context, *Rapsodia* [*Rhapsody*]. The most famous example of this topic is *Beethoven's 'Pastoral' Symphony (no. 6 in F major op. 68, of 1808) but there are also *Tomášek's *Eclogues* written over the period 1807–19.

'Pathétique' Sonata (Fr. 'Sonate pathétique')

Name given to *Beethoven's piano sonata no. 8, op. 13 in C minor (?1797–98, dedicated to Prince *Lichnowsky), which he called *Grande sonate pathétique*.

Pedal

A lever operated by the foot whose function, in the case of musical instruments, is to modify the sound while leaving the hands free. On keyboard instruments it fulfils those functions which were previously assigned to *stops or *genouillères (knee-levers). The principal pedals in the period 1760–1850 were:

(1) *The sustaining pedal* (damper, 'loud', 'forte', *la grande pédale, grande jeu, Fortezug*) (at the right on a modern piano) raises the dampers from the strings, allowing them to vibrate freely when the key(s) is/are no longer depressed. This was useful in sustaining the harmony when an arpeggiated bass-line was in use (as in many *nocturnes) or when there were wide leaps in the music. It was also used to create a 'halo' of sound (the effect asked for by, for example, *Beethoven in the reprise of the first movement of his piano sonata in D minor op. 31/2). In some pianos, this pedal could be divided, so that when the left half was depressed, it acted only on the dampers for the left half of the keyboard, and the right hand affected only the right half of the keyboard. (See Carew/MUSE, Pl. 13.)

(2) *The* una corda *[pedal]* (shift, soft pedal, *eine Saite, verschiebung*) (found on the left of modern grand pianos) shifted the piano's action from where the hammers struck the full complement of (usually) three strings, so that they struck only one, thus reducing the volume and

the richness of sound. Some instruments had the additional possibility of allowing the hammers to strike two of the three strings by raising or lowering a small block at the side of the keyboard; this was the *due corde*.

(3) *The soft pedal* (*piano* pedal, *jeu céleste, céleste, jeu de buffes,* buff, muffle, *Pianozug, il pedale del piano, flauto*) allowed the action to be moved closer to the strings so that the hammers had less distance to travel and produced a softer sound; thus the tone wasn't altered. This is found on modern upright pianos as the leftmost pedal.

(4) *The moderator pedal* ('moderator', *piano, pianissimo, Jeu Céleste, Jeu de buffe* or *Pianozug*) was another device for softening the sound and called for strips of soft leather or cloth to be applied between hammers and strings thus muffling the sound. Some early pianos had two such pedals with different degrees of muffling.

(5) *The lute pedal* (*sourdine, jeu de luth, jeu de harpe, Laute, sordino,* possibly also *Wornum's 'pizzicato pedal') causes a strip of felt or a fringe of wool or silk to be placed in contact with the strings to give an ethereal sound like a lute. Like the sustaining pedal, this was occasionally divided so that the upper and lower parts of the keyboard could be controlled separately. It must be pointed out that there is a good deal of interchange between the use of these last two terms (moderator and lute).

(6) *The bassoon pedal* (*basson, Fagott*) causes a strip of parchment or other medium-soft material to come into contact with the strings to give a buzzing

sound associated with a bassoon. It is often found as part of *Turkish Music applied to the piano.

(7) *The *Turkish Music pedals* comprise the bassoon pedal just described and a pedal controlling a drumstick (*tambour guerrier*, *Schlagzug*, *Bodenschlag*), 'triangle' (which could be a single bell, or three separate bells) and 'cymbals' (two or three strips of brass which are knocked against the bass strings); occasionally, the bells and cymbals had their own pedal separate from the drum. The 'drum' was usually the piano's soundboard which was hit by the felted drumstick as in the bass drum of the modern drum-kit, but there were cases of drumheads, or even real drums, being added.

(8) *The *coupler pedal* (which fulfilled a variety of functions, principally as the octave coupler, common on the harpsichord which was also applied to some pianos). By its agency, registers of strings an octave apart (above or below) could be coupled together so that they could be played by the same key simultaneously. It also activated and deactivated the 'extra' instrument in the case of *combination instruments (piano-harpsichord or piano-organ, for instance).

(9) There are other pedals which are much more specialized, either because they are rare or because they apply only to particular instruments, for example: the pedal for '*harmonic sounds*' by which a set of hammers or a bar touches the strings in the middle (or occasionally elsewhere) to create harmonics, giving the illusion of an echo; the *dolce compana*, by which the soundboard is alternately slightly pressured and released (sometimes

through the bridge) so that a kind of vibrato is produced. In *combination instruments involving an organ, one of the pedals would work the *bellows*, as it does on a harmonium or small organ.

(10) With the increasing number of pedals added to the piano, it was often the case that there would be *duplication* of the commonest pedals so that they could be used with either foot, thus allowing for more combinations.

(11) It was possible to have combinations of stops and pedals, either duplicating functions or adding to them. The device which operates several pedals or stops is called a *machine stop*, even though it may be activated by a pedal.

(12) Referring to larger organs or pedal-pianos, a *pedalboard* could be added to be played by the feet to the extent of several octaves. (See *Piano (9).)

While the sustaining pedal and either the *una corda* (usually, but not exclusively, on grands) or the soft pedal (*vis-à-vis* upright pianos) were nearly always present, it was by no means uncommon to have any or all of these pedals on the same instrument.

Pedal-board (see *Pedal (12))

Pedal-piano (see *Piano (9))

Perpetuum mobile (Lat.)**, Moto perpetuo** (It.)**, Motu perpetuo** (Lat.) (all meaning '[by] perpetual motion') (1) A musical technique which involves a constant (or almost constant) motion (usually rapid) for an entire movement. This may or may not involve the repetition of a particular characteristic rhythm.

(2) The second two of these terms are used as titles for pieces using the technique, but the first very rarely used so.

Phantasia, Phantasie, **Phantasy** (see **Fantasia*)

Philharmonic Society of London
A concert-giving body in London, growing from a meeting of P.A. Corri, William *Dance and *J.B. Cramer in early 1813, after which a society of thirty members was established, with unlimited associates; seven directors were chosen to manage the affair, which depended on aristocratic patronage for its functions. But all these personnel were musicians and the society included practically every musician of note active in the English capital, a great many of whom were foreigners. The pattern of concerts – eight in the 'season' – mid-February to June, but soon to be extended – followed that of aristocratic life migrating between London and country houses and the nucleus of its orchestra was drawn from the members supplemented by players from theatre and other orchestras in London. The music played tended to be modern and/or new to the city and vocal solos and concertos were initially not allowed. The ban on vocal solos lasted for three years – London concerts without singers were almost unheard of – and that on concertos a further four years, broken by Neate's performance of *Beethoven's First Piano Concerto. Orchestral standards, caused primarily by the lack of a permanent corps, were much criticized, and when *Spohr played with the orchestra in 1820, he left the violins and conducted in the present-day sense of the word (see *Conductor). The society got into financial difficulties and its future was in doubt. A credit balance of £300 after the 1846 season, when Michael Costa was conductor, convinced the society that a permanent appointment was necessary and he was eventually offered the post which he held for eight years. Wagner was appointed for the 1855 season on Costa's resignation to take up work elsewhere, but had a disastrous season and it fell to the next appointee, *Sterndale Bennett (1856), to regularize matters. He was still in office to conduct the fiftieth anniversary concert in 1853. The Society did not have a permanent orchestra until the foundation of the London Philharmonic Orchestra in 1932.

Phrase
Borrowed from prosody, it implies a short musical unit, longer than a motif and a subphrase, but shorter than a period (which is usually two phrases of the 'question-and-answer' kind) and a sentence, which is usually several periods.

Phrygian mode (see *Modes)

Piano[forte] (Piano-forte, Forte-piano)
(Fr. and It. *piano*; Ger. *Klavier*)
An instrument in which the sound is produced by striking taut strings – between one and four per pitched note, but usually two or three – with hammers attached to *keys on a *keyboard, which are activated by the fingers and thumbs of the player's hands. Its origins lie in the late medieval period, but it is generally agreed to have been invented by Bartolomeo *Cristofori, a harpsichord-maker at the court of Prince Ferdinand de' Medici in Florence from 1690; an inventory of 1700 shows that he had already made at least one piano. A contemporary description of the instrument as '*gravicembalo col piano e forte*' ('a harpsichord with soft and loud') is what gives it its name, usually

shortened to 'piano'. A full history of the instrument would be beyond the scope of this reference-work; suffice it to say that it has taken many forms during its subsequent history, of which some are given here (in more-or-less chronological order). See Carew/MUSE.

(1) The **fortepiano** is the name normally given to the **'Viennese' piano**, the first peak of excellence in the instrument's development, made by Austro-German makers, many – by no means all – of whom lived and worked in the Austrian capital. Composers such as *W.A. Mozart, *J. Haydn (for most of his life), *Beethoven, *Hummel and others wrote for it, although it was their preferred, not, as in the case of the last two their only, keyboard instrument.

(2) In Britain, the ***British piano** was a heavier instrument with a legato *touch much admired in slow movements and attracted composers such as many of those of the so-called *'London School', *Clementi and native British composers.
  Both (1) and (2) were grand pianos (see below), medium-sized instruments whose strings were in a parallel plane more-or-less perpendicular to the keyboards; other forms included:

(3) The **square piano**, a smaller domestic instrument with the strings parallel to the keyboard stretching left and right.

(4) The **upright piano**, again smaller and domestically-intended with strings stretching behind the keyboard from the floor upwards above the keyboard.

(5) The '**piccolo piano**', a smaller neater version of the upright, first patented by *Wornum.

(6) The **piano droit** (Fr.: 'right piano'), a small type of piano akin to and inspired by, *Wornum's piccolo piano (see (5) above). The first, by *Blanchet et Roller, was exhibited at the Paris Exhibition in the Louvre in 1827, causing a great sensation. The '**pianino**' was another name for this, although strictly speaking, this referred to very small pianos which were vertically strung (as opposed to the obliquely-strung piano droit).

(7) The **portable piano** is either small and/or light enough to carry, or one which can be folded up in some manner, to render it transportable. Many pianos, especially the 'Viennese' rested on trestles or tables and legs were inessential, or, if present, easy to remove, and were very light compared to later and modern instruments, so that they were relatively easy to carry from room to room. But some were constructed to be portable outside of the home also, such as the Verel portable (1783) which is about three feet long (c.95 cm) by one foot wide (c.30 cm) and six inches (c.15 cm) high. *Röllig [Rolling] (1795) also invented such instruments which could be strapped to the player when in use. These instruments were of great use during the eighteenth and early nineteenth centuries (before the advent of faster transport) for composers and performers during coach journeys and at overnight stops *en route*. It was also useful indoors for carrying from room to room or for rooms which were too small to support a larger piano. *W.A. Mozart is said to have had one for coach-travel made by Späth and Schmahl of Ratisbon. In Britain, such instruments were often called 'Conductor's pianos' and Sir George *Smart, founder-member and conductor of the *Philharmonic Society, had one and carried it with him

when travelling. In an age when most conductors still conducted from the keyboard rather than at the rostrum, the convenience in refreshing the memory *en route* can be appreciated.

(8) The **tangent piano** (Ger. *Tangentenflügel*) A type of grand piano invented by F.J. *Späth in Regensburg about 1751, although all the surviving instruments of this type were made after 1790. Like the *clavichord the strings were struck with *tangents, but they were wooden, unlike the metal tangents in clavichords. The *action was a simple piano action and there were several *stops in addition – buff, moderator – which in many cases could operate on treble and bass separately. The sound is reported to be particularly beautiful and a number of virginals (see *harpsichord) and *harpsichords had their actions converted to become tangent pianos. The principle was used by several other makers – some independently, such as *Marius – including *Stein.

(9) The **transposing piano** allowed music to be *transposed into different keys without changing the notes or fingering used. This was usually effected by shifting the *action up or down *vis-à-vis* the strings. The number of keys available for transposition rarely exceeded three or four, and depended on the instrument used.

(10) The **pedal-piano** was a regular instrument of the grand type with the addition of a *pedal-board operated by the feet on the lines of that in the *organ, either with its own set of strings and hammers, or *coupled to the host instrument. *Schumann, among others, wrote for it.

(11) The **concert grand** piano is at present the largest member of the family, in which the strings are perpendicular to the keyboard, stretching backwards for up to three metres (over nine feet) or more, even allowing for *overstringing. It can reach lengths of nearly ten feet (just over three metres).

(12) A smaller version, the **boudoir grand** (or **baby grand**) is a domestic substitute, being of similar shape and form, but under half the size of the grand.

(13) The *Pianola* is a brand-name for the **player piano** made by the Aeolian Corporation in the United States in the early twentieth century. These are mechanical pianos in which music is played automatically in response to the perforations on a roll of paper through which a performance has been recorded. Its great popularity was in the domestic circles in the early 1920s. Many eminent artists recorded for it.

(14) The various types of **electric pianos** and **electronic keyboards** are beyond the scope of this work.

Further reading (a selection only)
R. Benton, 'The Early Piano in the United States', *Hinrichsen's Musical Year Book*, xi (1961). C. Clutton, 'The Pianoforte', in A. Baines, ed., *Musical Instruments through the Ages* (London, 1961). E.D. Blackham, 'The Physics of the Piano', *Scientific American*, ccxiii (1965). P. Locard and R. Stricker, *Le piano* (Paris, 1966). W.L. Sumner, *The Pianoforte* (London, 1966). D. Wainwright, *The Piano Makers* (London, 1975). A. Dolge, *Pianos and their Makers* (California, 1911, R1972). D. Carew, *The Mechanical Muse: the Piano, Pianism*

and Piano Music c.*1760*–c.*1850* (2007).
Bie/HISTORY. Hipkins/PIANOFORTE.
Harding/PIANO-FORTE.Ehrlich/PIANO.
New Grove.

Pierson, [Pearson], **Henry Hugo** [Hugh]
British (naturalized German) composer
(b. 12 Apr 1815, Oxford; d. 28 Jan 1873,
Leipzig).

He was educated at Harrow School
and, although he studied medicine,
his simultaneous music studies with
*Attwood and Corfe convinced him of
his future path and he entered Trinity
College, Cambridge in 1836 to read
music, against his father's wishes. Pierson
went to Germany in 1839, staying five
years, studying with Rinck and Reissiger
and with *Tomášek in Prague and got to
know Mary Shelley, having an affair with,
and finally marrying, a poetic improviser,
Caroline Leonhardt, previously wife of
the poet Lyser; it was at this time that he
decided on the form of his name by which
he is now known.

He succeeded *Bishop as Reid
Professor of Music at Edinburgh
University, but resigned in less than a
year to settle in Germany with his wife,
who wrote the libretto for his opera
Lelia. He won great acclaim with this
and with other works in the German-
speaking countries, but success in
Britain eluded him; the British press was
extremely hostile and Pierson confined
his attentions to Germany, settling in
Stuttgart in 1863 and his pupils included
Parry.

Pierson's originality as a composer
was, in terms of melody, harmony and
orchestration, in the original mould,
though not on the level, of *Berlioz,
although it is his songs – solo and
choral, in German and in English –
which show him at his best; many are

settings of German translations of British
originals.

Works
Many solo songs including [five]
Characteristic Songs of Shelley (pub.
1840), six *Lieder* op. 7 (pub. 1842). Six
Gesänge for chorus with piano *ad lib*
op 9 (pub. *c.*1843). Stage works include
the operas *Lelia* (perf. 1848), *Fenice*
(perf. 1883) and the incidental music to
Goethe's *Faust* (perf. 1854).

Further reading
A. and B. Pollin, 'In Pursuit of Pierson's
Shelley Songs', *ML*, xlvi (1965).
N. Temperley, 'Henry Hugo Pierson,
1815–73', *MT*, cxiv (1973); cxv (1974).
MGG.

Pinto, George Frederick
British composer, pianist, violinist (b. 25
Sep 1785, Lambeth, London; d. 23 Mar
1806, Chelsea, London).

From a musical family on his mother's
side, he took his mother's maiden name as
his preferred surname. A child prodigy, he
learnt the violin and became *Salomon's
pupil, playing a concerto at his public
début at the age of 11 in London. His
friendship with the young *Field drew
him towards the piano, which became his
favourite instrument. Although a 'golden
boy', very beautiful, nature-loving,
humanitarian – he visited prisons, giving
his money to the prisoners – and cultured,
his drink problem caused his death at the
age of 20, although there is no medical
evidence.

His compositions, emotionally mature
beyond his years, excited much interest
in public and critics alike, who were
remarkably unanimous in their praise
– 'if he had lived and been able to resist
the allurements of society, England would

have had the honour of producing a second [W.A.] Mozart', said Salomon. In spite of his popularity, his compositions were forgotten within a couple of years of his death, with a brief revival in the 1840s. It is only since the 1960s that he has resurfaced in this capacity.

Pinto produced music remarkably quickly, but despite this, the proportion of trivia is nothing like as great as often results in such cases. His originality and energy are remarkable, and influence on *Beethoven has been suggested by a very respectable commentator, although it is unlikely. Influenced by *W.A. Mozart and *J.L. Dussek, his music shows anticipations of the later *Romantic composers, Beethoven, *Schubert, possibly *Chopin.

Works

For piano include *3 Favorite Airs with Variations* op. 2 (pub. ?1802), two *Grand Sonatas* op. 3 (Eb minor and A major), *A Grand Sonata* in C minor (both pub. 1803), three Sonatas op. 4 (G, Bb and C majors, pub. 1804–1805), Fantasia and Sonata in C minor (compl. *Wesley and *Wölfl). For violin, two sets of three duets for two violins and a set of three violin sonatas (piano with violin accompaniment, G minor, A major and Bb major). There are also 20 songs ('canzonets') and a lost violin concerto.

Further reading

N. Temperley, 'George Frederick Pinto', *MT*, cvi (1965); ed., *Music in Britain: the Romantic Age 1800–1914* (London, 1981). A.L. Ringer, 'Beethoven and the London Pianoforte School', *MQ*, lvi (1970). Newman/SSB.

Più (It.: 'more')
'More' as in *più piano* ('more soft', or 'softer').

Pixis, Johann Peter

German composer, pianist (b. 10 Feb 1788, Mannhein; d. 22 Dec 1874, Baden-Baden).

A child prodigy, he learnt piano (from his organist and composer father), violin and cello – accompanying his equally talented older brother, Friedrich Wilhelm, on tour – and composition. After moving to Vienna in 1806, the boys studied with Albrechtsberger and Johann Peter met *Meyerbeer, *Schubert and *Beethoven, and, on moving to Paris in 1823, *Cherubini, *Moscheles, Halévy, *Berlioz, *Liszt and *Rossini as well as Humboldt and Heine.

Pixis enjoyed great success as a pianist and teacher in Paris and had several concert tours, including one with the singer Sontag, to England in 1828. He moved to Baden-Baden in 1840 and remained there as a teacher until his death in 1874. As a virtuoso pianist-composer in the style of *Hummel, most of Pixis's works include the piano, in which he is seen at his best. He was criticized in his lifetime for superficiality and there is, perhaps, too much reliance on received forms as templates rather than launching-pads.

Works

Three sonatas and many sets of variations, dances, fantasias, etc. and character pieces for piano, and some chamber music – string quartets, piano trios and sonatas – as well as a symphony and pieces for piano and orchestra (a concerto, concertino and a *Fantaisie-militaire*). There are also four operas.

Further reading

H. Engel, *Die Entwicklung des deutschen Klavierkonzertes* (Leipzig, 1927). W. Stoll, 'Die Brüder Pixis',

Mannheimer Geschichtsblätter, xxix (1928). L. Schiwietz, *Johann Peter Pixis: Beiträge zu seiner Biographie, zur Rezeptionshistoriographie seiner Werke und Analyse seiner Sonatenformung* (Frankfurt, 1994). Fétis/*BIOGRAPHIE*.

Pizz. (see **Pizzicato*)

Pizzicato (It.: 'plucked')
Often abbreviated in scores to '*pizz.*', an instruction to string players – violin, viola cello, double bass – to pluck their instrument with fingers or nails, rather than use the bow in the conventional way; the requirement is cancelled by '*arco*' ('[with the] bow').

Plainchant [Plainsong, Gregorian Chant] (from Lat. *cantus planus*; Fr. *plainchant*; Ger. *Choral*; It. *canto plano*)
The devotional liturgical **monophonic chant, of the Christian churches, especially that of the Catholic Church, particularly with Latin texts. Traditionally sung by male voices in unison and without accompaniment, it was (and continues to be) written on a four-line staff with neumes – musical signs giving pitch, duration and method of articulation – as opposed to the later notes. The name 'Gregorian Chant' by which it is sometimes known refers to the belief that the Holy Spirit, in its traditional form of a dove, communicated the music to Pope Gregory the Great (590–604). It is likely that Gregory had a hand in the codification and organization of several different chant traditions into a more-or-less unified whole.

Plainsong (see **Plainchant*)

Plectrum
(1) A small, thin, hand-held device made of wood, ivory or plastic for plucking a stringed musical instrument such as a guitar or mandolin.

(2) In a harpsichord, the piece of quill or plastic which projects from the **jack which plucks the string.

Pleyel, Ignace Joseph [Ignaz Josef]
Austrian composer, piano-maker, music publisher (b. 18 Jun 1757, Ruppersthal, Austria; d. 14 Nov 1831, Paris).
Son of a schoolteacher, he is reputed to have had lessons from Vanhal in his youth. Count Erdödy made him a *protégé* and sent him to study with **J. Haydn, living in Eisenstadt, where his relatives, the **Esterházys, were the older composer's employers. The boy made great progress, composing a puppet opera and having it performed in the marionette theatre at Eisenstadt; he also wrote the overture for one of Haydn's similar works and dedicated his op. 1 String Quartets to Count Erdödy. In 1789 Pleyel was appointed **Kapellmeister* of Strasbourg Cathedral, also conducting public concerts in the city.
As a result of the French Revolution, religious functions were abolished and Pleyel took up the post of conductor of the Professional Concerts in London, staying for six months, during which time Haydn was also there. In spite of the newspapers' attempts to foment rivalry between the composers' two sets of concerts, the two, master and pupil, remained friends and attended each others' concerts. Like Haydn, during this period he also provided accompaniments for some of **Thomson's **Select Collection of Scottish Airs*.
On his return to France he bought a large *château* and settled in Paris, opening a music shop and founding a music-publishing business which featured works by most of the musical

luminaries of the time, including some who invested in the firm; it also issued the first miniature musical scores, beginning with some Haydn symphonies. Later, the output swung to the more popular composers and genres, *romances* and *chansons*, before Pleyel sold his stock to other publishing houses in 1834 and retired to his country retreat.

Pleyel's easy, approachable style, which was enormously popular, did not preclude a degree of originality in his earlier works, and he was adept at recycling his own works and allowing for the maximum possibilities for performance, such as his Concerto in C major performable on clarinet, flute or cello, for all of which he provided solo parts.

Pleyel also founded a piano-making firm in Paris in 1807, improving on current English models and specializing in *cottage pianos or 'pianinos' (see *piano (6)). His son Camille joined him in 1815 and the interest and investment of *Kalkbrenner greatly aided the venture. *Chopin's interest also boosted popularity; he made his Paris début on a Pleyel and owned a grand, of which he spoke highly. The Salle Pleyel was an important Paris venue for soloists and smaller ensembles.

Works

Some eight cello concertos and several *Symphonies concertantes as well as over a hundred symphonies, many of which appeared in multiple editions. His chamber music includes almost a hundred quartets, mostly for strings, but with occasional substitutions, almost as many again of keyboard trios, and quintets, sextets and septets as well as many duos, pieces for keyboard (mostly dances) and stage works.

Further reading
R. Benton, *Ignace Pleyel: a Thematic Catalogue of his Compositions* (New York, 1977); *Pleyel as Music Publisher: a Documentary Sourcebook of Early 19th-Century Music* (Stuyvesant, NY, 1990). E. Radant, 'Ignaz Pleyel's Correspondence with Hoffmeister & Co', *Haydn Yearbook 1981*.

Pohlmann, Johannes
German (English naturalized) harpsichord- and piano-maker (*fl.* 1767–93, London).

Like several other instrument makers, he emigrated to London after the Seven Years War (1756–63), setting up a harpsichord-making business in London, first in Soho and later in Bloomsbury (1777–94), becoming the foremost maker of *square pianos after *Zumpe, who outsourced his surplus work to him. In spite of this, his pianos were not reckoned to be very good.

Further reading
Harding/PIANO-FORTE. Loesser/MEN. Cole/PIANOFORTE.

Polacca, (alla) (see *polonaise*)

Polonaise
A Polish processional dance which also exists as an instrumental piece. It is in 3/4 time without an anacrusis, characterized by a rhythm of six quavers of which the second is divided into two semiquavers and a closing bar with a four-semiquaver first crotchet cadencing on the second, or occasionally, third. Its origins are in earlier Polish *folk song-dances with the same rhythmic characteristics, but differing in tempo and social function. The dance was taken up and developed in various ways by the aristocracy, becoming

a court favourite, and it is still danced and sung on ceremonial occasions and weddings

As an instrumental piece, the *polonaise* probably derived from the courtly type and appears in collections of dances in the seventeenth century. It is included among the works of many composers: *J.S. Bach, *Handel, *F. Couperin, *W.A. Mozart, *Beethoven, Prince *Ogiński, *Schubert (for piano duet) and *Chopin (whose essays in the *genre* benefited greatly from the Western European sympathy for Poland in the 1830s and remain a landmark in the *polonaise*'s literature) as well as *Kurpiński, *C.M. von Weber, *Liszt and Tchaikovsky.

The *polacca* (It. for 'Polish'), as well as being a type based loosely on the *polonaise*, is more common as a direction 'alla polacca', which often signifies little in terms of 'Polishness'. The type was popular as a *salon* or concert *bravoura* piece and as an operatic number with opportunity for showy vocalization.

Polyphony, polyphonic (from Gk. *polyphonia*, 'many sounds'; Fr. *polyphonie*; Ger. *Mehrstimmigkeit, Vielstimmigkeit*)
(1) Music in two or more parts in which the parts move independently on a melodic level; in this sense it is synonymous with counterpoint.

(2) The term particularly refers to music of the sixteenth century where religious *modal polyphony for voices produced a peak of achievement in the works of Victoria, Lassus and Palestrina.

Potter, (Philip) Cipriani (Hambly) [Hambley]
English composer (b. 3 Oct 1792, London; d. 26 Sep 1871, London).

The name Cipriani derived from his godmother and he was a cultured man with great mathematical and linguistic interests and ability. Apart from his father's musical tuition, he studied with *Attwood, *Crotch and, for five years, with *Wölfl. He became a member of the *Philharmonic Society and was one of a very small and select number of British composers to have a composition – two, in fact – commissioned by them.

However, lukewarm reception of his works in Britain prompted him to undertake further study on the Continent (1817) and, after much hesitation, he finally visited *Beethoven who thought well of his works and advised him. He studied with Aloys Förster and met J.B. *Streicher and, after visits to various German and Austrian cities and a spell in Italy, he returned to London in early 1819, embarking on a career as a concert pianist. In this capacity he played many of the *Mozart concertos and several of Beethoven's for the first time in England. One of the first piano teachers in the Academy of Music after its foundation, he became director of the practice orchestra and was appointed principal in 1859. In the meantime (from 1844) he was conductor of the Philharmonic Society and was much admired and respected. He stopped composing, to all intents and purposes, in 1837 because of his feelings of inadequacy in the face of the works of, among others, *R. Schumann and, later, *Brahms.

Works (mostly instrumental)
Nine symphonies, three or more concertos and other pieces for pf and orch., three pf trios op. 12, two pf sextets and a number of works for piano solo: three sonatas (opp. 1 in C, 3 in D and 4 in E minor (all 1818)), Studies in All the Major and Minor Keys (1826) and shorter occasional pieces.

Further reading
P.H. Peter, *The Life and Work of Cipriani Potter (1792–1871)* (diss., Northwestern U, 1972).

Praeludium (see *Prelude)

Prellmechanik
The earliest and simplest kind of *piano *action found exclusively in the *square type. It originally had no *escapement mechanism, but a slightly more developed form does possess one.

Prelude (Fr. *prélude*; Ger. *Vorspiel*; It. *preludio*; Lat. *praeludium*, *praeambulum*)
An instrumental piece played before another movement. Originally, it was intended as an *improvisatory check on the *tuning and *touch of an instrument before playing the chosen piece; it evolved into a genre of its own.

(1) Although the 'tuning' type of prelude was improvised, several composers wrote sets of unattached preludes in various keys which are intended for that purpose, but also serve the function of leading into pieces in the same key by exploring (however briefly) that key and mode; *Hummel's op. 67 set of 24 Preludes in all the major and minor keys (*c.*1814–15) are of this sort; so are *Moscheles's *50 Präludien* op. 73 (1827) specifically intended by him 'as short introductions to any movement'.

(2) Preludes were also written as dedicated to particular pieces which followed them, combining all of the functions mentioned under (1) but forming more discrete pieces, the first of a set of pairs. *J.S. Bach's *Wohltemperirte Clavier* with its 48

paired preludes and fugues features preludes of this kind. Similar works were written by *Felix Mendelssohn, *Liszt and *R. Schumann.

(3) The **Prélude**. This was a complete and unattached piece with, in almost all cases, no introductory function which was normally published as part of a set of such pieces in the early nineteenth century and probably intended for performance as a set or in groups. These tended to be longer than either of the types mentioned and were often *character pieces rather than of preludial intent. The best known are those in the set of 24 op. 28 by *Chopin (1836–39).

Prélude (see *Prelude (3))

Principes du clavecin ... (see *Saint-Lambert)

Private subscription
A system of publishing by private individuals or groups which bypassed publishers and publishing-houses proper. When the work to be published was decided upon, a list was sent round to prospective subscribers (individuals or institutions) who would guarantee to buy one or a number of copies, thus defraying the risk on an open market.

Prix de Rome
An annual prize for students of musical composition awarded by the Académie des Beaux-Arts from 1803 until 1968. It provided for the winner to spend four years at the Villa de Medici in Rome, with the fruits of their compositional labours being sent back to Paris. It set a number of composers on their feet in terms of a career, including, *Berlioz, Bizet and *Gounod.

Programme

(1) The schedule of a concert, usually furnished with information about the piece(s) and performer(s)

(2) As used in the term 'programme-music', the extramusical (usually literary) narrative underlying or being illustrated by a piece of music. The idea that the musical syntax and development should be independent of any programmatic considerations is a constant in composers' justifications of their forays into such music, although *Liszt (who invented the term) put it less strongly, noting that 'musical considerations, although they should not be neglected, have to be subordinated to the action of the given subject.'

Psaltery

A Medieval/early Renaissance instrument related to the harp and the zither in which strings stretched over a bridge on a sound-board or sound-box are plucked with the fingers, occasionally with a plectrum. It existed in a variety of shapes, the most common being harp-like (which seems to have been played similarly in an upright position) and the curved trapezoid shape which suggested a pig's snout (accounting for the Italian nickname of *strumento di porco*). The instrument was also played with beaters, especially in later centuries, giving the hammered *dulcimer. The psaltery was not confined to Europe, but had, and has, an important place in art-musics of the Near East.

Puget, Loïsa [Louise-Françoise]
French composer, singer (b. 11 Feb 1810, Paris; d. 27 Nov 1889, Pau).

Taught by her mother, a singer, Loïsa sang her own compositions – hundreds of simple sentimental romances with texts principally by her husband-to-be Gustave Lemoine – in the Paris salons (1832–42). She studied with Adolphe Adam and, as a result, wrote a one-act opera, *Le mauvais œil*, with the libretto by Scribe and Lemoine. It was performed at the Opéra-Comique in 1836 and well received. After her marriage, she almost ceased to compose.

Works
Include the operas *Le mauvais œil* (perf. 1836) and *La viellieuse, ou Les nuits de milady* (perf. 1869).

Further reading
F. Clément and P. Larousse, *Dictionnaire lyrique, ou Histoire des opéras* (Paris, 1867–69; enlarged 3/1905/R1969, ed. A. Pougin). A.B. Caswell, 'Louisa Puget and the French Romance' in *Music in Paris in the Eighteen-Thirties* (Northampton, MA, 1982). Fétis/*BIOGRAPHIE*.

Pyramid piano
A piano in which the soundboard and strings are mounted in an upright instead of the usual horizontal position, so that the longest (bass) strings stretch upward from directly behind the keyboard – and in front of the action – to the highest point giving the shape of a narrow pyramid. To accommodate this, the case is tapered symmetrically from the width of the keyboard up to a narrow blunt end, occasionally crowned by some decorative feature. Its invention is attributed to Christian Ernst *Friderici (although this is now disputed: see Pollens/EARLY), who also invented the first *square piano.

Further reading
Harding/PIANOFORTE.
Cole/PIANOFORTE.

Q

Quadrille (Fr., used in English etc.)
A lively dance, very popular in the nineteenth century, danced by groups of four, six or eight couples with elaborate steps. The name comes from the Spanish *cuadrilla* or the Italian *squadriglia*, and it was applied to a kind of *contredanse*, the *quadrille de contredanses*, and then shortened to the present word. Popular in Paris during the First Empire, it became popular in London and European cities, reaching Vienna in 1840.

The dance had five sections (or figures), which kept the names of the original *contredanses* which went to make it up: *Le pantalon* (in 6/8), *L'été* (2/4), *La poule* (6/8), *La pastourelle* (2/4) and a Finale. Occasionally *La Trénis* (after the dancer Trenitz) was substituted for *La pastourelle*, except in Vienna, where it made up a sixth dance. The music was usually adapted from popular stage works of the time, or had some other kind of easily recognizable or topical programme, such as *Jullien's *The British Army Quadrilles*. The ubiquity of the quadrille during its long heyday and the way in which the music chosen for it had to be adapted and squeezed into its rigid form became a source of musical jokes among composers, such as Chabrier's *Souvenirs de Munich*, which was based on themes from Wagner's *Ring*.

Quantz, Johann Joachim
German flautist, composer, theorist (b. 30 Jan 1697, Oberscheden, nr Hanover; d. 12 Jul 1773, Potsdam).

Son of a village blacksmith whose father died when he was 11, he was apprenticed to his musical uncle who was a town musician and learnt a variety of string and wind instruments, and harpsichord (with *Kiesewetter); later, however, he specialized in the transverse flute. Quantz joined the Dresden town band in 1716 and studied *counterpoint with one of Albrechtsberger's pupils, Zelenka, during a brief visit to Vienna. He was appointed oboist to the Polish chapel in Dresden and was exposed to the broader culture of Italian and French music there. 1724–27 he was studying in Italy – counterpoint with Gasparini in Rome – also visiting other centres, and met and impressed A. Scarlatti and Hasse. He also visited England and France, where he met *Handel, who tried to induce him to remain.

Accompanying his employer on a state visit to Berlin, Quantz met and began to teach flute to Prince *Frederick, visiting the city on a regular basis for the lessons. He declined an offer to join the Prince's retinue but, on becoming King of Prussia in 1740, Frederick appointed Quantz as his court composer and thenceforth he seems to have composed all his works for the King, who also composed and performed his own compositions at court.

Quantz's compositional style illustrates the transition from the *Baroque to the *Classical styles, the later works being more in the vein of the latter. He wrote an autobiography and other things, but his enduring achievement is his wide-ranging *Versuch* (treatise) on flute-playing which, like the two other great similar works by *C.P.E. Bach and *L. Mozart (on the keyboard and violin respectively) is much more than a primer for the player and deals with matters of performance and musical style generally.

Works
Many sonatas for flute and *continuo*, *trio sonatas, concertos and vocal

works. His theoretical works include the *Versuch einer Anweisung die Flöte traversiere zu spielen* (Berlin 1752, 3/1789) translated as *On Playing the Flute* (London 1985).

Further reading
E.E. Helm, *Music at the Court of Frederick the Great* (Norman, OK, 1960). E.R. Reilly, *Quantz and his Versuch: Three Studies* (New York, 1971). H. Augsbach, *Thematisch-zystematisches Verzeichnis der Werke von Johann Joachim Quantz* (Stuttgart, 1997). M.A. Oleskiewicz, *Quantz and the Flute at Dresden: his Instruments, his Repertory and their Significance for the Versuch and the Bach Circle* (diss., Duke U., 1998).

Quodlibet (Lat.: 'whatever you like')
A free, sometimes humorous, composition comprised of well-known tunes one after another, or combined. It began as part of non-musical *viva voce* examinations in European universities during the Middle Ages and into the seventeenth century when, in Germany, it became parodied by being based on incongruous lists of items associated with an absurd theme (such as items you don't need on your honeymoon). Musical quodlibets can be very skilful as well as being humorous, as is evinced by the last of *J.S. Bach's '*Goldberg' Variations, where two popular songs are combined with the theme of the set. Later examples are the music for the ball scene in *W.A. Mozart's *Don Giovanni* and the last movement of Ives's Symphony no. 2.

R

'Raindrop' Prelude

The title of no.15 of *Chopin's Préludes op. 28 in D♭ major; it is thought to have been suggested by the repetition of the note A♭, suggesting the dripping of the rain while he composed it. The set was written in 1836–39 during a visit to Majorca with George Sand and her children, during which it rained a great deal.

RAM (see *Royal Academy of Music)

Range (see *Compass; also *Tessitura)

Rank

(1) See *Organ.

(2) A row of *jacks.

Ranz des vaches (Ger. equiv. *Kuhreigen, Kuhreihen*)

Swiss mountain-song sung or played on an alphorn (and often improvised) by herdsmen to call their cows. The melodies usually involve arpeggiaic writing and *yodelling and are often wordless, though texts do survive. Several composers incorporated them in other works: the overtures to the operas *Guillaume Tell* by *Grétry (1791) and by *Rossini (1829); the shepherd's pipe tune in the finale of *Beethoven's Pastoral Symphony (1807–1808); in the 'Scène aux champs' in *Berlioz's *Symphonie fantastique* (1830).

Further reading
A.H. King, 'Mountains, Music and Musicians', *MQ*, xxxi (1945).

Recital

A musical concert given by (mostly) a single performer or a small group. It was first used in London in 1840 for *Liszt's solo concerts.

Recollections of ... (Fr. *Récollections de ...*; Ger. *Erinnerungen an ...*)

A piece of music designed to flatter the public of a particular country, geographical area or city, usually involving the use of *folk or popular tunes associated with them. 'Recollections' belonged to a series of pieces with similar intent, including 'Reminiscences of ...' (Fr. *'Réminiscences de ...'*; Ger. *'Erinnerungen an ...'*), '[The] Return to ...' (Fr. *'[Le] Rétour de ...'*), 'Farewell to ...' (Fr. *'Adieu à ...'*; Ger. *'Abschied an ...'*) and occasionally 'Homage to ...' (Fr. *'Hommage à ...'*). They are similar also to the operatic 'Reminiscences'.

Redichte

In *style galant* and music of the *Classical period, the technique of repeating a phrase more-or-less exactly. It is more purposeful than the *Baroque 'echo', where a short subphrase or motif is repeated with altered (usually softer) dynamics and, often, instrumentation.

Redoute [Ridotto] (Fr. from It. *ridotto*, 'reduced', 'arranged'; Ger. *Redout*)

A type of entertainment popular during the eighteenth century and into the nineteenth which mixed dancing and singing with music for listening to. It was introduced into London in 1722. The *Redouten-säle complex was built in Vienna to accommodate *redoutes*.

Redouten-Säle (Redoutensäle, Redoutensaal) (Ger.: 'Redout-Rooms')

A suite of two public ballrooms in Vienna, consisting of a large and a smaller one capable of accommodating some 3,000 people between them. (See *Redoute.)

Register

(1) See *Tessitura.

(2) See *Organ.

Reicha, [Rejcha], Antoine(-Joseph)
[Antonín, Anton]
Czech (French naturalized) composer,
theorist, teacher (b. 26 Feb 1770, Prague;
d. 28 May 1836, Paris).

Son of a town piper who died (at thirty)
before the boy was a year old, Reicha ran
away to his grandfather in Bohemia at
the age of ten and was later adopted by
an aunt and uncle, from whom he learnt
violin, piano and flute. When they moved
to Bonn in 1785, Reicha played in the
Hofkapelle (which his uncle directed)
with *Beethoven and *Neefe (from whom
he probably had composition lessons);
he was also introduced to *J.S. Bach's
keyboard works. He attended Bonn
university in 1789, meeting *J. Haydn and
fled to Hamburg when the French attacked
Bonn. Here he taught piano, harmony and
composition and devoted himself to the
latter. A year's stay in Paris, where he
hoped to break into the operatic scene,
proved unfruitful and he went to Vienna,
where he renewed his friendship with
Beethoven and Haydn and had lessons
from Albrechtsberger and Salieri. The
Empress Marie Therese commissioned an
opera from him (in which she herself sang)
and he declined the post of *Kapellmeister
to Prince *Lobkowitz.

He went to Paris in 1808, on the
invitation of Louis Adam and Sébastien
*Erard and wrote much music based on
*folk elements and, although operatic
success continued to elude him, he made
a great name for himself as a composer
and teacher. A recommendation for an
appointment for him at the Conservatoire
pointed out that many of his pupils

– among them Baillot, *Habeneck and
Rode – were already professors there
and Reicha was himself appointed
professor of *counterpoint and fugue in
1818 and one of his treatises (*Cours de
composition* ... (1816–18)) replaced the
official one of Catel. He married the same
year and the couple had two daughters;
*Rossini, *Felix Mendelssohn and
Balzac were counted among the family
friends. Criticism of Reicha by the 'old
guard' at the Conservatoire resulted in
factions being set up amongst students.
The anti-Reicha one, however, did not
include *Liszt and *Berlioz, both of
whom came to study with him in 1826,
but critical comments of a few of the
anti-brigade reached *Chopin's ears
when, in 1831, he intended to study at the
Conservatoire and he changed his mind.
Reicha was naturalized in 1829 and made
a Chevalier of the Légion d'honneur. His
influence was great, especially but by no
means exclusively in France and he was
admired by *Meyerbeer, *R. Schumann
and Smetana.

Works
Some 17 stage works, choral pieces
(including a requiem mass), half a dozen
symphonies,   overtures   and   several
concertos, as well as a large body of
chamber music of all sorts and piano
music. His theoretical works include
Traité de mélodie (pub. Paris 1814);
*Cours de composition musicale, ou Traité
complet et raisonné d'harmonie pratique*
(pub. Paris, ?1816–18; Eng. tr. 1854);
Traité de haute composition musicale
(pub. Pais 1824–26).

Further reading
J. Vysloužil, ed., *Zápisky o Antonínu
Rejchovi / Notes sur Antoine Reicha*
(Brno, 1970). O. Šotolová, *Antonín*

Rejcha (Prague 1977). Newman/SBE. *MGG*. Fétis/*BIOGRAPHIE*.

Reichardt, Johann Friedrich

German composer, writer on music (b. 25 Nov. 1752, Königsberg [now Kaliningrad]; d. 27 Jun 1814, Giebichenstein, nr Halle).

Son of a lutenist, he was a child prodigy on the violin and local musicians introduced him to the music of *J.S. and *C.P.E. Bach; however, his compositional training, like his general education, was lacking and incomplete. From the age of 15 he spent three years at Königsberg University and was influenced by Kant.

He went on several concert-tours, meeting *Schulz, F. Nicolai, *F. Benda – whose daughter was his first wife – J.A. Hiller, Klopstock, Lessing and C.P.E. Bach. Hearing that *Frederick the Great was seeking a *Kapellmeister for the royal Berlin opera, he recommended himself and secured the post in late 1775, at the age of 23. A trip enabled him to visit Klopstock, Goethe, *Galuppi and *Gluck and he heard Palestrina in Italy for the first time. When Frederick died in 1786, his successor Friedrich Wilhelm II allowed Reichardt to overhaul the opera and his own works were included. His enemies at court and his own somewhat petulant nature caused rifts and, after being denounced as a republican, he was dismissed without salary in 1794, also having bad relations with Goethe and Schiller, with both of whom he had happily collaborated. He was pardoned in 1796 and appointed director of a salt mine by Wilhelm and his estate at Giebichenstein became a haven for *Romantics and intellectuals, which included Tieck, the Schlegels, *E.T.A. Hoffmann, Schleiermacher, Fichte, Novalis and Voss. His home was destroyed by marauding French troops and he and his family were destitute; however, he managed and he was off travelling again and passing some months in Vienna where he was feted by his old friends. He was never recompensed for his property. In 1811 he received a small pension and his reputation soon waned.

Works

Many dramatic works and songs in styles ranging from the plainness of his Second *Berlin Lied School settings to dramatic ballades *à la* *Schubert – whom he much influenced. His non-vocal works suffer from the fact that he clung to the Doctrine of *Affections, making the music dull for its time. His many writings on musical matters (especially opera) were influential in their time.

Further reading

W. Salmen, *Johann Friedrich Reichardt: Konmponist, Schriftsteller, Kapellmeister und Verwaltunbgsbeamter der Goethezeit* (Freiburg and Zurich, 1963). N.B. Reich, *A Commentary on and a Translation of selected Writings of Johann Friedrich Reichardt* (diss., New York U., 1972).

Répertoire de musique

A collection of piano pieces by J.N. *Hummel aimed at the ladies of the German-speaking world, especially Vienna; the full title was *Répertoire de musique pour les dames, Ouvrage périodique et progressif composée par J.N. Hummel*.

Ries, Ferdinand

German pianist, composer, copyist (bap. 28 Nov 1784, Bonn; d. 13 Jan 1838, Frankfurt).

His father, an early teacher of *Beethoven, taught him violin and piano and he learned the cello from B.H.

Romberg. A hoped-for position in the electoral orchestra was not forthcoming – due to the court's disbanding – and he remained at home for further study. He became a pupil of Peter von Winter in Munich for a while and, by copying music, earned enough money to go to Vienna with a letter of introduction to Beethoven from his father.

Beethoven took good care of him as student and copyist and taught him piano; he studied composition with Albrechtsberger and was appointed pianist to Count von *Browne-Camus and to the service of Prince *Lichnowsky. Rejected for military service because of having lost an eye, he went to Paris in 1806 and scraped a living for two years before returning to Vienna in 1808, where a temporary estrangement from Beethoven over a misunderstanding was soon healed. Ries went on a series of financially-rewarding concert-tours from 1809–13, including an extensive one of Russia with his old cello-teacher, Romberg, and was made a member of the Swedish Royal Academy of Music in Stockholm. Shortly after (1813) he was in London and met Sir George *Smart and J.P. *Salomon, and was introduced to the *Philharmonic Concerts, where he and his works were often featured, both being well respected. He married an English lady and after 11 years retired to the Rhineland, finally moving to Frankfurt am Main where he died early in 1838.

Works
Many for and involving the piano: 14 sonatas (including op. 26, 'L'infortunée'); some 40 rondos, mostly on *folk and popular songs and arias; nearly 50 sets of variations on the same kind of material, as well as fantasias and others. His chamber music includes sonatas for violin, cello and flute, six piano trios, sextets, a septet and an octet, 26 string quartets and six quintets and orchestral music includes eight symphonies, overtures, a violin concerto and eight piano concertos as well as other works for piano and orchestra. There are also operas, partsongs, sacred works and 54 songs.

Further reading
D.W. MacArdle, 'Beethoven and Ferdinand Ries', *ML*, xlvi (1965). C. Hill, *The Music of Ferdinand Ries: a Thematic Catalogue* (Armidale, NSW, 1977); *Ferdinand Ries: a Study and Addenda* (Armidale, NSW, 1982).

Rigadoon, *rigadon* (see **Rigaudon*)

Rigaudon [*rigadon*, rigadoon]
French *folk dance and instrumental form beginning in southern France (especially the Languedoc and Provence). It became popular in the court of Louis XIV and was brought to Britain and Germany shortly after, becoming one of the *contredanses*. It was a joyful dance in duple *metre (often 6/8) with four-bar phrases and an anacrusis, or upbeat and could be danced by couples at balls or as a solo theatrical dance or, as mentioned, by several couples in the *contredanses*. It also occurred as an orchestral piece and especially in some *Baroque keyboard suites.

Further reading
P. Nettl, *The Story of the Dance* (New York, 1947). W. Hilton, *Dance of Court and Theater* (Princeton, NJ, 1981). F. Lancelot, *La belle dance: catalogue raisonné* (Paris, 1996).

Ritornello (It.; Fr. *ritournelle*)
Literally a 'little return' (diminutive of Italian *ritorno* ('return'). Very similar

in usage to the *rondo, the term refers in particular to the *tutti, or orchestral 'refrain' in a *Baroque concerto or aria which recurs throughout the movement. The ritornello usually gives the basic material of the movement in the tonic key and its recurrences are in a variety of different local keys – dominant, subdominant, relative – and in slightly different forms. These are interspersed with 'episodes' of soloistic writing (for the solo instrument(s) or voice), hence their alternative name of 'solos'. Thus the resulting 'ritornello form' can be summarized as

R[itornello] — Ep[isode] 1 — R — Ep. 2 — R — Ep. 4 . . . . . R.

Rococo

A style of art which flowered during the first half of the eighteenth century during the reign of Louis XIV, who called for a lighter and more youthful style of painting, and continuing into the reign of Louis XV. The term (pejorative at first) was coined retrospectively at the end of the eighteenth century in a revolutionary France as pleasing the frivolous taste of the aristocracy with forms and shapes like shells (rocailles). It was a revolt against academic strictures, and finds its most famous expression in Fragonard's The Swing (1767, Wallace Collection, London) with its twining branches and undergrowth and the swirl of the drapery, and in the work of Watteau, although it is Boucher who most epitomizes it.

The style also held sway in architecture and interior decoration and remains in the ethereal brightness and delicate tracery of the Princess's Salon in the Hôtel Soubise in Paris (1737–40), an oval room designed by Gabriel-Germain Boffrand and his team of designers, and in the interior of the Wieskirche (1745–54) in Bavaria, by the architect Dominkus Zimmermann.

The term rococo is more difficult to characterize in music and overlaps with the galant style. Opera, theatre and ballet-sets have certainly been influenced by it, and the existence of the French – and it is best confined to France or areas of French influence – opéra-ballet (Destouches, for example) and *pastoral were in the nature of a lighter antidote to the tragédie lyrique of Lully and others. Its most obvious expression is in the richly but delicately *decorated keyboard pieces on, very often, pastoral subjects of François *Couperin and Daquin.

Röllig [Rolling], Karl Leopold [Carl] Leopold

Viennese piano-maker (b. c.1740, ?Hamburg; d. 4 Mar 1804, Vienna).

Little is known about Röllig except that he invented a portable *piano (see *Piano (7)) in 1795, the 'Orphica' ['Orphika'], which could be strapped around the player's neck. It also had the distinction of having an iron frame – one of the very first of its kind.

Romanticism, Romantic

An artistic and cultural concept difficult to define as most of its characteristics can be applied to art and culture of all periods and all types. It is rather the particular concentration of these, perhaps during a particular time (c. 1790 – c.1915) which gives it the currency it enjoys in cultural criticism.

The term comes from the medieval Romance language of southern France and its literature, dealing with chivalry and brave adventures and couched in occasionally fantastic language freely expressed, and it was largely in that sense that the term was used in the eighteenth century, the Age of Enlightenment, as, in a sense, going against the trend. It is now used in music to describe the period between the high *Classic and the modern. Characteristics noted in that period include the primacy of matter over form and the predominance of emotional over rational matters, a high degree of emotionalism, an unassailable belief in the necessity and validity of personal expression, a concern with nature, the natural and the vernacular, and a preference for the spontaneous as opposed to the 'learned'. These can be discerned in the music of the period in various ways: a love of musical colour and occasionally exoticism, a penchant for *folk music, the belief in a composer's individualism and his (more rarely her) right – perhaps even duty – to stamp his/her works with that individualism, the spontaneity inherent in *improvisation, a love of virtuosity and the rise of public concerts.

Rondeau (see *Rondo)

Rondino (see *Rondo)

Rondo (It.; also adopted into Eng. and Ger.; Fr. *rondeau*)
A fundamental principle in music, that of recurrence of material either exactly or altered, it is also operative in the *da capo aria* and the *Ritornello forms. The material of the rondo's main section can be a theme or melody, or a medium-sized section of several themes, more-or-less complete in itself. Its returns – which can be modified, but are usually not significantly truncated – can be in various keys, normally closely-related ones such as the dominant, the subdominant, the relative, or the parallel mode, but as the nineteenth century progresses, also in keys a third away from the original.

The rondo material, or refrain, is often labelled 'A' in schematic diagrams and is interspersed with episodes (B, C, D, etc.). Rondo themes are commonly based on *folk or popular material or operatic arias. The basic rondo exists in two forms, the 'open' (with the scheme ABACADAE … ending with A) and the 'closed', with the palindromic ABACABA. Rondos can be free-standing works or could occur as middle (very rarely first) movements of larger works such as sonatas, and were particularly popular as finales in the *Classical and *Romantic periods.

Their use as finales gave rise to a hybrid 'Sonata-Rondo' [form], whereby the shape and all-important key-scheme of *Sonata Form is integrated with the looser Rondo form so that the latter's A corresponds with the Sonata Form's first subject [group], the B with the second subject [group] (often incorporating the transition), the repeat of the A as either codetta material, or the opening of the development section, the C section as the bulk of the Sonata Form's development, the A (or A1 if modified) as Sonata Form's recapitulated first subject, the B (or B1) as the second, and the final recurrence of A (or A1) as codetta or coda material. The key of the B section's first appearance would depend upon whether a major- or minor-key work was in question (see *Sonata Form).

The rondo principle is also found in its diminutives *rondino* and *rondoletto*.

Rondoletto (see *Rondo)

Rosenhain, Jacob [Jakob, Jacques]
German pianist, composer (b. 2 Dec 1813, Mannheim; d. 21 Mar 1894, Baden-Baden).
His teachers included Kalliwoda and he lived in Frankfurt am Main 1832–37.

After a very busy visit to London in 1837, he settled in Paris later the same year, becoming well-known for his evening chamber concerts, attended by such as *Cherubini, *Berlioz and *Rossini, and several of his operas were performed. He set up a piano school with *J.B. Cramer in 1843 and he settled in Baden-Baden in 1870, where he again became a prominent musical figure.

Works
Operas, including *Liswenna* (1836) (renamed *Le démon de la nuit* with a new libretto, perf. 1851) and *Volage et jaloux* (perf. 1863); three symphonies, a piano concerto (in D minor, op. 73 (pub. 1887)), four piano trios and many works for piano.

Further reading
E. Kratt-Harveng, *Jacques Rosenhain, Komponist und Pianist: ein Lebensbild* (Baden-Baden,1891).Fétis/*BIOGRAPHIE. MGG.*

Rossini, Gioachino (Antonio)
Italian composer (b. 29 Feb 1792, Pesaro; d. 13 Nov 1868, Passy).

Son of a horn-player and a singer, family life was disrupted by the Napoleonic Wars and the Rossinis finally settles in Bologna, where the boy forged ahead on the horn, keyboard and voice, and was made a member of the Accademia Filarmonica at the age of 12 and wrote his six Sonatas for String orchestra, which are still staple orchestral fare. In 1806 he joined the Liceo de Bologna and attended Padre Mattei's counterpoint class and wrote his first vocal works. A commission for a one-act farce for the Teatro San Moisè in Venice led to several others, including *La scala di seta*; he was exempted from military service. His need

to support himself and his parents led to frenetic opera-composition and his first international fame was simultaneous in comic and serious opera with *L'italiana in Algeri* (The Italian girl in Algiers) and *Tancredi* respectively (both 1813).

Rossini's operas were heard everywhere except in Naples, the shrine of Italian opera and very proud and protective of its position as the home of Cimarosa and *Paisiello. However, the far-seeing and powerful impresario of the Neapolitan theatres, Domenico Barbaia, invited Rossini to Naples as composer and musical and artistic director for his theatres, and Rossini accepted and remained in the city from 1815–22, the Neapolitan audiences being finally won over. It was an ideal situation for an operatic composer, working for a specific theatre (the San Carlo) and a cast with whom he was at home and an audience which he could – and did – mould to his ideas and innovations and he produced some of his greatest operas – *Otello* (1816), *Il barbiere di Siviglia* (*The Barber of Seville*, given in Rome in 1816, its disastrous first night only serving as an ironic foil to its later popularity), *La Cenerentola* (*Cinderella*, 1816), *La gazza ladra* (*The Thieving Magpie*, 1817), etc. He also became wealthy through his partnership with Barbaia in running the very successful gambling tables in the foyer of the theatre.

In 1822 he married the *prima donna* Isabella Colbran – who had been Barbaia's mistress – and toured Vienna (with the complete San Carlo company, 1822), and Paris and London in 1824. His operas were not particularly successful but he gained much financially by giving lessons to aristocrats' daughters and appearing at their musical gatherings; he was by now the most popular composer in the world.

That same year (1824) he was appointed musical director of the Théâtre Italien in Paris and for the next five years produced his greatest operas before retiring to his villa near Bologna, where he lived on with his second wife for another forty years in ill-health and composing only a few small pieces. He had a resuscitation in his last years, building a villa in Paris (in what was then the suburb of Passy) and wrote the *Péchés de viellesse* (*Sins of Old Age*) for piano and the *Petite messe solenelle*.

Works

The operas include *Il Signor Bruschino*, *Tancredi* and *L'italiana in Algeri* (*The Italian Girl in Algiers*) (all perf. 1813), *Otello* (1816), *La Cenerentola* (*Cinderella*) and *La gazza ladra* (*The Thieving Magpie*) (both 1817), *La donna del lago* (1819), *Semiramide* (1923), *Le Comte Ory* (1828) and *Guillaume Tell* (1829). Sacred works include several masses (the *Messa di gloria* (1820), *Stabat mater* (two versions: 1833 and 1841) and *Petite messe solenelle* (1863 and 1867)). Other works include six *sonate a quattro* for string orchestra (*c*.1804) and, for piano, *Péchés de viellesse* (*Sins of Old Age*) (13 vols, issued 1857–68).

Further reading

L.A. Bonnaccorsi, ed., *Gioacchino Rossini* (Florence, 1968). L.G. Rognoni, *Rossini* (Parma, 1956, 3/1977). H. Weinstock, *Rossini: A Biography* (New York, 1968). N. Till, *Rossini: his Life and Times* (London, 1983). R. Osborne, *Rossini* (London, 1986, 2/1987). A. Bassi, *Gioacchino Rossini* (Padua, 1992) G. Carli Ballola, *Rossini* (Florence, 1992). A. Kendall, *Gioacchino Rossini: the Reluctant Hero* (London, 1992).

Rousseau, Jean-Jacques

Swiss philosopher, author, theorist, composer (b. 28 Jun 1712, Geneva; d. 2 Jul 1778, Ermenonville).

Son of a poor, respectable Protestant watchmaker and dancing-master, his mother died in childbirth and when his father moved to France, he left him in the care of her relatives at the age of ten. Apart from some singing lessons, he was self-taught in music, using Rameau's *Traité de l'harmonie* (pub. 1722). At 16 he absconded from his apprenticeship to an engraver and wandered around Switzerland, Italy and France and, after meeting a young widow who was a kind of mother, then mistress, to him, he converted to Catholicism and lived with her in Chambéry 1731–40, moving alone to Paris in 1741.

Rousseau was much embittered that his newly-invented system of musical notation was not accepted by the Académie des Sciences. He was already composing operas and, on occasion, the libretti as well. In 1743 he went to Venice as secretary to the French ambassador and met Thérèse le Vaisseur, who was to become his long-term mistress and bear him five children and whom he married late in life. By 1745 he was back in Paris and collaborated with Diderot on the **Encyclopédie* and won first prize in a competition set up by the Academy of Dijon with his essay on the proposed topic *Discours sur les sciences et les arts* in 1750. He was involved in opera and his great musical triumph came at last in 1752 with the performance, before Louis XV at Fontainebleau, of his *intermède* (*intermezzo*) *Le devin du village* (*The Village Soothsayer*). It is a short work (about an hour) with only three characters, but in its amalgamation of pastoral setting with Italianate recitatives and simple, winsome airs, its success was instantaneous and long-lasting and the piece was given throughout Europe for over a half-century, with translations into all the major languages including English (by *Burney, for the London stage). Rousseau was drawn into the 'Querelle des Bouffons' on the Italian side and he expressed his reasons in his *Lettre sur la musique française* (1753), taking the view that opera was not possible in French – ironic, considering the success of *Le devin* – and he wrote the radically experimental spoken monodrama *Pygmalion* with most of the incidental music by another composer, whom Rousseau neglected to mention when it was performed in Paris. This led to charges of plagiarism, one which constantly recurred with respect to his music throughout his life. His extremely popular epistolary novel *Julie, ou la Nouvelle Heloise* was published in 1761 with its emphasis on feeling and sensibility, and in the same year his *Du Contrat Social* (*The Social Contract*) appeared, enshrining his ideas on republicanism. The following year *Emile, ou l'Education* outlined his ideas for a simple, virtuous, 'natural' education-system, removed from the corruptions of institutionalism, but his diatribes against, among other institutions, religion offended Catholics as well as Protestants and the book was banned, forcing him to flee to escape arrest and he wandered around Switzerland, England (where David Hume gave him asylum and where he began his self-justificatory but fascinating *Confessions*) and various French provinces. He returned to Paris in 1770, gradually losing his mind.

Rousseau's elevation of feeling over reason and of the natural over the artificial made him a patron saint of *Romanticism and, together with his mistrust of institutions and view of civilization as more

of a corrupting force than a 'civilizing' one, was of central importance in the philosophy behind the French Revolution. His *intermède Le devin du village* was the springboard for *opéra comique* and in his *Pygmalion* he can be said to have created *melodrama. Pestalozzi's educational reforms were a direct consequence of Rousseau's ideas on the subject.

Works
The music to most of his stage works is lost, but in the case of three, music and text remain: *Le devin du village* (*The Village Soothsayer*, perf. 1752), *Pygmalion* (perf. 1770), *Daphnis et Chloé* (unfinished, 1779). His musical writings include: *Discours sur les sciences et les arts* (*Discourse on the Sciences and the Arts*, 1750); *Lettre d'un symphoniste de l'Académe royale de musique à ses camarades de l'orchestre* (*Letter from a Symphonist of the Royal Academy of Music to his orchestral Colleagues*, 1753); *Lettre sur la musique française* (1753); *Essai sur l'origine des langues, où il est parlé de la mélodie et de l'imitation musicale* (*Essay on the Origin of Languages, in which Melody and Musical Imitation is discussed c.*1760). Other writings (selection): *Discours sur l'origine de l'inégalité* (*Discourse on the origins of Inequality*, pub. 1755); *Julie, ou la Nouvelle Heloise* (*Julie, or the New Heloise*, pub. 1761); *Du Contrat Social* (*The Social Contract*, pub. 1761); *Emile, ou l'Education* (pub. 1762); *Les Confessions* (1781–88, pub. posthumously) and *Les Rêveries du promeneur solitaire* (*Reveries of the Solitary Walker*, 1782).

Further reading
S. Starobinski, *Jean-Jacques Rousseau: Le transparence et l'obstacle* (Paris, 1971). J. Roussel, *Jean-Jacques Rousseau*

en France après la Révolution 1795–1830 (Paris, 1972). R. Cotte, *Jean-Jacques Rousseau, le philosophe musicien* (Braine-le-Comte, 1976). C. Blum, *Rousseau and the Republic of Virtue* (Ithaca, NY, 1986). B. Cannone, *Philosophies de la musique (1752–1780)* (Paris, 1990). C. Dauphin, *Rousseau musicien des Lumières* (Montreal, 1992). M. O'Dea, *Jean-Jacques Rousseau: Music, Illusion and Desire* (London, 1995). G. Dart, *Rousseau, Robespierre and English Romanticism* (Cambridge, 1999).

Royal Academy of Music
(1) An alliance of some of the nobility in London founded with royal patronage in 1718–19 to promote Italian opera in Britain, especially London. *Handel was closely associated with it.

(2) [**RAM**] A music conservatory founded in London in 1822 for the professional training of musicians; most of its professors were foreigners.

Rudolph (Johann Joseph Rainer)
Archduke of Austria [S.[erenissimus] R.[udolphus] D.[ux]]
Austrian music patron, pianist, composer (b. 8 Jan 1788, Florence; d. 24 Jul 1831, Baden, nr Vienna).

Youngest son of the Grand Duke of Tuscany, accompanied his father to Vienna when the latter became the Emperor Leopold II in 1790. Exempted from the traditional military career due to poor health, he interested himself in religion and the arts. *Beethoven taught him piano, composition and theory for almost twenty years on and off from 1803 and he became the composer's most staunch patron, becoming close friends in spite of Beethoven's intractability. In March 1809 he signed an agreement with

Princes *Lichnowsky and *Lobkowitz to pay Beethoven an annuity to ensure his continued presence in Vienna. Beethoven dedicated a number of works to Rudolph, including the Piano Sonata in E♭ major (*Lebewohl*, 'Farewell'), the Fourth Piano Concerto in G major and the *Missa Solemnis* in D major (1823). His interests included the theatre and he was created Archbishop of Olmütz (Olomuc) in 1819 and a cardinal. He was instrumental in the founding of the *Gesellschaft der Musikfreunde*, to which he donated his large music collection and wrote a clarinet sonata and variations on a theme by Beethoven as well as one for *Diabelli's variation-compilation.

Further reading
P. Nettl, 'Erinnerungen an Erzherzog Rudolph, den Freund und Schüler Beethovens', *Zeitschrift für Musikwissenschaft*, iv (1921–22). D.W. MacArdle, 'Beethoven and the Archduke Rudolph', *Beethoven-Jahrbuch 1959–60*. E. Forbes, ed., *Thayer's Life of Beethoven* (Princeton, NJ, 1964). S. Kagan, *Archduke Rudolph, Beethoven's Patron, Pupil and Friend: his Life and Music* (Stuyvesant, NY, 1988).

Rule Britannia[!]
A patriotic song appearing in the masque *Alfred* (1740) by James Thomson and David Mallet [Malloch] with music by *Arne; the words of the song are probably by Thomson. The song was very popular and was used later by *Handel, *Beethoven (a set of variations, WoO79 (1803) and in *Wellington's Victory at the Battle of Vitoria* (*'Battle Symphony', 1813)) and in an anthem by *Attwood. The chorus is:
    Rule Britannia! Britannia rule the
    waves! / Britons never never never
    shall be slaves.

S

Saint-Lambert, Monsieur de

French harpsichord-player, teacher, composer (*fl. c.*1700, Paris).

Nothing is known of his life except that he went to the French provinces to teach music to some of the local well-to-dos. He is known for two didactic works. His *Les principes du clavecin* (pub. Paris, 1702) comprises well-organized sections on the rudiments of music, on playing the harpsichord and a particularly important one on *ornaments. Similarly, his *Nouveau traité de l'accompagnement* (pub. Paris, 1707) is also exemplary in its clarity and its useful commentary on the harmonic theory of its day.

Works

Les principes du clavecin, contenante une explication exacte de tout ce qui concerne la tablature et le clavier [*Principles of the Harpsichord, containing a rigorous explanation of all that concerns Notation and the Keyboard*] (pub. Paris, 1702; Eng. tr., 1984). *Nouveau traité de l'accompagnement du clavecin, de l'orgue et des autres instruments* [*New Treatise on Accompanying on the Harpsichord, the Organ and on Other Instruments*] (pub. Paris, 1707; Eng. tr., 1991).

Further reading

R. Harris-Warwick, 'Introduction' to Saint-Lambert: *Principles of the Harpsichord* (Cambridge, 1984).

Salomon, Johann Peter

German violinist, impresario, composer (bap. 20 Feb 1745, Bonn; d. 28 Nov 1815 London).

He met *C.P.E. Bach and settled in London in 1781, where he was an important part of the musical life, organizing and conducting the series of *subscription concerts which came to be known as the 'Salomon Concerts'. He brought many international artists to London, notably *Joseph Haydn in1790–91 and 1794–95, for whose London concerts the latter wrote his last great 12 'Salomon' or 'London' Symphonies.

Further reading

H. Unverricht, 'Die Kompositionen Johann Peter Salomons: ein Überblick', *Studien für Musikgeschichte des Rheinlandes*, iii, ed. U. Eckart-Bäcker (Cologne, 1965). A. Tyson, 'Salomon's Will', *Studien zur Musikgeschichte des Rheinlandes*, iii, ed. U. Eckart-Bäcker (Cologne, 1965). R. Stowell, 'Johann Peter Salomon: Director or Co-Ordinator?', *Haydn Society Newsletter*, no. 8 (1988).

'Salomon Concerts' (see *Salomon)

Saltarello (It.: 'little jump'; Fr. *pas de Brabant*; Ger. *Hoppertanz, Hupfertanz*; Sp. *alta, alta danza*)

A name applied to several Italian dances in triple *metre and characterized by leaps. It was often used as an 'afterdance' to a pavan – and it was almost indistinguishable from its afterdance, the galliard – or to a *passamezzo*. At the end of the eighteenth century, a *folk *saltarello* began to become popular in Rome and then moving northwards. This was in 3/4 or 6/8 time, danced by one person or by a couple and characterized by increasingly frenzied leaping and gesticulating, accompanied by guitars and tambourine, with onlookers joining in with singing. *Felix Mendelssohn's two tunes in the finale (headed 'Saltarello') of his *Italian Symphony* (no. 4 in A major op. 90 (1833)) are probably based on real examples of the later type.

Sarabande (Fr. and Ger.; Eng. saraband (though the French was preferred generally); It. *sarabanda*; Sp. *zarabanda*) A very popular *Baroque dance and one of the core dances of the Baroque suite (along with the *allemande*, *courante* and *gigue*). It hardly ever has an anacrusis, is in slow triple *metre and very often syncopates the second beat. *J.S. Bach composed more of them than any other dance-type.

Further reading
R. Stevenson, 'The Sarabande, a Dance of American Descent', *Inter-American Music Bulletin*, no. 30 (1962); 'The Mexican Origins of the Sarabande', *Inter-American Music Bulletin*, no. 33 (1963). R. Gstrein, *Sarabande: Tanzgattung und musikalischer Topos* (Innsbruck, 1997).

Savoie (see *Savoy)   .

Savoy [Savoie]
An area of south-west France situated in the French Alps which included parts of Switzerland and Italy before being annexed to France during the Revolution. Like the areas of Switzerland and the provinces of Tyrol and Styria (both Austrian) which it borders, the *folk music is characterized by *yodelling, wide leaps and register-changes, and the use of *falsetto and arpeggiaic melodies. The adjective is *Savoyard(e)*.

Savoyard(e) (see *Savoy)

Scarlatti, (Giuseppe) Domenico
Italian composer, keyboard-player, teacher (b. 26 Oct 1685, Naples; d. 23 Jul 1757, Madrid).

Little is known of his early years, including his teachers, although, as a member of a musical dynasty and son of the famous composer Alessandro Scarlatti, he no doubt was instructed by him and other members of the family. At the age of 16 he was appointed organist and composer to the Neapolitan court where his father was *maestro di cappella*. It is possible that he met Bartolomeo *Cristofori on a visit to Florence with his father in 1702.

His father virtually ordered him to try his luck in Venice and Domenico spent four years there, no information about which survives, but he was appointed to the court of the Polish queen Maria Casimira who was in exile in Rome, for which he wrote six operas and some choral works. At the home of Cardinal Ottoboni he met many of the leading musicians of the period, including Corelli and *Handel, with whom he had a keyboard 'duel' in which, apparently, Handel won on the organ and Scarlatti on the harpsichord. He also met the young English musician Thomas Roseingrave, who became a great admirer and was of tremendous help in disseminating Scarlatti's music in Britain and elsewhere.

Such was his father's domineering that Domenico was forced to take out a legal injunction to determine his independence and he moved to Portugal in 1719 to the court in Lisbon. Little is known of his first nine years there because of the earthquake of 1755 which destroyed practically the whole city, but he travelled to Rome in 1724, meeting *Quantz and, perhaps, the celebrated *castrato* Farinelli. His duties at court included teaching keyboard to the talented Infanta Maria Barbara and her uncle, Don Antonio, who was directly responsible for the *corpus* of over 500 one-movement *Essercizi* (*'exercises', although usually called 'sonatas', even though they are in *binary, rather than *sonata, form) for keyboard. When the Infanta became queen of Spain in 1728, Scarlatti moved to Madrid with the court and remained there for the rest of his life (28 years) in comparative obscurity. A few facts have surfaced from these years, however. The *castrato* Farinelli was appointed to the court in 1738 as private singer and supervisor of theatrical productions, but their relationship or collaboration (if any) is unknown. Scarlatti's investiture as a Knight of the Order of Santiago is commemorated in a portrait, discovered in 1956, by Velasco in appropriate regalia.

Scarlatti's main legacy were his *Essercizi per gravicembalo* (London, 1738/R1967), 500-odd keyboard 'sonatas' in one movement, with their marvellous understanding of the keyboard and great harmonic and textural audacity which had much influence on subsequent keyboard music, in Spain (Antonio Soler, Félix Máximo López and Sebastián Albero) and Britain (Kelway and *Arne).

Works
Some 15 stage works, sacred and secular vocal works and many miscellaneous arias, cantatas and other works remain, together with 17 sinfonias and a doubtful harpsichord concerto. His most important contribution consisted of the *Essercizi per gravicembalo* (London 1738/R1967). Modern editions include: A. Longo, ed., *Opere complete per gravicembalo di Domenico Scarlatti* (Milan, 1906–1908), R. Kirkpatrick, ed., *D. Scarlatti: Complete Keyboard Works in Facsimile* (New York, 1970), K. Gilbert, ed., *D. Scarlatti: Sonates* (Paris, 1971) and E. Fadini, ed., *D. Scarlatti: Sonate per clavicembalo* (Milan, 1978).

Further reading
G. Pestelli, *Le sonate di Domenico Scarlatti: proposta di un ordinamento cronologico* (Turin, 1967). M. Bogianckino, *L'arte clavicembalista di Domenico Scarlatti* (Rome, 1956). R. Kirkpatrick, *Domenico Scarlatti* (Princeton, NJ, 1953 rev. 3/1968). M. Boyd, *Domenico Scarlatti, Master of Music* (London, 1986).

Schantz [Schanz], Johann
Austrian piano-maker (b. *c.*1762, Kladrob, Bohemia; d. 26 April 1828, Vienna).

Next to nothing s known about him except that he was working in Vienna around 1790. About 37 of his pianos (including two squares) survive and his instruments were recommended by *Beethoven, although he had occasion to return one to the maker because he was dissatisfied with it.

Further reading
M. Latcham, *The Stringing, Scaling and Pitch of Hammerflügel built in the Southern German and Viennese Traditions* 1780–1820 (Munich, 1999). Maunder/KEYBOARD.

Scherzando (see *Scherzo)

Scherzetto (see* Scherzo)

Scherzino (see *Scherzo)

Scherzo (It.: 'joke')
A type of musical movement or, occasionally, a free-standing piece, of a light, witty or boisterous kind, often in triple time. It is rarely found before the *Classical period, where it first came into prominence as a nickname for *J. Haydn's six op. 33 string quartets called 'Gli scherzi' ('The jokes'), as the *minuet

movements are all headed either 'scherzo' or '*scherzando*', although the reason is unclear, as they are in all respects, conventional minuets of their period. In *Beethoven's First Symphony, the movement headed 'Menuetto' is anything but that, being quite different in type and pace to its Classical counterpart and is in all respects a scherzo. In his other works, the minuet was gradually replaced by the faster 'scherzo' which, however, preserved the minuet-and-trio shape. A particular manifestation of the type can be found in the *Romantic period, often associated with music for or involving the piano, the 'demonic' scherzo, very often in a minor key and aspects of the grotesque began to intrude after 1850, for example in the symphonies of Mahler and Bruckner. Some composers substituted a national, *folk or other type of dance for the scherzo – Tchaikovsky the *waltz, Dvořák the *furiant*.

As a solo piece, the scherzo is first and best represented by *Chopin's four of the name, large-scale and generally *ternary in form, no. 1 in B minor op. 20 (1831–32), no. 2 in B♭ minor/D♭ major op. 31 (1837), no. 3 in C♯ minor op. 39 (1839) and no. 4 in E major op. 54 (1842); and *Brahms's Scherzo in E♭ minor op. 4 (1851).

Further reading
T. Russell, *Minuet, Scherzando, and Scherzo: the Dance Movement in Transition* (diss., U. of North Carolina, 1983). E. Platen, 'Scherzo' in G. Massenkeil, ed., *Das neue Lexicon der Musik* (Stuttgart and Weimar, 1996).

Schindler, Anton Felix
Moravian violinist, conductor, writer (b. 13 Jun 1795, Meedl, Moravia; d. 16 Jan 1864, Bockenheim, nr Frankfurt).

He was taught violin by his father and met *Beethoven when he moved to Vienna to study law in 1813; the composer became interested in him because of Schindler's political activities in demonstrations and his arrest. By now he had turned to music and become the leader of the Josephstadttheater and he also took over the duties of (unpaid) secretary and general factotum to Beethoven. Except for a brief breach in relations – common enough with Beethoven – he remained until Beethoven's death.

The problems with Schindler's accounts of Beethoven, in which he was in a unique position to deliver information unavailable from elsewhere to posterity, was his bias and notorious and often wilful inaccuracy. The most important documents of the composer's later life, contained in 'conversation-books' (which contain a written record of his half, occasionally more, of his intercourse with others) were systematically destroyed so that only a third remain, and those were liberally falsified and altered by Schindler long after the composer's death. The final (third) edition of his Beethoven *Biographie*, however, makes up, to some extent, for the hasty publication of the earlier ones but still has to be treated with caution.

Works
Biographie von Ludwig van Beethoven (Münster, 1840, 2/1845 w. two supplements: 'Auszüge aus Beethovens Konversationsheften' and 'Beethoven in Paris', 1860, Eng. tr. 1841); ed. D. MacArdle as, *Beethoven as I Knew Him* (London, 1966).

Further reading
D.W. MacArdle, Anton Felix Schindler, Friend of Beethoven', *MR*, xxiv (1963).

E. Forbes, ed., *Thayer's Life of Beethoven* (Princeton, NJ, 1964). E. Doernberg 'Anton Schindler', *MQ*, li (1965). P. Stadlen, 'Schindler's Beethoven Forgeries', *MT*, cxviii (1977).

Schobert, Johann [Jean]
Silesian harpsichordist, composer (b. *c.*1735, ?Silesia; d. 28 Aug 1767, Paris).

Little is known about him until his arrival in Paris in 1760 (or just after) in the court of the Prince of Conti, his marriage to a French woman, the disastrous reception of his only comic opera and his (and his wife and a child's) death after eating poisonous mushrooms.

His extant music shows, on the one hand, a lack of ability to develop successfully with a tendency to substitute the formulaic and, on the other, originality and freshness in a number of pieces. It was no doubt these which the seven-year-old *W.A. Mozart admired so much and which he strove to imitate.

Works
Sonatas for harpsichord and with violin *ad lib* as well as chamber music and concertos for harpsichord.

Further reading
H.C. Turrentine, *Johann Schobert and French Clavier Music from 1700 to the Revolution* (diss., U. of Iowa, 1962); 'The Prince de Conti, a Royal Patron of Music', *MQ*, liv (1968). L.E.R. Rush, *The Harpsichord Concertos of Johann Schobert* (DMA diss., U. of Northern Colorado, 1983). Newman/SCE. *MGG*.

schöne Müllerin, Die
Title of a song-cycle by *Schubert (D795, 1823) to a poem-cycle (originally a playlet with songs) of 20 numbers by *Wilhelm Müller (1817–20). It deals with a young apprentice-miller, seeking his fortune, who is drawn to a mill where he falls in love with the miller's daughter and she with him. However, she then gives her love to a dashing young huntsman and the miller-lad decides to leave in misery. His subsequent journey and slide into insanity are charted in Müller's *Die Winterresie* also set by Schubert.

The songs in the cycle are I. 'Das Wandern' ('Wandering') (B♭ major, 2/4, Mässig geschwind); II. 'Wohin?' ('Where to?') (G major, 2/4, Mässig); III. 'Halt!' (Halt!) (C major, 6/8, Nicht zu geschwind); IV. 'Danksagung an den Bach ('Thanksgiving to the Brook') (G major, 2/4, Etwas langsam); V. 'Am Feierabend' ('After the Day's Work') (A minor, 6/8, Ziemlich geschwind); VI. 'Der Neugierige' ('The Inquisitive One') (B major, 2/4, Langsam); VII. 'Ungeduld' ('Impatience') (A major, 3/4, Etwas geschwind); VIII. 'Morgengruß' ('Morning Greeting') (C major, 3/4, Mässig); IX. 'Des Müllers Blumen' ('The Miller's Flowers') (A major, 6/8, Mässig); X. 'Tränenregen' ('Rain of Tears') (A major, 6/8, Ziemlich langsam); XI. 'Mein!' ('Mine!') (D major, 2/2, Mässig geschwind); XII. 'Pause' ('Pause') (B♭ major, 4/4, Ziemlich geschwind); XIII. 'Mit dem grünen Lautenbande' ('With the Lute's Green Ribbon') (B♭ major, 2/4, Mässig); XIV. 'Der Jäger' ('The Huntsman') (C minor, 6/8, Geschwind); XV. 'Eifersucht und Stolz' ('Jealousy and Pride') (G minor, 2/4, Geschwind); XVI. 'Die liebe Farbe' ('The Beloved Colour') (B minor, 2/4, Etwas langsam); XVII. 'Die böse Farbe' ('The Hated Colour') (B major, 2/4, Ziemlich geschwind); XVIII. 'Trockne Blumen' ('Dry Flowers') (E minor, 2/4, Ziemlich langsam); XIX. 'Der Müller und der Bach' ('The Miller and the Millstream') (G minor, 3/8,

Mässig); XX. 'Des Baches Wiegenlied' ('The Millstream's Lullaby') (E major, 2/2, Mässig).

Further reading
S. Youens, *Schubert: Die schöne Müllerin* (Cambridge, 1992).

Schroeter, Johann Samuel
German pianist, composer (b. *c.*1752, ?Guben; d. 2 Nov 1788, London).

Taught first by his father, a good musician who fostered his children's careers, and then by J.A. Hiller in Leipzig (1763 on). He and his brother and two sisters – all musically talented – performed in the *Bach-Abel concerts in London in May 1772 and stayed behind when the rest went back to Germany. He was organist at the German Chapel and published several sets of chamber works and was patronized by an amateur composer Count Brühl, to whom he dedicated his op. 1. Schroeter. He was also befriended by *J.C. Bach and, like all musicians of German origin in Britain, benefited greatly from the arrival of the George III's German Queen Charlotte – indeed, on Bach's death in 1782 he was appointed music master to her. An elopement with one of his students to Scotland resulted in her wealthy family settling an allowance on him with the stipulation that he cease to perform in public, with which he complied to the letter, if not quite the spirit, as he performed in a number of concerts for the Prince Regent – not the most private of men. Schroeter died prematurely from a lung disease. His widow, Rebecca, became friendly, possibly more, with *J. Haydn on his London visits. As well as the harpsichord, Schroeter wrote idiomatically for the piano, with virtuosity and grace, especially in his concertos, which had a great influence on the young *W.A. Mozart during his London sojourn.

Works
Sonatas an some miscellaneous pieces for harpsichord and piano, others with violin *ad lib*, chamber music and some 'Scotch Songs' as well as a dozen keyboard concertos.

Further reading
K. Wolff, 'Johann Samuel Schroeter', *MQ*, xviv (1958). K. Komlós, *Fortepianos and their music: Germany, Austria, and England, 1760–1800* (Oxford, 1995).

Schröter, Christoph Gottlieb
German organist, composer, theorist, piano-maker (b. 10 Aug 1699, Hohnstein, Saxony; d. 20 May 1782, Nordhausen).

He was trained in childhood by his father and then joined the Dresden royal chapel choir, having keyboard lessons from the *Kapellmeister* J.C. Schmidt and, later, *fugue. In 1719 he began a five-year stint of European travel, giving lectures on the mathematical basis of the theory of music at Jena University, after which he held organist's posts at Minden and Nordhausen, where he remained for half a century. He wrote many theoretical books and essays. The occupying French soldiers sacked his home in 1761, destroying his library, including most of his own compositions and theoretical works, all unpublished.

Schröter was interested in the new piano and may possibly have been the first in Germany to arrive at its principles independently of *Cristofori. He apparently built a *down-striking as well as a normal up-striking piano, both of which he presented to the Dresden court and for which he received no acknowledgement.

Works

Chorales, fugues and cantata-cycles as well as theoretical works including *Deutliche Anweisung zum General-~Baß, in beständiger Veränderung des uns angebohrnen harmonischen Dreyklanges* (Halberstadt, 1772); *Christoph Gottlieb Schröters ... Letzte Beschäftigung mit musicalischen Dingen, nebst sechs Temperatur-Plänen und einer Noten-Tafel* (Nordhausen, 1782).

Further reading

H.T. David and H. Mendel, *The Bach Reader* (New York, 1945, rev 2/1966). R.N. 'Schröter's Piano action', *Musical Opinion*, lxxxvii (1963–64). F.T. Arnold, *The Art of Accompaniment from a Thorough-Bass* (London, 1931 /R1965). Harding/PIANO-FORTE.

Schubart, Christian Friedrich Daniel

German writer on music, poet, composer, journalist (b. 24 Mar 1739, Obersontheim, Swabia; d. 10 Oct 1791, Stuttgart).

He was taught music by his father as a child, but his parents sent him to study theology and he went to Erlangen University in 1758; he got into trouble, however, and was soon back at home. He became an organist to the Duke of Württemberg, and also court and opera-house harpsichordist. His loose living resulted in his dismissal and he went to Augsburg where he founded a periodical for music, literature and politics. He continued with this when he moved to Ulm in 1775 and offended the nobility to the extent that the Duke imprisoned him for ten years, during which he composed much and wrote important works, such as his *Ideen* (1784–85) and his *Leben und Gesinnungen* (1788–89). When released, he became court and theatre poet at Stuttgart, where he died after three years.

Schubart was well-thought-of as a keyboard player – excluding the piano – and he was popular as a lied composer also, providing his own texts. His other writings give a good picture of German music in the last half of his life and his ideas influenced *Beethoven and *R. Schumann; he had no time for the *galant* style and was one of the few of his time to recognize the worth of *J.S. Bach.

Works

Many lieder as well as keyboard works, particularly rhapsodies. Theoretical: *Leben und Gesinnungen, vom ihm selbst im Kerker aufgesetzt* [*Life and opinions of a falsely-imprisoned [man]*] (pub. 1971–73); *Ideen zu einer Ästhetik der Tonkunst* [*Ideas for a Musical Aesthetic*] (pub. Vienna, 1806 /R1969).

Further reading

R. Hammerstein, *Christian Friedrich Daniel Schubart, ein schwäbisch-alemanischer Dichter-musiker der Goethezeit* (diss., U of Freiburg, 1940). D. Ossenkop, *Christian Friedrich Daniel Schubart's Writings on Music* (diss., Columbia U., 1960); *The Earliest Settings of German Ballads for Voice and Clavier* (diss., Columbia U., 1968). T.A. DuBois, *Christian Friedrich Daniel Schubart's Ideen zu einer Ästhetik der Tonkunst: an Annotated translation* (diss., U. of Southern California, 1983). K. Honolka, *Schubart, Dichter un Musiker; Journalist und Rebell: sein Leben, sein Werk* (Stuttgart, 1985).

Schubert, Franz (Peter)

Austrian composer (b. 31 Jan 1797, Vienna; d. 19 Nov 1828, Vienna).

The only one of the great Viennese composers actually born in the city, he was taught music by his devoutly Catholic father, a schoolmaster, and piano by his elder brother; he later had lessons from the local organist, Holzer, who confessed himself to have been amazed at the boy's talent. No evidence has been found to support the reports of bad relations with his father at any time in their lives. In 1808 Schubert was a choirboy in the imperial court chapel and the Imperial and Royal City College, being examined by the directors Salieri and Eybler and by P. Körner; the boy was noted for his musicianship and general intelligence as well as his trustworthiness.

He left in 1813, the year of his father's remarriage after the death of Schubert's mother and, true to his parents' wishes, the boy enrolled in teacher-training school; his shortness of stature and defective sight prevented his being called-up for military service. A year later he was teaching at his father's school. His First Mass in F major was performed as part of the *Congress of Vienna celebrations. He also composed his first masterpiece, the song, now known as *Gretchen am Spinnrade [Gretchen at the Spinning-wheel, D118], after being bowled over by reading Goethe's Faust. In spite of lack of time, Schubert composed whenever possible, and the next few years saw the emergence of more songs, the first three symphonies, two masses and quite a number of piano and other pieces.

Having heard some of Schubert's music, the young composer Schober – the same age as Schubert – decided to seek him out and the two became friends. He tried to get Schubert to give up teaching and devote himself to composition, but it was a year before he ventured to do so. In the meantime, some of his Goethe-settings – including Gretchen and *Erlkönig – were sent to the man himself, but did not impress. About this time friends began

to arrange private concerts of his works – the *Schubertiade. Schober arranged for Schubert to live in his rich mother's house, where his compositions continued unabated. The situation only lasted for a year however, and Schubert was back at home and teaching as usual in 1817. Vienna was now suffering from *Rossini fever and the young Schubert could hardly miss it; he wrote a couple of *overtures in Italian – or, rather, Rossini – style, but when the family moved to a nearby district and another school, Franz went too.

However, in July 1818 he was appointed music-master to the children of Count Johann *Esterházy, which family *J. Haydn had served for most of his life; he resigned from his father's school and never returned there. The summer residence was in Zseliz, then in Hungary, and all seemed well until Schubert tired of the lip-service paid to music and longed for his Viennese friends. When the Esterházys returned to the capital for the winter, it was easier and Schubert continued to teach their children, but the ties had been loosened. The composer's name was now becoming widely known in the extensive and wealthy private musical circle in Vienna, and in the public domain as well (though less so), thanks to excellent semi-private performances of his works. In the summer of 1819 he accompanied his friend, the singer Vogl, to the beautiful countryside of Steyr, where they spent three idyllic months and which included the beginnings of the *'Trout' Quintet (D667), which was commissioned by a wealthy music-lover there. Back in Vienna, compositions continued to pour out, including some choral and dramatic music which were of limited public success.

In early 1821 Schubert found new lodgings and made a new friend in the

17-year-old painter Moritz von Schwind, who later painted the definitive picture of the musico-social Schubert, the *Schubert-Abend bei Joseph von Spaun* (*Schubert-evening at Joseph Spaun's*, 1726), showing a *Schubertiad* in full flow. He made many Goethe-settings that year but the puzzling lack of publishers' interest in Schubert's works caused his friends to get together and publish **Erlkönig* by *private subscription, which was a great success and led to the issuing of a score of songs in all.

In the summer of 1822 Schubert had a number of breaches with several friends occasioned, apparently, by his behaving uncharacteristically foppishly and living loosely. Although there were some reconciliations, one important development was his contraction of syphilis; the shining beacon of this time was the 'Unfinished' Symphony, no. 8 in B minor (D759). He moved back to his family's home and, needing money, became involved in a bad business deal which involved selling the rights to many of his works. His condition worsened and he was admitted to hospital in May 1823. During that time he began to set **Müller's verses, Die *schöne Müllerin*. He spent the late summer in Linz and Steyr, meeting his old friends there and being elected an honorary member of the Linz Musical Society. He was seriously ill several times during 1823 – including an attack while on holiday – but by the end of the year it seemed to have gone; unfortunately, it continued to affect his central nervous system leading to bouts of giddiness, pain and depression, which, again, strained relations with his friends. His various stage and operatic ventures were dogged by lack of success, due not to the music – apart from the rare instances of inappropriateness – but very often the

libretto or text. He began to write a series of chamber works and the first part of *Die schöne Müllerin* was published as his op. 25.

In the summer of 1824 he returned to the Esterházys at Zseliz as music-master and is thought to have fallen in love with one of the 'children' – now 20 – Caroline. Back in Vienna, meetings with out-of-town visiting singers saw his songs carried out into Europe; his more popular piano-works – dances and variations – were also becoming well known. Life also became more convivial and the *Schubertiade* recommenced.

In 1827 the dying **Beethoven* might have read some of Schubert's songs; according to the great man's unreliable amanuensis, **Schindler*, he is reported to have said 'Truly, in Schubert there is a divine spark'. Schubert himself briefly visited Beethoven's sickbed on 19 March – the first and only time they met – and was a torchbearer at the funeral the same year. Schubert began work on the **poem-cycle of Müller, Die Winterreise*. A visit to Graz to stay and compose for the Pachler family was a welcome diversion with daytime visits and evening *Schubertiads*, for which he improvised many dances, many of which were worked up for publication. On his return to Vienna, he was depressed and suffering various symptoms attributable ultimately to his syphilis. He finished his **Winterreise* and his friends were astounded by its power and bleakness, but warmed to it on further hearings, as Schubert said they would. The one and only full-scale concert of his works was given under the auspices of the **Gesellschaft der Musikfruende* in Vienna on 26 March to a full house of mostly friends and family. He could not afford a holiday that summer and moved in with his brother Ferdinand in the autumn, at which time he composed his last three piano sonatas, intending to dedicate them to *Hummel, but, when they were published in 1838, both composers were dead and the dedication went to *R. Schumann.

In October he fell ill and could not eat; he intended to study *counterpoint with *Sechter, but it is not known whether he did or not. He certainly did some work for him. His condition worsened in spite of professional and family care; he died in the afternoon of 19 November and was buried two days later within four graves of Beethoven.

Schubert enriched all genres except, possibly, opera – opera *qua* opera, one should perhaps say, as there is a great deal of beauty as well as mastery in his scores. He is best seen as a *Romantic Classicist rather than a true Romantic and his audacious harmonic shifts were commonplace by the time the greatest of his non-vocal music became better known (in the 1860s) and music had moved on.

Works
Theatrical and vocal include the *Singspiel Claudine von Villa Bella* (1815), the *melodrama *Die Zauberharfe* (*The Magic Harp*, 1820), the opera *Fierabras* (1823) and the incidental music to the play *Rosamunde, Fürstin von Zypern* (1823). There are also six masses and other religious music, many pieces for mixed, male and female voices and over a thousand songs, among them, *Gretchen am Spinnrade* [*Gretchen at the Spinning-wheel*, D118, 1814], *An den Mond* [*To the Moon*, D193], *An die Nachtigall* [*To the Nightingale*, D196] and *Erlkönig* [*The Erl-king*, D328, all 1815] as well as the song-cycles *Die schöne Müllerin* [*The Beautiful Miller-Maid*, D795, 1823–24]

and *Winterreise* [*Winter Journey*, D911, 1827]. Orchestral: nine symphonies including the 'Tragic', no. 4 in C minor (1816), 'Unfinished', no. 8 in B minor (1822) and the 'Great', no. 9 in C major (?1825–28), a Violin Concerto in D major (1816) and several overtures. Chamber: some 14 string quartets including the single-movement *Quartettsatz* in C minor (1820), 'Der Tod und das Mädchen' ('Death and the Maiden') in A minor (1824); the Piano Quintet in A major *'Die Forelle' (*'The Trout') and the String Quintet in C major; the Sonata in A minor D821, '*Arpeggione' (for that instrument) and some sonatas. There are also piano sonatas, many dances and variation-sets for piano and piano duet.

Further reading
From a huge literature: M.J.E. Brown, *Schubert: a Critical Biography* (London, 1958/R1977, 2/1961). E. Sams, 'Schubert's Illness Re-examined', *MT*, cxxi (1980). C. Osborne, *Schubert and his Vienna* (New York, 1985). E. Hilmar, *Schubert and his Time* (Portland, OR, 1988). E.N. McKay, *Franz Schubert: a Biography* (Oxford, 1996). *MGG*.

Schubertiad (pl. *-ade*; anglicized to Schubertiad(s))
A name given to any of the domestic concerts which *Schubert's friends arranged for him as occasions on which his works would be performed by himself and by others.

Schudi (see *Shudi)

Schulz, [Schultz] **Johann Abraham Peter**
German composer, conductor (b. 31 Mar 1747, Lüneburg; d. 10 Jun 1800, Schwedt an der Oder).

Son of a baker who wished him to become a churchman, he studied violin, flute, keyboard and theory with a local organist and at 15 went to Berlin, where he met *C.P.E. Bach and Kirnberger. However, he heeded the advice to complete his education at Lüneburg, which he duly did, and returned to Berlin to become a pupil of Kirnberger, who, in 1868, recommended him as teacher and accompanist to a Polish princess. He travelled throughout Europe for three years in her entourage, coming across *Gluck, *Grétry, *J. Haydn and making a firm friend of *J. Reichardt.

It was on the latter's recommendation that he was appointed music director to the new French theatre in Berlin in 1776, and two years later was music director at a private court theatre, finally becoming court composer to the Prussian royal family in 1780. However, the conservative royals found his penchant for new music too much and he resigned after seven years (1787), getting, in effect, promotion to the court in Copenhagen as *Hofkapellmeister* and also director of the Royal Danish Theatre; he made the city one of the most important cultural centres on the Continent. His tuberculosis caused him to retire prematurely with a pension, but it did stimulate his composition.

Schulz is best remembered for his *lieder as a member of the Second *Berlin Lied School, with their *folk-like melodies and fine texts, especially his original collection *Lieder im Volkston* (*Songs in Folk Style*, 1782–90). His influence was great on subsequent Danish music.

Works
Stage works include operas, *melodramas and *Singspiels* with over a hundred lieder (including *Lieder im Volkston* (*Songs in* Folk Style, 1782–90)) as well as oratorios, cantatas and other religious works.

Further reading
E. Schmitz, *Unverwelkter Folkslied-Stil: J.A.P. Schulz und seiner 'Lieder im Volkston'* (Leipzig, 1956). H. Gottwaldt and G. Hahne, eds, *Briefwechsel zwischen Johann Adam Peter Schulz und Johann HeinrichVoss* (Kassel, 1960). H. Hahne, 'Johann Heinrich Voss Versuch einer Gesamtaisgabe der Lieder Johann Abraham Peter Schulz', *Die Musikforschung*, xx (1967). *MGG*.

Schumann [née Wieck], **Clara (Josephine)**
German pianist, composer, teacher (b. 13 Sep 1819, Leipzig; d. 20 May 1896, Frankfurt).

She was the daughter of a well-known piano teacher who taught her and was determined that she would be a famous pianist. She appeared in public for the first time at the age of nine at the Gewandhaus, Leipzig, gave her first solo recital a few years later and undertook her first concert-tour with her father (including a visit to Paris) in 1831–32. She was famous throughout Europe by 1835, was acclaimed by, among others, Goethe, *R. Schumann, *Felix Mendelssohn. *Paganini, *Chopin and *Liszt and, in 1838, was appointed virtuoso pianist to the Austrian court – highly unusual for a non-Austrian, and a young one at that – and elected to the *Gesellschaft der Musikfreunde*.

When the young Robert Schumann arrived to live in Wieck's house as his piano-pupil, the two young people fell in love and wished to marry. Wieck had no intention of marrying his brilliant daughter to a penniless pianist-composer who also smoked and drank heavily and whose life, he suspected – correctly, as it happened – was far from chaste; in fact the young man was already suffering from the syphilis which would kill him. Wieck's response was to take Clara away, then forbid any contact of any kind between them until his irrational behaviour over three years caused them to resort to the law. After a series of suits and counter-suits, the court found in favour of the lovers and they were married the day before Clara's twenty-first birthday in 1840.

They lived in Leipzig (where a reconciliation of sorts with Wieck took place in 1843) then in Dresden (1844) and Düsseldorf (from 1850). Marriage was unexpectedly constricting for Clara, both in professional and in personal terms as she was not able to practise while Robert was composing – which he was most of the time. There were also children, eight in all in more-or-less rapid succession. Their final house in Düsseldorf (1853 on) was sufficiently large for the couple to play and/or compose simultaneously and Clara finished several works. The young *Brahms arrived to the Schumanns' acclaim in September 1853 and was hailed by Robert as a 'young eagle' in a famous review called 'Neue Bahnen' ['New Paths'] in the *Neue Zeitschrift für Musik, the periodical which he helped to found, for which he wrote and which he edited. After Robert's nervous breakdown, suicide attempt and final incarceration in a lunatic asylum – comfortable though the institution was – Brahms was a great comfort to Clara, and remained a stalwart friend, although he wished to be something more, though it is highly unlikely that he was; they destroyed most of their correspondence.

Clara's career continued apace and she toured regularly visiting Britain on an annual basis for 16 years. She was particularly noted for her performances of Robert's and Brahms's music. In 1857 she moved to Berlin to be close to her mother, who had divorced Wieck and married Adolf Bargiel and, after a spell in Baden-Baden, returned to Berlin where a series of tragedies involving her children occurred, two dying and one being committed for life to a mental asylum. She became head of piano-teaching at the Conservatory in Frankfurt and was also working on an edition of Robert's music and his letters for publication (appearing 1881–93 and 1885 respectively).

Clara had tremendous influence as a teacher and performer and her fine compositions – suffering the familiar oblivion of the non-*Canonic composer in general and the female composer in particular – should be better known; her Piano Concerto op. 7, in the same key as Robert's – A minor – is amazing for a fifteen-year-old.

Works

For piano include *Valses romantiques* op. 4 (?1833), *Quatre pièces caractéristiques* op. 5 (1833–36), *Soirées musicales* op. 6 (1834–36), Scherzo in D minor op. 10 (1838), *Quatre pièces fugitives* op. 15 (1841–44); some 60 songs; the Piano Concerto in A minor op. 7 (1833–36), Piano Trio in G minor op. 17 (1846) and *Drei Romanzen* for violin and piano op. 22 (1853).

Further reading

K.W. Leven, 'Clara Schumann's first Visit to England', *MT*, xcvii (1956). K. Walch-Schumann, ed., *Friedrich Wieck: Briefe aus den Jahren 1830–1838* (Cologne, 1968). J. Chissell, *Clara Schumann: A Dedicated Spirit* (London, 1983). N.B. Reich, *Clara Schumann: the Artist and the Woman* (Ithaca, NY, 2/1985, rev. 2000).

J. Klassen, *Clara Wieck-Schumann: die Virtuosin als Komponistin* (Kassel, 1990). B. Borchard, *Clara Schumann: ihr Leben* (Frankfurt, 1994).

Schumann, Robert

German composer, writer on music (b. 8 Jun 1810, Zwickau, Saxony; d. 29 Jul 1856, Endenich, nr Bonn).

Son of a publisher, author and bookseller with a nervous disorder, he was sent to private school locally at the age of six and had piano lessons from a local organist. Hearing *Moscheles play the piano fired him to emulate and throughout his later schooling at the Zwickau Lyceum (1820) music and music-performance were a prominent part of his life. By the time he left, with glowing reports, in 1828, several of the influences which were to shape his style were already in place: *Beethoven, *Hummel, Moscheles and *Schubert – after whose death in 1828 he cried for an entire night – and, in literature, Jean Paul from whom (he later said) he learnt more about *counterpoint than any music-teacher. His father, who encouraged his voracious reading, published some short articles of his in one of the periodicals he published. Although Robert's father wished him to study music, the death of the prospective teacher (*C.M. von Weber) and his own death put paid to that and, in deference to his mother's wishes, he went to Leipzig University to study law where, according to friends, he attended no lectures but improvised in music and in literature and drank champagne. However, he realized the need for proper musical training and enrolled for lessons with Friedrich Wieck, one of the foremost piano-teachers of the time in Leipzig. He met many of the local and out-of-town musicians at his home and, perhaps more important, Wieck's

piano-prodigy daughter, and Schumann's wife-to-be *Clara. As a result of letters from friends at Heidelberg University and his admiration for one of the law professors there, Justus Thibaut, whose book (*Über die Reinheit in der Tonkunst* (*On Purity in Musical Art*, 1825)) had impressed the young composer greatly, he cajoled his mother into allowing him to transfer there. In Thibaut's music society he learnt the music of the Renaissance choral masters and at the same time began a study of living masters (*Czerny, *Herz, Hummel and Moscheles), came across the music of *Chopin for the first time and heard *Paganini play (1830), both of which affected him greatly. He was finally allowed to change 'officially' from law to music and his first published opus, the *Thème sur le nom 'Abegg' varié pour le pianoforte* (*'Abegg' Variations*, 1831) shows his aptitude with pianistic experimentation and virtuosity.

Chopin inspired his other career, that in music criticism, giving rise to his first review in the influential periodical, the *Allgemeine musikalische Zeitung*, in which he began with the words 'Hats off, gentlemen, a genius!'. The style was in the vein of the novels of Jean Paul and *E.T.A. Hoffmann, commenting on style and effect rather than theoretical matters, True to his novelistic style, Schumann couched the majority of his reviews in dialogue, two characters representing the two different sides of his personality, Eusebius the dreamer and Florestan the fiery *Romantic, to which were added other characters later, representing his friends. These friends and he founded their own journal, the *Neue Zeitschrift für Musik* (1833), of which he soon became editor. His first compositions had been published by this time, the *Papillons* (*Butterflies*, 1832) op. 2, the

6 Studien nach Capricen von Paganini (*6 Studies after Caprices of Paganini*, 1832) op. 3 and the *6 Intermezzos* op. 4. A loss of feeling in Schumann's right hand meant that he had to abandon any thoughts of a performing career. Various reasons have been given for the affliction – the use of a mechanical device to help him cope with the virtuosity of Hummel's F♯ minor piano sonata and the cure, involving mercury, for the syphilis which he contracted because of his wild living are among them. Whatever the cause, it helped to concentrate his talents more on composition.

At this time also we learn of his growing affection for the fifteen-year old Clara and the reaction of her father, who, aware of Schumann's womanizing, heavy drinking and cigar-smoking, whisked her off on a concert-tour (January 1836). Then began a cat-and-mouse game of the lovers trying to see each other and Wieck trying to second-guess them, ending with a breaking-off of relations between both Wiecks and Schumann.

He was continuing to compose and continuing to try to find a teacher who would provide him with the musical grounding – *thorough-bass, *fugue, *counterpoint – which he felt he needed and which he finally tried to find in manuals. His *10 Impromptus über ein Thema von Clara Wieck* (*10 Impromptus on a Theme by Clara Wieck*, 1833) op. 5 was published shortly after it was written and the *Davidsbündlertänze* (*Dances of the league of David* – a reference to himself and his friends battling against the larger forces of musical mediocrity and philistinism, 1837) op. 6 and *Carnaval* op. 9 (1833–35) were published in 1837. Relationships between not only Schumann and Wieck but between Clara and Wieck began to worsen alarmingly

and led to a number of legal suits on both sides – Robert and Clara now having become formally betrothed. The final outcome was that the couple married, still in defiance of a frequently hysterical Wieck, in 1840, on the day before Clara's twenty-first birthday.

Schumann threw himself into composition and hundreds of songs poured forth as well as the First Symphony – the 'Spring' in B♭ major completed in just over a month – and other works. Clara's performing career also continued apace and the couple went on a number of tours, However, her new husband began to feel a little 'out of it', and on one occasion returned home early to compose, but lapsed into his old champagne-drinking and cigar-smoking habits; he did, however, begin a study of the string quartets of the Viennese Masters and his own efforts soon followed, especially after Clara's return. The two were reconciled with Wieck, to some extent, in 1843.

A tour to Russia, which Robert unsuccessfully tried to get out of, was finally made by the couple – by now with two children which they left with relations – and it was a triumph, although Robert suffered from depression and headaches, finally, three months after their return home, having a nervous breakdown. The couple and their children moved to Dresden in December 1844.

In the slower-paced environment he began to improve and persisted with his studies in counterpoint, from *Cherubini's *Cours de contrepoint*, in which Clara joined him, and wrote some fugues, being further stimulated by the arrival of a *pedal piano which he had obtained for organ-practice and for which he wrote some studies, 'sketches' and the *6 Fugues on B-A-C-H* op. 60 (1845). He also composed the Piano Concerto in A minor op. 54, or, rather, the Rondo finale, which he added to a recent slow movement prefaced by a Fantasie of 1841; Clara played it on New Year's Day 1846 in the Leipzig Gewandhaus. Together with Wagner and Hiller, he was engaged in founding a regular concert-series such as that existing in Leipzig. A trip to Vienna was something of a damp squib both in terms of Robert's compositions and Clara's playing. However, his creativity was improving and by mid-1847 he was on track again and a very productive six-year period began.

It saw the genesis and fruition of a large number of works including the 42 pieces of the *Album für die Jugend* (*Album for the Young*, 1848) op. 68 and the *3 Sonatas for the Young* (1853) – Clara continued to produce children, some of whom did not survive, as was so common at the time – the *Waldscenen* (*Woodland Scenes*, 1848–49) op. 82, the 14 *Bunte Blätter* (*Coloured Leaves*, compl. 1852) op. 99 all for piano; some 140 songs and partsongs, including patriotic works for men's chorus inspired by the Revolutions of 1848; chamber works, three symphonies (nos 2–4) and the *Concertstück* for piano and orchestra, as well as the opera *Genoveva* (op. 81, 1847–49) and the incidental music to Byron's *Manfred* (1848–49). They had to flee the riots in Dresden, giving them an excuse for a quiet month in the country.

Towards the end of the period, in 1852, the young *Brahms became a close friend – and would remain so to Clara for decades to come – and his career was helped by the couple. However, Robert was ailing again, with slurred speech and limitation of mobility and in 1854 this deteriorated alarmingly, ending with a failed suicide attempt. The same year he was confined to a comfortable private asylum where he was not allowed to see Clara until 1856, an absence of two years; he finally saw her two days before his death on 29 July 1856.

Works

For piano include *Thème sur le nom 'Abegg' varié pour le pianoforte* (*'Abegg' Variations*, 1830) op. 1, *Papillons* (*Butterflies*, 1830–31) op. 2, *6 Etudes pour le piano d'après les Caprices de Paganini* (*6 Studies after Caprices of Paganini*, 1832) op. 3, *6 Intermezzos* op. 4 (1832), *Davidsbündlertänze* (*Dances of the League of David*, 1837) op. 6, *Carnaval* (1834–35) op. 9, *Phantasiestücke* (*Fantasy-pieces*, 1837) op. 12, *12 Etudes Symphoniques* (*Symphonic Studies*, 1834–37) op. 13, *Kinderscenen* (*Scenes of Childhood*, 1838) op. 15, *Kreisleriana* (1838) op. 16, *Album für die Jugend* (*Album for the Young*, 1848) op. 68, *Waldscenen* (*Woodland Scenes*, 1848–49) op. 82 and *Bunte Blätter* (*Coloured Leaves*, pub. 1852) op. 99 as well as the Piano Concerto in A minor op. 54 (compl. 1845) and the Introduction and Allegro appassionato (*Concertstück*) for piano and orchestra op. 92 (1849). His orchestral works include four symphonies (1 in B♭ major, 'Spring', 1841; 2 in C major, 1845–46; 3 in E♭ major, 'Rhenish', 1850 and 4 in D minor, 1841, rev. 1851), overtures and incidental music (including that to *Manfred* (1848–49)) and the opera *Genoveva* (op. 81, 1847–48). Chamber works include three piano trios (D minor, F major and G minor) three string quartets (A minor and F and A majors) and a quartet and a quintet for piano (both E♭ major).

Further reading

M. Brion, *Schumann et l'âme romantique* (Paris, 1954, tr. G. Sainsbury as *Schumann and the Romantic Age*, London, 1956).

T.A. Brown, *The Aesthetics of Robert Schumann* (New York, 1968). J. Chissell, *Schumann* (London, 1948, rev. 2/1967). G. Eismann, *Robert Schumann: eine Biographie in Wort und Bild* (Leipzig, 1956, enlarged 2/1964; Eng. tr., 1964). L. Plantinga, *Schumann as Critic* (New Haven, CT, 1967). R. Taylor, *Robert Schumann: his Life and Work* (London, 1982). U. Rauchfleisch, *Robert Schumann, Leben und Werk: eine Psychobiographie* (Stuttgart, 1990). R.L. Todd, ed., *Schumann and his World* (Princeton, NJ, 1994).

Schuster, Vincenz

Austrian performer on the *Arpeggione.

Scotch snap

A melodic idiom in which a stressed short note is followed by a longer one. The origin of the term is not clear. In Italy and in France it was associated with Lombardy and is common in Purcell's music, so its appearance in printed Scottish strathspeys from 1760 was not new. It has been associated with Scottish *folk music, however, although it appears in a variety of Celtic musics, and has always carried rustic connotations, being used for this flavour by, for example, *Handel and *W.A. Mozart.

Scots Songs, A Selection of the Most Favourite (see *Napier)

Scots Songs in Three Parts: the Harmony by Haydn, A Selection of Original (see *Napier)

Scottish Airs, [Select Collection of] (see *Thomson)

Scottish Dialect, Poems, chiefly in the (see *Burns)

Sechter, Simon

Bohemian (Austrian naturalized) theorist, composer, organist (b. 11 Oct 1788, Freidberg [now Frimburk], Bohemia; d. 10 Sep 1867, Vienna).

He was taught music as a child and went to Vienna to further his education, meeting *Dragonetti and forming a lifelong friendship with the older man; he wrote piano accompaniments for Dragonetti's double bass concertos which brought him into the public eye. He taught piano and singing at the Blind School for fifteen years, during which time he became very well-known and many of his works played and published; in 1925 he became principal *Hoforganist* (Court Organist). Sechter became even better known as a theorist, the most important in the city, and taught many of the younger generation of composers and others, Pohl, Nottebohm, Umlauf, *Thalberg and the poet Grillparzer – even *Schubert had a lesson just before he died. He received many honours during his life and his successor at the Conservatory was Bruckner (1863).

Works

He wrote over eight thousand pieces, most of which are unpublished; those that were include his opera *Ali Hitsch-Hatsch* (1843), songs, *folk song arrangements and *contrapuntal pieces for piano. His most important theoretical writings are *Praktische Generalbaß-Schule* (*Basso continuo Tutor*) op. 49 (Vienna, c.1830) and *Die Grundsätze der musikalischen Komposition* (*The Basis of Musical Composition*) (3. vols, Leipzig, 1853–54).

Further reading

W.E. Caplin, 'Harmony and Meter in the Theories of Simon Sechter', *Music Theory Spectrum*, ii (1980). R. Wason, *Viennese*

Harmonic Theory from Albrechtsberger to Schenker and Schoenberg (Ann Arbor, MI, 1985). J.H. Chenevert, *Simon Sechter's 'The Principles of Musical Composition': a Translation of and Commentary on Selected Chapters* (diss., U. of Wisconsin, 1989). *MGG*.

Seguidilla [properly **'seguidillas'**, also *siguidilla*] (Sp. diminutive form of *seguida*, 'coda')
A Spanish song-dance (maybe of Moorish origin) in triple *metre of moderately-fast to (nowadays) fast tempo danced usually by two couples. It alternates sung passages (*coplas*) with guitar and castanet interludes and the text alternates five- and seven-syllable lines in (usually) four-line stanzas which are assonantal rather than rhyming. A short introduction (usually by guitar) leads to a 'false entry' by the singer and there is much repetition and variation throughout. Like the *bolero, it also uses the *bien parado*, a technique by which the dancers stop motionless over the accompaniment at the end of each section. Several Spanish provinces have their own variety. It was used by Albéniz as a piano piece and the example in Act I of Bizet's *Carmen*, though not very typical, has the general feel of the dance.

Seyfried, Ignaz (Xaver), Ritter **von**
Austrian composer, teacher, writer on music, conductor (b. 15 Aug 1776, Vienna; d. 27 Aug 1841, Vienna).

Brother of Joseph, a dramatist, he studied keyboard, probably with *W.A. Mozart and *Koželuch, and composition with Albrechtsberger and Winter, as well as philosophy in Prague (1792–93). His first ambitions were in the legal profession but music claimed him and he conducted in the Freihaus-Theater and the Theater an den Wien from 1797.

He also composed for these institutions, in fact his output was huge and in every field, though his music is not of great originality. *J. Haydn complimented him and *Beethoven thought enough of him to entrust the conducting of the premiere of *Fidelio* to him.

Works
Stage: *Der Wundermann am Rheinfall* (perf. 1799) and *Idas und Marpissa* (perf. 1807); incidental music to Schiller's *Die Räuber* (perf. 1808) and *Die Jungfrau von Orleans* (perf. 1811) and for the premiere of Grillparzer's *Die Ahnfrau* (perf. 1817).

Further reading
F. Hadamowsky, *Das Theater in der Wiener Leopoldstadt* (Vienna, 1934). O.E. Deutsch, *Das Freihaus-Theater auf der Wieden* (Vienna, 1937). A. Bauer, *150 Jahre Theater an der Wien* (Zurich, 1952); *Opern und Operetten in Wien* (Graz, 1955). B. von Seyfried, *Ignaz Ritter von Seyfried: thematisch-bibliographisches Verzeichnis, Aspekte der biographie und des Werkes* (Frankfurt, 1990).

Shudi [Schudi, Tschudi, Tshudi], **Burkat** [Burkhardt]
Swiss (English naturalized) harpsichord-maker (b. 1702, Schwanden (Glarus); d. 19 Aug 1773, London).

He arrived in England in 1718 and worked as a carpenter, married another Swiss in 1830 and set up on his own in business in 1739 in Soho (London), moving to Great Pulteney Street in 1842. John *Broadwood joined him in 1761, marrying his daughter and becoming a partner. *Zumpe had been amongst his apprentices. The *'Venetian Swell', allowing for an artificial kind of graded dynamics, was patented in 1769; it may have been invented in response to *Kirckman's *lid-swell. Shudi retired in 1771 and his son (also called Burkat) took over; after his death in 1803, Broadwood became owner, by this time the firm's output was almost exclusively pianos. Shudi's instruments were much admired for their tone and sold all over Europe, including its courts. *Frederick the Great (for whom he possibly invented the *machine stop), Maria Theresa, the Prince of Wales, Mrs Emma Hamilton *J. Haydn, his friends Gainsborough, Reynolds and *Handel all admired his instruments, and each owned at least one.

Further reading
W. Dale, *Tschudi the Harpsichord maker* (London, 1913). E. Halfpenny, 'Shudi and the "Venetian Swell"', *ML*, xxvii (1946). E.M. Ripin, 'Expressive Devices Applied to the Eighteenth-century Harpsichord', *Organ Yearbook*, i (1970). D. Wainwright, *Broadwood by Appointment: a History* (London, 1982). Boalch/HARPSICHORD. Russell/ HARPSICHORD. Hubbard/ HARPSICHORD.

Siciliana [siciliano] (It.; Old It. *ciciliano*; Fr. *sicilienne*)
Originally a dance form dating from the sixteenth century, it probably came from Sicily and its beginnings are very obscure. By the eighteenth century it was a popular aria-type in operas, and became a 'style' in the sense of the 'hunting style' etc. In ternary (ABA) form, minor mode and compound time, most commonly 6/8, its leisurely tempo and characteristic lilting rhythm gave it the character of a slow jig and it was associated with the *pastoral and the melancholy. *W.A. Mozart immortalized it in his use of it in minor

keys, as in the distraught F minor Adagio of the piano sonata in F major, K280 (189e), the beautiful slow movement of the A major piano concerto K488 and, above all, the magnificent Rondo in A minor K511.

Further reading
M. Little and C. Marsh, *La Danse noble: an Inventory of Dances and Sources* (Williamstown, MA, 1992).

Silbermann
German family of instrument-makers, especially organs.

Silbermann, Gottfried
German instrument-maker (b. 14 Jan 1683, Kleinbobritzsch; d. 4 Aug 1753, Dresden.)

Apprenticed, probably to a joiner, he went to Strasbourg in 1701, joining his elder brother to learn organ building. He made some first-class organs in Strasbourg and in France and settled in Freiberg in 1711. His work was admired by *J.S. Bach and J.L. Krebs.

He also built *pantaleons, including most of *Hebenstreit's, and much sought-after clavichords – one was *C.P.E. Bach's inseparable companion for half a century – as well as pianos, including those for *Frederick the Great – two of which survive – which J.S. Bach played and enjoyed.

Works
Some of his organs survive in Frauenstein, St Johannis's church and the Cathedral in Freiberg, the Sophienkirche and the Katholische Hofkirche in Dresden, and in St Georgen and St Marien in Rotha. A couple (possibly) of authentic clavichords survive as well as two of the pianos (c.1746) he built for *Frederick

the Great, in the *Staatliche Schlösser und Gärten Preußischer Kulturbesitz* in Potsdam.

Further reading
W. Müller, *Auf den Spuren von Gottfried Silbermann* (Kassel, 1968). M. Schaefer, 'Les anciens orgues Silbermann du Temple-Neuf à Strasbourg', in R. Minder, ed., *La musique en Alsace hier et aujourd'hui* (Strasbourg, 1970). W. Müller, *Gottfried Silbermann: Persönlichkeit und Werk* (Frankfurt, 1982). S. Pollens, 'Gottfried Silbermann's Pianos', *Organ Yearbook*, xvii (1986). Burney/ PRESENT. Boalch/HARPSICHORD. Hubbard/HARPSICHORD. *MGG*.

Sinfonia Concertante (see *symphony)

Smart, Sir **George (Thomas)**
British conductor, organist, composer (b. 10 May 1776, London; d. 23 Feb 1867, London).

He was a chorister at the Chapel Royal and studied with *Ayrton, Dupuis (organ) and Arnold (composition) after which he was organist at St James's Chapel and a violinist in *Salomon's orchestra, meeting *J. Haydn in the process. He also taught harpsichord and singing and was knighted by the Lord Lieutenant of Ireland for his services to concert life in Dublin. A founder-member of the *Philharmonic Society, he conducted – in the contemporary sense of 'presiding at the pianoforte' – the Lenten oratorio concerts annually for the next twelve years and the enterprizing City Amateur Concerts (which included *W.A. Mozart's piano concertos, *Beethoven's symphonies and newer music), as well as, of course, the Philharmonic Concerts themselves – including the British premiere of Beethoven's Ninth Symphony in 1826 –

for thirty-one years; he was also organist of the Chapel Royal.

Smart toured Europe in 1825 making copious notes and visiting Beethoven and *C.M. von Weber in Vienna; the latter died in Smart's house during his London visit a year later. He also introduced *Felix Mendelssohn's oratorio *St Paul to the British and saw to the musical arrangements for Queen Victoria's coronation; he was appointed one of the composers to the Royal Chapel.

Works
Include anthems, Kyries, glees and psalm tunes and he edited some music. His annotated concert-programmes, giving an inside view of their organization etc., are in the British Library.

Further reading
H.B. and C.L.E. Cox, *Leaves from the Journals of Sir George Smart* (London, 1907). A.H. King, 'The Importance of Sir George Smart', *MT*, xci (1950). C. Ehrlich, *First Philharmonic: A History of the Royal Philharmonic Society* (Oxford, 1995).

Sol-fa (see *Tonic Sol-fa)

Solfège (Fr.)**;** *solfeggio* (It.)
A system of vocal training popular in European conservatories (especially France and Italy) and schools, by which notes are sung to particular vowels or syllables; a more systematized example of this is *tonic sol-fa. *Solfège/solfeggio* is at the same time a basic technique for vocal training and an aid to sight-singing in helping the practitioner to recognize certain notes and intervals.

Solfeggio (see *Solfège*)

Sonata

A musical genre used to describe a multi-movement work for one or two instruments. Its meaning has changed since its first use in the *Baroque period up to the present and much of this history is beyond the scope of this book. To summarize, the term, which is the Italian for 'sounded', was used to distinguish it from the *cantata* or sung piece. Arcangelo Corell established the typical Baroque layout of movements in the sonata as being four, in the order slow—fast—slow—fast and at the end of the period it had largely become a three-part shape of fast—slow—fast. There was also the Baroque **trio-sonata** in which two principal instruments were accompanied by a *continuo part made up of a keyboard instrument and a bass string instrument.

The fast—slow—fast shape remained more-or-less constant in the ensuing *Classical period, although many of *J. Haydn's keyboard sonatas before his late works have two movements: a fast movement followed by a *minuet or a set of variations. *Beethoven's first piano sonatas had four movements (fast—slow—fast (minuet or scherzo)—fast) but this was not a reversion to Baroque practice, rather a proclamation that he considered the piano sonata to be capable of aspiring to the level of the *string quartet or the *symphony, both of which had this four-movement shape.

In the Baroque **duo-sonata** (for keyboard and a melody instrument) the participants had equal footing (facilitated by the largely *contrapuntal style) but in the early Classical era the vogue was for keyboard sonatas 'with the accompaniment of … (violin, flute etc.)' where, on occasion, the accompanying instrument's part was so incidental that it actually didn't have one, playing instead from the keyboard part and reading over the keyboardist's shoulder. It is a measure of the progression of the medium and the period that, by its end, equality between the instruments was restored. The first movement of a sonata in the Classical period was usually in *sonata form.

Sonata-allegro

The name given to the first movement of the *Classical sonata, which was fast (and usually in *sonata form). It is also used for the body of such a movement if there is a slow introduction.

Sonata Form

A musical structure used in movements of the *Classical and, to a great extent, *Romantic periods, which can be present in several forms. Its popularity as structure for the opening movement gave it the name 'first-movement form', but although this is largely true in practice, it is misleading.

(1) The *basic principle* is an amalgamation of the *Baroque and early *Classical *binary and *ternary forms, giving a tripartite structure dependent on melodic cohesion and key-underlay, as schematized very broadly in Figure 1.

The basic principle here is a harmonic one in which a key (the tonic) is established (in the First *Subject) and then temporarily replaced by another closely-related key – the shift being facilitated usually by a transition (or 'bridge') passage – in the Second Subject, which, with the Codetta, established the new key. The Development section has no specified plan, its function being simply to erode the new key by various modulations and other devices in which melodic material associated with each key-centre is tossed around until any association remaining

Section	Exposition				Development	Reprise			
Melody	1st subject	Trans- ition	2nd subject	Codetta		1st sub	Tr	2nd sub	Codetta
Harmony (maj key)	I_____	..............V_____		‖ ?	.... I__	..... I _____			‖
		(modul- ating)							
Harmony (min key)	i_____	..............III_____		‖ ?	.... i___	..... i _____			‖
		(modul- ating)							

Figure 1   Sonata Form, basic principle

is nullified. The Reprise restates all or most of the Exposition's material (with occasional variation or adaptation because of the lack of need for strong modulation) but now in the home key, in which the movement ends.

For most of the Classical period the exposition section is repeated fully (with suitable alternative links back to the beginning or forward to the Development) and so is the Development plus Reprise (also called Recapitulation) unit, again with alternative links if necessary. This repeat tended to fall out of use in the later Classical period and the Exposition repeat soon after.

(2) *Modifications* to the basic outline are (a) the addition of a slow introduction (which is hardly ever included in the repeat, being heard only once) and (b) of a Coda at the end which, again is not played until after the Development–Reprise repeat, when present; (c) in examples of sonata form after the Classical period – and occasionally in that period also – the subjects are multiple, i.e. there are several themes making up one or other (or both) of the subjects; in this case they are called 'subject groups'.

(3) Occasionally the term '*monothematic sonata form*' is encountered. This is extremely misleading as it does not mean that there is only one subject, but that the same theme or melodic material is used for both subjects (in their appropriate keys).

(4) So attractive was the basic principle, allowing for a satisfying excursion-and-return principle and allowing for longer and more varied movements than hitherto, that it was modified in several ways, such as *Slow-movement Sonata Form* in which the Development section is omitted, necessitating some compromises in the remaining sections, especially as the rigour of a full sonata form would have been felt to be inappropriate in a more 'relaxing' lyrical slow movement.

(5) The amalgamation of sonata form and *rondo form – Sonata-Rondo Form – was very popular, especially for finales. In this case the A and B sections of the rondo coincided with the first and second subjects of the sonata form and the rondo's C was a theme incorporated into the sonata form's Development section – and many *bona-fide* sonata-form

Development sections did have a 'new' theme in them. The sonata's Reprise mapped into the remaining A—B—A of the rondo in similar fashion.

(6) In the Classical and early *Romantic *concerto, the *tutti was followed by the soloist with the same or very similar material. It would clearly be inappropriate and anticlimactic to repeat the whole section as in the basic sonata form, so a kind of '*double-exposition*' was used, with, instead of a literal repeat, the soloist's material fulfilling that function. The other adjustments necessary (usually on the harmonic level) were tackled in different ways by different composers, some reserving the modulation out of the tonic for the soloist's exposition, some not.

Song cycle (Ger. *Liederkreis, Liederzyklus*)

Dating from the early nineteenth century, a group of songs for solo (or, more rarely, ensemble) voice(s) written to be performed as a group usually with instrumental accompaniment. It may be based on an extant poem cycle, but may be settings of poems chosen by the composer from a particular work of a particular poet, from various works of a particular poet, or from diverse poets. In all these cases the cycle is usually unified by a common poetic or musical idea, subject or mood. Examples are *Schubert's *Winterreise* (D911, 1827) and *Die schöne Müllerin* (D795, 1823), *Beethoven's *An die ferne Geleibte* (1816), *Schumann's *Frauenliebe und -leben* (1840), Schoenberg's *Pierrot lunaire* (1912) and Boulez's *Pli selon pli* (1957–62).

Further reading
D.L. Earl, *The Solo Song Cycle in Germany, 1800–1850* (diss., Indiana U.,

1952). W.D. Buckley, *The Solo Song Cycle: an Annotated Bibliography of Selected Published Editions, with an Historical Survey* (diss., U. of Iowa, 1965). R.O. Bingham, *The Song Cycle in German-Speaking Countries, 1790– 1840: Approaches to a Changing Genre* (diss., Cornell U., 1993).

Song-dance
A dance, the music of which is also a song which is sung while dancing it.

Song(s) Without Words (Ger. *Lied(er) ohne Worte*; Fr. *chanson*; *chant/romance sans paroles*)

A short lyrical piece, in practice, almost entirely confined to solo piano. It was invented by *Felix Mendelssohn as a title for his six groups of six pieces published between 1830 and 1845, in which a more-or-less clear distinction can be heard between the melody and the accompaniment. There are occasional examples of duets (i.e. two 'singers') also. Some of *Field's *Nocturnes (which predate the Mendelssohn works) were given this title, but that may be due to the editor (*Liszt).

Sordino (pl. *sordini*) (see *Mute)

Soundboard (Fr. *table d'harmonie*; Ger. *Resonanzboden*; It. *piano armonico, tavola armonica*)

A thin sheet of wood fairly close to the strings in a keyboard instrument which amplifies their sound and helps the tone quality. The soundboard is attached to one or more of the bridges over which the strings pass thus presenting a greater vibrating surface to the air than the individual strings alone. Their making involves a high degree of art on the instrument-maker's part, in choosing, cutting and processing the wood. *W.A. Mozart, in a letter to his father, describes how his favourite piano-maker, *Stein, seasoned the wood in various ingenious ways before using it.

Southwell, William
Irish piano-, harpsichord- and harp-maker (b. 1756, ?Dublin; d. 1842, Rathmines, Dublin).

He was apprenticed to Ferdinand Weber in Dublin in 1772 and set up his own business there in 1782. He was a pioneer in piano construction, inventing and patenting many important improvements, including the extending (upwards) of the compass of the square *piano, which was universally adopted. This patent also included the novel 'Irish *damper'. Many of his ideas were to circumvent the need to breach or cut away part of the soundboard, thus compromising the instrument's tone more-or-less seriously. His instruments were also particularly beautiful although, unfortunately, very few have survived. There is one (1790) in the National Museum of Ireland, one (1798) in the City Museum in Dundee and a *demilune* (semi-oval) in the Cobbe Foundation, Hatchlands Park, Surrey.

Further reading
T. de Valera, 'Two 18th-Century Dublin Musical Instrument Makers', *Dublin Historical Record*, xxxvi/4 (1982–83). A. Cobbe, 'Beethoven, Haydn and an Irish Genius: William Southwell of Dublin', *Irish Arts Review Yearbook*, xiii (1997). Harding/PIANO-FORTE. Cole/PIANOFORTE.

Späth, Franz Jakob
German organ and piano builder (b. 1714, Regensburg; d. 23 Jul 1786, Regensburg).

Son of an organ builder, he carried on the family tradition but also built pianos, for which he is best known. His instruments were much admired by *W.A. Mozart, C.D.F. *Schubart and others. Späth is best remembered for his invention of the *tangent piano. His son-in-law joined the business about 1774 and 'Späth and Schmahl' were very successful. Their pianos survive in several German collections.

Further reading
H. Herrmann, *Die Regensburger Klavierbauer Späth und Schmahl und ihr Tangentenflügel* (Erlangen, 1928). Harding/PIANO-FORTE. Boalch/HARP-SICHORD.

Sperl
Viennese dance-hall and beer-garden, built in 1807.

Spinner (Ger.: 'spinning-dance')
One of several Austrian popular – originally *folk – dances grouped together under the heading of *Deutscher* ('German dances') which were the forerunners of the *waltz. Like it, they were usually in triple time and moderately fast to fast in *tempo. Also like the waltz, they were couple dances danced for much of the time in close embrace.

Spohr, Louis [Ludewig, Ludwig]
German composer, violinist, conductor (b. 5 Apr 1784, Brunswick; d. 22 Oct 1859, Kassel).

Born into a musical family and showing talent at an early age, one of the local music-teachers arranged for him to go to Brunswick to further his training. He studied violin and theory and took part in concerts, occasionally playing his own works. A failed tour in 1799 resulted in his petitioning the Duke of Brunswick for financial assistance and he was so taken with the fifteen-year-old that he appointed him as a chamber musician. His exposure to opera caused him to revere *W.A. Mozart for the rest of his life. He then studied with Franz Eck, a violinist of the Mannheim School, and he copied the style of the French violinist Rode, whom he heard in Brunswick shortly after. His own debut was highly acclaimed and several tours followed; he accepted the post of *Konzertmeister* to the Gotha court. His seven years there (1805–12) were to provide him with a solid practical musical grounding and he was something of a pioneer in his use of the baton for conducting. He married a harpist and composed solo and joint works for their tours, of which there were many. His tours were punctuated by a couple of settled periods, as orchestra director at Vienna's Theater an der Wien (1813–15) and at Frankfurt am Main (1817) from which he resigned after two years because of disagreements with the shareholders. In early 1822 he accepted the post of *Kapellmeister* at Kassel, which C.M. von Weber had declined, suggesting Spohr, and he received a lifetime appointment. This was a good move: the new Elector, Wilhelm II wished to make the theatre an important national institution, subsidizing it generously and Spohr also had time and leave to tour and a say in programming.

After 1830 he suffered some setbacks, personal – his wife died – and professional, as political unrest caused the closure of the Opera and its reopening a year later on a subsidy which was almost halved; there were also differences of opinion with the future Elector who was co-regent, although these did not sour a relationship based on mutual respect.

Many honours were bestowed on him: memberships of important societies, both within and without Germany, and several university doctorates. He became very popular in Britain also. Toward the end of his life, his compositional output waned and he was buried with public mourning in Kassel cemetery.

As a virtuoso-composer from his period, Spohr's works are, for the most part, very good but typical examples of their era. He inherited a strong strain of chromaticism from *Cherubini which he refined and passed on to Wagner. His music is well-crafted and he excelled in violinstic lyricism, usually of a melancholic sort. His string quartets tend to favour the first violin, sometimes being miniature concertos; this was the result of the movement of the genre from the private to the public domain.

Works

Several operas and *Singspiel*s including *Faust* (1813) an *Zemir und Azor* (1818-9) and *Jessonda* (1823). Orchestral works include 10 symphonies, three of which are programmatic, overtures and dances, 15 violin concertos, no. 8 of which is subtitled 'in modo di scena cantante' ('in the style of a vocal scena'), four clarinet concertos (all except one in minor keys) and some double concertos. There are 36 string quartets and works for larger ensembles, such as the four double quartets, nonet, octet, sextet and eight quintets and, including piano, a Septet in A minor (flute, clarinet, horn, bassoon, violin and cello and piano), a Quintet for piano and winds and five piano trios. There are also some works with harp and solo works which include a Piano Sonata in A♭ major op. 125 (1843) and his pedagogical *Violin-Schule* (*Violin School*, 1830–31), together with choral and other vocal works.

Further reading

H. Heissner, 'Spohr der Künstler und seine Welt', *Hessische Heimat*, ix (1959–60). H. Homburg, 'Louis Spohr und die Bach-Renaissance', *Bach-Jahrbuch*, xlvii (1960); *Louis Spohr: Bilder und Dokumente seiner Zeit* (Kassel, 1968). M.F. Powell, 'Louis Spohr: a Retrospect of the Bicentenary', *MT*, cxxvi (1985). H. Peters, *Der Komponist, Geiger, Dirigent und Pädagoge Louis Spohr (1784–1859)* (Brunswick, 1987). *MGG.*

Square piano (see *Piano (3))

'S.R.D.' The abbreviated form of *Serenissimus Rudolphus Dux*, official title of The *Archduke Rudolph of Austria.

Stamitz [Stamic]
A family of Bohemian musicians who settled in Mannheim. **Johann (Wenzel Anton)** [Jan Waczlaw (Václav) Antonin (Antonín)]] was appointed to the Mannheim court *c.* 1741 and was *Konzertmeister* within four or five years. His duties were to compose orchestral and chamber (and possibly sacred) music and to lead the court orchestra, which he rapidly developed into the finest in Europe (see *Mannheim orchestra). His marriage produced children who were to continue his good work and become fine composers in their own right, particularly Carl and Anton Stamitz.

Staufer, J.G.
Inventor of the *arpeggione.

Steibelt, Daniel
German (French naturalized) composer, pianist (b. 22 Oct 1765, Berlin; d. 20 Sep/2 Oct 1823, St Petersburg).
    Son of a keyboard-instrument-maker, the crown prince (later Frederick Wilhelm II of Prussia) took an interest in him and sent him for lessons with Kirnberger. After publishing some songs at the age of 17, he joined the Prussian army, but deserted and fled Germany, travelling around for the following three years. He played in Saxony and Hanover in 1789 and the following year settled in Paris, having already gained a reputation there. On the rejection of his opera *Roméo et Juliette* by the Opéra, the piece was altered and provided with spoken dialogue, and enjoyed great success at the Théâtre Feydeau in 1793.
    A visit to London, where he appeared in the *Salomon concerts was very successful and his Third Concerto (which included a depiction of a musical storm) was very well received, among other works; he became a devotee of the *British piano and married an Englishwoman. After being officially pardoned for his military desertion, he was able to tour Germany and Austria, but a musical contest with *Beethoven affected his Viennese popularity. Back in Paris, he performed *J. Haydn's *The Creation* before Napoleon in 1800. Much of his piano music was composed in the first six years of the new century, but he was forced to flee Paris because of debts in 1808 and took up an appointment in St Petersburg as director of the French Opera and in 1810 was appointed *maître de chapelle* to the emperor after *Boieldieu's departure. Steibelt taught and wrote for the piano and got to know *Field, who became a generous friend. In 1820 he appeared in public, after an absence of six years, as soloist in his Eighth Concerto (with choral finale). He died after a long and painful illness and his family, who had been left fairly badly-off, were helped by benefit concerts.
    This may have been partly due to his endemic extravagance and vanity; he

also seems to have had a strong strain of dishonesty, often faking old works as new. His brilliant playing has often been remarked upon although the charge of superficiality runs through many reports and he seemed to be lacking in his left-hand technique. His music has not worn well, though the concertos are good examples of their kind and his operas well worth reviving.

Works
Stage works include the operas *Roméo et Juliette* (perf. 1793), *La princesse de Babylone* (*c.*1812, unpub.) and the ballets *Le retour de Zéphire* (perf. 1802) and *Le jugement de berger* (perf. London 1804). There are eight piano concertos including no. 3 in E major op. 33 ('L'Orage', 1799) and no. 5 in E♭ major op. 64 ('A la chasse', 1802), and some 180 piano sonatas for or including piano as well as dances, variations, fantasias, etc. for solo piano.

Further reading
G. Müller, *Daniel Steibelt: sein Leben und seine Klavierwerke* (Strasbourg, 1933, R/1973). K.A. Hagberg, *Cendrillon by Daniel Steibelt: a Critical Edition with Notes on Steibelt's Life and Operas* (diss., Eastman School of Music, 1976).

Stein, Johann (Georg) Andreas
German keyboard-instrument-maker (b. 6 May 1728, Heidelsheim; d. 29 Feb 1792, Augsburg).

He was trained by his father, an organ builder, and undertook his itinerant apprenticeship, first with a member of the *Silbermann family in Strasbourg (1748–49), then with *Späth in Regensburg (1749–50), and finally he settled in Augsburg, where the city's only organ builder had just died. Having built the organ for the Barfüsserkirche, he

was appointed organist there and, after a visit to Strasbourg and Paris, he married a local girl in Augsburg in 1760; *W.A. Mozart, on a visit, bought one of his portable *pianos.

Stein invented various *combination instruments (including a harpsichord/piano/organ), which cut little ice in the German-speaking lands, but took the French court by storm. He trained his own children (also as performers) – his daughter Nanette was a child prodigy – and they continued the business. Mozart was a great admirer of the pianos of both Stein generations and a letter of his gives some interesting details of their methods. One of Stein's most important inventions was a mechanism which prevented the hammers from jamming against the strings, which could be a problem in certain cases. Thirteen of his 'normal' pianos survive, including those in Nuremberg, Augsburg, Stuttgart, Leipzig and Munich.

Further reading
F.J. Hirt, *Meisterwerke des Klavierbaues* (Olten, 1955). A. Huber, 'Der Österreichische Klavierbau im 18. Jahrhundert', in G. Stradner, ed., *Klagwelt Mozarts* (Vienna, 1991). R. Maunder, 'Mozart's Keyboard Instruments', *Early Music*, xxi (1993). M.R. Latcham, 'The Pianos of Johann Andreas Stein', *Zur Geschichte des Hammerklaviers: Blankenburg, Harz, 1993*; reprinted in *Galpin Society Journal*, li (1998); *The Stringing, Scaling and Pitch of 'Hammerflügel' built in the Southern German and Viennese traditions, 1780–1820* (Munich, 2000).

Steinway
Firm of American piano makers (1853–present), founded by Heinrich Engelhard Steinway (Steinweg) (1797–1871) three

years after his emigration to New York in 1850. He exhibited and won great acclaim for a *cast-iron-framed overstrung (see *overstringing) *square piano (a type very popular there) and his application of these principles to the upright and, especially the grand made him the leading American maker. He was joined by his eldest son, C.F. Theodor Steinweg (1825–89) in about 1865.

Step
A musical interval of either a tone or a semitone.

Štěpán (Steffan/Stephan, Joseph Anton; Steffani Stephani, Giuseppe Antonio), **Josef Antonín**
Czech keyboard player, composer, teacher (bap. 14 Mar 1726, Kopidlno, Bohemia; d. 12 Apr 1797, Vienna).

Probably first taught by his father, an organist and schoolmaster, the child ran from the invading Prussians to Vienna, where he was patronized by a lord and learnt violin from his *Kapellmeister, eventually succeeding him. He also learnt harpsichord and composition from Wagenseil and soon achieved a good reputation as a composer, player and teacher in the city. In 1766 he was appointed *Klaviermeister* to the two royal princesses, one of whom – Maria Antonia – would become Queen of France. Although temporary blindness caused his resignation, he kept his salary and was in great demand in the best of the *salons* and continued to compose, although he died from a stroke, in obscurity.

Štěpán is an important forerunner not only of *Classicism but, it could be said, of *Romanticism also. His music is often strikingly original and includes programmatic and improvisational elements, without seriously compromising his structures, which are often quite individual. A devotee of the piano as opposed to the harpsichord in his mature years, his later piano concertos are of unusual layout, in their slow-movement minor-key introductions which include the soloist and in his view of the finale as being as weighty as the opening allegro, a feature which also applied to his sonatas.

Works
Some 45 concertos (including a small number of lost works) most of them for piano or harpsichord and many sonatas and smaller pieces for keyboard as well as sacred pieces and songs.

Further reading
D. Šetková, *Klavírní dílo Josefa Antonína Štěpána* [The Keyboard Works of Josef Antonín Štěpán] (Prague, 1965). M. Fillion, *The Accompanied Keyboard Divertimenti of Haydn and his Viennese Contemporaries (c.1750–1780)* (diss., Cornell U., 1892). H.J. Picton, *The Life and Works of Joseoh Anton Steffan (1726–1797) with Special Reference to his Keyboard Concertos* (New York, 1989). Fétis/*BIOGRAPHIE*. MGG. Newman/SCE.

Stevenson, Sir **John (Andrew)**
Irish composer (b. Nov 1971, Dublin; d. 14 Sep 1833, Kells, Co. Meath).

Son of a violinist in the State Band in Dublin, he was a chorister of Christ Church Cathedral and then in the choir of St Patrick's Cathedral for five years from 1775. An honorary MusD from Dublin was conferred on him in 1791, he was knighted in 1803 and appointed organist and music director at the Castle Chapel a year later. Although he composed music for the Dublin and London stages and many other works, he is best remembered for his 'symphonies' (i.e. piano introductions and accompaniments) to *Moore's Melodies.

Works
Comic and serious operas and many vocal works (canzonets, glees, etc.).

Further reading
J.S. Bumpus, *Sir John Stevenson: a Biographical Sketch* (London, 1893). T.J. Walsh, *Opera in Dublin, 1798–1820: Frederick Jones and the Crow Street Theatre* (Oxford, 1993).

Stodart
British firm of piano-makers.

Stodart, Robert
British piano-maker (bap. 19 Jul 1748, Walston, Lanarkshire; d. 10 Mar 1831, Edinburgh).

An engineer's apprentice in Dalkieth, he was then an apprentice to John *Broadwood in London and was involved with him and with *Backers in the construction of grand pianos. He invented a *combination piano/harpsichord in 1777 and his son, William, was a partner from the last decade of the eighteenth century. William set up in business on his own from about 1816. Two of his staff, Thom and Allen, invented the *'compensation frame' in 1820, which was made from tubular metal – an improvement on similar bracing – and it allowed for heavier strings to be used at higher tension, thus giving a stronger and fuller sound. When William's son Malcolm joined the firm c.1825 the firm was called William Stodart & Son, which closed in 1861.

Further reading
Boalch/HARPSICHORD.
Cole/PIANOFORTE.
Harding/PIANO-FORTE.

Stop
A lever operated by the hand whose function, in the case of musical instruments, is to modify the sound. On keyboard instruments it fulfils many of those functions which were previously assigned to *genouillères (knee-levers). They are mostly in the form of drawstops (that is, pulled and pushed to activate their mechanisms) although this term is usually reserved for the stops on the *organ.

The principal stops in the period 1760–1850 were:

(1) The *damper stop* ('loud', *'forte'*, *grande jeu*, *Fortezug*) raises the dampers from the strings, allowing them to vibrate freely when the key(s) is/are no longer depressed thus sustaining the sound until it dies or is dampened. It could also be used to create a 'halo' of sound (the effect asked for by, for example, *Beethoven in the reprise of the first movement of his piano sonata in D minor op. 31/2). In some pianos, this stop could be duplicated, so that the dampers affecting the left and the right halves of the keyboard could be treated separately.

(2) The *una corda [stop]* (shift, *eine Saite*, *verschiebung*) shifted the piano's action from where the hammers struck the full complement of (usually) three strings, so that they struck only one, thus reducing the volume and the richness of sound.

(3) The *moderator stop* (buff stop, moderator, *piano*, *pianissimo*, *Jeu Céleste*, *Jeu de buffe* or *Pianozug*) was another device for softening the sound and called for strips of soft leather or cloth to be applied between hammers and strings thus muffling the sound. Some

instruments had two such stops with different degrees of muffling.

(4) The *piano stop* (*jeu céleste*, *céleste*, *jeu de buffes*, buff, muffle, *Pianozug*, *flauto*) allowed the action to be moved closer to the strings so that the hammers had less distance to travel and produced a softer sound; thus the tone was not significantly altered.

(5) The *lute stop* (*sourdine*, *jeu de luth*, *jeu de harpe*, *Laute*, *sordino*) causes a strip of felt or other soft material to be placed in contact with the strings to give an ethereal sound like a lute. On the *harpsichord it refers to a set of *jacks which pluck the string near its end, giving a more genuinely lute-like sound.

(6) The *bassoon stop* (*basson*, *Fagott*) causes a strip of parchment or other medium-soft material to come into contact with the strings to give a buzzing sound associated with a bassoon. It is often found as part of *Turkish Music applied to the piano.

(7) *Turkish Music stop(s)* can occasionally be found comprising one or more of the following functions: bassoon stop (as just described); to control a drumstick (*tambour guerrier*, *Schlagzug*, *Bodenschlag*); 'triangle' (which could be a single bell, or three separate bells) and 'cymbals' (two or three strips of brass which are knocked against the bass strings). The 'drum' was usually the piano's soundboard which was hit by the felted drumstick, but there were cases of drumheads, or even real drums, being added.

(8) The *coupler stop* (which fulfilled a variety of functions, principally as the octave coupler, common on the harpsichord which was also applied to some pianos. By its agency, registers of strings an octave apart (above or below) could be coupled together so that they could be played by the same key simultaneously. It also activated and deactivated the 'extra' instrument in the case of *combination instruments (piano-harpsichord or piano-organ, for instance).

(9) There are other stops which are much more specialized, either because they are rare or because they apply only to particular instruments; for example, that for '*harmonic sounds*' by which a set of hammers or a bar touches the strings in the middle (or occasionally elsewhere) to create harmonics, giving the illusion of an echo; the *dolce compana*, by which the soundboard is alternately slightly pressured and released (sometimes through the bridge) so that a kind of vibrato is produced, in *combination instruments involving an organ.

(10) It was possible to have combinations of stops and pedals, either duplicating functions or adding to them. The device which operates several pedals or stops is called a *machine stop*, even though it may be activated by a pedal.

Strauss, Johann (Baptist) (I, or 'the Elder')
Austrian composer, conductor (b. 14 Mar 1804, Vienna; d. 25 Sep 1849, Vienna).

Son of an innkeeper, the family lived in Leopoldstadt and the boy was taught the violin and musical theory (by Ignaz von *Seyfried) and played in the dance orchestra of Michael Pamer, who was popularizing the *waltz. He became friendly with another player in the orchestra, Josef *Lanner and joined the latter's own dance-band in 1819. When this grew into a full orchestra, Lanner divided it (1824) and Strauss became second conductor.

However, after his marriage a year later Strauss split with Lanner and founded his own orchestra for which he composed his own waltzes, becoming very popular. His first real 'break' came with his engagement at the well-known *Sperl with its beer-garden and dance-hall at which Pamer was music-director. It was very popular with visitors from all parts of Europe and *Chopin and Wagner, among others, visited it and expressed their admiration for Strauss's music. As well as dances, Strauss introduced paraphrases of symphonic and other non-dance music to the audiences and he also included references to this music in his various dances, waltzes, cotillons (see *Contredanse). From 1833 he began to take his orchestra on European tours, being wildly acclaimed in all the major cities, winning the respect of art-musicians such as *Berlioz. On his return to Vienna he introduced the *quadrille which became very fashionable.

His first visit to Britain in 1838 – during which he and his orchestra were showered with praise – coincided with the coronation of Queen Victoria and his waltz dedicated to her (opp. 102 and 103 (1838)) was performed at Buckingham Palace and resulted in many engagements in other cities and stately homes throughout Britain. He died of scarlet fever, caught from one of his children, at the age of 45.

Works
Hundreds of *waltzes and *cotillons arranged in sets, many named after the establishments for which they were composed, as well as *galops, *quadrilles and marches (including the *Radetzky-Marsch*, associated with the might of the Habsburgs).

Further reading
M. Carner, *The Waltz* (London, 1948). H. Fantel, *Johann Strauss, Father and Son, and their Era* (Newton Abbott, 1971). J. Wechsberg, *The Waltz Emperors* (London, 1973).

Streicher
Austrian firm of piano-makers.

Streicher [Stein], **Nanette** (Maria Anna) Austrian piano-maker; daughter of J.A. *Stein (b. 2 Jan 1769, Augsburg; d. 16 Jan 1833, Vienna).

She was a child prodigy as a pianist and was taught by her father in this as well as in piano making and the business went so well that her husband, the composer and pianist J.A. Streicher, became her partner. She began to build pianos on her own account and the Stein firm (her brothers) moved to Vienna. Their instruments were admired as the best in Vienna, and they enjoyed the friendship of *C.M. von Weber, *Hummel – for whom they made a special *down-striking piano – and *Beethoven. The firm became 'Nanette Streicher geb, Stein und Sohn' when their son Johann Baptist Streicher (b. 3 Jan 1796, Vienna; d. 28 Mar 1871, Vienna) joined as a partner in 1823. They preferred the *'Viennese' Piano action to the *British and gave such an instrument to *Brahms in 1868, which he used throughout his composing life. J.B. Streicher's son (1836–1916) became a partner in 1857 and the firm ceased after his retirement.

Further reading
R.A. Fuller, 'Andreas Streicher's Notes on the Fortepiano', *Early Music*, xii (1984). Harding/PIANO-FORTE. Cole/PIANOFORTE.

Striking-place
The point at which a string on a piano is struck by the hammer. Within certain limitations, the striking-place affects the tone.

Strophic
A technique in vocal composition in which all the stanzas of a poem are set to the same music (excluding minor alterations to accommodate changes in prosody). It is seen as the opposite of through-composed (see *Durchkomponirt), in which each stanza is supplied with different music. Most *folk songs and ballads are strophic.

Studio per il pianoforte
Title of a piano *method by J.B. *Cramer; the revised edition was called the *New Studio* (1835).

Study (Fr. *étude*; Ger. *Etüde, Studie*; It. *studio*)
A piece of music designed for the perfection of some aspect of vocal or, in the vast majority of cases, instrumental technique. It should be distinguishable from the *exercise – a simple practice-piece which is usually and deliberately repetitious – in that it possesses some musical value, although the quality is variable. It came into its own with the ascendancy of the piano in the later eighteenth and the first half of the nineteenth centuries and many of the pianist-composers wrote sets of them: *J.B. Cramer, *Czerny, *Moscheles, *Hummel, *R. Schumann, *Chopin and

*Liszt in particular. Many of these used the French word '*Etude*' as a generic (or alternative) title, and it remained attached to, and was suggestive of, the more musical type of study such as Chopin's three sets (12 each of opp. 10 and 25 and the *Trois nouvelles études*).

Sturm und Drang (Ger.: 'storm and stress')
The phrase, from the title of a play by Maximilian Klinger (1776), is used to refer to a literary style in the German-speaking lands during the 1770s and 1780s which affected the other arts, including music. Its characteristics are the use of surprising, highly-charged or shocking images and the *sublime, and the emphasis is on the subjective and anti-rational often in extreme manifestations. It was a result of the Hamann-*Rousseau belief in the power of civilization to restrict and thwart the natural in humankind. The first real manifestation was in Goethe's play *Goetz von Berlichingen* (1773). In painting the subjects were often set in extreme natural locations or conditions – wild craggy Alpine (or 'primitive') scenery, storms on land or sea – and included shipwrecks and battles and are suffused with terror; there was a kinship with the slightly earlier Gothic movement which overlapped it.

Sturm und Drang's musical manifestations included the use of jagged themes, minor keys and bold harmonic juxtapositions (often involving chromatic harmony), vivid orchestration and use of extreme ranges or tessituras as well as agitated syncopated accompaniments. Good examples may be found in *J. Haydn's symphonies of the 1770s and *W.A. Mozart's early G minor Symphony, no. 25 K183 (173*d*/B, 1773).

Further reading

R. Pascal, *The German Sturm und Drang* (Manchester, 1953). H.C.R. Landon, 'La crise romantique dans la musique autrichienne vers 1770; quelques précurseurs inconnus de la Symphonie en sol mineur (KV 183) de Mozart', *Les influences étrangères dans l'œuvre de Mozart* (Paris, 1956). B.S. Brook, 'Sturm und Drang and the Romantic Period in Music', *Gesellschaft für Musikforschung Kongressbericht* (Bonn, 1970). E. Loewenthal, ed., *Sturm und Drang: kritische Schriften* (Heidelberg, 1972). A. Huyssen, *Drama des Sturm und Drang: Kommentar zu eine Epoche* (Munich, 1980). B. Plachta and W. Winfried, eds, *Sturm und Drang: Geistiger Aufbruch 1770–1790 im Spiegel der Literatur* (Tübingen, 1997).

Style brisé (Fr.: 'broken style')

(1) A technique used by Renaissance and *Baroque lutenists by which a melody becomes integrated with an arpeggiaic accompaniment and/or is spread between different strings and parts.

(2) A term used to describe the appliance of a similar technique to keyboard instruments, using different registers and dividing material arpeggiaically between the hands.

Style galant (Fr.: 'gallant or galant style'; Ger. *galanter Stil*; It. *stile galante*)

An eighteenth-century style, especially in music, whose aim is to be pleasant and untaxing. In music it is associated with melodies of even, two-plus-two, or four-plus-four bars of phrasing, easy melodies and an unobtrusive accompaniment involving largely *diatonic harmonies.

Styria (see *Savoy)

Subject

A term used in certain musical forms to refer to the principal items or groups of melodic material, which may range from a few notes to a full-blown melody. Implicit in the use of the term – as opposed to, say, 'theme' – is that the material will be developed or altered in the course of the piece, movement or section. Thus, the main melodic material of, for example, *sonata form, *fugue, etc., is called the subject.

Sublime

In the eighteenth and nineteenth centuries, a sense of the sublime was the feeling of awe felt in the presence, or, by implication, the contemplation of, the extremes in nature which threatened to engulf or overpower, most commonly the wildernesses and high mountains – the Alps, Scotland – but also the sea, caverns and dungeons. In the last, there is an overlap with the Gothic and awe of the sublime is often referred to in novels belonging to that movement. This awe is often soon accompanied by feelings of transport or rapture and subsides to feelings of reverence and respect and a sense of cleansing, possibly akin to religious salvation or the promise of it.

In Edmund Burke's enormously influential *Enquiry into the ... Sublime and the Beautiful* (see below for full title), he talks of the sublime exciting 'ideas of pain and danger' and that its 'ruling principle' is 'terror' and threat to self-preservation. In a rather unfortunate gender-appropriation, he sees the sublime as a rough male preserve, and contrasts it with the beautiful, which he sees soft, round, vulnerable, bright and feminine. For the *Romantics, the sublime was associated with the power of the imagination, as opposed to the more plodding reason, the soul as opposed to the body, nature as opposed to ordered society; the high point (literally) in the Grand Tour was the crossing and contemplation of the Alps.

In art, the sublime can be seen in the paintings of Fuseli, Barry, J. Casper David and Turner, in literature in the Gothic novels, the Ossianic poetry of Macpherson and the works of Young, James Thomson, Wordsworth, Byron and Shelley and in music in the symphonies of *Beethoven.

Further reading
E. Burke, *An Enquiry into the Origin of our Ideas of the Sublime and the Beautiful* (London, 1757, R/1990 Oxford). T. Weiskel, *The Romantic Sublime: Studies in the Structure and Psychology of Transcendence* (Baltimore, MD, 1976, R/1986). P. De Bolla, *The Discourse of the Sublime: Readings in History, Aesthetics, and the Subject* (Oxford, 1989). F. Ferguson, *Solitude and the Sublime: Romanticism and the Aesthetics of Individuation* (New York, 1992). B.C. Freeman, *The Feminine Sublime: Gender and Excess in Women's Fiction* (Los Angeles, CA, 1995).

Subscription [series/concert(s)]
(1) *Published works* A method of limiting losses usually perpetrated by the composer him/herself, by which an intended series of musical pieces or other musical work was notified to enthusiasts (usually known to the composer) in advance of engraving, publication and so on, and who would commit themselves to purchase the work(s) when eventually published. *W.A. Mozart used this method – to his occasional disappointment – and *Hummel's Pianoforte School was also advertised in this way.

(2) *Concerts* A more-or-less public concert or (more often) concert-series in which possible patrons were circulated in advance and requested to commit themselves to attendance with advance payment. They were a regular feature of private or semi-private concert-giving associations such as the *Philharmonic Society in London.

Suite (Fr. ['succession'], *ordre*; Ger. *Partita, Partie*; It. *partita*)
(1) Any series of linked pieces of music intended to be played as a unit.

(2) A group of pieces taken from a larger work for separate performance, as in Bizet's *L'Arlésienne Suite* (from his incidental music to the play of that name) and Tchaikovsky's *Nutcracker Suite* (from his own ballet).

(3) In the *Baroque period, a set of instrumental (often keyboard) pieces in the same key, many of which were dance-types (whether so-titled or not) or related to dances. The core of the suite were the four dances, *Allemande, *Courante, *Sarabande and *Gigue, but other dances (such as the Loure, *Bourrée and, very commonly, *Minuet) and non-dance pieces such as the *Prelude and *Aria or Air(e) were often found. *J.S. Bach wrote sets of French, English and German suites for keyboard (the latter called *Partitas*).

Swell
A device for gradation of sound-volume on keyboard instruments.

(1) In the organ, the 'Swell organ' is a *manual with a *rank or ranks of pipes enclosed in a box (the 'swell-box') one side of which consists of individually-hinged slats as in a Venetian blind. These

can be opened or closed (thus giving the listener the impression of increasing or decreasing volume) by raising or depressing a *pedal.

(2) In the harpsichord, a similar principle was applied, called the '*Venetian*' or '*nag's head*' swell, where the case and action were covered with hinged slats capable of being opened and closed by the release and depression of a *pedal, giving a semblance of graded dynamics.

(3) On some square pianos (and some early harpsichords), a '*lid swell*' was fitted by which the hinged lid, or a part of it, was attached to a *pedal which could be gradually opened and closed as an extra device for sound-gradation. In these cases, the tone of the instrument is also affected, becoming muffled as the lid is closed.

Symphonic poem (Fr. *Poème symphonique*; Ger. *Symphonische Dichtung*)

An orchestral piece, also called 'tone-poem', which is based on a non-musical programme, which may be literary (a poem or story), artistic (for example a painting) or a person(ality) (living, historic or mythical).

Stemming from the *Romantic period's interest in the extramusical, as shown in pieces such as operatic (later purely concert) overtures and such works as *Beethoven's 'Pastoral' Symphony (no. 6 in F op. 68, 1808), with its imitations of birdsong, and *Berlioz's *Symphonie Fantastique* (op. 14, 1830), whose subtitle, *épisode de la vie d'un artiste* ('an episode from an artist's life'), underlines its programmatic, and in this case almost autobiographical, intent.

It was *Liszt who coined the term (in German) and many of his works

have programmatic bases or content, not only shorter orchestral pieces such as *Hunnenschlacht* (describing the battle between Christians and Huns in 451) but also longer pieces such as the *Dante* and *Faust* symphonies and very many of his piano pieces as well. The symphonic poem declined in the early twentieth century when Romantic features were overtaken by others.

Symphonie fantastique

*Berlioz's own alternative title for his symphonic work *Episode de la Vie d'un Artiste*. *Symphonie fantastique et monodrame lyrique* (*Episode from the Life of an Artist*, 1830), op. 14. The symphony, in five movements, is autobiographical with a *programme, printed copies of which Berlioz asked to be distributed to the audience – or at least that the titles of the movements mentioned – whenever the piece was performed. He did add, however, that he hoped the symphony would interest on purely musical grounds. He used an *idée fixe*, a theme which recurred in various transparent guises, and the technique had a lasting effect on subsequent composers, as soon as the work began to be disseminated. The programme charts his then-unrequited love for the Irish actress, Harriet Smithson who was part of a British Shakespearian troupe visiting Paris; she is also commemorated in her frequent role of Juliet in Berlioz's own symphony *Roméo et Juliette* (1839). The five movements of the *Symphonie fantastique* are: i. Rêveries (Passions): Largo, C minor, 4/4 – Allegro agitato e appassionato assai (C major); ii. Un bal (A Ball): Valse Allegro non troppo, A major, 3/8; iii. Scène aux champs (Scenes in the Country): Adagio, F major, 6/8; iv. Marche au supplice (March to the Gallows): Allegretto non troppo, G minor, 4/4; v. Songe d'une nuit du Sabbat (Dream of a Witches' Sabbath): C major, 4/4 – Ronde du Sabbat (Witches' Round-Dance).

Symphony (from Gk. *syn* ['together'] and *phone* ['sounding'] through Lat. *symphonia*; Fr. *simphonie, symphonie*; Ger. *Sinfonie*; It. *sinfonia*)
The name given to an extended work for orchestra. In the *Classical and *Romantic periods it was the principal orchestral form and considered as the most important musical manifestation.

(1) In its early meaning in the Middle Ages and Renaissance, it denoted an instrumental ('sounded') as opposed to vocal ('*cantata*' or sung) piece and was, in the *Baroque period, applied to the instrumental introduction to, and sometimes to orchestral interludes within, an *opera, *oratorio, *cantata or *aria; the introductory piece would later be called an '*overture'.

(2) In the *Classical and *Romantic periods it acquired its generally-accepted meaning of an orchestral work in four, less commonly five, separate but related movements. The first and last movements were in the *tonic key but at least one of the internal ones was almost always in a closely related key (dominant, subdominant, submediant – occasionally flat submediant); these keys became more remote as the nineteenth century progressed. An extra introductory more-or-less short, slow, movement was frequently added, leading into the main first movement – usually an *Allegro – and any of the movement could be linked in various ways to that following.

(3) The choral symphony had an added choir, and optional soloist(s), for one or more movements.

T

Tangent

The part of a *clavichord's action which touches the string, causing it to vibrate to produce the sound. It is usually a small metal (usually brass) oblong of about a millimetre's thickness set into the *key.

Tangent piano (see *Piano (8))

Tarantella (It. also *tarandla*, *tarantela*, *tarantelle*; Fr. *tarantelle*)

A *folk dance from southern Italy whose name comes from the ancient city of Taranto (Tarantum) in Apulia. Characterized by 6/8 (or occasionally triple) time, it alternates major and minor modes and increases in speed. Melodically, it is characterized by scalic motion, use of the upper and lower *auxiliary notes and repetition of notes. It is normally a couple-dance, miming courtship, with a circle of onlookers who occasionally sing, and accompanied by tambourines and castanets. The connection with the tarantula spider, which also takes its name from Taranto, in that the dance was supposed to be a way of 'sweating' the venom from the creature's bite from the body, is coincidental; in any case the bite is only of mild toxicity. The disease of tarantism, reported in the fifteenth, sixteenth and seventeenth centuries was almost certainly hysterical. The tarantella resurfaced in art music and was popular in the nineteenth and early twentieth centuries, especially as a piano piece, with examples in the music of *Chopin (his op. 43), *Liszt (in the *Années de pèlérinage*), *Gottschalk (op. 67), *Heller (op. 85) and Rakhmaninov (op. 17).

Further reading
A.G. Bragaglia, *Danze popolare Italiane* (Rome, 1950). B. Galanti, *Dances of Italy* (New York, 1950).

Taskin, Pascal (-Joseph)

Flemish harpsichord-maker (b. 1723, Theux, nr Liège; d. 1793, Paris).

He worked in the employ of *Blanchet and took over the business when he married his widow in 1766 and became a master-builder of instruments. In 1774 he was made court instrument-maker, bringing his nephew in to help, and continued to make harpsichords with other members of his family. He was appointed as keeper of the royal instruments and also made much-admired pianos.

Further reading
J. Koster, 'Two Early French Grand Pianos', *Early Keyboard Journal*, xii (1994). Boalch/HARPSICHORD. Hubbard/HARPSICHORD. Russell/HARPSICHORD.

Temperament

The systems according to which an instrument is tuned (see *Tuning).

What follows is a broad summary of the main systems used at present and since the *Baroque period for keyboard instruments.

(1) Equal temperament is obtained when the octave is divided into twelve equal ('pure') semitones and is the modern standard; it has been used only very occasionally in the past (see *Das *Wohltempierte Clavier*) as it has been considered relatively characterless. Its advantage is that it allows for the full range of pitches to be used without distortion, thus allowing free modulation.

(2) In mean-tone temperament in which the third interval is tuned slightly sharp or flat, but divided into equal tones; this results in slightly mistuned ('sour' or 'wolf') fifths, but means that the farther one gets away from the scale (or key) in which the instrument is tuned, the more perceptive the mistunings become. This system, in which each key has its own characteristic sound, is favoured for musical periods in which remote modulation was not desirable or necessary.

Further reading
A.R. McClure, 'Studies in Keyboard Temperaments', *Galpin Society Journal*, i (1948). J.M. Barbour, *Tuning and Temperament: a Historical Survey* (East Lansing, MI, 1951, 2/1953). M. Lindley, 'Temperaments: a Brief Survey' (Oxford, 1993) [Bate Collection handbook]; and R. Turner-Smith, *Mathematical Models of Musical Scales: a New Approach* (Bonn, 1993).

'Tempest' Sonata
Title given to *Beethoven's Piano Sonata no. 17 in D minor op. 31/2. The name comes from *Schindler's request to the composer as to what the dramatic work 'meant'; he was told to 'read Shakespeare's *The Tempest*'. The sonata was written in 1802, just before his impending deafness caused him to write the 'Heiligenstadt Testament'. The movements are: i. [Introduction] Largo, D minor, 4/4 – Allegro (with modified recurrences of the introduction); ii. Adagio, B♭ major, 3/4; iii. Allegretto, D minor, 3/8, a *perpetuum mobile*.

Tempo (It.: 'time')
The speed at which a musical work is performed, and which may change many times during its course. It is specified in two ways:

(1) A more-or-less absolute method is given by counting the number of beats (or stressed notes) per minute and expressing it as an equation, thus ' ● [crotchet] = 60', means that there are sixty crotchets to a minute, i.e. each lasts one second; in compound time this would be a dotted note (appropriate to the time-signature). This is the reason for the *metronome, a mechanical, electrical or electronic device.

(2) Specifying subjectively by the use of tempo directions, traditionally in Italian but, nowadays, not necessarily so. These are formed from relative directions (*Allegro (happily, therefore fast), Adagio (slowly), Largo (slowly and broadly, Vivace (lively) etc.), and qualifiers, of which the most common are *più (more) *meno (less) *molto* (very [much]) and *quasi* (almost). These directions arrived comparatively late in music history, as, in a smaller, more homogeneous world, period style was common currency and the character of the music would immediately suggest the tempo and manner of execution without further stipulation. The directions became more elaborate from the *Classical period onwards, and especially so in the *Romantic period, with its emphasis on individuality, creativity and music as property, when composers wished to have greater control over the way their works were interpreted, especially as the importance of the professional (non-composing) performer grew.

Tempo giusto (It.: 'correct' time)
(1) A general instruction to play a piece at the right or appropriate speed, whether specified, or deduced from its style.

(2) A specific instruction to keep to (if the style of the music suggests otherwise), or to return to (after a permitted deviation) the strict time, of a piece implied in the most recent *tempo direction(s).

Tempo ordinario (It.: 'ordinary' speed)
(1) An instruction to play a piece at 'ordinary' speed whether expressed as a specified speed in the tempo directions or deduced from the piece's style.

(2) Another term for 'common time' (or a time signature of 4/4).

Ternary form

A musical form which was in two sections, labelled as A and B, each of which was usually repeated, but the latter of which included a repeat (wholly or mostly) of the A section, thus suggesting the underlying tripartite shape. The same, or recognizably similar, melodic material was used for each section, the first of which remained (apart from transient modulations) in the tonic. The second section began in another key and modulated back to the tonic, closing with the A section or a close variant. Both sections were repeated.

Melodic material ||:A   :||: B   A   :||
(and sections)
Key (major)   I___ ?_ ?_ I___
Key (minor)   i___ ?_ ?_ i___

Most of the *minuets in the *Baroque *suite and the *Classical period were cast in ternary form.

Terraced dynamics

A description used to indicate that an instrument was incapable of graded dynamics, but could only increase or decrease sound-volume by fixed increments. It is most often used of the *harpsichord.

Terzverwandtschaft (Ger.: 'third-relationship')
The use of notes in a melody, or of keys (in modulation) – such as moving between, say C major or minor and E♭ or A♭ majors – which are separated by the interval of a third. It became more common in *sonata-form movements, as the *Romantic period waxed, in substitution for the usual dominant.

Tessitura (It.: 'texture')
A term for describing the vocal (especially) or instrumental pitch-compass in which a piece of music is set (high, low, etc.), at a given section in the music; thus, it is similar to *'register' but less definite. A piece or part is said to have a high *tessitura* if much of it lies in the upper range.

Teutscher
An alternative name for *Deutscher*.

Thalberg, Sigismond (Fotuné François)

German or Austrian pianist, composer (b. 8 Jan 1812, Pâquis, nr Geneva; d. 27 Apr 1871, Posillipo, nr Naples).

His ancestry is unclear. He was possibly the illegitimate son of Count Moritz von Dietrichstein and Baroness von Wetzlar, but his birth certificate gives his parents as Joseph Thalberg and Fortunée Stein with wording which suggests that they were not married to each other, but to others. It may be that the Count persuaded the 'father' to assume paternity.

Sigismond was sent to Vienna for a diplomatic career but studied music concurrently, with lessons in theory from a bassoonist, then with *Sechter, and piano with *Hummel. He played in many of the fashionable *salons* from the age of 14 and published his first works. He toured the European mainland and Britain from 1830, and then studied with *Pixis in Paris and *Moscheles in London, gaining great fame in the former city. In Paris he was a rival to *Liszt who publicly wrote badly of his compositions, but *Fétis defended him; on the other hand, *Berlioz was on the Liszt side. Matters came to a head when the two were induced to perform in a concert for the Princess de Belgiojoso, after which they were reconciled and agreed to join four other virtuosi in the *Hexameron*, a six-piano extravaganza to which they (with *Pixis, *Herz, *Chopin and *Czerny) each contributed a variation. Afterwards, Thalberg's fame increased and he travelled to the New World – where he lived for several years – Havana and Brazil. He spent his last years producing wine on his estate in Posillipo, near Naples.

Thalberg is, by common consent, one of the two greatest virtuosi of the mid-nineteenth century, with Liszt. His famous *'three-handed' technique, although impressive, was quite simply a siting of the main melody in the centre of the keyboard played by the thumbs of both hands with bass and treble figuration below and above, all controlled by deft pedalling. His compositions were reviewed with admiration by *R. Schumann – not one to have much time for virtuosos. Thalberg's great advantage was to temper Lisztian virtuosity with Hummelian *bel canto*.

Works
Apart from two unsuccessful operas, a few chamber works and some songs, all his works were for piano – a large quantity of operatic fantasias and variations (*Don Giovanni*, *Les Huguenots*, *Oberon*, etc.) and improvisational pieces, as well as miscellaneous works and a pedagogical work, *L'art du chant appliqué au piano* (*The Art of Singing applied to the Piano*) op. 70.

Further reading
L. Plantinga, *Schumann as Critic* (New Haven, CT and London, 1967). V. Vitale, 'Sigismondo Thalberg a Posillipo', *Nuova rivista musicale italiana*, vi (1972). I.G. Hominick, *Sigismond Thalberg (1812–1871), Forgotten piano Virtuoso: his Career and Musical Contributions* (DMA diss., Ohio State U., 1991). Marmontel/*PIANISTES*. Fétis/*BIOGRAPHIE*. *MGG*.

Thomson, George
British (Scottish) publisher, music editor (b. 4 Mar 1757, Limekilns, Fife; d. 18 Feb 1851, Leith).

After a childhood in northern Scotland, he moved to Edinburgh in 1774 and six years later became a clerk to the Board of Trustees for the Encouragement of Art and Manufactures in Scotland. He then devoted his spare time to music, becoming a violinist in the Edinburgh Musical Society (1780), taking part in both the choir and the orchestra, and his interest in Scottish *folksong was kindled. It was not the indigenous product, however, or its native performers which interested him, but the concertized drawing-room versions into which potentially lucrative market he determined to tap.

With great conviction he decided to publish a collection of Scots folksongs in arrangements by the most prestigious composers of the time which became, effectively, his life's work over the half-century 1791–1841. When *J. Haydn arrived in London for the first of his two visits in 1791 the ailing publisher *Napier (also a Scot) was financially rehabilitated by signing Haydn for a similar project to Thomson's and the latter promptly engaged *Pleyel, one of Haydn's pupils, who was also in the British capital at the time; the first part of Thomson's *Select Collection of Scottish Airs* was issued in Edinburgh in 1793.

For his second part of his *Collection*, Thomson amassed an impressive list of arrangers, including Haydn, with 187 settings, *Hummel, *Koželuch, *C.M. von Weber, *Bishop and no less than *Beethoven who set 126 numbers. Some of the results are curiosities, partly through general (though not universal) ignorance in matters such as the style of the melodies (which were subjected to Viennese *Classical harmonic settings) but also not helped by the fact that the melodies were already bowdlerized and were not accompanied by the words, so the sentiments were often very much at odds with the settings, even with the best will in the world. Beethoven was particularly put out when Thomson simplified his piano-parts for the domestic market, who was also responsible for the laundering of the texts, again by some well-known figures, such as *Burns, Hogg and Baillie. The entire collection was of some 300 songs in six volumes (1793–1841); it was viewed as a curiosity and never attained the iconic status for which Thomson hoped. His granddaughter married Charles Dickens in 1836.

Works
Select Collection of Scottish Airs (6 vols, 1793–1841). *Welsh Airs* (3 vols, 1809, 1811, 1817); *Irish Airs* (2 vols, 1814, 1816); an account of the Edinburgh Musical Society's activities in the 1780s included in R. Chambers, *Traditions of Edinburgh* (Edinburgh, 1868).

Further reading
C. Hopkinson and C.B. Oldman, 'Thomson's Collection of National Song', *Transactions of the Edinburgh Bibliographical Society*, ii (1940). J. Sachs, 'Hummel and George Thomson of Edinburgh', *MQ*, lvi (1970). D. Johnson, *Music and Society in Lowland Scotland in the 18th Century* (London, 1972).

'Three-handed technique' (see *Thalberg)

Thoroughbass (Thorough-bass) (see *Basso continuo*)

**Through-composed (see *Durchkomponiert*)

Timbre
The characteristic quality of a particular instrument's sound.

Tirolienne (see *Tyrolienne)

Toccata (It.: 'touched')
A virtuoso piece almost exclusively for keyboard and free in form; in the *Baroque period, a concluding *fugue was understood and *moto perpetuo* was a characteristic. Little used in the *Classical period, though there are a couple of notable *Romantic examples – *R. Schumann's in C major op. 7 – it was revived in the twentieth century, especially among organ composers (Widor, Vierne) but also, for instance, the finale of Debussy's *Pour le piano*, Ravel's *Le tombeau de Couperin* and Prokofiev's op. 11.

Toccatina
Diminutive form of *Toccata.

Tomášek, Vacláv Jan Křitel
[Tomaschek, Wenzel Johann]
Bohemian composer, teacher (b. 17 Apr 1774, Skuteč; d. 3 Apr 1850, Prague).

He was the youngest of thirteen children and showed musical aptitude from an early age. From his ninth until his twelfth year he studied violin and singing with a local choirmaster and at thirteen became an alto in a monastery choir which helped to fund his Gymnasium schooling. He was taught theory and organ by a friend, Schuberth – his only formal training – and studied alone from then on from the works of Fux (the *Gradus ad Parnassum*) Kirnberger and Marpurg. In 1790 he went to study at the Gymnasium in Prague, teaching piano to support himself, and he may have had lessons from F.X. Dussek. He was at the University from 1794 and spent three years in the study of history, aesthetics, philosophy and mathematics and then went on to study law in 1797.

His reputation as a teacher had grown and one of the noble families for whom he worked, that of Count Buquoy, appointed him as tutor and composer with good conditions and pleasant surroundings. Tomášek remained in this post for 16 years before becoming freelance in Prague. He married in 1824 and his home was a kind of unofficial city conservatory, attracting many eminent pupils – Kittl, Dreyschock, Hanslick and Voříšek. He travelled to Vienna, meeting *J. Haydn (1801) and *Beethoven (1814) as well as Salzburg and Bayreuth and met and corresponded with Goethe. All the prominent visiting musicians paid calls to his home when they were in Prague.

Tomášek was a keyboard pioneer of *Classic/*Romantic transition and an important figure in the *character piece. His eclogues, rhapsodies and similar pieces influenced later composers such as *Schubert and *R. Schumann.

Works
He wrote many short piano pieces, solo and part-songs and some stage and choral works.

Further reading
V. Thompson, *Wenzel Johann Tomaschek: his Predecessors, his Life, his Piano Works* (diss., U. of Rochester, 1955). V.M. Postler, *V.J.Tomášek: Bibliografie* (Prague, 1960).

Tomkison, Thomas
British (English) piano-maker (*fl.* 1798 – bef. Dec 1853).

Little is known of this figure, who worked, between late 1798 and mid-1851, in Dean Street in London's Soho. He made squares and grands, one fine example being for the Prince Regent at Brighton Pavilion, which was reconstructed by Nash. In fact his instruments carried the title of 'Maker to his Royal Highness the Prince Regent' and, later, 'Maker to His Majesty'. He built some 9,000 instruments in all.

Further reading
C.F. Colt with A. Miall, *The Early Piano* (London, 1981).

Tonal
Referring to the use of major and minor and, within their framework, chromatic scales and the harmonic framework associated with them as the basis of musical composition. Each piece begins and ends within a specified key and although, in the case of multi-movement works, one or more inner movements may have their own keys (different from the overall) the multi-movement piece

as a whole conforms to the tonic key in which the first and last movements are cast. Within each key – and it is the same for all keys – there is a hierarchy of chords with functions which serve to preserve the basic key, even though this may be temporarily substituted by one or more of them. The term atonal refers to music which does not operate within tonal principles and, although it could be used to describe modal music, it usually refers to more radical departures such as twelve-note music.

Tone-poem (see *Symphonic poem)

Tonic Sol-fa
A kind of musical notation for vocal music and the system of sight-singing to which it gives rise, using letters (called by two-letter syllables) and punctuation marks. It is based on the scale of C major and can be transposed into any key without change. It was devised to improve congregational singing in 1842 in England by John Curwen, based heavily on a previous system by a schoolmistress, Sarah Glover, for teaching children without using standard musical staff notation. The degrees of the scale were given letters d ('doh') r ('ray') m ('me'), etc. with variants for accidentals – for example C♯ was 'de' and D♯ 're' – and the rhythm was indicated by punctuation marks, for example, in 4/4 time the first four notes of the scale, C—D—E—F, shown in crotchets would be:

| d : r | m : f |

Touch
On a keyboard instrument, the amount of effort needed to produce a sound with the added qualification, in the case of the *clavichord and *piano, that the amount of force used is in direct proportion to the volume produced. This is not a universal quantity, but depends on the *action – its type, weight, stiffness and so on – of the particular instrument; also involved is the amount of *key-dip on the instrument. Although the matter of touch can only be a strictly quantitative matter – a mathematical proportion as outlined above – the term 'touch' has had a qualitative aura attached to it, based on the player's ability to relate the sounds produced.

***Traité** [d'instrumentation]*
Abbreviated title for *Berlioz's *Grand traité d'instrumentation et d'orchestration modernes* op. 10. First published in Paris in 1843, it was a compilation of articles he wrote on orchestration for the periodical *La Revue et gazette musicale*. A second edition, pub. 1855, has an additional section, *Le Chef d'orchestra: Théorie de son art* (*The Conductor: a Theory of his Art*) and it received its first English translation in the same year. A translation from a treatise by R. Strauss (reflecting late *Romantic orchestration) was published in New York in 1944 as *Treatise on Instrumentation* and reprinted in 1991 (New York). A modern translation by the Berlioz scholar Hugh Macdonald – *Berlioz's Orchestration Treatise: A Translation and Commentary* – was published in Cambridge in 2002.

Transpose
To write, play or sing music in a key other than that in which it was intended to be. It is sometimes done when a piece is played on a different instrument, or sung by a different voice, from the original, or if it is too high or too low. Transposing pianos (see *piano (9)) were built at various times during the eighteenth and nineteenth centuries and some instruments (*'transposing instruments')

automatically transpose the music played on them into a different key from that written.

Transposing instruments
An instruments which, when played, sounds at a different pitch from the music's written equivalent. There are various reasons for this, mainly to do with allowing the player being able to play the same music on several instruments of the same family without altering the fingering. Thus the same music can be played in different keys on the clarinets in B♭ or in A without alteration and the same applies to various differently-pitched trumpets. The most commonly-encountered transposing instruments in the modern orchestra are the clarinets, cor anglais, trumpets, horns, saxophones and the double bass, which plays the music given to it down an octave.

Transposing piano (see *Piano (9))

Transposition
The result of *transposing music.

Tremolando (see *Tremolo)

Tremolo (It.: 'trembling', quivering')
A musical technique characterized by rapid changes in volume of, or fast repetition of, single notes. On string instruments the related direction '*tremolando*' is more commonly used for the same effect. It has been used to create excitement and tension in music – especially operatic music – since the *Baroque period.

Trésor des pianistes, Le
A collection of keyboard music covering 300 years, including contemporary composers. It was issued in Paris in 23 volumes between 1861 and 1874 by Aristide *Farrenc with the assistance of his wife, *Louise, who completed the programme after his death in 1865. Some of the more prominent (in the editors' opinion) had a whole volume, or more than one, dedicated to them.

Trio-sonata (see *Sonata)

Trichord [trichord-strung, trichord stringing]
Of the piano, having three strings with the same tuning for each note of the same pitch sounded simultaneously with a single hammer.

Trill (Shake) (Fr. *cadence, tremblement, trille*; Ger, *Triller*; It. *trillo*)
A musical *ornament consisting of the fast alternation of a main note and an adjacent note, mostly associated with *cadences. It is most commonly shown on scores by the letters *tr* with or without a following wavy line (*tr* ᰃ), although signs for the trill in past periods varied a good deal.

Trois nouvelles études ['Three new Studies']
By *Chopin (see **Méthode des méthodes*).

'Trout' Quintet
Name given to the piano quintet (pf, vn, va, vc and db) in A major D 667 (1819) by *Schubert in five movements of which the fourth is a set of variations on the melody of his own song *Die Forelle ('The Trout').

Tschudi (see *Shudi)

Tuning
(1) The adjustments made to a musical instrument before a performance, to

ensure that the sound-producing agents (strings, pipes, etc.) produce sounds in accordance with the accepted pitch-ranges, scales and within the prevalent *temperament.

(2) The set of pitches to which particular instruments are tuned, as in, for example, the four strings of the violin, tuned to G—D—A—E (working upwards).

Turca, Alla (see *Turkish Music)

Türk, Daniel Gottlob
German theorist, composer (b. 10 Aug 1750, Claussnitz, nr Chemnitz; d. 26 Aug 1813, Halle).

Son of a musical hosier, he received his first lessons from his father and learnt a number of wind instruments from his friends. He was then taught by a pupil of *J.S. Bach and then, while studying at Leipzig University, under Hiller, and used *C.P.E, Bach's *Versüch. In 1774 Hiller recommended him for a Kantorship at Halle and he remained there for the rest of his life, soon becoming the city's leading musical light and restoring music after the Seven Years War (1756–63). In 1779 he additionally became director of music at Halle University and received a doctorate; he married in 1783 and was appointed to a professorship in 1808. When he was appointed to organist and musical director of the Marktkirche (Liebfrauenkirche), he relinquished the Gymnasium, which required him to teach general subjects as well as music. Türk is best remembered for his Clavierschule (see below).

Works
Many keyboard works and vocal pieces. His pedagogical writings include the Clavierschule, oder Anweisung zum Clavierspielen für Lehrer und Lernende ... nebst 12 Handstücken (Halle 1789, 2/1802; Eng. tr., 1982).

Further reading
E.R. Jacobi. 'Nachwort', *D.G. Türk: Klavierschule*, Documenta Musicologica, 1st series, *Druckschriften-Faksimiles*, xxiii (1962, rev. 2/1967). R.H. Haagh, *Introduction to D.G. Türk: School of Clavier Playing* (Lincoln, NE, 1982) [Eng. tr. of Clavierschule].

Turkish music [Janissary music] (Ger. türkische Musik, Janischären Musik; It. banda turca; Turkish mehter)
A musical expression of the fashion for things Turkish – dress, symbols, etc. – which had begun in the eighteenth century as a result of the Turkish wars. The military music of the Sultan's private bodyguard, the Janissaries, was well-known to the servicemen who had been involved and such 'Janissary music' had a strong impact on military music in the West. After the treaty with the Ottoman Empire, many European army regiments incorporated Turkish instruments into their own bands and Western royalty vied with each other in forming private Turkish bands, including Catherine the Great, the King of Prussia and the Austrian Emperor. Some took trouble to seek advice from Turkish musicians and even employ them. By the late eighteenth century it was common to include a Turkish percussion section in many European regimental bands.

The sound of the music was characterized by the contrasting sonorities of the shrillness of the several Turkish hautboys, flute, cymbals and triangle, and the dull sound of kettle- and bass-drums, and the fact that they played in unison or octaves.

Westernized parodies were common, immortalized in the rondo finale, *Alla Turca*, of *W.A. Mozart's piano sonata in A major, K331, in the parallel minor with a recurring episode in the major, in which mode it ends. The finale has the traits traditionally associated with the Western 'Turkish music' – a simple melody, more rhythmic than melodic and heavily reliant on repeated figures, a four-square, regular accompaniment of the 'um-cha[-cha]' type and a very restricted harmonic ambit, basically *diatonic and confined to the three primary chords, a slow rate of harmonic rhythm and the use of the dominant minor. The implied effects suggest the cymbals, triangle (or bells) and bass drum which later pianos equipped with Turkish music could provide, although a drum alone could also be found, occasionally operable by a different pedal. (See Carew/MUSE, Plates 17 and 18.) Many composers used the device, such as *Gluck, in *La rencontre imprévue* (perf. 1764) and W.A. Mozart in *Die Entführung aus dem Serail* (perf. 1782). The vogue for Turkish music lasted into the early nineteenth century and can be found, for example, in *Bethoven's Ninth (1822–24) and 'Battle' (1813) Symphonies and in the Turkish March from his incidental music (1811) to *Die Ruinen von Athen* (*The Ruins of Athens*).

Further reading
E.H. Powley, *Turkish Music: an Historical Study of Turkish Percussion instruments and their Influence on European Music* (diss., Rochester U., 1968). E.R, Meyer, 'Turquerie and Eighteenth Century Music', *Eighteenth-Century Studies*, vii (1974). M. Head, *Orientalism, Masquerade and Mozart's Turkish Music* (London, 2000).

Tutti (It.: 'all'; plural of *tutto*)
(1) Indicating, in orchestral or chamber music, that the whole group or orchestra is to partake after only some have been involved.

(2) In the *concerto it indicates the purely orchestral passages, particularly, in the *Classical concerto, the orchestra's introductory section in which it outlines the main thematic material of (usually) the opening movement.

Tyrol (see *Savoy)

Tyrolienne (Tirolienne) (Fr.: 'Tyrolese', 'Tyrolean')
A fast dance and type of song in triple *metre akin to the slower *Ländler. The dance was best known from its use in ballet, purporting to represent the dancing of Bavarian and Austrian peasants, and the song-type was all the rage on both sides of the Atlantic during the second and third quarters of the nineteenth century. The style, popularized by several waves of touring 'Swiss families', was characterized by *yodelling and echo effects, arpeggiaic melodies and simple harmonizations in parallel thirds with sentimental 'homely' texts. *Moscheles arranged a number of the tunes for piano, and the best-known example of the style is probably the 'chœur tyrolienne' in Act III of *Rossini's *Guillaume Tell* ('A nos chants viens mêler tes pas').

U

Una corda (see *Pedal (2) and *Stop
(2))

Upright piano (see *Piano)

V

Valse (Fr. for *waltz)

Variation
A variation may occur singly or in a set and the set may be free-standing or part of a larger work. The theme is usually stated first in its more-or-less basic form and the variation(s) follow(s), giving the common 'theme and variations' format. The theme may be anything from a motif (rare) to a melody of several *phrases (most common). Variations always imply alteration but some connection, however tenuous, with the theme remains; variations more remote from the theme tend to occur in longer sets. Variation is carried out in two principal ways which may coexist in the same set, or alternate or even blend into each other.

(1) *Alteration of the theme*   Any aspect or aspects of the theme may be altered. In terms of melody, the notes, motifs subphrases, *phrases, sections, or the whole melody may be subjected to changes, and any or all of these at the same time. The result may be anything from the addition of simple decorations and *passing-notes (similar to the *double or the *Figuralvariation*, based on figuration involving mostly such decorations) to a wholesale re-jig. Rhythm may be similarly varied and harmony also, chords may be substituted for the original ones which, in turn, may lead to further melodic or rhythmic changes. The time-signature may be substituted by another, although radical alterations, such as the change of a triple to a quadruple *metre, are rare before the late *Classical period. The character (happy, serious, dance-like,

aria-like) may also be varied, as well as the tempo.

(2) *Alteration of the setting*   In this case the theme's melody (including rhythm) remains the same and other aspects of the music are altered, such as the harmony and/or the instrumentation. This type enjoyed popularity in the early nineteenth century, and the variation-movement in *Schubert's *'Trout' Quintet D667 in A major for violin, viola, cello, double bass and piano (1819) is a good example.

(3) *Special types*   In certain cases, the theme takes the form of a harmonic sequence, or a bass-line, over which variations are written or played. An example of this type is the triple-*metre *chaconne* (Fr.; Elizabethan Eng. chacony; It. *ciacona*; Sp. *chacona*) – a famous example being in *J.S. Bach's Solo Violin *Partita* no. 2 in D minor BWV1004 (1720) – or the *passacaglia* (It.; Eng. ground bass; Fr. *passacaille*; Sp. *passacalle*) which was not restricted to triple metre; an example of this is the finale of *Brahms's Fourth Symphony, op. 98 in E minor (1884–85).

'Venetian Swell' (see *Swell (2))

Versuch (see *Versuch über die wahre Art ...*)

Versuch über die wahre Art das Klavier zu spielen ('Essay on the True Art of Playing Keyboard Instruments')
A treatise on keyboard playing by *Carl Philipp Emmanuel Bach published in two parts (1753 and 1762). It is a practical instruction-manual and a compendium of eighteenth-century practice with the best of it clearly laid out for the student. Topics dealt with include *basso continuo*,

*improvisation, instrumental techniques – with reference to the different keyboard instruments of the time – *decoration and *fingering. In spite of the author's favourite instrument being the *clavichord, the piano is not neglected. Bach wrote several sets of pieces to illustrate the principles expounded in the *Versuch*, as the continuation of its title shows: *'mit Exempeln und Achtzehn Probe-Stücken in sechs Sonaten erläutert'*. The first complete translation in English was W.J. Mitchell, *Essay on the True Art of Playing Keyboard Instruments* (New York, 1949).

Vibrato (It.: 'shaken', from Lat. *vibrare*, 'to shake')
A slight and largely irregular wavering of pitch used to intensify and enrich the voice and many instruments, its use and degree, not to mention its desirability, varying with period and culture. In modern times it is usually expected and composers who specifically do not wish its use must write *'senza vibrato'* ('without vibrato') on vocal or instrumental parts scores. Vibrato is sometimes confused or interchanged with *tremolo.

Vienna, Congress of (1 Nov 1814 – 9 Jun 1815)
A meeting, after the Napoleonic Wars and the abdication of Napoleon Bonaparte, of the statesmen and representatives of the allied forces (Russia, Prussia, Austria and Great Britain) in Vienna during the dates given. The purpose was to decide the fate of Europe after the wars. It provided much social life for the city and several composers, including *Beethoven and *Hummel, living or visiting the city were commissioned to write music for various state and public occasions, mainly dances. The news that Napoleon had escaped from Elba interrupted proceedings, which were resumed after Waterloo.

'Viennese' Piano
The first peak of perfection in piano-making, the instrument was called the fortepiano, to distinguish it not only from later models, but from the *British piano, with which for a while it vied for popularity, until makers began to amalgamate the best qualities from each during the nineteenth century.

The features of the pianos of this kind (compared with the British model and even more so compared with the modern one) were a greater degree of lightness in *touch and action with a shallower *key-dip, a smaller and thinner (but perfectly-controllable) sound, a crisp staccato due to the excellent damping, very small hammers, largely *bichord stringing with thinner strings and a concave (upwards) soundboard. In addition, the case was separate from the instrument itself, whereas in the British model it was often integral. The style of music associated with the instrument was brilliant and light, though it was capable of powerful sound and could easily hold its own against an orchestra of the period.

Viols
A group of bowed instruments, precursors to and shaped like, the violin family with frets and six strings as opposed to the modern violin's four. Their shoulders were more sloping than the violins and they were held downwards, resting on the lap or between the legs. The shape of many modern double basses is descended from the bass viol. or *violone*.

Voice
The original musical instrument, produced by the human larynx in association with

the lungs. The word is used in various senses in music.

(1) The human voice in its different registers (soprano, alto, etc.) including *falsetto.

(2) An individual melody-line in music is sometimes called a 'voice', especially if it functions independently as in *contrapuntal or *polyphonic music. This usage is not confined to vocal music and is often applied to instrumental lines also.

Volkslied (Ger.: 'folk song')
A term coined by *Herder. (See *Folk song.)

Volti (**Volti subito**) (**v. s.**) (It.: 'turn [over]' ('turn over quickly'))
A direction often found at the bottom of pages in musical parts as a warning to the player or singer that the (usually fast-paced) music continues immediately over the page or that there is something unexpected following.

Von Himmel hoch (Ger.: 'From Heaven On High')
A *chorale which *J.S. Bach set several times during his life, but is manifested at its finest in the set of *canonic variations BWV769, which he wrote in 1747 as a membership-offering for a musical society to which he applied. It is a *tour-de-force* of *Baroque *contrapuntal writing.

W

Waldstein, Count (see * *'Waldstein'
Sonata*)

'Waldstein' Sonata

Title given to *Beethoven's Piano
Sonata no. 21 in C major op. 53 (1804)
because of its dedication to one of his
patrons, Count Waldstein. It is a virtuoso
work, revelling in the piano's orchestral
sonorities. The movements are: i. Allegro
con brio, C major, ₵; ii. Introduzione:
Adagio molto, modulating, 6/8, leading
to iii. Rondo: Allegretto molto, C major,
2/4 – Prestissimo, C.

Walter, (Gabriel) Anton

German (Austrian nationalized) piano-
maker (b. 5 Feb 1752, Neuhausen an der
Fildern, nr Stuttgart; d. 11 April 1826,
Vienna).

He married in Vienna in 1780 and ten
years later was entitled Imperial Royal
Chamber Organ and Instrument Maker.
His stepson became his partner in 1800.
*W.A. Mozart admired his pianos and his
own Walter is now in the Mozarteum in
Salzburg.

Further reading
U. Rück, 'Mozarts Hammerflügel erbaute
Anton Walter, Wien', *Mozart-Jahrbuch
1955*. J. A. Rice, 'Anton Walter: Instrument
Maker to Leopold II', *JAMS*, xv (1989).
M.R. Latcham, 'Mozart and the Pianos of
Gabriel Anton Walter', *Early Music*, xxv
(1997). Maunder/KEYBOARD.

Waltz (Fr. *valse*; Ger. *Walzer*)

A couple-dance in triple (normally 3/4)
time which was popular throughout the
nineteenth and early twentieth centuries.
It was also popular as an instrumental

piece with many composers contributing
to its literature.

In spite of the many schemes later
assigned, the waltz was at first informal,
without prescribed steps or patterns,
characterized by couples in intimate
bodily contact whirling in and out of a
crowd of others. It filtered upwards from
socially lower strata, belonging to a group
of (mostly) triple-time dances known
simply as *Deutscher* (German dances).
These featured embracing couples with
names derived from words which, like
the German root of the title – *'walzen'*
(to rotate) – itself, drew attention to their
shared characteristic twirling or twisting
motion – *Dreher*, *Weller*, *Spinner* and
the generic term, *Ländler*, which was
originally a kind of slow waltz. There
was so much cross-fertilization, however,
that it was eventually impossible to
distinguish the types from each other, and
'waltz' became the blanket term, almost
by chance.

Owing to the usually large number
of dancers, their peasant garb (including
hobnail boots for the men) and the
vigour of the movements – the female
partner was frequently thrown over the
shoulders of the male – it was an outdoor
dance. With their general atmosphere
of freeness, and their association with
inns and alcohol, they were particularly
popular in the Vienna Woods and suburbs
in the *Heurigen*, the vineyard inns which
continued to retain their rural simplicity,
despite being close to the glitter of a
dance-crazy Vienna, and it would not
be long before these happy abandoned
dances infiltrated Viennese society. It had
become popular by the last decade of the
eighteenth century.

Vienna already had a large public
venue for dancing, the *Redouten-
säle*, consisting of a large and a smaller

ballroom capable of accommodating about 3,000 people, and such was the increasing popularity of public dancing that two more were added (1807 and 1808). The first of these, the *Sperl, had a beer-garden and was a great haven for tourists, and an idea of the sumptuousness of the *Apollosaal (or *Apollosäle*, 1808), catering for 4,000 (or in some accounts, 6,000), included five great mirrored dance-halls with pillars and crystal chandeliers, together with over twenty *rococo-styled drawing rooms, three glass-domed gardens with waterfalls and swans and thirteen kitchens. Similar establishments in other cities also included gaming-rooms and concert-halls. The choice of this gay, elegant and – under the iron hand of Metternich's secret police – politically stable city to host the *Congress of Vienna (1815–16) where the leaders of Europe gathered to chop up 'their' continent, was a great boost.

If the waltz threatened to wane in popularity in the 1820s, it underwent a blood-transfusion in the hands of a group of vigorous young composer/bandleaders who dedicated themselves to its well-being, led by Joseph *Lanner and Johann *Strauss the Elder. Once Strauss began to tour that continent with his orchestra in the 1830s, the popularity became a craze and dance-halls and pleasure gardens designed to include musical performance and dancing opened up everywhere.

Following its revival, the waltz attracted even the very greatest, composers, who were more than happy to supply single waltzes as well as sets, for public as well as private dancing. These included *Chopin and *Liszt but waltzes were also included in the most exalted genres such as the symphony, for example in *Berlioz's *Symphonie fantastique* (1830), and it still makes an occasional appearance.

Further reading
M. Carner, *The Waltz* (London, 1948). M. Schönherr and K. Reinöhl, *Das Jahrhundert des Walzers: Johann Strauss Vater* (Vienna, 1954). R.T. Flotzinger, 'Und walzen umatum ... zur Genealogie des Wiener Walzers', *Österreichisches Musikzeitschrift*, xxx (1975). R. Hess, *La valse* (Paris, 1989).

'Wanderer' Fantasy
Name given to *Schubert's *Fantasia* (*'Wandererfantasie'*) in C D 760 (1822) because the Adagio section is a set of variations on his song *Der Wanderer* D 489 (1816).

Weber, Carl Maria (Friedrich Ernst) von
German composer, conductor, pianist, critic (b. ?18 Nov 1786, Eutin; d. 5 Jun 1826, London).

Son of the manager of a travelling theatre troupe, whose appropriation of the noble 'von' was without foundation, he was a sickly child with a permanent limp who picked up music as he travelled with the troupe. As soon as he had regular lessons he made swift progress and went on to study with *Michael Haydn in Salzburg, under whose tutelage he produced his first mass and his third opera, *Peter Schmoll*. Weber moved to Vienna intending to study with *Joseph Haydn but went to Abbé Vogler instead. Again, he made rapid progress, interested himself in *folk songs and was recommended for the post of *Kapellmeister* at Breslau, which he gained and, taking his father with him, he arrived in the summer of 1804; he was only 17 years of age.

The latter fact was a source of resentment for many, as were the various new arrangements he instigated; after an eight-week illness he returned to work to find them all undone and he resigned. In 1807, after a concert-tour, he was appointed secretary to the Duke of Stuttgart's brother and the duke and the brother, who was the ruler, did not get on, which made life difficult for all ranks involved. There was, however some compensation in the artistic life of the city, some of whose musical figures encouraged him to compose, and he produced a number of piano and chamber works. Interference from his father, who arrived to stay with his son, resulted in legal proceedings over misappropriation of funds and, soon after, banishment from Württemberg early in 1810. His one-act *Singspiel*, *Abu Hassan*, was well received, encouraging him to consider an operatic career, and he was appointed to direct the opera in Prague, in 1813, which he transformed on all levels, concentrating on German and then French opera, which expanded his musical palette greatly. He also began to write music criticisms for the local newspapers.

The royal equerry Count Vizthum, who was already aware of Weber's music and had met him and presented him with the gift of a snuffbox, offered him the post of Royal Saxon *Kapellmeister* in Dresden with a brief to develop German opera. Standards were low and, again, he transformed the company and the theatre, although the Royal *Kapellmeister*, Morlacchi had a strong faction promoting Italian opera, which caused difficulties. He married a long-term sweetheart and managed to compose instrumental works with what little spare time he had. He was also writing a novel, *Tonkünstlers Leben* (*A Musician's Life*).

The production of his new opera, *Der Freischütz* (*The Freeshooter*, 1821) – his greatest – was a great triumph and he became known throughout Europe.

He was commissioned to write an opera for the Kärntnerthortheater in Vienna and set to work amidst pleasant enough interruptions such as visits from Spontini, Tieck, Jean Paul and *Wilhelm Müller (who dedicated his publication of *Die schöne Müllerin* and *Die *Winterreise* to him). At the same time, his health was deteriorating. He went to Vienna to direct rehearsals, meeting *Beethoven; the opera, *Euryanthe*, was a moderate success, as the city was in the grip of *Rossini-fever – which Weber himself shared. His health – he was tubercular – continued to deteriorate and he was given two years to live.

An invitation from Charles Kemble, manager of Covent Garden Theatre in London, to conduct a production of *Freischütz* brought in its train a commission for an opera and the Shakespearian character of Oberon was decided upon as a subject. *En route* to London in early 1826, he spent a fortnight in Paris, where he met Paer, Catel Auber, *Cherubini and *Rossini but missing *Berlioz, who spent a good deal of time trying to find him. By March that year he was in London, staying with Sir George *Smart. On the first of his rehearsals the audience gave him a standing ovation. He gave a number of concerts, mainly to make sufficient money to ensure his family's security after his death. That came all too soon, in June after a successful première of *Oberon*. He was buried in Moorfields Chapel and in 1844 Wagner had his coffin taken back to Germany where he was re-buried in Dresden Cemetery.

His greatest work was *Freischütz*, whose combination of *folk-like melody, a supernatural theme imbued with Germanic folk-references and with forward-looking motivic treatment was enormously influential on opera in the German-speaking lands and on *Marschner and Wagner.

Works

Stage: *Abu Hassan* (*Singspiel*) (1810–11), *Der Freischütz* (*The Freeshooter*, 1817–21), *Euryanthe* (1822–23) and *Oberon* (1825–26). Many choral works, cantatas, etc., and songs. Orchestral: two symphonies (1807), two piano concertos (C major, 1810 and E♭ major, 1812), and the *Konzertstück* in F minor (1821) and two clarinet concertos and a Concertino. Smaller works include a Piano Quartet and Clarinet Quintet and the *Grand duo concertant* for clarinet and piano, as well as fugues, variations and four sonatas for piano solo.

Further reading

W. Becker, *Die deutscher Oper in Dresden unter der Leitung von Carl Maria von Weber, 1817–1826* (Berlin, 1962). J. Warrack, *Carl Maria von Weber* (London, 1968, 2/1976); ed., *Carl Maria von Weber: Writings on Music* (Cambridge, 1981). S. Goslich, *Die deutsche romantische Oper* (Tutzing, 1975). G. Jones, *Backgrounds and Themes of the Operas of Carl Maria von Weber* (diss., Cornell U., 1972).

Well-tempered Clavier (see *Wohltemperirte(s) Clavier, Das*)

Wesley, Samuel

British (English) composer, organist (b. 24 Feb 1766, Bristol; d. 11 Oct 1837, London).

A precociously musical child, who composed an oratorio at the age of eight, his father discouraged music until he had had a proper *Classical education. He learnt piano and violin as well as organ and was very drawn to Catholic music, even to the extent that he was reputed to have converted from his Methodism, which he did, in 1784, to his family's chagrin. However, he regretted this later, expressing his dislike for the doctrines of the Church of Rome, while retaining his love of the music and its ritual.

A serious accident damaged his skull and, refusing treatment, he suffered much from depression and irritability throughout his life. While his condition was, no doubt, exacerbated by the accident, it is unlikely to have been the cause, or the sole reason, for it. He was something of a freethinker and his marriage lasted only a couple of years; he had to support his wife and three children for the rest of his life although his income was inadequate to it. A mistress bore him several more children. He was frequently in financial need and imprisoned for debt at one stage, although he took pupils and had a freelance performing schedule of sorts. Wesley was an important figure in the *[J.S.] Bach revival in England and christened his son Sebastian after him; his works range from Classically-oriented chamber works and symphonies to more lucrative pot-boilers.

Works

A huge body of sacred and secular music and songs; many organ works and works (sonatas, sonatinas, variations, rondos, dances) for harpsichord and piano.

Further reading

N. Temperley, 'Samuel Wesley', *MT*, cvii (1966). P. Holman, 'The Instrumental and Orchestral Music of Samuel Wesley', *The Consort*, no. 23 (1966). J. Schwartz jr, *The Orchestral Music of Samuel Wesley* (diss., U. of Maryland, 1971); 'Samuel and Samuel Sebastian Wesley, the English *Doppelmeister*' *MQ*, lix (1973). J. Marsh, *The Latin Church Music of Samuel Wesley* (diss., U. of York, 1975). P.J. Olleson, 'Samuel Wesley and the *European Magazine*', *Notes*, lii (1995–96); *Samuel Wesley: the Man and his Music* (Aldershot, 2003); 'Samuel Wesley and the Music Profession', in C. Bashford and L. Langley, eds, *Music and Culture, 1785–1914: essays in Honour of Cyril Ehrlich* (Oxford, 2000); and M. Kassler, *Samuel Wesley: a Sourcebook* (Aldershot, 2001).

Wieck, Clara (see *Schumann, Clara)

Wieck, Friedrich
(b. 1785; d. 1873) Father of *Clara Wieck-Schumann (see Clara and Robert *Schumann).

Winterreise
A *song-cycle in two books by *Schubert for male voice, D911 (op. 89) composed in 1827 to a poem-cycle by Wilhelm *Müller (pub. 1823–24). The 24 numbers are: Book I: 1. 'Gute Nacht' ('Good Night'), Mässig in gehender Bewegung, D minor, 2/4; 2. 'Die Wetterfahne' ('The Weathervane'), Ziemlisch geschwind, A minor, 6/8; 3. 'Gefror'ne Thränen' ('Frozen Tears'), Nicht zu langsam, F minor, ₵; 4. 'Erstarrung' ('Numbness'), Ziemlich schnell, C minor 4/4; 5. 'Der Lindenbaum' ('The Lime Tree'), Mäasig, E major, 3/4. 6. 'Wasserfluth' ('Flood'), Langsam, F♯ minor, 3/4; 7. 'Auf dem Flusse' ('On the River'), Langsam, E minor, 2/4; 8. 'Rückblick' ('Backward Glance'), Nicht zu geschwind, G minor, 3/4; 9. 'Irrlicht' ('Will-o'-the-Wisp'), B minor, 3/8; 10. 'Rast' ('Rest'), Mässig, D minor (also a C minor version), 2/4; 11. 'Frühlingstraum' ('Dream of Spring'), A major, 6/8; 12. 'Einsamkeit' ('Loneliness'), Langsam, D minor (also a B minor version), 2/4; Book II: 13. 'Die

Post' ('The Post'), Etwas geschwind, E♭ major, 6/8; 14. 'Der greise Kopf' ('The Grey Head'), Etwas langsam, C minor, 3/4; 15. 'Die Krähe' ('The Crow'), Etwas langsam, C minor, 2/4; 16. 'Letzte Hoffnung' ('Last Hope'), Nicht zu geschwind, E♭ major, 3/4; 17. 'Im Dorfe' ('In the Village'), Etwas langsam, D major, 12/8; 18. 'Der stürmische Morgen' ('The stormy Morning'), Ziemlisch geschwind, doch kräftig, D minor, 4/4; 19. 'Täuschung' ('Delusion'), Etwas geschwind, A major, 6/8; 20. 'Der Wegweiser' ('The Signpost'), Mässig, G minor, 2/4; 21. 'Das Wirthshaus' ('The Inn'), Sehr langsam, F major, 4/4; 22. 'Muth' ('Courage'), Ziemlich geschwind, kräftig, A minor, 2/4; 23. 'Die Nebensonnen' ('Phantom Suns'), Nicht zu langsam, A major, 3/4; 24. 'Der Leiermann' ('The Hurdy-gurdy Man'), Etwas langsam, B minor (also an A minor version), 3/4.

Wohltemperirte(s) [*wohltemperierte(s)*]
Clavier, Das (*The Well-tempered Clavier*)
Also called '*48* [*Forty-Eight*] *Preludes and Fugues*' or, simply, '*The 48*' ['*The Forty-Eight*']
   A keyboard work in two books by *J.S. Bach, each book containing paired sets of *preludes and *fugues in all the major and minor keys in ascending chromatic order from C (major). The fugues are mostly in three or four parts with a few in five, and a single two-part one. The first book dates from 1722, during Bach's sojourn at Cöthen and the second from 1744, when he was at Leipzig.
   The 'well-tempered' of the title does not necessarily call for the equal *temperament system of tuning, as there are several others possible – at least five – which would allow a sufficiently in-

tune performance of the whole work at one sitting without re-tuning.

Wölfl [Wölffl, Woclfl], Joseph

Austrian composer, pianist (b. 24 Dec 1773, Vienna; d. 21 May 1812, London).

He appeared in a public recital on the violin at seven and sang in the cathedral choir at Salzburg where he was taught by *Michael Haydn, *Leopold Mozart and possibly *W.A. Mozart also. The latter certainly had a hand in Wölfl's appointment as composer to Count *Oginsky and many of the noble Polish families. He returned to Vienna in 1795 and, after marrying a singer, became famous and much sought-after as a composer and pianist, gaining the respect of even *Beethoven, with whom he had an *improvisation duel. Wölfl took up residence in Paris in 1801 and was lionized there, but a stormy personal life caused him to decamp to London and he arrived there in 1805. As elsewhere, he soon became enormously successful in his dual roles. He died in the middle of 1812.

Works
Various operatic works, seven piano *concertos, some *programmatic — 'Le coucou' op. 49 in D (1810), 'Military', and 'Le calme' in G op. 36 (1807) — two symphonies and orchestral dances, various chamber works (12 string quartets, six pf trios, six wind sextets) and some 30 piano sonatas as well as accompanied sonatas, solo piano variations, rondos etc.

Further reading
W. Hitzig, 'Die Briefe Joseph Wölfls an Breitkopf & Härtel', *Der Bär* (1926).

R. Baum, *Joseph Wölfl: Leben Klavier-Werke* (Kassell, 1928).

Word-painting (Ger. *Wortmalerei*)
The depiction by musical means of the meaning of a word or of ideas associated with it, such as a descending motion for 'low' or 'deep'. It was very common in the Renaissance and *Baroque periods, but fell out of favour later. However, examples can be found, for example, in *Schubert – the rippling accompaniment depicting water in his song *Die Forelle *(*The Trout*).

Wornum [Wornham], Robert
British (English) piano-maker, music publisher (b. 19 Nov 1780, London; d. 29 Sep 1852, London).

Born into a family business of instrument-making and publishing, he went into partnership in a piano-making business 1810–13 (Oxford Street, London) and continued in his family's business after his father's death in 1815, moving to Store Street in 1832. His work on the development of the upright piano was important from the point of the instrument's marketability and its evolution, as he invented diagonal and vertical stringing (1811–13) and patented his own version of the tape-check for uprights which was much imitated and remains the basis for modern upright actions. His son joined him and continued the business until trading ceased in 1900.

Further reading
Hipkins/PIANOFORTE.Harding/PIANO-FORTE. Loesser/MEN. Ehrlich/PIANO.

Y

Yodel, yodelling (Ger. *jodeln*)
Singing (or calling) in a manner which alternates rapidly between vocal registers, especially when one is *falsetto. It is common in mountainous areas of the world and in the music of the African pygmies, but is best known from its use in Alpine areas of Europe and their *folk music, whence it has been imported into transcriptions of them, or original pieces based on them. Yodelling is part of the style of the *tyrolienne and features strongly in Swiss music.

Z

Zelter, Carl Friedrich

German composer, conductor, teacher (b. 11 Dec 1758, Berlin; d. 15 May 1832, Berlin).

Son of a stonemason involved in the building of Sanssouci (the palace of *Frederick the Great at Potsdam), he followed his wishes and footsteps in spite of his aptitude for music. He was allowed to sit as a child in the orchestra pit in Potsdam and, at the age of seventeen, learnt piano and violin rapidly while recuperating from smallpox. After this he made secret visits to a musician's home and joined an amateur orchestra in Berlin of which he later became conductor. Wishing to compose, and being aware of his theoretical drawbacks, he studied (1784–86) with Carl Fasch, a leading figure in court musical circles.

Having attained the rank of master-mason in 1783 he devoted himself to music in the 1790s and took over Fasch's conducting duties of his choir, the *Singakademie* – soon to become one of the leading vocal institutions in Germany, and of which he had also been a member – and established another choir also. Like Fasch, he continued to promote the work of *J.S. Bach and passed his love onto his pupils; one of them, *Felix Mendelssohn, was particularly susceptible and went on to arrange the first performance, since its composer's death, of Bach's *St Matthew Passion* in the spring of 1829.

Zelter was now composing lieder in a style which would become that of the First *Berlin Lied School, of which he can be said to have been a founder-member. His first published collection included settings of Goethe who, when he heard them, wrote to congratulate Zelter, thus beginning both a close lifelong friendship and a long and important correspondence. Zelter was particularly interested in musical education and as a result of a series of published essays was appointed to the Royal Academy of Arts (Berlin) and was made professor of music at the university after its founding in 1809.

Zelter's influence on musical life in Berlin was great and touched all aspects of it; his pupils included, apart from Mendelssohn, Otto Nicolai, Eduard Devrient, *Loewe and *Meyerbeer. He made the *Singakademie* into a formidable body – the seed of the later Berlin Philharmonic – and the *Liedertafel* (a male choir after the manner of the Meistersinger guild) which he founded in 1809 was the model for many others which sprang up in the German-speaking lands.

Works
Keyboard works, much sacred and choral music and a very important body of lieder.

Further reading
R. Barr, *Carl Friedrich Zelter: a Study of the Lied in Berlin during the Late Eighteenth and Early Nineteenth Centuries* (diss., U. of Wisconsin, 1968). W. Victor, *Carl Friedrich Zelter und seine Freundschaft mit Goethe* (Berlin and Weimar, ?1958). G. Wittmann, *Das klavierbegleitete Sololied Karl Friedrich Zelters* (Giessen, 1936). D. Fischer-Dieskau, *Carl Friedrich Zelter und das Berliner Musikleben seiner Zeit: eine Biographie* (Berlin, 1997).

Zumpe, Johannes [Johann Cristoph]

German (British naturalized) keyboard-instrument-maker (b. 14 Jun 1726, Fürth, nr Nuremburg; bur. 5 Dec 1790, London).

He came to London (like several others) after the Seven Years War (1756–63) and possibly worked in the *Silbermann workshop and for *Shudi before setting himself up in 1761 near Hanover Square. He was soon building pianos exclusively, as there was a flourishing market for them in London and *J.C. Bach gave the piano's first public solo performance in London on a Zumpe square. Zumpe went into partnership with Gabriel Buntebart from 1769 to 1788 and they were joined by another maker in 1778.

Further reading
W.H. Cole, 'The Early Piano in Britain Reconsidered', *Early Music*, xiv (1986). R. Maunder, 'The Earliest English Square Piano', *Galpin Society Journal*, xlii (1989). Harding/PIANO-FORTE. Loesser/MEN. Cole/PIANOFORTE.

Zumsteeg [Zum Steeg], **Johann Rudolf** German composer, conductor (b. 10 Jan 1760, Sachsenflur, nr Mergentheim; d. 27 Jan 1802, Stuttgart).

Son of a military father in personal service, he attended the military academy founded by his father's employer (the Duke of Württemberg) and became friendly with Schiller and the sculptor Dannecker. He himself was destined to be a sculptor but his musical talents resolved otherwise and he studied cello and composition with the *Kapellmeister*, Poli and composing his first works, including several cello concertos. Zumsteeg was solo cellist in the court orchestra from 1781 and wrote operas and ceremonial vocal music as well as songs which were printed in various publications; he also edited some of these collections himself. He became music-master in his old school and took over the duties of director of German music

at court after the death of *Schubart in 1791 and, two years later, was promoted to *Konzertmeister* on Poli's retirement. Unlike the Italian Poli, he concentrated on German operatic productions including some of his own works. His lieder and ballads became very popular and he became an important member of the Second *Berlin Lied School. Zumsteeg's most important works are those within this field, the lieder conforming to the '*folk' type, but the ballads being much more adventurous in harmony, setting and accompaniment.

Works
Apart from operas, orchestral and choral works, many lieder and ballads including seven volumes of *Kleine Balleden und Lieder* (*Little Ballads and Lieder*) (1800– 1805, pub. 1932).

Further reading
K. Haering, 'Johann Rudolph Zumsteeg: Opern- Balladen- und Liederkomponist, Konzertmeister   1760–1802', *Schwäbische Lebensbilder*, ii (Stuttgart 1941). E.G. Porter, 'Zumsteeg's Songs', *MMR*, lxxxviii (1958). G. Maier, *Die Lieder Johann Rudolph Zumsteegs und ihr Verhältnis zu Schubert* (Goppingen, 1971). R. Nägele, ed., *Johann Rudolph Zumsteeg (1760–1802) – der andere Mozart?*, Württembergischen Landesbibliothek, 9 Oct – 23 Nov 2002 (Stuttgart, 2002) [exhibition catalogue with other essays].

Żywny, Wojciech [Adalbert] [Živný, Vojtech; Zhyvny, Ziwny, Ziwny, Zwiny] Bohemian (naturalized Polish) piano teacher, composer (b. 13 May 1756, Bohemia; d. 21 Feb 1842, Warsaw).

He studied the piano, violin, harmony and counterpoint in Bohemia and after stays in Stuttgart and Zweibrücken, arrived in Poland between 1764 and 1795. After three years at a provincial court, he moved to Warsaw and became the most sought-after piano teacher in the city. His many pupils included *Chopin (from 1816 to 1822), who thought highly of him and is his main claim to fame.

Works

Piano pieces and lieder, mostly lost and none published.

0–9

'48' [Forty-Eight] (see *Wohltemperirte
Clavier*)

Index

Works mentioned under the heading '*Works*' in composers' entries are not indexed, unless they appear elsewhere. Names of relevant people appearing in '*Works*' or '*Further reading*' are indexed, but not bibliographical names or places, except those occurring in titles. 'i' and 'ii' after page numbers refers to columns.

Bold type indicates that a heading has its own entry and the pagination is also in **bold** type.